# TAXATION AND BUSINESS PLANNING FOR PARTNERSHIPS AND LLCS

2020–2021 Client File

DD Pizzeria LLC (Operating Partnership)

# TAXATION AND BUSINESS PLANNING FOR PARTNERSHIPS AND LLCS

## 2020–2021 CLIENT FILE

## DD PIZZERIA LLC (OPERATING PARTNERSHIP)

BRADLEY T. BORDEN
*Professor of Law*
*Brooklyn Law School*

ASPEN
PUBLISHING

To contact Customer Service, e-mail customer.service@aspenpublishing.com, call 1-800-950-5259, or mail correspondence to:

Aspen Publishing
Attn: Order Department
PO Box 990
Frederick, MD 21705

Printed in the United States of America.

1 2 3 4 5 6 7 8 9 0

ISBN 978-1-5438-0932-9

## About Aspen Publishing

Aspen Publishing is a leading provider of educational content and digital learning solutions to law schools in the U.S. and around the world. Aspen provides best-in-class solutions for legal education through authoritative textbooks, written by renowned authors, and breakthrough products such as Connected eBooks, Connected Quizzing, and PracticePerfect.

The Aspen Casebook Series (famously known among law faculty and students as the "red and black" casebooks) encompasses hundreds of highly regarded textbooks in more than eighty disciplines, from large enrollment courses, such as Torts and Contracts to emerging electives such as Sustainability and the Law of Policing. Study aids such as the *Examples & Explanations* and the *Emanuel Law Outlines* series, both highly popular collections, help law students master complex subject matter.

**Major products, programs, and initiatives include:**

- **Connected eBooks** are enhanced digital textbooks and study aids that come with a suite of online content and learning tools designed to maximize student success. Designed in collaboration with hundreds of faculty and students, the Connected eBook is a significant leap forward in the legal education learning tools available to students.
- **Connected Quizzing** is an easy-to-use formative assessment tool that tests law students' understanding and provides timely feedback to improve learning outcomes. Delivered through CasebookConnect.com, the learning platform already used by students to access their Aspen casebooks, Connected Quizzing is simple to implement and integrates seamlessly with law school course curricula.
- **PracticePerfect** is a visually engaging, interactive study aid to explain commonly encountered legal doctrines through easy-to-understand animated videos, illustrative examples, and numerous practice questions. Developed by a team of experts, PracticePerfect is the ideal study companion for today's law students.
- The **Aspen Learning Library** enables law schools to provide their students with access to the most popular study aids on the market across all of their courses. Available through an annual subscription, the online library consists of study aids in e-book, audio, and video formats with full text search, note-taking, and highlighting capabilities.
- Aspen's **Digital Bookshelf** is an institutional-level online education bookshelf, consolidating everything students and professors need to ensure success. This program ensures that every student has access to affordable course materials from day one.
- **Leading Edge** is a community centered on thinking differently about legal education and putting those thoughts into actionable strategies. At the core of the program is the Leading Edge Conference, an annual gathering of legal education thought leaders looking to pool ideas and identify promising directions of exploration.

# Contents

*Explanation of the Client File* ix

INTRODUCTION
**Demonstration of Problem Analysis** 1
Memorandum #X (Self-Employment Income) 2
Steps of Legal Analysis 3
Sample Write-Up 18

FOLDER I
**Memoranda** 25
Memorandum #1 (New Client) 27
Memorandum #2 (Choice of Entity) 29
Memorandum #3 (Partnership Tax Accounting) 30
Memorandum #4 (General Allocations) 32
Memorandum #5A (Compensatory Interests) 34
Memorandum #6A (Section 704(c) Allocations) 36
Memorandum #5B/6B (Property Contributions) 37
Memorandum #7 (Distributions) 38
Memorandum #8 (Non-Partner Capacity) 40
Memorandum #9 (Tax-Partnership Liabilities) 42
Memorandum #10 (Disguised Sales with Liabilities) 43
Memorandum #11 (Nonrecourse Deductions) 45
Memorandum #12 (Transfers of Tax-Partnership Interests) 47
Memorandum #13 (Mergers and Divisions) 49

FOLDER II
**DD Pizzeria Documents** 51
DD Pizzeria LLC Operating Agreement 53

FOLDER III
**DD Pizzeria Financials** 73

FOLDER IV
**11 Duffield Documents** 97
11 Duffield LLC Operating Agreement 99
11 Duffield Mortgage Note 132
11 Duffield Mortgage and Security Agreement 138
11 Duffield Guaranty of Payment 181
11 Duffield ADA and Environmental Indemnity Agreement 195
11 Duffield Assignment of Leases and Rents 209

FOLDER V
**11 Duffield Financials** 223

FOLDER VI
**The Amarillo Documents** 231
The Amarillo Mortgage Note 233
The Amarillo Guaranty of Payment 240

FOLDER VII
**Recent Legal Developments** 255
*Castigliola v. Commissioner* 257
*Hardy v. Commissioner* 266
Choice-of-Entity Analysis: Effective Tax Rates 275
Choice-of-Entity Considerations: Reasonable Compensation versus Passthrough 280
Carried Interests Tax 285

# Explanation of the Client File

The Client File for DD Pizzeria LLC includes memoranda with information about hypothetical parties to hypothetical scenarios that a typical transactional lawyer could see in practice over a number of years. In addition to presenting information about the client's situation, the memoranda request research and analysis related to situations that arise throughout the course of typical business operations. The Client File also includes several documents that attorneys draft or work with in providing advice. This Client File does not focus on drafting, but the documents are relevant to analyses particular to several memoranda. Spreadsheets also accompany the client file and include financial information about the operation of DD Pizzeria LLC and real estate investments of one DD Pizzeria LLC's members.

Successful completion of the assignments in each memorandum requires an understanding of the law and other concepts presented in the accompanying casebook, Taxation and Business Planning for Partnerships and LLCs, or other source and readings of the materials and information in the Client File, including financial statements, entity and loan documents, and facts presented in the memoranda. The entire semester will be dedicated to matters that arise with respect to DD Pizzeria LLC or its members. The parties' situations evolve as the semester and their business progresses, so work in later memoranda often requires an understanding of materials and information presented in earlier memoranda. This is reminiscent of law practice, which often requires remembering a client's situation over several years of representation.

Constraints caused by classroom study affect the manner in which the material is presented and the facts develop. The events presented in the materials occur over several years, but most tax law courses span not more than a dozen weeks. Thus, students must pay attention to the dates of each memorandum. The dates are given in generic years and are not intended to correspond to any specific calendar year. Thus, the law of the year during which the course is offered applies to all situations. Unlike a practice setting in which attorneys cannot predict the type of work that a client will bring to the firm, the classroom setting allows students to foresee the materials that will be covered later in the semester by perusing the materials in the casebook and client file. Another deviation of practice is the direction that the memoranda provide with respect to research. Each memorandum refers to materials in the casebook that provide the research needed to complete the memoranda assignments. In the practice setting, attorneys often must find the relevant legal sources on their own. The direction in this setting helps move the analysis along but leaves to students the responsibility of learning the presented law. Other venues provide the opportunity for developing research skills.

**Note on Legal Analysis and Tax Planning:** Successful analysis of the problems requires learning and knowing the law that applies. Partnership tax is particularly known for being challenging.[1] The law is complex, the situations to which the law applies are often complex. Much of partnership tax law is in regulations, and many of the provisions have never been the subject of litigation or clarification. Consequently, the study of partnership tax often requires the ability to work to understand the meaning of no more than several words. Understanding the factual situation also often requires similar effort. Thus, analysis and planning in the partnership tax area often requires thinking more about a limited number of words and phrases than other areas of the law. Such thought processes may require diagramming structures, outlining provisions of the law, and breaking down and scrutinizing individual words, both in promulgated rules and in agreements that clients use. Analysis also often requires anticipating how advice will affect clients. For instance, if members of a tax partnership are able to choose the manner in which the law will apply to a particular situation, they will generally want advice from their tax attorney regarding the effect the different alternatives will have on the parties' respective tax situations. An example illustrates how students should approach problems in the Client File.

**Recent Developments:** Because it is updated frequently, the Client File provides the opportunity to include recent developments that are relevant to problems in the Client File. The problems will cite to relevant recent developments that are reproduced in the Client File or in primary source material. New versions of the accompanying casebook will incorporate the recent developments to help ensure that portion of the Client File does not become unwieldy. Including recent updates in the materials is undoubtedly a deviation from practice. Typically, an assignment from a partner to an associate would not include the relevant legal authority. Instead, the assignment would implicitly require the associate to find the relevant legal source and apply it. The materials are designed for a non-research course, so the presentation of recent developments is consistent with that aspect of the design.

**Spreadsheets and Financial Information:** More and more tax attorneys express a need to understand spreadsheets and financial information. The Client file includes a spreadsheet that includes several years of financial information. That information can help answer questions about the parties' prior practices, which may help determine how they are interpreting provisions of the operating agreement. The spreadsheets also provide templates for students who are working on problems that

1. *See, e.g.*, Twenty Mile Joint Venture v. Commissioner, 200 F.3d 1268, at 1272 (10th Cir. 2000) ("We are mindful that 'partnership taxation is . . . generally regarded as the most difficult area of the Internal Revenue Code.'").

require presenting financial information. Thus, the Client File provides an opportunity to learn to work with spreadsheets. Students are best served by immersing themselves early in the use of spreadsheets, even if they have no prior experience working with them. The problems in the Client File require increasingly complicated spreadsheet presentations, so students are best served by working with the spreadsheet in the earliest problems to which it applies. Doing so provides an opportunity to spreadsheet novices to begin to develop some skills. Those skills can grow significantly over even a few weeks of working with the spreadsheet and then watching others work with it.

**Use of Client File in an Inverted Classroom:** In an inverted classroom, students read and learn substantive law outside of class, allowing in-class time to focus on analysis and application of the law. The Client File is designed to facilitate and drive such an inverted classroom. Students begin their study of a topic by reading the assigned memorandum, which presents facts, questions, and the chapter that contains the relevant legal sources. After reading the problems, students the learn the law by reading the relevant chapter and cited primary sources. Students can then analyze the problems and prepare short write-ups of their analyses to share with classmates and the professor. That process requires students to learn the law, so class time can be devoted to issues that the analysis raised and testing each other's knowledge of the law and its application. In-class discussions can also focus on policy matters that the problems raise. The Author uses the inverted classroom for his courses. He assigns students problems to present. The expectation is that students assigned to a problem will distribute a brief write-up of the analysis to the members of the class prior to meeting to discuss the problem. The assigned student will then have an opportunity to lead the discussion of the problem and answer questions and address comments that classmates and the professor have related to the problem.

**Acknowledgements:** Students and teachers face the challenge in the academy of finding documents that reflect real-world transactions. Fortunately, Benjamin Weinstock, Phillip Pepper, and Sean Cassidy shared documents that are the basis for those presented in this client file. Sarah Hains was instrumental in creating the design and formatting for this product. The author is extremely grateful for their generous contributions.

# DEMONSTRATION OF PROBLEM ANALYSIS

The client-file method, which requires analyzing real-life legal problems, will be new to many people who study these materials. The client-file method adopts a pedagogical approach known as error-correction. Students analyze problems, present the problems, and receive feedback that helps them identify aspects of their analyses that could be done better. Students should implement the feedback in future problem analyses, receive feedback, and reiterate this cycle over and over throughout the course of a semester.[1] The opportunity to analyze several problems and receive feedback throughout a course, provides a challenging, yet excellent learning experience. Students should use the feedback to understand whether their preparation was sufficient to enable them to understand and apply the law. They should use the feedback to improve their methods of learning and analysis on future problems. The error-correction approach is most effective when it begins with a demonstration of an analysis. A classroom demonstration can be fleeting, so these materials provide the following example as a demonstration of how to

1. Error-correction focuses on process and skills, perhaps more than on substantive knowledge. Students should work to develop the skills needed to obtain knowledge of the law from the materials, the skills needed to apply that law to a legal problem, and the skills needed to present the application of the law to the problem. Feedback in class discussions should help students recognize errors that may have occurred in any aspect of the preparation process. Students should recognize that errors are almost inevitable, especially when analyses require learning applying new knowledge and skills. Feedback can be a beneficial part of the learning process when students incorporate the feedback in future work and learn avoid making the same errors in the future. Errors may include reading and applying irrelevant law, failing to study the relevant law with sufficient care and attention to detail, failing to recognize subtle aspects of the facts, failing to apply the law correctly. Over the course of a semester students should recognize any of these types of errors and work to eliminate them from their analyses. Early in a semester, the professor will be more active in providing feedback, often through questions the test students' application of the required skills and their mastery of the relevant materials. As the semester progresses, students should take on more active roles in monitoring themselves, and the professor should be able to become more of a participant in a discussion about the law and problems. This requires significant effort from the students. This scaffolding technique empowers students to apply their legal skills. An overview of some of these general instructional concepts appear in M. David Merrill, *First Principles of Instruction*, 50 EDUC. TECH., RES. AND DEV. 43 (2002).

approach problems in this Client File. The demonstration begins with the facts and questions presented in Memorandum #X.

**MEMORANDUM #X**
**(SELF-EMPLOYMENT INCOME)**

To: Tax Associate
From: Tax Partner
Subject: Self-Employment Income of Partners
Date: September 1, Year 1

***Research Sources: Materials in Chapter 1***

Beverly and Jinhua are members of Bevhua Partnership, a general partnership in the business of preparing and selling food in Downtown Brooklyn from a cart it owns. Jinhua and Beverly both contributed capital to Bevhua Partnership, but Jinhua manages the partnership. Jinhua receives $225,000 a year for managing the partnership and an equal share of the Bevhua Partnership's profits (computed after deducting the services payment to Jinhua), which average around $450,000 per year. Jinhua and Beverly have both been treating the payments they receive from Bevhua Partnership and allocations of its profits as self-employment income. Jinhua has contacted us to ask if their treatment of the payments and allocations as self-employment income is correct. If it is, she would like to know if there is anything they can do to change the character of the payments and allocations of profits to avoid the tax on self-employment income. Please prepare an analysis of the questions that Jinhua has asked us to consider.

This simple fact pattern will most likely overwhelm most people who are not familiar with the laws that apply to it. The only way to fully understand and analyze the problem is to become familiar with the applicable law. Notice that the memorandum refers to materials in Chapter 1 of the accompanying casebook, which provide the law needed to analyze the problem. Also notice that the problem does not ask for a description of the law, but an analysis of the problem. This demonstration shows that although the analysis requires a thorough understanding of the law, it also requires application of the law, not a mere description of it. A sophisticated analysis also requires an orderly synthesis of the rules and coherent presentation. The best analyses flow from a multiple-step process that requires learning and applying the law. Students will gain the most from this demonstration by working through the steps on their own before they read the description. The multiple-step process is not the exclusive, process for analyzing a legal problem. Nonetheless, every effective legal analysis includes several common components.

**Common Components of Effective Legal Analysis**

- Preciseness.
- Attention to detail.
- Critical scrutiny of what you read.
- Focus on best result, not winning a debate.
- In-depth knowledge of the law and the facts.
- Critical scrutiny of your interpretations and conclusions.
- Articulate and organized written and oral presentation of analysis.

Notice how the following analysis incorporates these components.

## STEPS OF LEGAL ANALYSIS

**Step 1: Read the fact pattern and the problem.** Reading the fact pattern and problem before studying the law puts information in your mind and allows your mind to begin processing the information and subconsciously begin the analysis. A general knowledge of the fact pattern also provides a basis for searching for the law that may apply to the problem. The client-file method is problem-driven, meaning the problem dictates the law you should learn.

**Step 2: Quickly read the relevant materials.** After reading the problem, quickly read the referenced materials that apply to the problem—in this case, Chapter 1, including the cited references. The chapters in the accompanying casebook provide brief treatise-like commentary that describes relevant concepts and cites to applicable legal authority. The legal authority cited in chapter footnotes is essential to the analysis. The commentary leads you to the relevant legal authority. The legal authority will be the foundation of your analysis.

Most people must thoughtfully read legal sources multiple times before they understand them sufficiently to apply them effectively to a problem. The first reading is not to obtain a perfect understanding of the materials, but simply to know what law the materials include. As you read the materials, make note of your general understanding of the topic each source covers. During the analysis, you will return to the sources that apply to the problem and study them closely to fully understand them.

**Note on Sources**
**(Be willing to do more with less.)**

All of the legal sources needed to analyze the problems in the Client File are cited in the casebook that accompanies the Client File or included in the Client File. Instead of searching for additional outside sources to help understand the law (which in many cases will not exist), learn to spend the requisite time to piece together the information in the cited authorities. Sophisticated legal work often requires doing more with less. Many analyses require understanding, interpreting, and applying concepts that the law expresses in relatively few words. Sometimes words in statutes have been interpreted by courts or the Internal Revenue Service in regulations or rulings, but the law has many gaps, and many provisions have not been considered by the courts or the IRS (thus, even exhaustive research often fails to directly address a question about a particular rule). The casebook attempts to present all published authorities that are relevant to analyses that the Client File requires. Understanding the relevant law often requires diligent study of the available authorities. Be willing to take time to think critically about words you are reading in primary sources. Be prepared to stop and think about those words and read them again and again while thinking about them and the situations to which they apply until you begin to understand what they mean. Doing more with less requires periods of thought and analysis in between reading. It may also require outlining or diagramming a statute, regulation, or other source of the law. Learn to rely upon your own efforts to figure things out instead of always looking for a study aid to help. But know where to start the analysis to ensure you are considering the relevant law.

An astute and accomplished practitioner observed that many new attorneys do not fully appreciate the proper way to find and use commentary and legal sources.[2] When an attorney approaches a topic for the first time, the attorney should first gain a general understanding of the law by reading secondary sources, such as treatises and articles. The commentary in the accompanying casebook can serve as such secondary source for this Client File. After gaining a general understanding from the secondary source, the attorney should carefully study the cited legal authority. Citations to the relevant primary authority are often found in the footnotes. Be certain to carefully study everything in the footnotes that relates to the relevant commentary. That authority, not the commentary, will become the basis of the analysis. Good commentary provides insight and generally describes the law correctly, but sometimes secondary sources misinterpret the law or have

2. *See, e.g.*, Mark Herrmann, The Curmudgeon's Guide to Practicing Law, 19–22 (2006). This book is one that every student should consider reading.

gaps. Attorneys must develop the skill and confidence required to recognize when commentary should and should not be disregarded in light of a contradictory meaning in primary sources of the law. In practice, attorneys would also do research to ensure that there are no new developments that would change what the secondary source stated. Students will most often use the Client File in doctrinal courses, not research courses, so they generally would not be expected to do additional research. The Client File cites and presents recent developments that are relevant to the analyses (unless developments occur after the submission of the Client File manuscript for publication).

**Step 3: Identify the legal sources that apply to the problem.** After reading through the materials, return to the problem and carefully read it again. Consult notes and textual annotations from your first reading of the chapter and identify legal sources that appear to apply to the problem. Because the problem asks about self-employment income, your prior reading should lead you back to Part C of the chapter. As you reread the text of that part and examine the cited legal authority carefully, you should notice that section 1402(b) defines "self-employment income" to include net earnings from self-employment. Section 1402(a) defines "net earnings from self-employment" to include income an individual derives from carrying on a trade or business plus the individual's distributive share of income from a partnership. These two concepts appear relevant to the fact patter and question, so you will most likely want to study them closely.

Recognize that you may have misidentified some of the legal sources and may have to read through some of the materials again to determine whether their subject matter applies. Also, recognize that you may leave some legal sources off your initial list of sources that may apply, and as you analyze the problem, you may need to return to the materials to find additional sources that will enable you to fully analyze the problem.

### Note on Vocabulary and Precision

Notice that section 1402(a), which will become the focus of the analysis, uses the term "net earnings from self-employment" instead of the term "self-employment income" used in the memorandum. Jinhua may not have used the term "self-employment income" to describe the taxes that her and Beverly are paying, but perhaps the attorney who spoke with her verified what she was talking about. The memorandum also provides that Jinhua and Beverly are partners in a general partnership. Jinhua may have used the more generic term partnership, without realizing that it is a general partnership. The tax partner who spoke with her apparently made certain that Bevhua Partnership is a general partnership.

Attorneys must use vocabulary precisely. Legal terms generally have technical definitions, such as the term "net earnings from self-employment" and "general partnership." Attorneys must understand that clients may not use technical terms appropriately or may fail to use the appropriate technical term. Attorneys who speak with clients must understand that clients may use terms in their non-technical sense, and it is the attorney's responsibility to determine exactly what a client is talking about. Attorneys should not assume that a client's use of a technical term was intended to have technical meaning. For instance, a client may refer to a fellow business owner as a partner, even though they are members of a limited liability company, and not technically partners. Attorneys must be able to recognize what clients are talking about and verify with specificity when necessary.

Attorneys must speak precisely. If they determine that using technical terms when speaking with a client is not appropriate, they must ensure that their message properly expresses the application of the law. Attorneys also must speak precisely about the parties and rules involved in a fact situation. Those who are new to this type of precision may find themselves using pronouns instead of actual names, but precision generally requires using the actual names of parties and proper use of technical and non-technical terms.

**Step 4: Understand the stakes.** Analyzing problems generally requires considerable effort. Before doing the analysis, it is important to understand what is at stake. With tax planning, an amount of tax generally is at stake. If the amount at stake is too low, then the potential tax savings (or potentially lost tax benefits) may not justify the effort to do an analysis.[3] Often a general estimate of the tax situation will be sufficient to understand the stakes and know whether additional analysis is justified.

3. An example of costs of failing to understand the stakes comes from an anecdote a practitioner shared with the Author. The practitioner was a tax partner in a large national law firm. He gave an assignment to an associate to consider the tax aspects of a disposition of property and the acquisition of another like-kind property. The associate did the analysis and showed how the transaction could be structured as a tax-free exchange under section 1031. Structuring the transaction to come within section 1031 would require legal work and cause the client to incur additional transaction costs. Often the tax savings on the sale of property with unrealized gain would justify the costs, but in this situation, the property being sold had unrealized losses, so structuring the transaction as a section 1031 exchange would deprive the client of losses that would offset gain from other sources. If the associate had first considered the tax consequences of simply disposing of the property in the taxable transaction, then he would not have expended effort to design a tax-free disposition. This example illustrates the importance of knowing the stakes before beginning an analysis of a problem. Of course, in an academic setting, even if the tax stakes might appear to be low, students are expected to analyze assigned problems, but attempting to understand the stakes may also alert students that they are pursuing an incorrect analytical thread.

Part C of the casebook cites to sections 1401(a) and (b) which apply a 12.4% Social Security rate and a 2.9% Medicare rate, respectively, to self-employment income. To apply those rules, you must you fully understand the definition of self-employment income. Section 1402(b)(1) provides that for purposes of the tax imposed by section 1401(a) (the 12.4% amount), self-employment income does not include net earnings from self-employment that exceed the "contribution and benefit base." The amount is further reduced by wages paid to an individual. This should cause you to wonder if the payment to Jinhua for services comes within the definition of wages. A footnote in Part C cites to Rev. Rul. 69-184, which provides that amounts paid to partners are not wages, so Jinhua's guaranteed payment would not affect the contribution and benefit base. The memorandum does not indicate whether Jinhua has wages from other sources, but it does provide that she has been treating the payments as self-employment income. Based on that information, you would likely move forward with the analysis, assuming she does not have wages from other sources, but make a note that her amount of self-employment income would be reduced by her wages.

Another footnote in Part C cites to the Social Security website that provides the contribution and benefit base, which can fluctuate from year to year. For 2017, the base is $127,200, so assuming she asked us to analyze the amount of tax for 2017, only self-employment income of an individual up to that amount will be subject to the 12.4%. All self-employment income will be subject to the 2.9% portion.[4] With that information, you can do computations to approximate how much self-employment tax Beverly and Jinhua might owe based upon the information Jinhua provided.

| Estimated Self-Employment Taxes for Jinhua and Beverly | | |
|---|---|---|
| | **Jinhua** | **Beverly** |
| Total Potential S-E Income | $475,000 | $225,000 |
| Amount Subject to Soc. Sec. Tax ($127,200 base) | $127,200 | $127,200 |
| Soc. Sec. Rate | 12.4% | 12.4% |
| Soc. Sec. Tax | $15,773 | $15,773 |
| Amount Subject to Medicare | $475,000 | $225,000 |
| Medicare Rate | 2.9% | 2.9% |
| Medicare Tax | $13,775 | $6,525 |
| Total S-E Tax for Each Partner | $29,548 | $22,298 |
| Total Aggregate Tax on S-E Income | **$51,846** | |

4. As part of your analysis, you will notice that section 1401(b)(1) imposes an additional 0.9% tax on self-employment of high-income individuals. That could apply to Beverly and Jinhua, but unless that amount becomes relevant to the analysis, at this point, you might decide to not consider its application, but make a note that the taxes could be higher than your estimate due to that additional amount.

The quick computations show that Jinhua and Beverly could be paying around $50,000 for self-employment taxes for the year. That amount could rise each year as the contribution and benefit base rises. They would naturally be interested to receive confirmation that the law requires them to pay that amount under their current arrangement and whether there is a way for them to reduce the amount of self-employment taxes they are paying. The amount of self-employment taxes at issue also appears significant enough to justify incurring costs to explore ways to minimize it.[5]

**Best Attorneys Understand the Business Arrangement**

As you join the practice of transactional law, you will hear people say, "The best attorneys are those who understand their clients' businesses." Be sure to devote time as a developing transactional attorney to learn about business in general and to learn about your clients' businesses in particular. Also, be certain to spend the time needed to understand what your clients are asking and how your advice will add value to them. You should spend time learning about business, even if you are unable to bill it.

**Step 5: Apply the law to the fact pattern.** At this point, you know that the key to the definition of self-employment income, as defined in section 1402(b), is the definition of net earnings from self-employment, as defined in section 1402(a). You also know that Jinhua and Beverly could be paying enough tax on their self-employment income to justify expending effort on the issue.

After identifying section 1402(a) as the applicable law, the next step is to carefully read the law and apply it to the facts. A somewhat careful reading of section 1402(a) reveals that it appears to include two components in the definition of net earnings from self-employment: (1) income an individual derives from the individual's trade or business and (2) an individual's distributive share of partnership income. The analysis must consider whether either or both of these components apply to Jinhua and Beverly. The final clause of section 1402(a) appears to include an exception to the general rules regarding the definition of net earnings from self-employment. If your analysis of the two components confirms that Beverly's and Jinhua's shares of Bevhua Partnership's income and the payments to Jinhua are net earnings from self-employment income, you must consider whether any of the exceptions apply.

*First Component*

The first component of section 1402(a) includes gross income derived by an individual from a trade or business the individual carries on less deductions allowed with respect to that trade or business. Both Beverly and Jinhua are individuals,

5. The $50,000 alone could justify the costs, but because they are paying about that much annually, the costs to them over time are significant.

i.e., human beings, so this rule could apply to them. It would not, however, apply to other types of persons, such as corporations.

The next question (using exact language from the Code) is whether income allocated to Beverly and Jinhua from Bevhua Partnership is "income derived by an individual from any trade or business carried on by such individual." Beverly and Jinhua both appear to derive income from Bevhua Partnership, which is in the business of operating a food cart. The quoted language requires income to be derived from a business carried on by the individual. Thus, the application of the rule requires knowing whether the food cart business is carried on by Beverly and Jinhua. Because partnerships are legal fictions, they cannot do anything on their own and need human actors to conduct trades and businesses. One might, therefore, reason that the food cart business is carried on by Beverly and Jinhua,[6] and income they derive from Bevhua Partnership comes within the definition in the first component. The facts indicate that Bevhua Partnership owns and operates a food cart, so one might also reason that the partnership is carrying on a trade or business through Jinhua and Beverly.

Another reading of the first component is that it only applies to sole proprietors who are carrying on their own trades or businesses. Because neither Beverly nor Jinhua operate the food truck as sole proprietors, income they derive from Bevhua Partnership would not come within the first component's definition of net earnings from self-employment. At this point, the application of the first component may be unclear. Perhaps an analysis of the second component will help with the interpretation of the first component. Before examining the second component, consider how the law connects the first and second components.

*Components Connector*

Section 1402(a) provides that net earnings from self-employment include an individual's gross income (less allowed deductions) from the first component *plus* the individual's distributive share of income or loss from the second component. The "plus" connector suggests that the first and second components of the definition are distinct (otherwise an item of income that came within both components would be double counted). Consequently, any income that comes within the first component will not come within the second component, and vice versa. Thus, if the analysis determines that Beverly's and Jinhua's shares of Bevhua Partnership's income comes within the second component, those shares will not come within the

6. The language in the fact pattern provides that Jinhua is the manager. In that context, the term "manager" does not appear to have technical significance. It could mean that Jinhua works at the food cart preparing and serving food. Operating the food cart most likely also requires ordering product, maintaining the cart, and dealing with government agencies that grant permission to operate the food cart. Those activities may or may not come within the definition of management, as used in the fact pattern. They may, however, come within the section 1402(a) definition of carrying on a trade or business. If Beverly participates in any of those activities, the question of whether Bevhua Partnership's trade or business is carried by them, would apply equally to Beverly and Jinhua. If Beverly is a totally passive investor in Bevhua Partnership, then perhaps the argument could be made that income she derives from Bevhua Partnership is not derived from a business she carries on. That issue will be moot, however, if the first component does not apply to either Beverly or Jinhua in this instance.

first component. Such a determination suggests that the first component applies to the income of sole proprietors, not income members derive from partnerships.

*Second Component*

The second component of section 1402(a) provides that the definition of net earnings from self-employment includes an individual's "distributive share (whether or not distributed) of income or loss described in section 702(a)(8) from any trade or business carried on by a partnership of which he is a member." This clause contains several elements that the analysis must consider.

First, the language recognizes that partnerships carry on trades and businesses, which relates to the carryover question from the first component. That question considered whether Beverly and Jinhua are carrying on a trade or business individually within the meaning of the first component when they act on behalf of the partnership. The language in the second component recognizes that partnerships carry on trades or businesses. Because partnerships need human actors to carry on a trade or business, the actions of the partners in carrying on the trade or business of a partnership must be imputed to carrying on the trade or business of the partnership. Thus, one should be able to conclude that the operation of the food cart is a trade or business carried on by Bevhua Partnership through its agents,[7] Beverly and Jinhua, but Beverly and Jinhua do not carry on that trade or business individually. They act as agents for the partnership. This suggests that Beverly's and Jinhua's shares of income from Bevhua Partnership do not come within the definition of net earnings from self-employment under the first component.

**Note on Critical Thinking and Statutory Construction**

A person who quickly reads the first component for the first time could conclude that it applies generally to income a partner receives from a partnership the partner manages. Critical thinking requires the person to not only read the law critically but to be open to the possibility that a preliminary understanding of what the person read may not be correct. Thus, legal analysis requires attorneys to think critically about their own thoughts and interpretations of the law and to be open to the possibility that their interpretations are not correct. Human inclination is to prefer one's own easily-obtained interpretation or understanding over one that may require more effort or require considering what another person is explaining.[8] A common mistake is to quickly assume that another person's interpretation of

7. According to section 1402(c), the term "trade or business" generally has the same meaning in this context that it has when used in section 162. Students should recall from their basic tax course that a section 162 business is an activity carried on for profit with continuity and regularity. *See* Commissioner v. Groetzinger, 480 U.S. 23 (1987). Recalling the definition of "trade or business" may require revisiting the materials you used in your basic tax course.

8. *See* Daniel Kahneman, Thinking, Fast and Slow 44–46 (2011).

something that differs from one's own interpretation is incorrect, instead of considering whether our own understanding is wrong. Lawyers must be willing to challenge their initial understanding of concepts and situations.

In the context of statutory construction (which applies equally to regulations), critical thinking requires more than merely reading a statute and accepting one's first understanding of it. Critical thinking is a deliberate process of breaking the statute down into its elements and thinking carefully about each element. That process often requires thinking carefully about what each word means. Words may be defined elsewhere in the statute, in a regulation, in a ruling, or in a case. If a word or concept is not defined elsewhere, the analysis requires understanding the situations to which the rule applies and interpreting the rule in that context. For various reasons, some statutes and rules are not interpreted or expounded in other sources. For instance, a newly-enacted statute, or recently-promulgated regulation, may not have any other sources interpreting it. Some issues are not litigated or considered for further interpretation. Reasons for such failure could be lack of government resources to devote to an issue, lack of concern by the government about the taxpayer practices with respect to the law, or other practical or policy reasons. Analyses should be thorough enough to identify existing relevant authorities but also open-minded enough to recognize that the existing authorities are all that consider an issue. Once an analysis determines the extent of existing authorities (in a closed-research course, those authorities are the ones presented in the materials), it must use those authorities with well-reasoned analysis to draw conclusions.

Too often people who are new to the legal profession take a position and aggressively advocate it, with an apparent goal of winning an argument. Some people appear to rely on force of personality in such discussions, instead of sound legal analysis. That practice can be disastrous in a transactional setting. A transactional attorney must analyze the law and situation to which the law applies from many perspectives to maximize the likelihood that the position the attorney recommends is sound. Transactional attorneys must have the humility to focus on getting to the best result and not let the analysis become personal and turn into a fight to have a viewpoint adopted. Humility, properly balanced with the confidence needed to present and discuss an interpretation of the law, is a critical part of legal analysis.

Second, the second component only applies to members of a partnership. Beverly and Jinhua are both members of Bevhua Partnership, so the second component appears to apply.

Third, the second component provides that a partner's "distributive share...of income or loss described in section 702(a)(8)" from a partnership's trade or business comes within the definition of net earnings from self-employment. The application of this provision requires knowing what a distributive share is and what income is described in section 702(a)(8). Section 702(a) requires partners to take into account their distributive shares of listed partnership tax items when computing their income tax. Section 701 provides that partners, not partnerships are liable for income tax on a partnership's income. A partner's distributive share of a partnership's income thus must be the amount of the partnership's income that the partner must consider in determining the partner's income tax. Beverly's and Jinhua's distributive shares of Bevhua Partnership's income would appear to be their respective shares of its profits.[9]

The income or loss described in section 702(a)(8) is the partnership's taxable income exclusive of other items described in section 702(a)(1) through (7). Those excluded items include capital gains and losses, charitable contributions, dividends, and certain taxes. The facts do not provide that Bevhua Partnership has any of the excluded items, so its section 702(a)(8) income would appear to include all amounts presented in the fact pattern.[10]

Finally, the parenthetical in the second component clarifies that the definition of net earnings from self-employment include both distributed and undistributed distributive shares of partnership section 702(a)(8) income.[11] Thus, any portion of Bevhua Partnership's income allocated to Beverly and Jinhua could come

9. The memorandum provides that Beverly and Jinhua share "profits," which is a term that is not used in section 702(a)(8). Profits could differ from "taxable income" used in section 702(a)(8). A complete analysis in practice might require asking Jinhua how she and Beverly define profits to determine whether their definition deviates from the definition of taxable income. Often, partnership and LLC agreements will define profits to reflect taxable income. *See, e.g.*, Article I of DD Pizzeria LLC Operating Agreement. In this example, because Bevhua Partnership is an operating business that appears to have little working capital, profits will most likely be fairly similar to taxable income, so proceeding on that assumption appears to be reasonable. Recognize, however, that profits could be different from taxable income, and if you were to present the analysis to Jinhua, you might have to verify with Jinhua that their definition of profits reflects taxable income.

10. In practice, at this point, the attorney might ask Jinhua if Bevhua Partnership's income derived from any of the excluded items. Knowing the exact breakdown of the income may not, however, be important to the analysis. Bevhua Partnership operates a food cart. It might have some income that is excluded from section 708(a)(8), but most of its income likely comes within section 702(a)(8). Because Jinhua asked whether income from Bevhua Partnership comes within the definition of self-employment income, a report back to her could provide that any income derived from the operation of the food cart would come within the definition, but, to the extent Bevhua Partnership has any of the excluded types of income, such income would not come within the definition.

11. The use of "distributive" and "distributed" in the provision reinforces the need to read critically and use legal language precisely. The parenthetical provides that distributive shares of income "(whether or not distributed)" come within the definition of net earnings from self-employment. This indicates that distributive shares of income may not be distributed. Thus, distributive shares of income are not synonymous with distributions. Distributions are actual transfers of money from a partnership to a partner. Distributive shares of income are allocations of income to members, representing the amount of income each partner must report on the partner's tax return. A critical reading of the statute requires recognizing those words have different meanings, and full understanding of the provision requires knowing the definitions of the respective words.

within the definition of net earnings from self-employment. Unless the allocated amounts come within one of the exceptions, they will be self-employment income.

***Exceptions***

The final clause of the lead-in language of section 702(a)(8) provides "*except* that in computing the gross income and deductions and such distributive share of partnership ordinary income or loss. . . ." (Emphasis added.) The "except" provision indicates that exceptions apply to the general rules in the two components. The only way to determine whether any of the exceptions apply is to read them. Exception (13) should raise some interest because it excludes "the distributive share of any item of income or loss of a limited partner." The second component address distributive shares of income, so this exception appears to have some connection to that component. It also only applies to limited partners. The fact pattern provides that Bevhua Partnership is a general partnership, which would not have limited partners. Limited partners are members of limited partnerships, so the exception would not appear to apply to Beverly or Jinhua, who are not limited partners. Thus, Beverly's and Jinhua's distributive shares of Bevhua Partnership's income appear to come within the definition of net earnings from self-employment.

The exception also contains language that should spark additional analysis. The exception for limited partners has an exception for guaranteed payments (as defined in section 707(c)) to a partner who receives the payments as remuneration for services provided to the partnership. Thus, such payments to a limited partner would not be excluded from the definition of net earnings from self-employment. Even though that guaranteed-payments exception to the exception for limited partners does not apply under the current facts, it raises the question of how the general rule should treat the payments that Jinhua receives for managing Bevhua Partnership, which might be guaranteed payments. The statute does not clearly provide how to treat guaranteed payments, which are not distributive shares of partnership income. If they are not subject to the exception of limited partners, they would appear to fall within the general rule, but they do not appear to fall nicely within either component.

If a statute is unclear, sometimes the regulations provide clarity, as is the case in this situation. Treas. Reg. §1.1402(a)-1(b) provides that gross income derived from an individual's trade or business includes payments that are determined without regard to the partnership's income. Thus, the regulations deem guaranteed payments to be net earnings from self-employment under the first component. The memorandum provides that Jinhua receives $225,000 for managing Bevhua Partnership. Section 707(c) defines guaranteed payments as payments to a partner that are determined without regard to the income of the partnership. The payments to Jinhua for managing Bevhua Partnership appear to come within that definition, and, if so, they would be net earnings from self-employment under the first component.

**Step 6: Consult the supporting documents and financial information as needed to help with the analysis.** The Client File includes the operating agreement, financial information, and other documents for the relevant entities and transactions. The availability of the operating agreement and financial information could prove useful in answering some factual questions that the memoranda do not answer. For instance, the Bevhua Partnership agreement (which is not available in this demonstration), might provide that Jinhua will receive payment for managing the partnership, without regard to the partnership's income. Such a provision in the partnership agreement would confirm that she is receiving guaranteed payments.

**Step 7: Draw a conclusion.** The distributive shares of income from a general partnership and guaranteed payments for services provided to a partner come within the definition of net earnings from self-employment. Thus, the payments Jinhua receives for services would be net earnings from self-employment under the first component. Each person's distributive shares of Bevhua Partnership's income would be net earnings from self-employment under the second component.

**Step 8: Consider whether planning opportunities would allow parties to mitigate any unfavorable results of the analysis.** You should be able to deduce that Beverly and Jinhua would prefer that their income from Bevhua Partnership not come within the definition of net earnings from self-employment—by avoiding coming within definition, their income would not be subject to the tax on self-employment income. You should therefore consider whether Beverly and Jinhua can take any steps to change that result. Having studied the exception for the distributive shares of limited partners, one idea that should come to mind is recommending that Beverly and Jinhua consider converting Bevhua Partnership to a limited partnership.

Under such a structure, Jinhua could continue as general partner and Beverly and Jinhua could both be limited partners. The partnership agreement could provide that Jinhua will provide services in her capacity as general partner, and receive guaranteed payments in that capacity. Beverly and Jinhua would share in profits as limited partners. Section 1402(a)(13) contemplates a person having a distributive share as a limited partner and receiving guaranteed payments for services, so the structure would appear to have a possibility of shielding Jinhua's distributive share from self-employment income.

They may also consider whether the guaranteed payments being made to Jinhua reflect market rates for her services. If the payments do not reflect market rates, Beverly and Jinhua should consider adjusting the amounts of the payments to ensure that they do, so the IRS and courts will respect the distributive shares. The analysis at this point should call to mind the reading in Part C of the casebook regarding compensation planning in the S corporation context. You should recall that the discussion cited to *Watson v. United States*, 757 F.Supp. 2d 877 (S.D. Iowa 2010). When you revisit that case to read it more carefully, you will note that the taxpayer in that case was an individual CPA who was a member S corporation, through which he provided accounting services. The taxpayer received a small salary from the S corporation and paid employment taxes on it and received distributions of profit from the corporation.[12] The court determined that the salary was unreasonably low and recharacterized some of the distribution as compensation, subjecting it to employment taxes. The principles in that case should apply to the payments that Jinhua receives.

**Note on Critical Thinking and Application of Case Law**

Tax planning often occurs in gray areas of the law—i.e., those areas for which the law is not perfectly settled. The application of *Watson* to a person who holds both a general partner interest and limited partner interest in a limited partnership is such an area. *Watson* is an S corporation case, so it does not directly apply to a limited partnership. The aspect of *Watson* that is useful in this setting is the ruling regarding reasonable compensation. If a person holds both general partner and limited partner interests in a limited partnership, and the person provides services for compensation to the limited partnership, one could argue that the IRS could insist upon that compensation being reasonable for purposes of applying section 1402. Application of case law (and rulings) requires identifying the extent to which the facts of the case are similar to the facts of the current situation. If the facts are similar, the ruling should be very informative. Otherwise, its only application may be by analogy.

Even minor deviations from facts of cases can be significant. A case that denies favorable tax treatment under one set of facts probably is not support for favorable tax treatment under different facts. Being able to distinguish the facts of a situation from the facts of a case with a negative taxpayer result may be sufficient to get comfortable that no negative authority exists with respect to the position. Critical analysis of cases requires understanding their facts and rulings and being able to apply the ruling to the situation under consideration, or recognizing the inapplicability of the case. Such critical analysis requires very careful readings of cases and thoughtful application of them to the facts under consideration.

**Step 9: Consider economic consequences of tax planning.** If Jinhua wishes to have all of her distributive share of income excluded from self-employment income, she should work with Beverly to ensure that the guaranteed payments are not less than market value of her services. If the payments exceed market rates, they may consider paying Jinhua less and converting the excess to distributive shares of

12. Compensation from an S corporation is not self-employment income, so the corporation withheld and paid the employment taxes. The analysis should consider whether the difference affects the application of the case to the question of reasonableness of compensation. This demonstration assumes the case is relevant to that question in the instant situation.

income. If they make such a conversion, they must consider whether they will alter the profit-sharing arrangement to be something other than equal sharing. If Jinhua gives up some of her rights to guaranteed payments, she would most likely request that she receive more than a 50% of the profits. Beverly may recognize that she is doing Jinhua a favor by agreeing to alter the agreement and insist that she also share in some of Jinhua's tax savings. The parties must reconcile their preferences.

The facts do not indicate the market value of Jinhua's services, so Beverly and Jinhua might want to consider what the economic results would be if the market for her services is alternatively greater than or less than what she currently receives. For instance, if they determine that the market value of her services is $175,000, the profits, after paying the guaranteed payment, would become $525,000. Alternatively, if the market value of the services is $300,000, the profits, after paying the guaranteed payment, would be $400,000. Some simple computations show the amounts that each person would receive under the two alternatives, assuming they continue to share profits equally.

**Effect of Changing Guaranteed Payment**

| Current | Jinhua | | Beverly |
|---|---|---|---|
| Guaranteed Payment | $250,000 | | |
| Profits | | $450,000 | |
| Equal Sharing | $225,000 | | $225,000 |
| Total Share | **$475,000** | | **$225,000** |
| | **Alternative 1** | | |
| Guaranteed Payment | $175,000 | | |
| Profits | | $525,000 | |
| Equal Sharing | $262,500 | | $262,500 |
| Total Share | **$437,500** | | **$262,500** |
| | **Alternative 2** | | |
| Guaranteed Payment | $300,000 | | |
| Profits | | $400,000 | |
| Equal Sharing | $200,000 | | $200,000 |
| Total Share | **$500,000** | | **$200,000** |

In each of the two alternatives, the parties would receive amounts that differ from the amounts they receive under the current arrangement. If the profits are fairly predictable, they could adjust the profit-sharing ratio to ensure that the payments to the parties do not change. Under the current arrangement, Beverly's total share of payments and profits is $475,000. For her to receive that same amount under Alternative 1, her share of the profits would have to be $300,000 or about 57% of total profits ($300,000/$525,000). Under Alternative 2, her share of profits would have to be $175,000 or about 44% of total profits ($175,000/$400,000). The parties could consider whether they would make such adjustments, if they were to adjust the guaranteed payment to reflect market value.

**Step 10: Revisit the math.** Having completed the analysis, you are now in a position to determine how much self-employment tax the parties might save if they were to convert Bevhua Partnership to a limited partnership. To do this analysis, you might assume that the guaranteed payments reflect market value. Based upon that assumption, Jinhua's $250,000 guaranteed payment would be self-employment income. The distributive shares of income to the members as limited partners would not be self-employment income. Some quick computations show what each partner's self-employment tax would be, if your prescribed structure is valid.

**Estimated Self-Employment Taxes for Jinhua and Beverly, Assuming Conversion to Limited Partnership**

| | Jinhua | Beverly |
|---|---|---|
| Total Potential S-E Income | $250,000 | $0 |
| Amount Subject to Soc. Sec. Tax ($127,200 base) | $127,200 | $0 |
| Soc. Sec. Rate | 12.4% | N/A |
| Soc. Sec. Tax | $15,773 | $0 |
| Amount Subject to Medicare | $250,000 | $0 |
| Medicare Rate | 2.9% | N/A |
| Medicare Tax | $7,250 | $0 |
| Total S-E Tax for Each Partner | $23,023 | $0 |
| Total Aggregate Tax on S-E Income | **$23,023** | |

This simple computation shows that converting to a limited partnership would reduce the aggregate self-employment tax from $51,846 to $23,023, resulting in close to $30,000 of annual tax savings. Most of the savings go to Beverly. The parties would have to consider whether they would want to make any changes to the profit-sharing arrangement to share the savings more equally. They could do that by increasing Jinhua's share of the profits sufficiently to account for the necessary portion of the savings that would ensure that each partner shares in the tax savings equally. At a minimum, the analysis shows that tax planning can help the reduce the parties' overall self-employment tax liability.

Some classroom formats may require students to prepare a brief write-up to present their analyses of problems to the class. The legal profession requires transactional attorneys to be able to communicate in various media with varying levels of formality. Some communication will be written and be very formal with formal Bluebook citations and professional writing and not be accompanied by an oral discussion. Other written communication will be less formal with the minimum detail needed to communicate the relevant information and informal references to the supporting legal authority. Such communication often is appropriate when the author will provide an oral explanation of the written document.

If a doctrinal course requires written analyses of problems, those analyses generally should be informal and provide sufficient detail to demonstrate a thorough analysis of the problem, a comprehensive grasp of the relevant law, an understanding of economic consequences of any recommendations, and the computations needed to show the analysis and facilitate discussion. The write-up should also present an organized structure of the analysis, stepping through the facts and law in an orderly, deliberate manner. The constraints of a doctrinal course, which requires students to spend most of their preparation time learning complex law and analyzing challenging problems, generally do not afford students the opportunity to prepare formal professional writing and citation formatting. A student's informal written product should be sufficient to support a rigorous discussion of the analysis. Readers of such write-ups should be able to identify the writer's analysis with a fairly quick reading of the write-up. Some write-ups that require presentation of financial information will include a very skeletal outline of the analysis with accompanying financial information that presents the results of the analysis, and others will include computations in the spreadsheet that accompanies the Client File. Some should also include diagrams—remember that a picture is worth a thousand words. They all should be based in the law and draw upon the available facts. The following is an example of a write-up of the analysis for Bevhua Partnership self-employment income problem.

## SAMPLE WRITE-UP

**Student:** Stanislav

**Question:** Jinhua has asked us if her and Beverly's treatment of the payments and allocations from Bevhua Partnership as self-employment income is correct. If it is, she would like to know if there is anything she and Beverly can do to change the character of the payments and allocations of profits. Please prepare an analysis of the questions that Jinhua has asked us to consider.

**Answer:** Section 1401 imposes two types of taxes on self-employment income—Social Security at 12.4% and Medicare at 2.9%. The definition of self-employment income in section 1402(b), includes net earnings from self-employment and a ceiling for the amount of earnings from self-employment that is subject to the Social Security portion of the tax. Treas. Reg. §1.1402(a)-1(b) deems the guaranteed payments from a partnership to be income from an individual carrying on a trade or business, which is net earnings from self-employment under the first component of section 1402(a). Section 1402(a) also treats partners' distributive shares of income as net earnings from self-employment. Consequently, both the guaranteed payments and the partners' shares of Bevhua Partnership's profits (assuming they are the same as taxable income and do not include any of the section 702(a) excluded items) will be subject to self-employment income, computed as follows.

| Estimated Self-Employment Taxes for Jinhua and Beverly | | |
|---|---|---|
| | **Jinhua** | **Beverly** |
| Total Potential S-E Income | $475,000 | $225,000 |
| Amount Subject to Soc. Sec. Tax ($127,200 base) | $127,200 | $127,200 |
| Soc. Sec. Rate | 12.4% | 12.4% |
| Soc. Sec. Tax | $15,773 | $15,773 |
| Amount Subject to Medicare | $475,000 | $225,000 |
| Medicare Rate | 2.9% | 2.9% |
| Medicare Tax | $13,775 | $6,525 |
| Total S-E Tax for Each Partner | $29,548 | $22,298 |
| Total Aggregate Tax on S-E Income | **$51,846** | |

Section 1402(a)(13) provides an exception to the general rule about partners' distributive shares by excluding from the definition of net earnings from self-employment a limited partner's distributive share of income. Beverly and Jinhua appear to be able to reduce the amount of tax that they pay on self-employment income by converting Bevhua Partnership to a limited partnership. If they were to convert it to a limited partnership and the treatment of their distributive shares were respected, the tax on their self-employment income would be as follows.

| Estimated Self-Employment Taxes for Jinhua and Beverly, Assuming Conversion to Limited Partnership | | |
|---|---|---|
| | **Jinhua** | **Beverly** |
| Total Potential S-E Income | $250,000 | $0 |
| Amount Subject to Soc. Sec. Tax ($127,200 base) | $127,200 | $0 |
| Soc. Sec. Rate | 12.4% | N/A |
| Soc. Sec. Tax | $15,773 | $0 |
| Amount Subject to Medicare | $250,000 | $0 |
| Medicare Rate | 2.9% | N/A |
| Medicare Tax | $7,250 | $0 |
| Total S-E Tax for Each Partner | $23,023 | $0 |
| Total Aggregate Tax on S-E Income | **$23,023** | |

Converting to a limited partnership would thus significantly reduce the amount of tax they pay on self-employment income each year. Beverly and Jinhua may also consider whether the guaranteed payments reflect market value of Jinhua's services. If the payments are below market value, the IRS could, relying upon *Watson*, recharacterize a portion of Jinhua's distributive share as compensation. If they adjust the amount of guaranteed payment to reflect market value, then they will have to consider whether they want to adjust their profit-sharing ratios to compensate for the change in guaranteed payment. The following table illustrates how adjusting the guaranteed payment amount without adjusting the profit-sharing ratio could affect the total payments to which Beverly and Jinhua might be entitled.

| Effect of Changing Guaranteed Payment | | | |
|---|---|---|---|
| **Current** | **Jinhua** | | **Beverly** |
| Guaranteed Payment | $250,000 | | |
| Profits | | $450,000 | |
| Equal Sharing | $225,000 | | $225,000 |
| Total Share | $475,000 | | $225,000 |
| | **Alternative 1** | | |
| Guaranteed Payment | $175,000 | | |
| Profits | | $525,000 | |
| Equal Sharing | $262,500 | | $262,500 |
| Total Share | $437,500 | | $262,500 |
| | **Alternative 2** | | |
| Guaranteed Payment | $300,000 | | |
| Profits | | $400,000 | |
| Equal Sharing | $200,000 | | $200,000 |
| Total Share | $500,000 | | $500,000 |

The write-up is very brief, but it demonstrates significant effort went into the analysis. First, the write-up shows that Stanislav understands sections 1401 and 1402. Second, it shows he understands that section 1402(a)(13) might provide an opportunity for Beverly and Jinhua to reduce their taxes. Third, it shows that he is thinking that they might be able to further reduce their taxes, if the guaranteed payment to Jinhua exceeds the market value of her services. Fourth, it shows that changing the amount of guaranteed payments would affect the dollar amounts of profits the parties receive (assuming partnership income remains constant), so they may have to adjust their profit-sharing ratio to account for that difference. Finally, it demonstrates ability to find and apply the relevant law in the materials, and does not include any materials that are not relevant to the analysis. Stanislav appeared to use his time learning and applying only the relevant rules.

Notice that the write-up does not include any reproduction of the law. The primary authorities are available to everyone in the class, so the write-up does not need to present them to the class members. Students who prepare an analysis can expect questions from classmates and the professor that will test the students' underlying knowledge, interpretation, and application of the rules. The write-up forms the basis for discussion, but it does not need to be overly formal or reproduce block quotes of the law.

By demonstrating an understanding of the law and its implications in this write-up, Stanislav creates an opportunity to use class time to discuss issues that this structure raises. For instance, the class discussion could consider whether the rules are fair. All of a general partner's income is self-employment income, but a limited partner's distributive share of income and distributions from S corporations are not. The discussion can also consider whether the section 1402(a)(13) exception applies to a limited partner who is both a limited partner and a general partner.

*In a doctrinal course that adopts the Client File and requires written analyses, most time and effort devoted to class preparation, which will be significant, should be spent on understanding the facts and materials and applying the law to the facts. The write-up should consume a small fraction of that preparation time, so it should be informal, but should effectively communicate the knowledge obtained studying and applying the material. The write-up most likely will, however, help clarify your thinking and should present an organized analysis of the problem. It should include the relevant supporting numerical representations when appropriate.*

### Transactional Tax Practice Is Different from Litigation

This Demonstration of Problem Analysis in the transactional tax setting reveals that the analysis relies upon law and facts. It combines those elements in a coherent way to draw conclusions, address the client's questions, make recommendations, and anticipate other issues that the advice might raise. The demonstration illustrates how anticipation in the practice of transactional law differs from advocacy in litigation.

Good transactional attorneys must anticipate how language in documents, deal structures, and tax plans will affect the relevant parties. They also must anticipate how other parties will exploit or attack weaknesses in structures, document language, and tax-reporting positions. A transactional tax attorney must recognize how language in a document or a deal structure will affect a client and ensure that the client's interests are met. Notice in the demonstration, how the analysis considered how changing the amount of the guaranteed payment could affect the amount of profits that the parties would share. An attorney representing Jinhua would anticipate the effect that such a change would have and recommend that she consider changing the profit-sharing ratio, if she were to receive a smaller guaranteed payment. In that sense, the transactional attorney both anticipates the effect of a recommendation and advocates for the client.

Litigators by contrast advocate particular interpretations of the law on behalf of their clients. They look for every argument possible to support the position. Some might proclaim that litigation in the business setting is the result of a transactional attorney messing up. For instance, a dispute over ambiguous contract language often indicates a mistake in drafting the contract. After such a contract is executed and an ambiguity becomes a point of contention, the advocate would argue on Jinhua's behalf in favor of the interpretation that favors Jinhua. The attorney would "win" by prevailing and obtaining a ruling in Jinhua's favor. Advocating for a particular interpretation of an ambiguous provision in the drafting stage is unwise. At that stage, the goal generally is to identify and eliminate ambiguity. In the planning and documentation phase of a transaction, a transactional attorney should be open to and explore all reasonable interpretations of the law and document to identify weaknesses in a proposal. After carefully considering reasonable interpretations, the attorney would make a professional judgment about the meaning and application of the law. A transactional attorney would be unwise to apply the advocacy of a litigator to a point of view that could end up being incorrect. Nonetheless, a transactional attorney must develop knowledge of the law and facts that provide the confidence needed to advise a client.

Transactional tax attorneys should do everything in their power to understand the law and apply it. They should also be prepared to listen to others who have devoted similar time to a problem and have come up with a different interpretation. After informed discussion, people with different views of the meaning or application of a rule (1) may recognize that one view is better than another, (2) may recognize that both views are incorrect and an alternative view is superior, or (3) may recognize that some combination of the different views is the best interpretation and application of the law. Preparation and open-mindedness will greatly facilitate the learning process and help the transactional tax attorney come up with the best advice. The practice of analyzing legal problems also helps attorneys sense when an analysis is complete and when some issues remain unresolved. Repeated exposure to problem-solving helps attorneys develop that sense, or recognize when an analysis is incomplete.

Finally, even though transactional law is not debate or litigation, transactional attorneys must be able to articulate their understanding of the law and its application. Transactional attorneys' analyses should step through the application of the law in a manner that communicates their understanding of the law to other attorneys and clients of all levels of legal and tax sophistication. A thorough knowledge and orderly application of the law allows a transactional attorney to defend a position, while remembering to listen to and learn from others in pursuit of the best outcome.

An example illustrates the difference between debate and pursuit of knowledge. Imagine two persons who interpret the application of the first component of section 1402(a) differently. One interprets it to apply to income allocated to partners, and one interprets it to apply only to sole proprietors. They would make little progress in resolving their dispute by sharing their thoughts and feelings about the wording in the first component. If they focus on legal analysis, however, they would read the second component and the "plus" that connects the two components, recognizing that partnerships carry on trades or businesses and partners who provide services for such partnerships are not carrying on a trade or business as individuals. By applying tenets of statutory construction, the parties would realize that the second component would not have meaning, if it included partners providing services for the partnership. Focusing on the law and searching for a best interpretation instead of trying to win a debate should help both people understand the law better.

**Transactional Tax Practice Requires "Hard" (Not "Soft") Analysis**

When new to transactional legal analysis, people often preface comments with phrases such as "I think," "I feel," or "in my opinion." Such phrases could be hollow introductions to sophisticated analyses, but typically they merely introduce thoughts that are not supported by law or sound legal reasoning. Comments that actually relate to personal thoughts, feelings, and opinions represent "soft" analysis, which rarely lead to good legal outcomes (and would lead to such outcomes by chance, if at all). Comments that further discussion generally reference a specific provision of a statute, case, regulation, ruling, or agreement. Informed comments may also draw upon the facts of a case that relate to the transaction under consideration. Comments based in law and fact allow transactional attorneys to do "hard" analysis.

Examining operating agreements and other documents in the transactional context also requires hard analysis. An operating agreement is a contract among the parties to which contract law applies. If language appears to be ambiguous, the focus should be understanding what the parties may intend it to mean. The Client File provides numerous sources of facts that may help identify that intent, including information in the memoranda about the facts, the financial statements, and agreements as a whole. The parties' prior practice may provide some insight into their intentions. Understanding the intention of the parties also generally requires considering how reasonable interpretations of an agreement may benefit or harm specific parties to the agreement. Hard analysis must draw upon legal principles and facts.

FOLDER I

# MEMORANDA

# MEMORANDUM #1

## (New Client)

To: Tax Associate
From: Tax Partner
Subject: Potential New Client Matter
Date: January 25, Year 6

---

***Research Sources: Materials in Chapter 1***

Our firm has been approached by the members of Debby's Deep Dish Pizzeria to review their current structure, assist them with any obvious tax-planning alternatives, and help them with future matters that may arise, i.e., serve as outside tax counsel. They have also given us the attached financial statements and a copy of their operating agreement. In addition, they provided the following background information. Debby Day is a very well-known chef. Several years ago, she was the winner of Super Chef, a nationally televised cooking competition. She leveraged that fame to obtain capital to open her first Debby's Deep Dish Pizzeria about five years ago on January 1, Year 1. As initial investors in Debby's Deep Dish Pizzeria, Ella Baurdain put up $1,250,000 and Farzan Vater put up $750,000. The plan was for Debby to create the menu and manage the restaurant and for Ella and Farzan to play passive roles. They formed DD Pizzeria LLC to run the business and agreed to divide profits as provided for in the DD Pizzeria LLC Operating Agreement.

The Pizzeria used the $2,000,000 original investment to enter into a lease for restaurant space, purchase equipment and furniture for the restaurant, and fund the first six months of operations. DD Pizzeria has done well since. It now has five locations and is always looking to expand.

Before we accept this representation, we must be sure that doing so would not violate any ethical rules. We also need to know who would be our ideal client. Please research and provide answers to the following questions.

1. If Debby contacted us, can we accept an engagement with DD Pizzeria LLC (assume we are licensed attorneys with our current knowledge and legal experi ence working together as a firm)?
2. If Ella and Farzan agreed to grant an equity interest in DD Pizzeria LLC to Grace, who could we represent in that transaction?
3. Debby has been paying herself $150,000 as salary from DD Pizzeria LLC. Farzan recently asked Debby where she got the authority to do that. Debby asked us to confirm whether she can unilaterally cause DD Pizzeria LLC to pay her the salary.
4. Debby has learned of the so-called employment tax loophole that many people use with S corporations, and she wonders whether she can use the same strategy for herself with respect to distributions that she might receive from DD Pizzeria LLC. She has been paying self-employment tax on her $150,000 salary. So far, she has not received any other distributions, but as DD Pizzeria LLC begins to turn a profit, she believes that she will start to receive distributions, and she

would like to not report those distributions as self-employment income. What does the law provide on this issue? In addition to other sources that you will consider, you should be certain to consider whether the recently-decided *Castigliola v. Commissioner*, T.C. Memo 2017-62 and *Hardy v. Commissioner*, T.C. Memo. 2017-16 (reproduced in the Recent Developments section of this Client File), are relevant to the analysis.

5. Debby has asked us to write an opinion letter stating that any allocations to her or distributions she receives from DD Pizzeria LLC are not self-employment income. What level of opinion can we give?
6. If we were unable to get comfortable giving an opinion about the employment tax treatment of distributions to Debby, what obligation do we owe to Debby, DD Pizzeria LLC, Ella, and Farzan?
7. What should we do if Debby informs us that she will not pay the self-employment taxes on allocations or distributions to her (assuming we were to advise her that she must)?
8. If Debby owed but did not pay employment taxes on distributions DD Pizzeria LLC made to her, would she owe penalties in the event the IRS audited her and challenged her treatment of the distributions?

# MEMORANDUM #2

## (Choice of Entity)

To: Tax Associate
From: Tax Partner
Subject: Choice-of-Entity Matters
Date: February 15, Year 6

---

***Research Sources: Materials in Chapter 2***

Debby has asked us to examine her entity structure and recommend any changes we might have. Please do research and provide suggestions with respect to the following questions:

1. What other state-law entities are available to Debby, Ella, and Farzan for operating their Pizzeria and owning property? Do any of the other alternatives provide a better choice of state-law entity for them? Please provide some detail that we can share with Debby that supports your recommendation.
2. What tax entities are available to Debby, Ella, and Farzan for operating their Pizzeria and owning property? Do any of the other alternatives provide a better choice of tax entity for them? Would you recommend any restructuring? Please provide detail that we can share with Debby that supports your recommendations.
3. Debby is considering a lease for a new DD Pizzeria location. The owner of the property has suggested that the lease include a relatively low flat monthly rental payment and an annual payment of a share of DD Pizzeria LLC's profits. Please look into whether such a structure raises any tax or legal concerns. The property owner also said that he would consider accepting a share of DD Pizzeria LLC's gross receipts in exchange for keeping the monthly rental payments low. Would that make a difference?
4. Debby is considering purchasing a small office building and she would like DD Pizzeria LLC to use a portion of the building as its corporate headquarters. What issues does this purchase raise?
5. If Debby can obtain the required financing and overcome any other issues that you discover, how would you recommend that she structure the ownership of the office building she would like to purchase?
6. If Debby wanted to use separate entities for each of the various restaurant locations, what alternatives does she have? What would be the advantage of using separate entities for each location?

# MEMORANDUM #3

## (Partnership Tax Accounting)

| | |
|---|---|
| To: | Tax Associate |
| From: | Tax Partner |
| Subject: | General Treatment of Partnership Tax and Economic Items |
| Date: | March 1, Year 6 |

***Research Sources: Materials in Chapter 3***

Debby provided the attached financial information for Year 1 through Year 5 and asked us to provide her guidance about she would treat those items. Please do the necessary research and provide answers to the following questions with respect to DD Pizzeria LLC and its partners based upon the Year 5 financial information:

1. Questions related to the computation of taxable income.
   a. What is DD Pizzeria LLC's Year 5 taxable income and who pays tax on that income?
   b. Which Year 5 items must DD Pizzeria LLC separately state? Debby probably does not understand why partnerships separately state certain items. Please provide a description of why the law requires some items to be separately stated.
   c. Will any of the members of DD Pizzeria LLC qualify for the 20% deduction under section 199A? Two articles, *Choice-of-Entity Analyses: Effective Tax Rates* and *Choice-of-Entity Considerations: Reasonable Compensation versus Passthrough*, in the Recent Developments section of this Client File may direct you to provisions of section 199A that may help with this analysis.
2. Questions related to the nature and character of tax-partnership income.
   a. Can the parties deduct their allocable shares of DD Pizzeria LLC's interest expense?
   b. Farzan has an account of securities that he regularly trades. That activity makes him a trader with respect to those securities, and any gain or loss that he recognizes from those sales are ordinary. How does Farzan's trading activity affect the character of gain or loss that DD Pizzeria LLC recognizes on the sale of its securities? How does it affect the character of gain or loss allocated to Farzan?
3. DD Pizzeria LLC's Available Cash for Year 5 equals the amount of distributions presented in the statement of cash flows. When and to whom does Debby distribute that cash? Will the distributions affect the manner in which DD Pizzeria LLC will allocate taxable income to the members?
4. DD Pizzeria LLC purchased about $175,000 of new equipment and furniture in Year 5. Ella and Farzan have expressed conflicting preferences for how they would like to treat the cost recovery of the equipment. Farzan would like deduct the cost of the equipment as quickly as possible, so he would like to make a section 179 election. Debby, on the other hand, would prefer to recover the cost of the new equipment under the normal depreciation rules. Ella would prefer to

delay the cost recovery, so she would rather not make the section 179 election, and she would like to elect to depreciate the equipment using the straight-line method. Can each of the parties elect to treat their respective shares of the cost differently? If not, how can they resolve this difference?

5. How does the DD Pizzeria LLC Operating Agreement require Debby to allocate the Year 5 taxable income to the members, assuming Debby distributes the amount in the statement of cash flows and does not make any election with respect to the property it places in service in Year 5?
6. How will Year 5 tax-item allocations and distributions affect the members' outside bases? Explain why the outside-basis adjustments must reflect the allocations of the various items and the distributions. How will the allocations and distributions affect the members' capital account balances? Complete the balance sheet and tax information for the end of Year 5.
7. What are the income tax consequences to Debby and the other members of DD Pizzeria LLC paying Debby's salary in Year 5?
8. The city is planning to do some infrastructure work outside two of DD Pizzeria's locations, which could adversely affect the revenue of those locations. If the work proceeds as planned, Debby anticipates that DD Pizzeria LLC will have as much as $150,000 of losses for Year 6. Debby has also entered a cooking competition. If she wins, she will have an extra $250,000 of income in Year 6, which will put her in the highest income tax bracket. Debby would like to avoid that possibility by allocating all of the $150,000 potential losses to herself in Year 6. Would she be able to allocate all of that loss to herself in Year 6? If she can make that allocation, what would be her tax consequences?

# MEMORANDUM #4

## (General Allocations)

| | |
|---|---|
| To: | Tax Associate |
| From: | Tax Partner |
| Subject: | Allocations of Partnership Tax Items |
| Date: | April 1, Year 6 |

***Research Sources: Materials in Chapter 4***

Debby called to inform us that Farzan is under IRS audit. Debby wants to be prepared if the IRS asks questions about the DD Pizzeria LLC allocations and would like us to examine the operating agreement and advise her with respect to the validity of the allocations through Year 5.

1. Is the DD Pizzeria LLC Operating Agreement compliant with the economic effect safe harbor or the alternate test for economic effect? If not, what would it take to make it compliant, and should we advise Debby to amend the agreement to make it compliant?
2. Do tax-item allocations made pursuant to the DD Pizzeria LLC Operating Agreement have economic effect? Include in your analysis an illustration of how hypothetical book-value liquidations help determine whether allocations have economic effect. To keep things simple, the CPA asked that we use the Year 1 and Year 5 allocations to illustrate the analysis required to answer this question.
3. Are tax-item allocations made pursuant to the DD Pizzeria LLC Operating Agreement in accordance with the members' interests in DD Pizzeria LLC? If not, how would the IRS reallocate the tax items for any or all of the first four years of DD Pizzeria LLC operations (assuming each tax year is still open for audit)?
4. Farzan's tax advisor assured him that the IRS will not raise the allocation provisions on audit because the audit rules are too complex. Farzan anticipates that he will have tax losses from outside DD Pizzeria LLC for Year 5 and the next few years, so he will not be able to use some of the deductions that DD Pizzeria LLC would otherwise allocate to him. Ella has asked Debby and Farzan to agree to allocate Farzan's share of DD Pizzeria LLC's depreciation deductions to her during that period of time. The allocation will have economic effect. Debby has asked for our opinion about whether she can make that allocation. Analyze each of the following questions:
   a. What results would obtain under the DD Pizzeria LLC operating agreement in Year 5 and future years if she made the allocation? Show how the economic effect of the allocation is or is not substantial under the general test.
   b. Show how the economic effect of the allocation is or is not substantial under the overall tax effects test.
   c. Show how the economic effect of the allocation is or is not substantial under the test for transitory allocations.

5. Learning that Farzan will have tax losses this year, Ella would like to ask him to agree to take her distributive share of any taxable interest income. In exchange, she will take an equal amount of his distributive share of interest from tax-exempt bonds. Ella has asked for our opinion about whether she can allocate those items in that manner.

# MEMORANDUM #5A

## (Compensatory Interests)

To: Tax Associate
From: Tax Partner
Subject: Compensatory Transfer of a Tax-Partnership Interest
Date: August 1, Year 6

***Research Sources: Materials in Chapter 5***

1. Debby is still under an IRS audit for Year 1. The audit agent noticed that Debby did not contribute any capital upon formation of DD Pizzeria LLC, and she did not recognize any income when she received her DD Pizzeria LLC interest. She noticed that Debby currently has a positive capital account balance in DD Pizzeria LLC, so she asked why Debby did not report income upon receipt of the interest. TEFRA does not prevent the IRS from challenging Debby's reporting position.

   What type of interests did Debby, Ella, and Farzan receive when they formed DD Pizzeria LLC? Is it possible for the recipient of a profits-only interest to have a positive capital account balance after receiving the interest? Does the IRS have any basis for challenging Debby's original treatment of the receipt of her interest in DD Pizzeria LLC based upon her current positive capital account balance?
2. The answer to Question 1 will be timely because Debby is very impressed with work that Ignacio is doing as a manager of DD Pizzeria, and she would like to give him an equity interest in DD Pizzeria LLC. She is thinking about granting Ignacio a 10% Class B interest. Because Ignacio does such good work, she is concerned that he might entertain offers from other restaurants. If he leaves within three years after the grant of the interest, she would want that interest to automatically revert back to DD Pizzeria LLC. Debby asked us to consider the legal, tax, and accounting implications of granting the interest, which she would like to make effective as of August 10, Year 6.
   a. What are the tax consequences of granting the Class B interest to Ignacio? Prepare a revised Schedule A to reflect the granting of the interest.
   b. What would be the tax consequences if Ignacio leaves DD Pizzeria within three years after the grant of the interest?
3. As part of the Tax Cuts and Jobs Act of 2017, Congress enacted section 1061. How, if at all, will that provision affect the interests that Debby holds and the interest that Ignacio may receive? If any gain from the sale of the Cheez Corp stock were allocated to Debby, would that provision affect the character of such gain? The article *Carried Interests Tax* in the Recent Developments section of this Client File may direct you to provisions of section 199A that may help with this analysis.

4. Debby has asked how granting the interest during the partnership's taxable year will affect allocations. Please research the necessary law and answer each of the following questions.
   a. How should DD Pizzeria LLC apportion cash flows and taxable income to the period prior to the grant of the interest and to the period following the grant of the interest? For this Problem 3.a. only, consider the following two scenarios. How would the apportionment change if construction outside of two locations during January, February, and March resulted in $350,000 less in total revenue during those months (sales and all other items otherwise remain the same)? Alternatively, what if a sudden rise in the cost of ingredients in September resulted in an additional $250,000 of costs for September, October, November, and December that Debby had not expected (costs and all other items otherwise remain the same)?
   b. Does the DD Pizzeria LLC Operating Agreement or tax law require Debby to make book adjustments when it grants Ignacio the Class B interest for services? Why might Debby decide to make book adjustments, even if the operating agreement and law do not require her to do so?
   c. What would be the book and tax situation immediately prior to DD Pizzeria LLC making a book adjustment?
   d. How would book adjustments affect DD Pizzeria LLC's book and tax amounts, and what would DD Pizzeria LLC's book and tax situation be following the adjustment?

# MEMORANDUM #6A

## (Section 704(c) Allocations)

| | |
|---|---|
| To: | Tax Associate |
| From: | Tax Partner |
| Subject: | Allocations after a Compensatory Transfer of a Tax-Partnership Interest |
| Date: | March 25, Year 7 |

***Research Sources: Materials in Chapter 6***

Debby booked-up DD Pizzeria LLC's assets according to our guidance when she granted the Class B interest to Ignacio, effective on August 10, Year 6. She has contacted us for more specific advice about the Year 6 tax-item allocations.

1. What are the book and tax depreciation and amortization amounts for the portion of the year following the grant of the interest? Can we use an aggregation method with any of these assets?
2. How should DD Pizzeria LLC allocate Year 6 depreciation and amortization deductions under each of the following methods? Which method would each of the respective members of DD Pizzeria LLC prefer, and which method should DD Pizzeria LLC adopt?
   a. The traditional method.
   b. The traditional method with curative allocations.
   c. The remedial allocation method.
3. How should DD Pizzeria LLC allocate the loss under each of the section 704(c) methods if it sold the Cheez Corp Stock for $12,000 on December 31, Year 6? Which method would each of the respective members of DD Pizzeria LLC prefer and which method should DD Pizzeria LLC adopt?
4. How should DD Pizzeria LLC allocate book and tax items related to accounts payable and accounts receivable?
5. How will DD Pizzeria LLC allocate all other profit and loss items for Year 6? What will DD Pizzeria LLC's book and tax situation be at the end of Year 6?

# MEMORANDUM #5B/6B

## (Property Contributions)

To: Tax Associate
From: Tax Partner
Subject: Admission of a Property-Contributing Member
Date: October 6, Year 7

---

***Research Sources: Materials in Chapters 5 and 6***

Debby called to notify us that she is considering granting a Class A interest to Jada. As you probably know, Jada is the owner of ChezeGlaze™, which makes grilled cheese sandwiches on glazed donuts. Jada basically wants to retire, and Debby wants to expand DD Pizzeria LLC's menu. Nonetheless, Debby does not want to take on more restaurants and does not particularly like the way Jada has managed her operations. Consequently, they propose that instead of having DD Pizzeria LLC acquire Jada's chain of restaurants, Jada will transfer her ChezeGlaze™ trademark in exchange for a Class A interest. Jada paid $150,000 to acquire the ChezeGlaze™ trademark on May 20, Year 1. Debby and Jada agree that the value of the ChezeGlaze™ is now $435,000. Before finalizing the deal, Debby wants to know what the tax and legal consequences will be to DD Pizzeria LLC and Jada if they move forward with this plan. Before we get back to Debby, we should have answers for the following questions:

1. What will be the tax consequences to DD Pizzeria LLC and Jada on the transfer of the ChezeGlaze™ trademark in exchange for a Class A interest? What changes to the DD Pizzeria LLC Operating Agreement will Debby have to make to reflect the exchange?
2. Explain how DD Pizzeria LLC will apportion Year 7 cash flows, taxable income, and book income to the periods before and after November 15, Year 7, assuming Jada joins DD Pizzeria LLC on that date.
3. Should DD Pizzeria LLC book up its assets when it transfers a Class A interest in exchange for the ChezeGlaze™ trademark? If so, how will the book-up affect capital accounts?
4. Explain what DD Pizzeria LLC will have to do to allocate tax and book items for Year 7. Will the ceiling rule apply to allocations of the amortization deduction of the ChezeGlaze™ trademark?
5. Consider which section 704(c) method each of the members will prefer.

# MEMORANDUM #7

## (DISTRIBUTIONS)

| | |
|---|---|
| To: | Tax Associate |
| From: | Tax Partner |
| Subject: | Distribution |
| Date: | December 3, Year 8 |

***Research Sources: Materials in Chapter 7***

Debby has contacted us with the following questions about the Year 8 distributions. She plans to make the UPR distribution to Ella and Jada and would like to distribute an amount to Ella that is sufficient to cover her UCC, either in the form of cash or by distributing the ChezeGlaze™ trademark to her. DD Pizzeria LLC's CPA warned Debby that either distribution could trigger ordinary income under section 751(b) and possibly raise other tax issues, so she called for our advice. She does not yet have financial information for Year 8, so, to the extent necessary to determine book and tax values of property, we'll have to begin with end-of-Year-7 amounts and adjust as needed. She provided the projected values and financial and tax information for the end of Year 8 in the attached spreadsheet. Do the necessary research and analysis and provide answers to the following questions.

1. Describe generally how DD Pizzeria LLC would allocate gain or loss if it were to sell the ChezeGlaze™ trademark at the end of the year for its projected fair market value.
2. General Application of the Distribution Rules.
   a. If DD Pizzeria LLC makes the contemplated distributions in either of the respective forms, what would be the total amount it transfers to Ella in Year 8? What would be the composition (for both book and tax purposes) of the amount DD Pizzeria LLC transfers to Ella?
   b. How would a cash distribution affect the members, if section 751(b) does not apply?
   c. How would a distribution of the ChezeGlaze™ trademark affect the members, if section 751(b) does not apply?
   d. Should DD Pizzeria LLC book-up its assets if it transfers either the cash or ChezeGlaze™ trademark? Illustrate how the book-up will affect the members.
3. General Application of Section 751(b).
   a. What will be the tax and book values of DD Pizzeria LLC's unrealized receivables, inventory items (i.e., section 751 property), and other items (i.e., non-section 751 property) on December 31?
   b. What will be Ella's interest in the section 751 property and non-section 751 property? Would a distribution of cash or property to Ella be an exchange of 751 property for non-section 751 property? Would section 751(b) apply to a UCC cash distribution to Ella?

4. <u>Section 751(b) Tax Consequences of the Cash Distribution.</u>
   a. If section 751(b) does apply to the cash distribution, what would be the character and amount of gain or loss that each member would recognize on the distribution?
   b. What would be the book value and basis of each property following a UCC cash distribution and what would be the amount of each member's capital account balance and outside basis?
5. <u>Section 751(b) Tax Consequences of the Property Distribution.</u>
   a. If section 751(b) applies, how much gain would each member of DD Pizzeria LLC recognize if Debby makes a UCC distribution using the ChezeGlaze™ trademark?
   b. What would be the book value and basis of each property following a UCC distribution of the ChezeGlaze™ trademark and what would be the amount of each member's capital account balance and outside basis?

# MEMORANDUM #8

## (NON-PARTNER CAPACITY)

| | |
|---|---|
| To: | Tax Associate |
| From: | Tax Partner |
| Subject: | Partner-Partnership Transactions |
| Date: | December 19, Year 8 |

***Research Sources: Materials in Chapter 8***

I just spoke with Debby, and DD Pizzeria LLC continues to grow and enjoy success, but some discord already exists between Jada and the other members. Several matters have arisen, and she has asked for our advice regarding them.

1. If Jada received a UPR distribution at the end of Year 8, what would be the proper tax treatment of that distribution?
2. The members have encouraged Debby to make a cash distribution to Jada that would satisfy her UCC and UPR. She asked us to consider how the distribution would affect Jada and the other members and whether they could do any planning to help the other member's tax situation. Please research and answer the following questions:
   a. Could the distribution possibly result in a disguised sale to Jada?
   b. What would be the tax consequences to Jada and the other members if the distribution is not part of a disguised sale?
   c. What would be the tax consequences to Jada and the other members if the distribution is part of a disguised sale?
   d. Would Debby and the other members prefer the distribution be part of a disguised sale? What would Jada prefer? What, if anything, can Debby do to influence whether the distribution is part of a disguised sale?
   e. Debby is a little bit worried that if they simply liquidate Jada's interest that she may accuse her of bad-faith dealing. She has asked what the tax consequences would be if, instead of cashing Jada out, she redeems Jada's Class A interests by distributing cash sufficient to meet all of her UPR and UCC and issue her a Class C interest that provides that Jada will receive annual payments for the next eight years equal to 4.5% of the value of the Cheze-Glaze™ trademark at the time Jada transferred it to DD Pizzeria LLC. What would be the proper tax treatment of those annual payments?
3. Now that DD Pizzeria is a thriving business enterprise, Ignazio would like to renegotiate his employment contract to get a larger share of company profits. He presented a plan with the following features:
   a. He will forego compensation increases for seven years and perhaps consider waiving a portion of his current salary.
   b. DD Pizzeria LLC will issue a new class of interests (Class D interests) that will provide the holders with a right to preferential distributions of profits. DD Pizzeria LLC will make those preferential distributions after it has returned all of the UCC but before it makes any profits distributions to

holders of Class B interests. (Debby anticipates that she will make the final UCC distributions this year or next.)

c. The amount distributable under the Class D interest will equal 11% of any net increase in Available Cash for the year.

What will be the tax consequences to DD Pizzeria LLC and Ignazio, if they adopt Ignazio's proposal and DD Pizzeria LLC makes Class D payments?

4. The members of DD Pizzeria LLC would like to develop a more aggressive marketing plan. They are in talks with Francesca to hire her to help develop and implement a marketing plan. Francesca said that she would like a share of DD Pizzeria LLC's profits. If DD Pizzeria LLC grants Francesca some Class D interests in DD Pizzeria LLC, would payments pursuant to the Class D interests be compensation or distributions? Would the classification of the payments significantly affect the tax consequences to the members?

# MEMORANDUM #9

## (Tax-Partnership Liabilities)

| | |
|---|---|
| To: | Tax Associate |
| From: | Tax Partner |
| Subject: | Allocations of Tax-Partnership Liabilities |
| Date: | October 12, Year 14 |

***Research Sources: Materials in Chapter 9***

Recall from Memorandum #2 (dated February 15, Year 6) that Debby was considering purchasing an office building. She ended up purchasing 11 Duffield for $14,600,000 on January 1, Year 14, through 11 Duffield LLC with Manage Great Realty LLC (MGR), a property-management company. Upon formation, Debby contributed $3,150,000 and MGR contributed $120,000 to 11 Duffield LLC. 11 Duffield LLC granted a mortgage and borrowed another $12,175,000 to purchase 11 Duffield for $14,600,000.

11 Duffield LLC would like to maintain about $850,000 of cash reserves. It recognizes, however, that it may have to borrow to fund operations in its early years. Consequently, it has secured a $1,000,000 line of credit. It will draw on that line of credit whenever necessary to prevent the year-end cash balance from going below $10,000, and will repay the outstanding line of credit during any year in which available cash would otherwise be greater than $10,000. MRG is a single-member disregarded LLC wholly owned by MGR Parent LLC. MGR generally maintains no more $75,000 of cash reserves and its only asset is its interest in 11 Duffield LLC.

Debby has provided us with the operating agreement, loan documents, and pro forma financial information for 11 Duffield LLC (attached hereto) and has asked us to advise her about various tax aspects of this arrangement, and we need to consider the following questions.

1. Will the mortgage be recourse or nonrecourse under section 752?
2. How would 11 Duffield LLC allocate the mortgage liability at the end of Years 14–20, assuming the actual results match the pro forma?
3. What are the tax consequences of changes to the members' shares of the tax-partnership liabilities?
4. Will money drawn down from the line of credit come within the section 752 definition of liability?
5. Assuming that any money draw down from the line of credit comes within the section 752 definition of liability, analyze the following problems.
   a. Will the line-of-credit liability be recourse or nonrecourse under section 752?
   b. How, if at all, will MGR's structure affect the allocation of the line-of-credit liability?
6. Debby indicated that MGR might agree to indemnify her if she pays any of the guaranty. What effect would such an indemnity have on the members' shares of 22 Duffield LLC's liabilities? Would the answer change if one of MGR's principals were to agree to indemnify Debby for any payments she makes under the guaranty?

# MEMORANDUM #10

## (Disguised Sales with Liabilities)

| | |
|---|---|
| To: | Tax Associate |
| From: | Tax Partner |
| Subject: | Tax-Partnership Liabilities and Disguises Sales |
| Date: | October 9, Year 20 |

***Research Sources: Materials in Chapter 10***

Debby called to inform us that she would like to contribute anther property to 11 Duffield LLC. Debby has been a member of another real estate venture, Multiple Real Estate Holdings LP, that is dissolving. As part of the dissolution, Debby will receive The Amarillo, a commercial building with the following information.

| | |
|---|---|
| Value: | $5,300,000 |
| Adjusted Basis: | $3,832,284 |
| Mortgage: | $3,830,000 |

The Amarillo is in need of some capital improvements and repairs. Debby has approached MGR inquiring whether it would be interested in having Debby contribute The Amarillo to 11 Duffield in exchange for Class A interests. 11 Duffield could then borrow against both properties to fund the improvements. She anticipates that she would receive and transfer the property to 11 Duffield LLC on January 1, Year 21. Debby has asked us to advise her with respect to the tax treatment of the possible contribution of The Amarillo to 11 Duffield LLC.

Debby indicated that 11 Duffield LLC's financial performance over the last several years has closely matched the pro forma projections she provided a few years ago, so we can use those numbers, along with our prior analysis of liability allocates, as needed for the analysis. Debby also indicated that the rent revenue of The Amarillo, after accounting for operating expenses, is about 3% of its value. For now, assume that Debby will transfer The Amarillo to 11 Duffield LLC subject to its current liability. She provided a copy of the note and the guarantee for that liability and says the other loan documents are very similar to the 11 Duffield loan documents.

1. Debby indicated that the other partnership incurred the liability to acquire The Amarillo three years ago. Please research and provide an analysis of the following issues.
   a. Will the liability be recourse or nonrecourse after 11 Duffield LLC assumes it?
   b. How will 11 Duffield LLC allocate the liability, and how will that allocation affect Debby's share of the liability before and after the contribution?
   c. What will be the tax consequences to Debby of transferring The Amarillo to 11 Duffield LLC?
2. Debby has indicated that she may be able to take The Amarillo subject to no liabilities, by giving up rights to other assets owned by the dissolving investment arrangement. If so, she would like to know what the tax consequences would be

to her if she were to draw cash out of the property before or after transferring it to 11 Duffield LLC. I believe she has two alternatives that would allow her to draw cash by borrowing against the property. Please consider the tax consequences of each alternative.

a. First, prior to contributing The Amarillo to 11 Duffield LLC, Debby could borrow $3,830,000 against it and then contribute it subject to the new loan.
    i. Can the newly-procured loan be a qualified liability?
    ii. What would be the tax consequences to Debby and 11 Duffield LLC if she transfers The Amarillo subject to the newly-procured loan to 11 Duffield LLC?
b. Second, she could transfer The Amarillo to 11 Duffield LLC free and clear of any liabilities, but shortly after Debby transfers The Amarillo to 11 Duffield LLC, 11 Duffield LLC would borrow $3,830,000, which would be secured by The Amarillo. After securing that financing, 11 Duffield would distribute the $3,830,000 to Debby. What would be the tax consequences to Debby and 11 Duffield LLC under this alternative?
c. What, if anything, can Debby do to improve her tax situation upon transfer of The Amarillo under these two scenarios?

3. Debby also asked us whether she might risk recognizing gain on the transfer of The Amarillo from the other investment arrangement, which is a tax partnership. She will receive the property in complete liquidation of her interest in that arrangement. Would a liquidating distribution to her of The Amarillo cause her or the dissolving partnership from which she will receive The Amarillo to recognize gain?

# MEMORANDUM #11

## (NONRECOURSE DEDUCTIONS)

To: Tax Associate
From: Tax Partner
Subject: Allocations of Nonrecourse Deductions
Date: February 10, Year 22

---

***Research Sources: Materials in Chapter 11***

Debby called with a concern about how 11 Duffield LLC has accounted for gain and loss allocations following a refinancing of 11 Duffield LLC on January 1, Year 19. Because the property has appreciated significantly, National Bank was willing to restructure the loan. She has asked us to consider the allocations and describe how 11 Duffield LLC should make those allocations, based upon the following general information about the restructuring. As part of the restructuring, National Bank agreed to increase the outstanding loan balance to $11,700,000 by paying 11 Duffield LLC $954,827, which it applied toward operating expenses and reserves. National Bank agreed to have the loan secured by nothing other than 11 Duffield LLC and waived any guaranty requirement. The loan carries 4.5% cumulative simple interest with of the interest due at the end of Year 23, 20% of the outstanding principal is due at the end of Year 21, with the balance due at the end of Year 23.

Debby did not have exact financial information about 11 Duffield LLC's financial performance in Year 21 and did not have projections for Year 22 and Year 23. She estimated that rent revenue from the two properties that Duffield LLC holds was about $2,700,000 and operating expenses were about $1,500,000 in Year 19. For purposes of analysis, she suggested that we treat those amounts as increasing by about 6% each year.

To assist Debby, we must analyze the following the matters.

1. What effect, if any, did the loan restructuring have on the member's shares of the 11 Duffield loan? What affect does accrued interest have on their shares of liability?
2. Did 11 Duffield LLC have any minimum gain in Year 19 or Year 20?
3. If the restructuring results in minimum gain, will 11 Duffield LLC have nonrecourse deductions? Explain how the concept of economic effect relates to nonrecourse deductions.
4. How should 11 Duffield LLC allocate the tax items related to any increases in minimum gain in Year 19 and Year 20?
5. What effect doe the repayment of principal in Year 21 have on minimum gain? What are the tax consequences of a change in minimum gain resulting from the loan repayment?
6. I asked Debby if 11 Duffield LLC had distributed any of the proceeds of the Year 19 loan restructuring. She could not recall, but asked whether it would make a difference if it had. Would a distribution of all or a portion of the $954,827 of cash that 11 Duffield LLC received when it restructured the loan have affected the computation of minimum gain?

7. If, in Year 22, Debby were to guarantee $100,000 of the 11 Duffield loan, how would that guarantee affect the computation of 11 Duffield LLC's minimum gain? How would 11 Duffield LLC allocate the items related to the $100,000 guaranty?
8. Debby suggested that she and MGR are considering selling 11 Duffield LLC at the beginning of Year 23 for around $15,000,000. How would gain from that disposition be allocated to Debby and MGR?
9. Does 11 Duffield LLC have any exculpatory liabilities? If so, how should it allocate the tax items associated with those liabilities?

# MEMORANDUM #12

## (Transfers of Tax-Partnership Interests)

| | |
|---|---|
| To: | Tax Associate |
| From: | Tax Partner |
| Subject: | Transfers of Interests in Tax Partnerships |
| Date: | May 5, Year 24 |

***Research Sources: Materials in Chapter 12***

11 Duffield LLC ended up selling 11 Duffield on January 1, Year 23 for $15,000,000. Debby is now in talks with Keun to sell two-thirds of her Class A interest in 11 Duffield LLC to him for $1,550,000. She has asked us to provide tax advice related to that potential sale. She indicated that the actual performance of 11 Duffield LLC was very close to the 6.5% changes that she had estimated for Year 22. Because 11 Duffield LLC sold 11 Duffield, its rent revenues for Year 23 were about $850,000 and operating expenses were about $685,000. She estimates those numbers will increase about 5% in Year 24. Please analyze and prepare to discuss the following questions.

**Note on changes to tax law:** When considering the materials in Chapter 12 of the casebook, recognize that Congress repealed Section 708(b)(1)(B) as part of the Tax Cuts and Jobs Act of 2017.

1. What effect, if any, does the transfer have on the continuation of 11 Duffield LLC?
2. If the sale occurs at the end of Year 24, how much gain or loss will Debby recognize on the sale?
3. What would be the character of any gain or loss that Debby recognizes on the transfer of the interest and at what rates would that gain or loss be taxed?
4. What basis would Keun take in his acquired interests and what would be his capital account balance?
5. Does 11 Duffield LLC have a section 754 election in effect? Consider what the effect would be of having such an election in effect:
   a. What would be the amount of any basis adjustment under section 743?
   b. How would 11 Duffield LLC apportion any basis adjustment? Debby estimates The Amarillo will be worth about $5,000,000 at the end of Year 24, and it will likely have about $25,000 of due but unpaid rent at that time.
   c. How would 11 Duffield LLC account for the basis adjustment in Year 25?
6. What would be a reason not to make a section 754 election? If 11 Duffield LLC did not make the election, how might Debby, Keun, and 11 Duffield LLC account for the potential additional tax that results from not making the election?
7. Keun has expressed some concern about joining an 11 Duffield LLC because of its prior ownership of 11 Duffield, and he would like to consider migrating the LLC from New York to Delaware.
   a. What types of transactions would allow the parties to migrate 11 Duffield LLC from New York to Delaware?

b. Would such a migration affect the continuation of 11 Duffield LLC if it occurred as part of the transfer of Debby's interests?
c. Keun is more familiar with owning real estate in limited partnerships and has asked if Debby and MGR would consider converting 11 Duffield LLC into a limited partnership as part of the migration.
   i. How could the parties accomplish the conversion as part of the migration?
   ii. Would the conversion affect the continuation of 11 Duffield LLC?

# MEMORANDUM #13
## (Mergers and Divisions)

| | |
|---|---|
| To: | Tax Associate |
| From: | Tax Partner |
| Subject: | Mergers and Divisions of Tax Partnerships |
| Date: | November 12, Year 26 |

***Research Sources: Materials in Chapter 13***

Debby, Keun, and MGR would like to separate ownership of 11 Duffield and The Amarillo. The plan is to move The Amarillo from 11 Duffield LLC into a different tax partnership Diversified Properties LP owned by Debby, Keun, MGR and other investors. Debby suggested that we can continue to use the financial information she provided in Year 22 to analyze and give advice with respect to the proposed transaction. She provided the attached summary balance sheet for Diversified Properties LP as of the end of Year 25. Its general partner/manager is Diversified Property Management LLC, which is wholly owned by Property Syndicator LLC. Them manager of Diversified Property Management LLC is Joline, who indicates that Diversified Properties LP still owns the same properties and has the same ownership structure today that it had at the end of Year 25. The Amarillo will be the first property that they have added to Diversified Properties LP through contribution. All of the other members of Diversified Properties LP are the original investors. We will have to address the following matters to provide advice.

1. Debby believes that at the end of Year 26, when the transaction would occur, 11 Duffield will be worth $14,000,000 and The Amarillo will be worth $7,000,000. What tax form will the transfer from 11 Duffield LLC and to Diversified Properties LP take with each of the following transaction alternatives (in each situation, The Amarillo will transfer subject to the outstanding liability?
   a. 11 Duffield LLC contributes The Amarillo to Diversified Properties LP and then distributes the LP interests to Debby, Keun, and MGR.
   b. 11 Duffield LLC distributes The Amarillo to Debby, Keun, and MGR, and they immediately contribute it Diversified Properties LP.
   c. 11 Duffield LLC forms a DropCo LLC and contributes The Amarillo to DropCo LLC. DropCo LLC then merges with Diversified Properties LP.
   d. 11 Duffield LLC forms DownCo LLC, contributes 11 Duffield to DownCo LLC, and then distributes the interests in DownCo LLC to Debby, Keun, and MGR. Diversified Properties LP then merges into 11 Duffield LLC.
   e. 11 Duffield LLC forms DownCo LLC, contributes 11 Duffield to DownCo LLC, and then distributes the interests in DownCo LLC to Debby, Keun, and MGR. Diversified Properties LP then contributes its assets and liabilities to 11 Duffield LLC in exchange for interests in 11 Duffield LLC and then distributes those interests to its members in complete liquidation.
   f. Diversified Properties LP contributes its assets and liabilities to ComboCo LLC in exchange for interests in ComboCo LLC, and 11 Duffield LLC

contributes The Amarillo to ComboCo LLC in exchange for interests in ComboCo LLC. Diversified Properties LP then distributes its interests I ComboCo LLC to its members in liquidation, and 11 Duffield LLC distributes its interests in ComboCo LLC to Debby, Keun, and MGR.

2. Does the tax form of the transaction affect the tax consequences to the members of the two tax partnerships? Identify the different tax consequences, if any, of the following transactions.
   a. 11 Duffield LLC is treated as distributing The Amarillo to Debby, Keun, and MGR who are treated as then contributing it to Diversified Properties LP.
   b. 11 Duffield LLC is treated as contributing The Amarillo to Diversified Properties LP in exchange for interests in Diversified LP and then distributes the interests to Debby, Keun, and MGR.
   c. 11 Duffield LLC is treated as distributing 11 Duffield to Debby, Keun, and MGR, after which Diversified Properties LP is treated as contributed its assets and liabilities to 11 Duffield LLC in exchange for interests in 11 Duffield LLC, following which Diversified Properties LP is treated as distributing the interests in 11 Duffield LLC to its members.
   d. 11 Duffield LLC is treated as distributing 11 Duffield to Debby, Keun, and MGR, after which Diversified Properties LP is treated as distributing its assets and liabilities to its members in complete liquidation, following which they are treated as contributing the assets and liabilities to 11 Duffield LLC.
3. Debby indicated that she would like to take some cash out of the transaction and take a proportionately smaller interest in either the tax partnership that owns 11 Duffield LLC, the one that owns The Amarillo, or both. How could the parties structure the transaction to allow Debby to take some cash out of the transaction, and what would be the tax consequences of doing so?

**Diversified Properties LP**
**Summary Balance Sheet as of December 31, Year 14**

| Assets | | | Liabilities and Equity | |
|---|---|---|---|---|
| | Adjusted Basis | FMV | | |
| Cash | $550,000 | $550,000 | Liabilities | $11,096,868 |
| Triumph Towers | $4,512,492 | $6,250,000 | DPM (GP) | $250,000 |
| Myro Lergo | $7,259,376 | $7,150,000 | LPs | $975,000 |
| Total | $12,321,868 | $13,950,000 | Total | $12,321,868 |

FOLDER II

# DD PIZZERIA DOCUMENTS

# DD PIZZERIA LLC OPERATING AGREEMENT

This OPERATING AGREEMENT ("**Agreement**") of DD Pizzeria LLC, a New York limited liability company ("**Company**"), dated as of January 1, Year 1, by and among the initial Manager and the Members set forth on Exhibit A hereof, as amended from time to time.

## ARTICLE I

### Definitions

1.1 Definitions. For purposes of this Agreement, capitalized terms used herein and not otherwise defined shall have the meanings set forth in this Section 1.1:

"Act" means the New York Limited Liability Company Law as in effect on the date hereof, as such Act may be hereafter amended from time to time, and any successor provision or provisions thereto.

"Adjusted Capital Account" means, with respect to any Member, the Member's Capital Account as of the end of the relevant Fiscal Year, after giving effect to the following adjustments:

(a) crediting to such Capital Account any amount that such Member is obligated to restore pursuant to Treas. Reg. §1.704-1(b)(2)(ii)(c) or is deemed to be obligated to restore pursuant to Treas. Reg. §§1.704-2(g) or 1.704-2(i); and

(b) debiting to such Capital Account the items described in Treas. Reg. §§1.704-1(b)(2)(ii)(d)(4), (5), and (6).

"Assignee" means a person who or which has been assigned a Membership Interest in the Profits and Losses of the Company, including without limitation, the right to receive Distributions from the Company, but has not been admitted as a Substituted Member pursuant to this Agreement.

"Available Cash" means the cash reserves of the Company in excess of that required: (a) to satisfy current liabilities; (b) to reasonably provide for the payment of long-term liabilities of the Company; and (c) to reasonably set aside a reserve for future needs, contingencies, and liabilities of the Company, as determined from time-to-time by the Manager.

"Capital Account" means the capital account established and maintained for each Member in accordance with Treas. Reg. §1.704-1(b)(2)(iv) or any successor section thereto. If a Member shall transfer all or any part of such Member's Membership Interest, a proportional share of such Member's Capital Account shall become the Capital Account of such Assignee or Substituted Member.

"Capital Contribution" means the amount of cash and the net fair market value of any property contributed to the Company.

"Class A Member" means the initial Member or Members, as set forth in Schedule A, which shall be amended from time-to-time as necessary to reflect Transfers and Successor Members hereunder.

"Class A Percentage Interest" means a Class A Member's aggregate rights in the Company, including, without limitation, the Class A Member's right to a share of the Profits and Losses of the Company, and right to receive Distributions of the Company.

"Class B Member" means the Members, as set forth in Schedule A, which shall be amended from time-to-time as necessary to reflect Transfers and Successor Members hereunder.

"Class B Percentage Interest" means a Class B Member's aggregate rights in the Company, including, without limitation, the Class B Member's right to a share of the Profits and Losses of the Company, right to receive Distributions of the Company, and right to vote and participate in the management of the Company.

"Code" means the Internal Revenue Code of 1986, as amended, and in effect from time-to-time.

"Distribution" means money or the fair market value of property transferred by the Company to one or more of its Members in their capacity of as Members.

"Majority" means one or more Class B Members who or which, collectively, own Class B Membership Interests constituting more than 50% of the Class B Percentage Interests of the Company.

"Manager" means, initially, Debby, or his or her successor or successors as appointed from time-to-time in accordance with Section 5.2 herein.

"Member" means each Person designated as a Member on Schedule A, attached hereto, as amended from time-to-time to remove Members who or which have withdrawn from the Company and to add Persons who or which have been duly admitted as additional Members or Substitute Members in accordance with Section 3.2 herein and the provisions of the Act. The term Member shall mean either a Class A Member or a Class B Member, as appropriate, depending on the context, and the term Members shall refer to both Class A Members and Class B Members.

"Membership Interest" means each Member's aggregate rights in the Company, including, without limitation, such Member's right to a share of the Profits and Losses of the Company, right to receive Distributions from the Company, and right to vote and participate in the management of the Company, if applicable.

"Net Profit" and "Net Loss" means the net amount of the items of Profit and Loss for the taxable year, but excluding those items of Profit or Loss to the extent that they are specially allocated under Sections 4.2(c) or 4.2(d) herein for the taxable year.

"Percentage Interest" means each Member's aggregate share of the Profits and Losses of the Company as set forth in Schedule A, attached hereto, as amended from time-to-time.

"Person" means any association, corporation, joint stock company, estate, general partnership (including any registered limited liability partnership or foreign limited liability partnership), limited association, limited liability company (including a professional service limited liability company), foreign limited liability company (including a foreign professional service limited liability company), joint venture, limited partnership, natural person, real estate investment trust, business trust or other trust, custodian, nominee or any other individual or entity in its own or any representative capacity.

"Preferred Return" means, with respect to a Class A Member, the amount that shall accrue at the rate of ten percent (10.00%) per annum on the amount of such Class A Member's Unreturned Capital Contribution. The Preferred Return shall be cumulative, but not compounded, and shall accrue for the benefit of such Class A Member for each year or portion thereof (based on a 360-day year consisting of twelve 30-day months). The Preferred Return shall be recomputed monthly, not earlier than a date five (5) days prior to the date of any Distribution, or from time-to-time, as necessary and appropriate.

"Profit" and "Loss". For purposes of computing the amount of any item of Profit or Loss of the Company, the determination, recognition, and classification of any item of income, gain, loss, or deduction to be allocated pursuant to Article 4 and to be reflected in the Capital Accounts shall be the same as its determination, recognition, and classification for federal income tax purposes (including the method of depreciation, cost recovery, or amortization used for such purposes); provided, however, that:

(i) Profit shall include those items of income and gain which are not includable in the gross income of the Company or are exempt from federal income tax.

(ii) Loss consisting of expenditures described in Section 705(a)(2)(B) or treated by Treas. Reg. §1.704-1(b)(2)(iv)(i) as expenditures described in Section 705(a)(2)(B), and not otherwise taken into account in computing Profit or Loss herein, shall be excluded from Profit and Loss.

(iii) Loss consisting of depreciation, amortization, and cost recovery deduction with respect to property having a book value that differs from the adjusted tax basis of such property shall be computed by reference to such property's book value in accordance with Treas. Reg. §1.704-1(b)(2)(iv)(g).

(iv) If property of the Company is revalued pursuant to Treas. Reg. §1.704-1(b)(2)(iv)(e) or (f), the Capital Accounts shall be adjusted to reflect the manner in which the unrealized income, gain, loss, and deduction would be allocated among the Members if there were a taxable disposition of such property for the fair market value of such property on the date of such revaluation.

(v) Items of income, gain, loss, or deduction that are allocated pursuant to Section 4.2(c) or (d) herein shall be excluded from the computation of Profit and Loss for purposes of Section 4.2(a) and (b) herein.

To the extent an actual adjustment to the adjusted tax basis of any property of the Company pursuant to Sections 732(d) or 734(b), or a notional adjustment to the adjusted tax basis of any property of the Company with respect to the transferee Membership Interest pursuant to Section 743(b), is required, pursuant to Treas. Reg. §1.704-1(b)(2)(iv)(m), to be taken into account in determining Capital Accounts, the amount of such adjustment to the Capital Accounts shall be treated as an item of gain (if the adjustment increases the basis of the property) or loss (if the adjustment decreases the basis of the property).

"Substituted Member" means an Assignee who or which has been admitted as a Member pursuant to Section 3.2 herein, to the extent of the Membership Interest assigned.

"Transfer" means any direct or indirect sale, exchange, transfer, disposition, assignment, pledge, grant, or hypothecation of a Membership Interest, absolute or as security or encumbrance, whether such Transfer occurs voluntarily, involuntarily, knowingly, unknowingly, or by operation of law.

"Treasury Regulations" (abbreviated hereinafter as "Treas. Reg.") means the final, temporary, and proposed regulations promulgated by the U.S. Department of the Treasury pursuant to the Code.

"Undistributed Preferred Return" means, with respect to a Class A Member, the amount of the excess (if any) of: (1) the cumulative amount of Preferred Return that such Member has accrued during the current year, or portion thereof, and all prior years; over (2) the cumulative amount of distributions to such Member under Sections 4.1(b)(i). A Class A Member's Undistributed Preferred Return shall be determined monthly, or from time-to-time, in order to determine Distributions.

"Unreturned Capital Contribution" means, with respect to a Member, the amount of the excess (if any) of: (1) the cumulative amount of Capital Contributions by such Member over (2) the cumulative amount of distributions to such Member pursuant to Sections 4.1(b)(ii) to (iv), until such Capital Contributions are returned.

## ARTICLE II

### Organizational Matters

2.1 Formation. The Company has been formed as a New York limited liability company under the Act. The undersigned parties desire to set forth the rights, powers, duties, and obligations of the Members and Manager of the Company in accordance with the terms and conditions set forth herein.

2.2 Place of Business. The principal office of the Company shall be located at 100 Main Street, New York, NY or at such other place as the Manager may designate from time-to-time.

2.3 Business Activities. The Company has been organized to pursue any lawful business activity or activities, excluding any business activity that under applicable New York law specifically requires a natural person or a legal entity other than a New York limited liability company.

2.4 Powers. In furtherance thereof but subject to other provisions of this Agreement the Company may exercise all of the powers as provided in the Act.

2.5 Term. The Company shall continue to exist until the Company is dissolved or terminated as herein provided, as set forth in the Certificate of Formation, or as provided by law. The Company shall forthwith be terminated and dissolved and its business and affairs liquidated upon the occurrence of any one of the following events or conditions:

(a) the sale (other than an exchange under Section 1031 of the Code), taking, condemnation, destruction, or any other disposition of all or substantially all of the Company's property;

(b) upon the determination of the Manager and the affirmative vote a Majority of the Class B Members to terminate and dissolve the Company;

(c) the death, dissolution, expulsion, incapacity or withdrawal of the last remaining Manager, or in the occurrence of any other event that precludes the last remaining Manager from acting as such, unless within forty-five days after such event, a Majority of the Class B Members make an affirmative vote to appoint one or more successor Managers; or

(d) the entry of a decree of judicial dissolution under the Act.

## ARTICLE III

### Admission to Membership; Capital Contributions

3.1 Initial Members. The Members shall make Capital Contributions to the Company as set forth on Schedule A hereto. Each Member's Membership Percentage shall be the percentage set forth opposite such Member's name on Schedule A hereto and shall be subject to subsequent adjustment as provided in this Agreement.

3.2 Admission to Membership. The Manager is authorized to admit Persons as additional Members in exchange for such Capital Contributions and upon such terms and conditions as the Manager shall deem to be in the best interest of the Company. The Manager is authorized to admit Assignees as Substituted Members upon such terms and conditions as the Manager shall deem to be in the best interest of the Company. In the event any additional Members are admitted to the Company pursuant to this Section 3.2 hereto, the Membership Percentages of the then existing Members (as shown on Schedule A hereto) shall be reduced pro rata in an aggregate amount equal to the aggregate Membership Percentage in the Company acquired by the new Member or Members. To accomplish the purposes of this Section, the Manager is authorized to do all things necessary to effectuate the admission of such additional Members (including the recomputation and revision of Schedule A hereto), each of whom shall become a signatory hereto, whereby each such additional Member shall be deemed to have adopted and to have agreed to be bound by all of the provisions of this Agreement.

3.3. Withdrawal from Membership. No Member shall have the right to withdraw from the Company without the express permission or consent of the Manager. Any attempt by a Member to withdraw from the Company in violation of this Agreement shall be ineffective and void ab initio.

## ARTICLE IV

### Distributions and Allocations

4.1 Distributions. Except as otherwise provided herein, for each fiscal year, Available Cash shall be distributed as follows:

(a) Tax Distributions. The Manager shall make reasonable efforts to Distribute to the Members amounts sufficient to pay their respective federal and state tax liabilities, as determined in the Manager's sole discretion, arising from transactions of the Company for each taxable year. The tax distributions made to any Member shall be treated as an advance to such Member and shall reduce the amount of the Distribution such Member is entitled to receive under Section 4.1(b) below.

(b) Distributions of Available Cash. Except as otherwise provided herein, for each fiscal year, Available Cash shall be distributed from time-to-time as the Manager shall determine, in his or her sole discretion, in the following order of priority:

(i) First, to the Class A Members, in proportion to the amounts of their respective Undistributed Preferred Returns, until the total amount distributed shall equal the total amount of such Undistributed Preferred Returns for all Class A Members;

(ii) Second, to the Class A Members, in proportion to the amounts of their respective Unreturned Capital Contributions, until the amounts distributed shall equal the total amount of such Unreturned Capital Contributions for all Class A Members;

(iii) Third, to the Class B Members, in proportion to their respective Unreturned Capital Contributions, until the amounts distributed shall equal the total amount of such Unreturned Capital Contributions for all Class B Members; and

(iv) Thereafter, to the Class B Members, in proportion to their respective Percentage Interests.

4.2 Allocations of Profit and Loss.

(a) Net Profit with respect to each Fiscal Year shall be allocated among the Members in the following order of priority:

(i) First, among the Class A Members, pro rata in proportion to their relative Class A Percentage Interests, until the aggregate amount of Net Profit allocated pursuant to this Section 4.2(a)(i) shall equal the aggregate amount of the Preferred Returns distributed pursuant to Section 4.1(b)(i) above;

(ii) Second, among the Class A Members, pro rata in proportion to the total amount of the excesses of (x) their relative Unreturned Capital Contributions over (y) their relative Adjusted Capital Account balances, until the amounts allocated shall equal such excesses;

(iii) Third, among the Class B Members, pro rata in proportion to the total amount of the excesses of (x) their relative Unreturned Capital

Contributions over (y) their relative Adjusted Capital Account balances, until the amounts allocated shall equal such excesses; and

(iv) Thereafter, among the Class B Members, pro rata in proportion to their relative Class B Percentage Interests.

(b) Net Loss with respect to each Fiscal Year shall be allocated among the Members in the following order of priority:

(i) First, among the Class B Members, pro rata in proportion to the total amount of the excesses of (x) their relative Adjusted Capital Account balances over (y) their relative Unreturned Capital Contributions, until such excesses have been eliminated;

(ii) Second, among the Class B Members, pro rata in proportion to their Adjusted Capital Account balances, until such balances have been reduced to zero;

(iii) Third, among the Class A Members, pro rata in proportion to the total amount of the excesses of (x) their relative Adjusted Capital Account balances over (y) their Unreturned Capital Contributions, until such excesses have been eliminated; and

(iv) Thereafter, among the Class A Members with positive Adjusted Capital Account balances, pro rata in proportion to their relative positive Adjusted Capital Account balances, until such balances have been reduced to zero.

(c) Regulatory Allocations. Prior to making any allocations of Net Profit or Net Loss under Sections 4.2(a) or (b) herein, income (including, without limitation, gross income, if necessary), gain, loss or deduction shall be specially allocated among the Members to the extent required as follows:

(i) Minimum Gain Chargeback. This Agreement incorporates by reference the "minimum gain chargeback" requirement in Treas. Reg. §1.704-2(f). The items of Profit and Loss allocated hereunder shall be determined under Treas. Reg. §1.704-2(j)(2).

(ii) Qualified Income Offset. This Agreement incorporates by reference the "qualified income offset" requirement in Treas. Reg. §1.704-1(b)(2)(ii)(d).

(d) Special Allocations. After taking into account the allocations under Section 4.2(c) herein, and prior to making any allocations of Net Profit or Net Loss under Sections 4.2(a) or (b) herein, income, gain, loss, or deduction shall be specially allocated among the Members as follows:

(i) Nonrecourse Deductions. Except as otherwise provided herein or as agreed to by the Members and incorporated herein, deductions that are treated as nonrecourse deductions within the meaning of Treas. Reg. §1.704-2 shall be specially allocated among the Class B Members, pro rata in proportion to their relative Percentage Interests.

(ii) Corrective Allocations. This Section 4.2(d)(ii) is intended to preserve the contemplated economic arrangement among the Members and is to be applied in a manner reasonably consistent with that intent. If any allocation is made pursuant to Sections 4.2(a) or (b) herein that distorts the contemplated economic arrangement among the Members, then items of Profit (including, without limitation, gross income, if necessary) and Loss shall be allocated among the Members as soon as possible (in a manner consistent with the requirements of Section 704(b) and the Treasury Regulations thereunder) to restore the Capital Accounts to the balances that would have existed, and to achieve the allocation of Profits and Losses and items thereof that would have been achieved, if such allocations pursuant to Sections 4.2(a) and (b) had not occurred. The manner in which such allocations are made shall be determined by the Manager in his or her reasonable discretion.

(e) Tax Allocations. Notwithstanding any provision herein, tax items of income, gain, loss, and deduction with respect to property having an adjusted tax basis different from its book value shall be allocated among the Members so as to take account of the variation between the adjusted tax basis and book value of such property in accordance with the principles of Section 704(c) or any successor section thereto.

(f) Alternative Minimum Tax. All Company items of income, gain, loss, deduction and credit shall be allocated for purposes of the alternative minimum tax in a manner that satisfies the requirements of Treas. Reg. §1.704-1(b).

(g) Proration of Allocations. If a Member Assigns or Transfers a Membership Interest, the transferor Member and the transferee Member shall take into account their distributive shares of the Net Profits and Net Losses of the Company in accordance with the varying interest rule set forth in Section 706 and the Treasury Regulations thereunder.

4.3 Conforming Amendments. The allocations set forth herein shall be amended as may be required from time-to-time, and as may be necessary to comply with the Code and Treasury Regulations thereunder.

## ARTICLE V

### Management

5.1 Duties and Powers of the Manager.

(a) The Manager shall possess and enjoy any and all of the management rights and powers provided in the Act, except as otherwise modified or limited by this Agreement. Except as otherwise specifically provided herein, the Manager shall conduct and manage the business of the Company in accordance with the provisions of the Act and the terms of this Agreement. The Manager shall not be required to devote any amount of such Manager's time and attention to the Company's business. The Manager may receive reasonable compensation for any management services provided by him or her. The Manager shall be reimbursed for out-of-pocket expenses incurred on behalf of the Company.

(b) Without limiting the foregoing general powers, the Manager is hereby authorized and empowered on behalf and in the name of the Company to:

(i) admit additional Members on such terms and conditions as he or she shall determine;

(ii) appoint, delegate authority to, remove and terminate such employees, officers and agents as he or she considers appropriate;

(iii) sell, exchange, pledge, or otherwise transfer all or any portion of the assets of the Company;

(iv) approve any merger or consolidation of the Company with or into another limited liability company or other business entity;

(v) borrow or lend money on behalf of the Company on such terms and conditions as he or she shall determine;

(vi) make all tax elections on behalf of the Company;

(vii) invest the assets of the Company in stock, debt obligations, and other securities of, any issuer, wherever such issuer may be located, organized or operated, whether within or without the United States of America, without limitation as to marketability of the securities or other interests reflecting such investments, and in options and other rights with respect to such securities;

(viii) employ one or more custodians of the assets of the Company;

(ix) possess, lend, mortgage, hypothecate, write options on, lease and otherwise deal in, or take other action with respect to, any or all of the assets of the Company;

(x) vote, give assent and otherwise exercise all rights, powers, privileges and other incidents of ownership or possession with respect to assets of the Company and execute and deliver proxies or powers of attorney to such person or persons as she shall deem proper, granting to such person or persons such power and discretion with relation to the Company's assets as she shall deem proper;

(xi) institute, prosecute, defend, settle, compromise or otherwise adjust all claims (including but not limited to claims for taxes) and litigation arising out of the conduct or the affairs of the Company or in the enforcement of obligations due it, including all rights of appeal;

(xii) employ or consult with such agents or independent contractors as he or she may deem necessary or advisable, including without limitation, brokers, auditors, counsel, investment advisers or manager or specialists in any field of endeavor whatsoever, including such persons or companies as may be Members or affiliated with any Member;

(xiii) pay all expenses, fees, charges, taxes and liabilities incurred or arising in connection with the conduct of the affairs of the Company;

(xiv) enter into joint ventures, general or limited partnerships and any other combinations or associations;

(xv) endorse, accept or guarantee the payment of any notes, drafts or other obligations of any Person and make contracts of guaranty or suretyship, or otherwise assume liability for payment thereof;

(xvi) purchase and pay for such insurance as he or she shall deem necessary, desirable or appropriate for the conduct of the business of the Company;

(xvii) make, issue, accept, endorse and execute promissory notes, drafts, bills of exchange, guarantees and other instruments and evidences of indebtedness, and secure the payment thereof by mortgage, pledge, or assignment of or security interest in all or any part of the assets then owned or thereafter acquired by the Company;

(xviii) adopt, amend and repeal by-laws not inconsistent with this Agreement providing for the conduct of the Company's business;

(xix) enter, make and perform such other contracts, agreements and other undertakings as may be necessary, desirable or advisable or incidental to the carrying out of any of the foregoing powers, objects or purposes, including contracts, agreements and undertakings with affiliates of any Member; and

(xx) execute all other instruments of any kind or character and take all action of any kind or character which he or she may in his or her sole discretion determine to be necessary or appropriate in connection with the business of the Company.

(c) If, at any time, there is more than one acting Manager, the actions set forth in Sections 4.1 (b) (i), (iii), (iv), (v) and (xiv) herein shall require the unanimous consent of all of the Managers, which consent shall not be unreasonably withheld.

(d) No Member, solely by reason of being a Member, shall be an authorized agent of the Company.

(e) Each Manager shall be an agent of the Company for the purpose of its business, and the act of any one Manager, including the execution in the name of the Company of any agreement, document or instrument for apparently carrying on in the usual way, the business of the Company (including but not limited to deeds, notes, mortgages and related documents) shall bind the Company, unless (i) the Manager so acting has in fact no authority to act for the Company in the particular matter and (ii) the person as to which such Manager is dealing has knowledge of the fact that such Manager has no such authority.

5.2 <u>Appointment of the Manager</u>. The initial Manager shall be Debby. So long as Debby can fulfill the obligations of Manager hereunder, she may not be removed as a Manager. The Manager or, if more than one, the Managers, may appoint in writing additional Managers by unanimous vote. Each Manager may appoint in writing his or her successor Manager. If at any time Debby ceases to serve as Manager and has failed to appoint a successor Manager, then a Majority of the Class B Members may appoint one or more successor Managers.

5.3 <u>Indemnification of Members and Such Manager</u>.

(a) Each Member and each Manager (including any executor or administrator of any such Member or Manager) and, to the extent any such Member or Manager is not a natural person, each Member's or Manager's directors, officers, employees or agents acting on its behalf (hereinafter "Indemnified Parties") shall be held harmless and indemnified by the Company from any liability, loss, cost or expense (including, without limitation, judgment, fines, amounts paid in settlement, attorneys' fees and expenses actually and necessarily incurred) arising out of any action or proceeding arising out of any act taken in the capacity of a Member or Manager (or a director, officer, employee or agent thereof) or any failure to take action in such capacity in connection with activities of the Company; provided, however, that no indemnification may be made to or on behalf of any Indemnified Party if a judgment or other final adjudication adverse to the Indemnified Party establishes (a) that the acts in question were committed in bad faith or were the result of active and deliberate dishonesty and were material to the cause of action so adjudicated, or (b) that the Indemnified Party or a principal of the Indemnified Party personally gained in fact a financial profit or other advantage to which the Indemnified Party or any such principal was not legally entitled. The Company shall advance to each Indemnified Party any expenses incurred by the Indemnified Party in the defense of any action or proceeding arising out of any act taken in the capacity of a Member or Manager (or a director, officer, employee or agent thereof) or any failure to take action in such capacity in connection with activities of the Company upon the written undertaking of the Indemnified Party to reimburse the Company therefor in the event that such Indemnified Party is ultimately found not to be entitled to indemnification as a result of the proviso set forth above.

(b) A Manager (including any executor or administrator of such Manager) and, to the extent a Manager is not a natural person, each of such Manager's directors, officers, agents or employees acting on its behalf (hereinafter "Exculpated Parties") shall not be liable to the Company or any Member for any damages suffered by the Company or any Member as a result of any breach of duty by any Exculpated Party in the capacity of a Manager, except to the extent that a judgment or other final adjudication adverse to the Exculpated Party, or a principal of such Exculpated Party, establishes that the acts or omissions of the Exculpated Party, or a principal of such Exculpated Party, were in bad faith or involved intentional misconduct or a knowing violation of law or that the Exculpated Party, or a principal of such Exculpated Party, personally gained in fact a financial profit or other advantage to which the Exculpated Party, or a principal of such Exculpated Party, was not legally entitled or that with respect to a Distribution the subject of subdivision (a) of Section 508 of the Act the acts the Exculpated Party, or a principal of such Exculpated Party, were not performed in accordance with Section 409 of the Act.

5.4 Outside Interests. A Member or a Manager may, directly or indirectly, own, manage, operate, control, be employed by, participate in, be financially interested in, or represent, or render any advice or services in any other business, regardless of whether the activities of such other business may conflict with, may be competitive with, or may be similar to that of the Company.

5.5 Books, Records, and Reports.

(a) The fiscal year and accounting period of the Company shall be the calendar year and at all times during the continuance of the Company the Manager shall keep or cause to be kept full and true books of account in which shall be entered fully and accurately each transaction of the Company. All of the books of account, together with (i) a current list of the full name set forth in alphabetical order and last known mailing address of each Member, together with the Capital Contribution and the Membership Percentage of each Member or information from which such Membership Percentage can be readily derived; (ii) a copy of the Certificate of Formation and all amendments thereto, or restatement thereof, together with executed copies of any powers of attorney pursuant to which any certificate of amendment has been executed; (iii) a copy of this Agreement, any amendments thereto and any amended and restated Operating Agreement; and (iv) a copy of the Company's Federal, state and local income tax or information returns and reports, if any, for the three most recent fiscal years, shall at all times be maintained at the principal office of the Company, or at such other office as the Manager may designate by written notice to all Members. Any Member or his duly authorized representative may inspect and copy at his own expense for any purpose reasonably related to the Member's interest as a Member the records referred to herein, any financial statements maintained by the Company for the three most recent fiscal years and other information regarding the affairs of the Company as is just and reasonable, at any time during regular business hours upon reasonable prior notice to the Company.

(b) All financial statements and income tax returns referred to in this Agreement shall be prepared by such accountant as may be engaged by the Manager. Such financial statements shall be prepared on the basis employed by the Company for Federal income tax purposes and otherwise shall follow, to the extent possible or practicable, sound accounting practice consistently applied.

(c) The Company shall deliver to each Member within one-hundred twenty (120) days following the end of the Company's fiscal year, or at such later date as may be recommended by the accountant for the Company, information necessary for the preparation by each Member of his Federal income tax return as to the Company's income, gain, and loss or deductions, if any.

5.6 <u>Tax Matters</u>.

(a) Debby shall be appointed as the "tax matters partner" of the Company as such term is defined under the Code.

(b) The expenses of professional representation during any tax audit controversy or dispute shall be a Company expense payable out of Company funds.

(c) The Manager may in his or her sole discretion settle or dispose of any tax controversy or dispute affecting the Company or any of the tax positions taken by the Company.

5.7 <u>Status of Members</u>.

(a) No Member shall be subject to calls or assessments for Capital Contributions in excess of such Member's agreed Capital Contributions, nor shall any Member in the capacity of a Member, be bound by, or be personally liable for, any expense, liability or obligation of the Company, except to the extent of such Member's agreed Capital Contributions.

(b) No Member shall have the right to demand the return any Capital Contributions to the Company, except upon dissolution of the Company.

5.8 Action by Members or Manager Without a Meeting.

(a) Whenever Members or a Manager are required or permitted to take any action by vote, or any consent of Members or a Manager are required hereunder, such action may be taken, or such consent given, without a meeting, without prior notice and without a vote, if a consent or consents in writing, setting forth the action so taken shall be signed by (i) the Manager or (ii) the Members who hold Membership Interests representing not less than the minimum number of Membership Interests that would be necessary to authorize or take such action at a meeting at which all of the Members entitled to vote thereon were present and voted. All such consents shall be delivered to the principal office of the Company, or a Manager, employee or agent of the Company having custody of the records of the Company. Delivery made to the principal office of the Company or Manager, employee or agent shall be by hand or by certified or registered mail, return receipt requested.

(b) Every written consent shall bear the date of signature of each Manager and/or each Member who signs the consent, and no written consent shall be effective to take the action referred to therein unless, within sixty (60) days of the earliest dated consent, written consents signed by (i) the Manager or (ii) holders of sufficient Membership Interests to authorize or approve the action are delivered to the principal office of the Company or a Manager, employee or agent of the Company having custody of the records of the Company. Delivery made to such principal office or Manager, employee or agent shall be by hand or by certified or registered mail, return receipt requested.

(c) Prompt notice of the taking of the action without a meeting by less than unanimous written consent of all Members shall be given to those Members who have not consented in writing, but would have been entitled to vote thereon had such action been taken at a meeting.



## ARTICLE VI

## Membership

6.1 Members' Liability. The liability of each Member, as such, shall be limited to the amount of such Member's Capital Contributions in accordance with the provisions hereof. None of the Members shall have any further personal liability to contribute money to or in respect of the liabilities or the obligations of the Company, nor shall any Member be personally liable for any other obligations of the Company. Each Member understands, however, that, to the extent required by Section 508 of the Act, if such Member knowingly receives a Distribution from the Company in violation of subdivision (a) of 508 of the Act, such Member may be liable to the Company for the amount of such Distribution; but nothing herein is intended to or shall expand the rights, if any, that a creditor may have under applicable law apart from this Agreement.

6.2 Negative Capital Account. A "Negative Capital Account" resulting from any Distribution in accordance with the provisions of this Agreement, or from losses, is hereby recognized as a possibility under this Agreement, and such Negative Capital Account shall not affect a Member's participation in the Profits and Losses of the Company. Except as otherwise provided by allocations in Section 4.2(a)(ii)(3), Section 4.2(c), or Section 4.2(d), in no event shall a Member be required to make an additional Capital Contribution to personally restore a Negative Capital Account or shall such Negative Capital Account be considered a liability of such Member or an asset of the Company.

6.3 Interest. Class B Members shall not be entitled to receive any interest on their Capital Contributions to the Company.

6.4 Provisions of Agreement Not for Benefit of Any Creditor. None of the provisions of this Agreement shall be construed as existing for the benefit of any creditor of any of the Members or of the Company, nor shall any such provision be enforceable by any party not a signatory to this Agreement.

## ARTICLE VII

### Transfers of Membership Interests

7.1 Restriction on Transfer. Except as expressly permitted by this Article VII, a Member may not Transfer all or any portion of a Membership Interest, nor enter into any agreement as a result of which any other person shall become interested in the Company, including any purported assignment of the economic rights only, without the prior written consent of the Manager.

7.2 Death, Dissolution, Bankruptcy Event, Incapacity, or Other Involuntary Transfer. In the event of the death, incapacity, Bankruptcy Event or other event which results in an involuntary Transfer of a Member's interest in the Company (including, without limitation, a transfer by way of attachment, levy, foreclosure, sheriffs' or other judicial sale, or pursuant to a divorce decree), the executor, administrator, guardian, other personal representative or successor in interest to such Member shall become an Assignee of the economic rights of such Member, but shall not acquire any right to vote or consent or participate in the management of the Company subject to Article IX. In the event any Member that is a corporation or limited liability company is dissolved, or any Member that is a trust or other entity is liquidated, or any case if the legal existence of an entity is otherwise terminated, the legal representative or successor to such Member shall become an Assignee of the economic rights of such Member, but shall not acquire any right to vote or consent or participate in the management of the Company except as otherwise provided herein.

7.3 Relationship of Assignees and Substituted Members.

(a) No Assignee shall have the right to participate in the management of the Company, inspect the books of account of the Company or exercise any other rights of a Member until admitted as a Substituted Member. An Assignee shall be entitled to share in the Profits and Losses of the Company and receive Distributions from the Company, to the extent distributions are made, provided, however, that no assignment shall be binding on the Company until written notice thereof is received by the Company. An Assignee may become a Substituted Member only upon the terms and conditions set forth in subsection (b) below.

(b) In order to become a Substituted Member, an Assignee of a Membership Interest must first obtain the prior consent of the Manager. The admission of a Substituted Member shall be conditioned upon the Substituted Member's written acceptance and adoption of all of the terms and provisions of this Agreement.

## ARTICLE VIII

### Dissolution and Liquidation

8.1 Dissolution. Upon the dissolution of the Company, the Manager, or if none, a liquidating agent selected by a Majority of the Class B Members, shall proceed to the orderly liquidation of the Company. Such persons winding up the Company's affairs may, in the name of and for and on behalf of the Company, prosecute and defend suits, whether civil, criminal or administrative, settle and close the Company's business, dispose of and convey the Company's property, discharge the Company's liabilities and distribute to the Members any remaining assets of the Company. The proceeds of such liquidation shall be applied first to the payment of the debts and liabilities of the Company and expenses of liquidation and to the setting up of any reserves which the Manager or liquidating agent may deem reasonably necessary for any contingent or unforeseen liabilities or obligations of the Company (other than debts, liabilities or capital contributions owed to any Member or its affiliates). Said reserve shall be paid over by the Manager or liquidating agent to a bank designated by the Manager or liquidating agent, as escrow agent, to be held for the purpose of disbursing such reserve in payment of any of the aforementioned contingencies and, at the expiration of such period as the escrow agent shall deem advisable, to distribute the balance thereafter remaining in the order of priority set forth in Section 8.2 herein.

8.2 Distributions Upon Dissolution. Each Member shall look solely to the assets of the Company for all Distributions in connection with a Dissolution of the Company, and no Member shall have recourse therefor (upon dissolution or otherwise) against any Manager or any other Member. The proceeds of the Company, including reserves released from escrow, shall be paid or Distributed in the following order of priority:

(a) to the payment or satisfaction of all outstanding obligations of the Company to the creditors of the Company, including Members who or which are creditors, and to reasonably set aside a reserve for the expenses of liquidation (including a reasonable reserve for contingent, conditional, or unmatured claims or obligations of the Company and all claims and obligations which are known but which the identity of the claimant is unknown);

(b) to the payment and discharge of all of the obligations of the Company for Distributions to Members; and

(c) thereafter, to the Members in proportion to their positive Capital Account balances (if any) as of the date of such Distributions, after giving effect to all Capital Contributions, Distributions, and allocations for all periods, including the period during which such Distributions occurs.

8.3 Allocation of Taxable Gain or Loss on Dissolution and Liquidation. Except as otherwise provided herein, in connection with a dissolution and liquidation of the Company pursuant to Section 4.1 herein, any Profit, Loss, Net Profit, or Net Loss of the Company shall be allocated in the same manner as provided in Section 4.2 herein.

8.4 Liquidation of Member's Interest. If there is a liquidation of a Member's interest in the Company, any liquidating Distribution pursuant to such liquidation shall not be less than the positive Capital Account balance, if any, of such Member for the taxable year during which such liquidation occurs after proper adjustments for allocations and Distributions for such taxable year up to the time of liquidation. Such Distributions shall be made by the end of the taxable year of the Company during which such liquidation occurs, or if later, within 90 days after such liquidation.

8.5 Distributions in Kind. In the event it becomes necessary to make Distributions of Company property in kind, such property shall be transferred and conveyed to the Members or their Assignees so as to vest in each of them, as a tenant in common, an undivided interest in the whole of said property, equal to such Member's Membership Percentage as if the property had been sold and the proceeds of sale were being distributed as provided in Section 4.1 herein. Furthermore, the Manager may, in his or her sole discretion, make distributions of property in kind disproportionately to a single member as a return of capital in such Member's capital account.

8.6 Orderly Liquidation. A reasonable time shall be allowed for the orderly liquidation of the assets of the Company and the discharge of liabilities to creditors so as to minimize the losses normally attendant upon liquidation.

8.7 Statements on Liquidation. On liquidation, each of the Members shall be furnished promptly with a statement which shall set forth the assets and liabilities of the Company as at the date of liquidation, and each Member's share thereof and a final Federal partnership tax return. Within ninety (90) days following the date of dissolution, the Manager, or the liquidating agent if there be one, shall execute and cause to be filed Articles of Dissolution of the Company.

## ARTICLE IX

### Miscellaneous

9.1 Title to Property. Title to all assets of the Company shall be held in the name of the Company.

9.2 Notices. Except as otherwise provided herein, all notices, demands or other communications hereunder shall be in writing and shall be deemed to have been given upon personal delivery thereof, or, if by Federal Express or another overnight delivery service to the parties at the addresses set forth below, two (2) days following deposit of same with such overnight delivery service, or, if mailed by certified or registered mail, postage prepaid, return receipt requested to the parties at the addresses set forth below, five (5) days following deposit of same in the United States mail. Notices shall be delivered as follows:

(a) To the Company at the principal office of the Company;

(b) To any Member or Manager at the address for such Member or Manager set forth on Schedule A hereto, with a copy to the Company.

Any party may change an address by giving notice to the Company and each Member and each Manager in the manner provided above, effective upon receipt thereof.

9.3 Further Assurances. The Members and/or Manager will execute and deliver such further instruments and do such further acts and things as may be required to carry out the intent and purpose of this Agreement.

9.4 Integration. This Agreement constitutes the entire agreement among the parties pertaining to the subject matter hereof and supersedes all prior and contemporaneous agreements and undertakings of the parties as Members and/or Manager in connection herewith. No covenant, representation or condition not expressed in this Agreement shall affect, or be effective to interpret, change or restrict, the express provisions of this Agreement.

9.5 Successors in Interest. Except as otherwise provided herein, all provisions of this Agreement shall be binding upon, inure to the benefit of, and be enforceable by and against the parties hereto and each of their respective heirs, executors, administrators, personal representatives, successors and assigns. However, none of the provisions of this Agreement shall be for the benefit of or enforceable by any creditors of the Company.

9.6 Governing Law. This Agreement shall be construed in accordance with the laws and decisions of the State of New York. In the event any provision hereof shall be judicially declared invalid or inoperative, the Members agree that this Agreement shall remain in full force and effect and that all other provisions hereof shall be carried out to the extent legally possible.

9.7 Counterparts. This Agreement may be executed in one or more counterparts each of which shall constitute one Agreement, binding on all parties hereto, even though all the parties are not signatory to the original or the same counterpart and such counterpart signature may be effected by execution of a Certification Signature Page.

9.8 Headings. The headings of the Articles, Sections and subsections of this Agreement are inserted for convenience of reference only and shall not be deemed to be part of this Agreement.

9.9. Amendments. This Agreement may be amended from time to time in the Manager's reasonable discretion; provided, however, that any such amendment of this Agreement may not materially diminish the economic interests of any Member.

If any Amendment materially diminishes the economic interests of a Member, the Amendment shall require such Member's prior written consent.

9.10 <u>Remedies</u>. The Members and the Manager agree that they will be irreparably damaged in the event that this Agreement should not be specifically enforced. If any dispute arises concerning any transfer or other disposition of any Membership Interest under this Agreement, a court of competent jurisdiction may issue a temporary restraining order, injunction or decree of specific performance, without any bond or other security being required and without proof of actual damage. Such remedies shall be cumulative and not exclusive, and shall be in addition to any other remedies which the parties may have.

9.11 <u>Gender/Plural</u>. The neuter gender herein shall be deemed to include the masculine and/or feminine and vice versa, the masculine gender shall be deemed to include the feminine and vice versa, and the singular shall be deemed to include the plural and vice versa wherever necessary or appropriate or required by the context.

IN WITNESS WHEREOF, each of the undersigned parties hereto has executed this Agreement as of the date first written above.

<u>MANAGER</u>:

*Debby Day*
Debby Day, as Manager

<u>MEMBERS</u>:

*Debby Day*
Debby Day, as Member

*Ella Baurdain*
Ella Baurdain, as Member

*Farzan Vater*
Farzan Vater, as Member

## SCHEDULE A

Capital Contributions and Percentage Interests

| Name and Address | Contribution | Class A Membership Percentage | Class B Membership Percentage |
|---|---|---|---|
| Debby<br>785 NW State Street<br>Big City, Illinois<br>99919 | $0 | 0% | 20% |
| Ella<br>942 Elm Street<br>DUMBO,<br>New York<br>88853 | $1,250,000 | 100% | 0% |
| Farzan<br>444 Fulton Avenue<br>Cobble Hill,<br>Georgia 77732 | $750,000 | 0% | 80% |
| Total | $2,000,000 | 100% | 100% |

# DD PIZZERIA FINANCIALS

An electronic version of these financial statements is available on the Aspen Publishing product page for *Taxation and Business Planning for Partnerships and LLCs, 2020-2021 Client File* by Bradley Borden under the Student Resources tab.

## Statement of Cash Flows for Year Ended 12/31/01

| | |
|---|---|
| **Cash Flows from Operations** | |
| Sales Receipts | $415,345 |
| Interest on Cash Account | $2,000 |
| Dividends Received | $0 |
| Interest from Tax-Exempt Bonds | $0 |
| Employee Compensation | ($425,000) |
| Pizza Ingredients | ($166,138) |
| Rent | ($55,200) |
| Accident Insurance | ($3,588) |
| Interest | $0 |
| Contribution to Charity | $0 |
| Employee Health Insurance | ($24,921) |
| **Net Cash from Operations** | ($257,502) |
| **Cash Flows from Investment** | |
| Sale or Disposition of Property, Plant, and Equipment | $0 |
| Sale or Maturity of Investment | $0 |
| Purchase of Property, Plant, and Equipment | ($215,000) |
| Purchase of Investments | $0 |
| **Net Cash from Investment** | ($215,000) |
| **Cash Flows from Financing** | |
| Loan Proceeds | $0 |
| Loan Repayment | $0 |
| Contributions | $2,000,000 |
| Distributions | $0 |
| **Net Cash from Financing** | $2,000,000 |
| **Net Cash Flows** | $1,527,498 |

## Depreciation Schedule for Year 1

| | Cost | Placed in Service | Year 1 |
|---|---|---|---|
| Location #1 | $215,000 | 1/1/01 | $30,724 |
| Total | $215,000 | | $30,724 |

Depreciation Table

| Year | Percentage |
|---|---|
| Year 1 | 14.29% |
| Year 2 | 24.49% |
| Year 3 | 17.49% |
| Year 4 | 12.49% |
| Year 5 | 8.93% |
| Year 6 | 8.92% |
| Year 7 | 8.93% |
| Year 8 | 4.46% |
| | 100.00% |

## Rent and Compensation for Year 1

**Rent**

| | Square Feet | Rent/sq. ft. | Monthly Rent | Rent for Year |
|---|---|---|---|---|
| Location #1 | 2,000 | $2.30 | $4,600 | $55,200 |
| Location #2 | | $2.25 | $0 | $0 |
| Total | | | | $55,200 |

**Compensation**

| | |
|---|---|
| Debby | $150,000 |
| Location #1 | $275,000 |
| Total | $425,000 |

## Taxable Income for Year Ended 12/31/01

| **Gross Income** | | **Separately Stated Items** |
|---|---|---|
| Sales Receipts | $415,345 | $0 |
| Dividends Received | $0 | $0 |
| Interest on Cash Account | $2,000 | $0 |
| Interest from Tax-Exempt Bonds | $0 | $0 |
| Gains from Sales of Capital Assets Held More Than One Year | $0 | $0 |
| Gains from Sales of Capital Assets Held Less Than One Year | $0 | $0 |
| Total Receipts | $417,345 | $0 |
| **Deductions** | | |
| Employee Compensation | ($425,000) | $0 |
| Pizza Ingredients | ($158,138) | $0 |
| Rent | ($55,200) | $0 |
| Accident Insurance | ($3,588) | $0 |
| Contribution to Charity | $0 | $0 |
| Interest | $0 | $0 |
| Employee Health Insurance | ($24,921) | $0 |
| Depreciation Deductions | ($30,724) | $0 |
| Amortized Rent Deduction | $0 | $0 |
| Loss from Sales of Capital Assets Held More Than One Year | $0 | $0 |
| Loss from Sales of Capital Assets Held Less Than One Year | $0 | $0 |
| Total Deductions | ($697,570) | $0 |
| Taxable Income (Loss) | ($280,225) | |
| Net Amount | | ($280,225) |

## Distributions and Allocations for Year 1

- 4.1(a) is 35% of prior year allocation made before 4/1; 4.1(b) amounts are made on 12/31

| **Distributions** | UPR | UCC | 4.1(a) | 4.1(b)(i) | 4.1(b)(ii) | 4.1(b)(iii) | 4.1(b)(iv) | **Total** |
|---|---|---|---|---|---|---|---|---|
| Ella | $125,000 | $1,250,000 | $0 | $0 | $0 | $0 | $0 | $0 |
| Debby | $0 | $0 | $0 | $0 | $0 | $0 | $0 | $0 |
| Farzan | $0 | $750,000 | $0 | $0 | $0 | $0 | $0 | $0 |
| Total | | | | | | | | $0 |

| **Allocations** | 4.2(a)(i) | 4.2(a)(ii) | 4.2(a)(iii) | 4.2(a)(iv) | 4.2(b)(i) | 4.2(b)(ii) | 4.2(b)(iii) | 4.2(b)(iv) | **Total** |
|---|---|---|---|---|---|---|---|---|---|
| Ella | $0 | $0 | $0 | $0 | $0 | $0 | $0 | $0 | $0 |
| Debby | $0 | $0 | $0 | $0 | $0 | $0 | $0 | $0 | $0 |
| Farzan | $0 | $0 | $0 | $0 | $0 | ($280,225) | $0 | $0 | ($280,225) |

| **Capital Account Adjustments** | |
|---|---|
| Ella | $0 |
| Debby | $0 |
| Farzan | ($280,225) |

## Balance Sheet as of 12/31/01

| | **Assets** | | | | **Debt & Equity** | | |
|---|---|---|---|---|---|---|---|
| | Value | Book | Tax | | Value | Book | Tax |
| Cash | $1,527,498 | $1,527,498 | $1,527,498 | Accounts Payable | | $0 | $0 |
| Accounts Receivable | | $0 | $0 | Long-Term Debt | | $0 | $0 |
| Food Inventory | $8,000 | $8,000 | $8,000 | | | | |
| Furniture & Equipment | $92,000 | $215,000 | $215,000 | | | | |
| Accumulated Depr. | | ($30,724) | ($30,724) | Ella's Capital Account | | $1,250,000 | $1,250,000 |
| Leaseholds | $0 | $0 | $0 | Debby's Capital Account | | $0 | $0 |
| Accumulated Amort. | $0 | $0 | $0 | Farzan's Capital Account | | $469,775 | $469,775 |
| Investments | $0 | $0 | $0 | | | | |
| | **$1,627,498** | **$1,719,775** | **$1,719,775** | | | **$1,719,775** | **$1,719,775** |

## Statement of Cash Flows for Year Ended 12/31/02

| | |
|---|---|
| **Cash Flows from Operations** | |
| Sales Receipts | $980,325 |
| Interest on Cash Account | $1,527 |
| Dividends Received | $0 |
| Interest from Tax-Exempt Bonds | $0 |
| Employee Compensation | ($748,025) |
| Pizza Ingredients | ($343,114) |
| Rent | ($102,225) |
| Accident Insurance | ($6,645) |
| Interest from Taxable Bonds | $0 |
| Contribution to Charity | $0 |
| Employee Health Insurance | ($112,204) |
| **Net Cash from Operations** | ($330,360) |
| **Cash Flows from Investment** | |
| Sale or Disposition of Property, Plant, and Equipment | $0 |
| Sale or Maturity of Investment | $0 |
| Purchase of Property, Plant, and Equipment | ($232,500) |
| Purchase of Investments | $0 |
| **Net Cash from Investment** | ($232,500) |
| **Cash Flows from Financing** | |
| Loan Proceeds | $0 |
| Loan Repayment | $0 |
| Contributions | $0 |
| Distributions | $0 |
| **Net Cash from Financing** | $0 |
| **Net Cash Flows** | ($562,860) |

## Depreciation Schedule for Year 2

| | Cost | Placed in Service | Year 1 | Year 2 | Total |
|---|---|---|---|---|---|
| Location #1 | $215,000 | 1/1/01 | $30,724 | $52,654 | $83,377 |
| Location #2 | $232,500 | 2/15/02 | – | $33,224 | $33,224 |
| Total | $447,500 | | $30,724 | $85,878 | $116,601 |

Depreciation Table

| Year | Percentage |
|---|---|
| Year 1 | 14.29% |
| Year 2 | 24.49% |
| Year 3 | 17.49% |
| Year 4 | 12.49% |
| Year 5 | 8.93% |
| Year 6 | 8.92% |
| Year 7 | 8.93% |
| Year 8 | 4.46% |
| | 100.00% |

## Rent and Compensation for Year 2

**Rent**

| | Square Feet | Rent/sq. ft. | Monthly Rent | Rent for Year |
|---|---|---|---|---|
| Location #1 | 2,000 | $2.30 | $4,600 | $55,200 |
| Location #2 | 2,200 | $2.25 | $4,950 | $47,025 |
| Total | | | | $102,225 |

**Compensation**

| | |
|---|---|
| Debby | $152,250 |
| Location #1 | $280,500 |
| Location #2 | $315,275 |
| Total | $748,025 |

## Taxable Income for Year Ended 12/31/02

| **Gross Income** | | **Separately Stated Items** |
|---|---|---|
| Sales Receipts | $980,325 | $0 |
| Dividends Received | $0 | $0 |
| Interest on Cash Account | $1,527 | $0 |
| Interest from Tax-Exempt Bonds | $0 | $0 |
| Gains from Sales of Capital Assets Held More Than One Year | $0 | $0 |
| Gains from Sales of Capital Assets Held Less Than One Year | $0 | $0 |
| Gross Income | $981,852 | $0 |
| **Deductions** | | |
| Employee Compensation | ($748,025) | $0 |
| Pizza Ingredients | ($336,114) | $0 |
| Rent | ($102,225) | $0 |
| Accident Insurance | ($6,645) | $0 |
| Contribution to Charity | $0 | $0 |
| Interest | $0 | $0 |
| Employee Health Insurance | ($112,204) | $0 |
| Depreciation Deductions | ($85,878) | $0 |
| Amortized Rent Deduction | $0 | $0 |
| Loss from Sales of Capital Assets Held More Than One Year | $0 | $0 |
| Loss from Sales of Capital Assets Held Less Than One Year | $0 | $0 |
| Total Deductions | ($1,391,090) | $0 |
| Taxable Income (Loss) | ($409,237) | |
| Net Amount | | ($409,237) |

## Distributions and Allocations for Year 2

• **4.1(a) is 35% of prior year allocation made before 4/1; 4.1(b) amounts are made on 12/31**

| **Distributions** | **UPR** | **UCC** | | **4.1(a)** | **4.1(b)(i)** | **4.1(b)(ii)** | **4.1(b)(iii)** | **4.1(b)(iv)** | **Total** |
|---|---|---|---|---|---|---|---|---|---|
| Ella | $250,000 | $1,250,000 | | $0 | $0 | $0 | $0 | $0 | $0 |
| Debby | $0 | $0 | | $0 | $0 | $0 | $0 | $0 | $0 |
| Farzan | $0 | $750,000 | | $0 | $0 | $0 | $0 | $0 | $0 |
| Total | | | | | | | | | $0 |
| **Allocations** | 4.2(a)(i) | 4.2(a)(ii) | 4.2(a)(iii) | 4.2(a)(iv) | 4.2(b)(i) | 4.2(b)(ii) | 4.2(b)(iii) | 4.2(b)(iv) | **Total** |
| Ella | $0 | $0 | $0 | $0 | $0 | $0 | $0 | $0 | $0 |
| Debby | $0 | $0 | $0 | $0 | $0 | $0 | $0 | $0 | $0 |
| Farzan | $0 | $0 | $0 | $0 | $0 | ($409,237) | $0 | $0 | ($409,237) |
| **Capital Account Adjustments** | | | | | | | | | |
| Ella | $0 | | | | | | | | |
| Debby | $0 | | | | | | | | |
| Farzan | ($409,237) | | | | | | | | |

## Balance Sheet as of 12/31/02

| | **Assets** | | | | **Debt & Equity** | | |
|---|---|---|---|---|---|---|---|
| | **Value** | **Book** | **Tax** | | **Value** | **Book** | **Tax** |
| Cash | $964,639 | $964,639 | $964,639 | Accounts Payable | $2,700 | $0 | $0 |
| Accounts Receivable | $3,500 | $0 | $0 | Long-Term Debt | | $0 | $0 |
| Food Inventory | $15,000 | $15,000 | $15,000 | | | | |
| Furniture & Equipment | $217,000 | $447,500 | $447,500 | | | | |
| Accumulated Depr. | | ($116,601) | ($116,601) | Ella's Capital Account | | $1,250,000 | $1,250,000 |
| Leaseholds | $0 | $0 | $0 | Debby's Capital Account | | $0 | $0 |
| Accumulated Amort. | $0 | $0 | $0 | Farzan's Capital Account | | $60,537 | $60,537 |
| Investments | $0 | $0 | $0 | | | | |
| | **$1,200,139** | **$1,310,537** | **$1,310,537** | | | **$1,310,537** | **$1,310,537** |

## Statement of Cash Flows for Year Ended 12/31/03

| | | |
|---|---|---|
| **Cash Flows from Operations** | | |
| Sales Receipts | $2,654,397 | |
| Interest on Cash Account | $965 | |
| Dividends Received | $0 | |
| Interest from Tax-Exempt Bonds | $0 | |
| Employee Compensation | ($936,414) | |
| Pizza Ingredients | ($1,061,759) | |
| Rent | ($134,580) | |
| Accident Insurance | ($8,748) | |
| Interest | $0 | |
| Contribution to Charity | $0 | |
| Employee Health Insurance | ($140,462) | |
| **Net Cash from Operations** | $373,399 | |
| | | |
| **Cash Flows from Investment** | | |
| Sale or Disposition of Property, Plant, and Equipment | $0 | |
| Sale or Maturity of Investment | $0 | |
| Purchase of Property, Plant, and Equipment | ($197,350) | |
| Purchase of Investments | ($89,000) | • 200 shares of Cheez Corp, 3/15; Tax-Exempt Bonds, 12/31 |
| **Net Cash from Investment** | ($286,350) | |
| | | |
| **Cash Flows from Financing** | | |
| Loan Proceeds | $0 | |
| Loan Repayment | $0 | |
| Contributions | $0 | |
| Distributions | ($123,500) | |
| **Net Cash from Financing** | ($123,500) | |
| | | |
| **Net Cash Flows** | ($36,451) | |

## Depreciation Schedule for Year 3

| | Cost | Placed in Service | Year 1 | Year 2 | Year 3 | Total |
|---|---|---|---|---|---|---|
| Location #1 | $215,000 | 1/1/2001 | $30,724 | $52,654 | $37,604 | $120,981 |
| Location #2 | $232,500 | 2/15/2002 | – | $33,224 | $56,939 | $90,164 |
| Location #3 | $197,350 | 8/15/2003 | – | – | $28,201 | $28,201 |
| | $644,850 | | $30,724 | $85,878 | $122,744 | $239,345 |

Depreciation Table

| Year | Percentage |
|---|---|
| Year 1 | 14.29% |
| Year 2 | 24.49% |
| Year 3 | 17.49% |
| Year 4 | 12.49% |
| Year 5 | 8.93% |
| Year 6 | 8.92% |
| Year 7 | 8.93% |
| Year 8 | 4.46% |
| | 100.00% |

## Rent and Compensation for Year 3

**Rent**

| | Square Feet | Rent/sq. ft. | Monthly Rent | Rent for Year |
|---|---|---|---|---|
| Location #1 | 2,000 | $2.30 | $4,600 | $55,200 |
| Location #2 | 2,200 | $2.25 | $4,950 | $59,400 |
| Location #3 | 1,850 | $2.40 | $4,440 | $19,980 |
| Total | | | | $134,580 |

**Compensation**

| | |
|---|---|
| Debby | $154,534 |
| Location #1 | $286,110 |
| Location #2 | $321,581 |
| Location #3 | $174,189 |
| Total | $936,414 |

## Taxable Income for Year Ended 12/31/03

| **Gross Income** | | **Separately Stated Items** |
|---|---|---|
| Sales Receipts | $2,654,397 | $0 |
| Dividends Received | $0 | $0 |
| Interest on Cash Account | $965 | $0 |
| Interest from Tax-Exempt Bonds | $0 | $0 |
| Gains from Sales of Capital Assets Held More Than One Year | $0 | $0 |
| Gains from Sales of Capital Assets Held Less Than One Year | $0 | $0 |
| **Gross Income** | $2,655,362 | $0 |
| | | |
| **Deductions** | | |
| Employee Compensation | ($936,414) | $0 |
| Pizza Ingredients | ($1,056,759) | $0 |
| Rent | ($134,580) | $0 |
| Accident Insurance | ($8,748) | $0 |
| Contribution to Charity | $0 | $0 |
| Interest | $0 | $0 |
| Employee Health Insurance | ($140,462) | $0 |
| Depreciation Deductions | ($122,744) | $0 |
| Amortized Rent Deduction | $0 | $0 |
| Loss from Sales of Capital Assets Held More Than One Year | $0 | $0 |
| Loss from Sales of Capital Assets Held Less Than One Year | $0 | $0 |
| Total Deductions | ($2,399,706) | $0 |
| **Taxable Income (Loss)** | $255,655 | |
| | | |
| **Net Amount** | | $255,655 |

## Distributions and Allocations for Year 3

• 4.1(a) is 35% of prior year allocation made before 4/1; 4.1(b) amounts are made on 12/31

| **Distributions** | UPR | UCC | 4.1(a) | 4.1(b)(i) | 4.1(b)(ii) | 4.1(b)(iii) | 4.1(b)(iv) | **Total** |
|---|---|---|---|---|---|---|---|---|
| Ella | $375,000 | $1,250,000 | $0 | ($123,500) | $0 | $0 | $0 | ($123,500) |
| Debby | $0 | $0 | $0 | $0 | $0 | $0 | $0 | $0 |
| Farzan | $0 | $750,000 | $0 | $0 | $0 | $0 | $0 | $0 |
| Total | | | | | | | | ($123,500) |

| **Allocations** | 4.2(a)(i) | 4.2(a)(ii) | 4.2(a)(iii) | 4.2(a)(iv) | 4.2(b)(i) | 4.2(b)(ii) | 4.2(b)(iii) | 4.2(b)(iv) | **Total** |
|---|---|---|---|---|---|---|---|---|---|
| Ella | $123,500 | $0 | $0 | $0 | $0 | $0 | $0 | $0 | $123,500 |
| Debby | $0 | $0 | $0 | $0 | $0 | $0 | $0 | $0 | $0 |
| Farzan | $0 | $0 | $132,155 | $0 | $0 | $0 | $0 | $0 | $132,155 |
| | | | | | | | | | $255,655 |

| **Capital Account Adjustments** | |
|---|---|
| Ella | $0 |
| Debby | $0 |
| Farzan | $132,155 |

## Balance Sheet as of 12/31/03

| | Assets Value | Assets Book | Assets Tax | | Debt & Equity Value | Debt & Equity Book | Debt & Equity Tax |
|---|---|---|---|---|---|---|---|
| Cash | $928,188 | $928,188 | $928,188 | Accounts Payable | $2,450 | $0 | $0 |
| Accounts Receivable | $4,250 | $0 | $0 | Long-Term Debt | | $0 | $0 |
| Food Inventory | $20,000 | $20,000 | $20,000 | | | | |
| Furniture & Equipment | $295,000 | $644,850 | $644,850 | | | | |
| Accumulated Depr. | – | ($239,345) | ($239,345) | Ella's Capital Account | | $1,250,000 | $1,250,000 |
| Leaseholds | $0 | $0 | $0 | Debby's Capital Account | | $0 | $0 |
| Accumulated Amort. | – | $0 | $0 | Farzan's Capital Account | | $192,693 | $192,693 |
| Cheez Corp Stock | $14,300 | $14,000 | $14,000 | | | | |
| Tax-Exempt Bonds | $74,650 | $75,000 | $75,000 | | | | |
| | **$1,336,388** | **$1,442,693** | **$1,442,693** | | | **$1,442,693** | **$1,442,693** |

## Statement of Cash Flows for Year Ended 12/31/04

| | | |
|---|---|---|
| **Cash Flows from Operations** | | |
| Sales Receipts | $3,329,768 | |
| Interest on Cash Account | $928 | |
| Dividends Received | $700 | |
| Interest from Tax-Exempt Bonds | $2,625 | |
| Employee Compensation | ($1,354,134) | |
| Pizza Ingredients | ($1,331,907) | |
| Rent | ($234,068) | |
| Accident Insurance | ($15,214) | |
| Interest | $0 | |
| Contribution to Charity | $0 | |
| Employee Health Insurance | ($203,120) | |
| **Net Cash from Operations** | $195,578 | |
| **Cash Flows from Investment** | | |
| Sale or Disposition of Property, Plant, and Equipment | $0 | |
| Sale or Maturity of Investment | $0 | |
| Purchase of Property, Plant, and Equipment | ($237,789) | |
| Purchase of Investments | ($77,000) | • 70 shares of Whole Grain Co on 9/1 |
| **Net Cash from Investment** | ($314,789) | |
| **Cash Flows from Financing** | | |
| Loan Proceeds | $21,000 | • $14,000 for WGC stock; $7,000 for operations |
| Loan Repayment | $0 | |
| Contributions | $0 | |
| Distributions | ($71,254) | |
| **Net Cash from Financing** | ($50,254) | |
| **Net Cash Flows** | ($169,465) | |

## Depreciation Schedule for Year 4

| | Cost | Placed in Service | Year 1 | Year 2 | Year 3 | Year 4 | Total |
|---|---|---|---|---|---|---|---|
| Location #1 | $215,000 | 1/1/2001 | $30,724 | $52,654 | $37,604 | $26,854 | $147,834 |
| Location #2 | $232,500 | 2/15/2002 | – | $33,224 | $56,939 | $40,664 | $130,828 |
| Location #3 | $197,350 | 8/15/2003 | – | – | $28,201 | $48,331 | $76,532 |
| Location #4 | $213,789 | 4/15/2004 | – | – | – | $30,550 | $30,550 |
| | $858,639 | | $30,724 | $85,878 | $122,744 | $146,399 | $385,745 |
| Rent Amortization | | | | | | $600 | |

Depreciation Table

| Year | Percentage |
|---|---|
| Year 1 | 14.29% |
| Year 2 | 24.49% |
| Year 3 | 17.49% |
| Year 4 | 12.49% |
| Year 5 | 8.93% |
| Year 6 | 8.92% |
| Year 7 | 8.93% |
| Year 8 | 4.46% |
| | 100.00% |

## Rent and Compensation for Year 4

**Rent**

| | Prepaid | Square Feet | Rent/sq. ft. | Monthly Rent | Rent for Year |
|---|---|---|---|---|---|
| Location #1 | | 2,000 | $2.30 | $4,600 | $55,200 |
| Location #2 | | 2,200 | $2.25 | $4,950 | $59,400 |
| Location #3 | | 1,850 | $2.40 | $4,440 | $53,280 |
| Location #4 | | 2,300 | $2.35 | $5,405 | $40,538 |
| Location #5 | $24,000 | 2,250 | $3.80 | $8,550 | $25,650 |
| Total | | | | | $234,068 |

**Compensation**

| | |
|---|---|
| Debby | $156,852 |
| Location #1 | $291,832 |
| Location #2 | $328,012 |
| Location #3 | $355,346 |
| Location #4 | $222,092 |
| Total | $1,354,134 |

| Taxable Income for Year Ended 12/31/04 | | |
|---|---|---|
| **Gross Income** | | **Separately Stated Items** |
| Sales receipts | $3,329,768 | $0 |
| Dividends Received | $0 | $700 |
| Interest on Cash Account | $928 | $0 |
| Interest from Tax-Exempt Bonds | $0 | $2,625 |
| Gains from Sales of Capital Assets Held More Than One Year | $0 | $0 |
| Gains from Sales of Capital Assets Held Less Than One Year | $0 | $0 |
| Gross Income | $3,330,696 | $3,325 |
| **Deductions** | | |
| Employee Compensation | ($1,354,134) | $0 |
| Pizza Ingredients | ($1,311,907) | $0 |
| Rent | ($234,068) | $0 |
| Accident Insurance | ($15,214) | $0 |
| Contribution to Charity | $0 | $0 |
| Interest | $0 | $0 |
| Employee Health Insurance | ($203,120) | $0 |
| Depreciation Deductions | ($146,399) | $0 |
| Amortized Rent Deduction | ($600) | $0 |
| Loss from Sales of Capital Assets Held More Than One Year | $0 | $0 |
| Loss from Sales of Capital Assets Held Less Than One Year | $0 | $0 |
| Total Deductions | ($3,265,442) | $0 |
| Taxable Income (Loss) | $65,254 | |
| Net Amount | | $68,579 |

## Distributions and Allocations for Year 4

• 4.1(a) is 35% of prior year allocation made before 4/1; 4.1(b) amounts are made on 12/31

| **Distributions** | UPR | UCC | | 4.1(a) | 4.1(b)(i) | 4.1(b)(ii) | 4.1(b)(iii) | 4.1(b)(iv) | **Total** |
|---|---|---|---|---|---|---|---|---|---|
| Ella | $376,500 | $1,250,000 | | $0 | ($25,000) | $0 | $0 | $0 | ($25,000) |
| Debby | $0 | $0 | | $0 | $0 | $0 | $0 | $0 | $0 |
| Farzan | $0 | $750,000 | | ($46,254) | $0 | $0 | $0 | $0 | ($46,254) |
| Total | | | | | | | | | ($71,254) |
| **Allocations** | 4.2(a)(i) | 4.2(a)(ii) | 4.2(a)(iii) | 4.2(a)(iv) | 4.2(b)(i) | 4.2(b)(ii) | 4.2(b)(iii) | 4.2(b)(iv) | **Total** |
| Ella | $25,000 | $0 | $0 | $0 | $0 | $0 | $0 | $0 | $25,000 |
| Debby | $0 | $0 | $0 | $0 | $0 | $0 | $0 | $0 | $0 |
| Farzan | $0 | $0 | $43,579 | $0 | $0 | $0 | $0 | $0 | $43,579 |
| **Capital Account Adjustments** | | | | | | | | | |
| Ella | $0 | | | | | | | | |
| Debby | $0 | | | | | | | | |
| Farzan | ($2,676) | | | | | | | | |

## Balance Sheet as of Year 4

| **Assets** | Value | Book | Tax |
|---|---|---|---|
| Cash | $758,723 | $758,723 | $758,723 |
| Accounts Receivable | $7,280 | $0 | $0 |
| Food Inventory | $40,000 | $40,000 | $40,000 |
| Furniture & Equipment | $332,000 | $858,639 | $858,639 |
| Accumulated Depr. | – | ($385,745) | ($385,745) |
| Leaseholds | $24,100 | $24,000 | $24,000 |
| Accumulated Amort. | – | ($600) | ($600) |
| Whole Grain Co Stock | $76,400 | $77,000 | $77,000 |
| Cheez Corp Stock | $15,250 | $14,000 | $14,000 |
| Tax-Exempt Bonds | $73,360 | $75,000 | $75,000 |
| | **$1,327,113** | **$1,461,017** | **$1,461,017** |

| **Debt & Equity** | Value | Book | Tax |
|---|---|---|---|
| Accounts Payable | $6,350 | $0 | $0 |
| Long-Term Debt | | $21,000 | |
| Ella's Capital Account | | $1,250,000 | $1,250,000 |
| Debby's Capital Account | | $0 | $0 |
| Farzan's Capital Account* | | $190,017 | $211,017 |
| | | **$1,461,017** | **$1,461,017** |

*Assumes (for the sake of simplicity) all liability is allocated to Farzan.

## Statement of Cash Flows for Year Ended 12/31/05

| | | |
|---|---|---|
| **Cash Flows from Operations** | | |
| Sales Receipts | $4,729,376 | |
| Interest on Cash Account | $759 | |
| Dividends Received | $4,550 | |
| Interest from Tax-Exempt Bonds | $2,625 | |
| Employee Compensation | ($1,505,899) | |
| Pizza Ingredients | ($1,891,750) | |
| Rent | ($335,340) | |
| Accident Insurance | ($21,797) | |
| Interest | ($945) | |
| Contribution to Charity | ($12,000) | |
| Employee Health Insurance | ($225,885) | |
| **Net Cash from Operations** | $743,693 | |
| **Cash Flows from Investment** | | |
| Sale or Disposition of Property, Plant, and Equipment | $0 | • 40 shares WGC at $1,000, 7/15; 50 shares Cheez at $90, 10/20 |
| Sale or Maturity of Investment | $44,500 | |
| Purchase of Property, Plant, and Equipment | ($175,000) | |
| Purchase of Investments | $0 | |
| **Net Cash from Investment** | ($130,500) | |
| **Cash Flows from Financing** | | |
| Loan Proceeds | $0 | |
| Loan Repayment | ($21,000) | -on 9/1 |
| Contributions | $0 | |
| Distributions | ($785,253) | |
| **Net Cash from Financing** | ($806,253) | |
| **Net Cash Flows** | ($193,059) | |

## Depreciation Schedule for Year 5

| | Cost | Placed in Service | Year 1 | Year 2 | Year 3 | Year 4 | Year 5 | Total |
|---|---|---|---|---|---|---|---|---|
| Location #1 | $215,000 | 1/1/2001 | $30,724 | $52,654 | $37,604 | $26,854 | $19,200 | $167,034 |
| Location #2 | $232,500 | 2/15/2002 | – | $33,224 | $56,939 | $40,664 | $29,039 | $159,867 |
| Location #3 | $197,350 | 8/15/2003 | – | – | $28,201 | $48,331 | $34,517 | $111,049 |
| Location #4 | $213,789 | 4/15/2004 | – | – | – | $30,550 | $52,357 | $82,907 |
| Location #5 | $175,000 | 6/1/2005 | – | – | – | – | $25,008 | $25,008 |
| | $1,033,639 | | $30,724 | $85,878 | $122,744 | $146,399 | $160,120 | $545,864 |
| Rent Amortization | | | | | | $600 | $2,400 | |

Depreciation Table

| Year | Percentage |
|---|---|
| Year 1 | 14.29% |
| Year 2 | 24.49% |
| Year 3 | 17.49% |
| Year 4 | 12.49% |
| Year 5 | 8.93% |
| Year 6 | 8.92% |
| Year 7 | 8.93% |
| Year 8 | 4.46% |
| | 100.00% |

| Rent and Compensation for Year 5 | | | | | | | |
|---|---|---|---|---|---|---|---|
| **Rent** | **Prepaid** | | | | | **Compensation** | |
| | | Square Feet | Rent/sq. ft. | Monthly Rent | Rent for Year | Debby | $159,205 |
| Location #1 | | 2,000 | $2.30 | $4,600 | $55,200 | Location #1 | $297,669 |
| Location #2 | | 2,200 | $2.25 | $4,950 | $59,400 | Location #2 | $334,572 |
| Location #3 | | 1,850 | $2.40 | $4,440 | $53,280 | Location #3 | $362,453 |
| Location #4 | | 2,300 | $2.35 | $5,405 | $64,860 | Location #4 | $237,000 |
| Location #5 | $24,000 | 2,250 | $3.80 | $8,550 | $102,600 | Location #5 | $115,000 |
| Total | | | | | $335,340 | Total | $1,505,899 |

## Depreciation Schedule for Year 8

| | Cost | Placed in Service | Year 1 | Year 2 | Year 3 | Year 4 | Year 5 | Year 6 | Year 7 | Year 8 | Total |
|---|---|---|---|---|---|---|---|---|---|---|---|
| Location #1 | $215,000 | 1/1/2001 | $30,723.50 | $52,653.50 | $37,603.50 | $26,853.50 | $19,199.50 | $19,178.00 | $19,199.50 | $9,589.00 | $215,000.00 |
| Location #2 | $232,500 | 2/15/2002 | – | $33,224.25 | $56,939.25 | $40,664.25 | $29,039.25 | $20,762.25 | $20,739.00 | $20,762.25 | $222,130.50 |
| Location #3 | $197,350 | 8/15/2003 | – | – | $28,201.32 | $48,331.02 | $34,516.52 | $24,649.02 | $17,623.36 | $17,603.62 | $170,924.84 |
| Location #4 | $213,789 | 4/15/2004 | – | – | – | $30,550.45 | $52,356.93 | $37,391.70 | $26,702.25 | $19,091.36 | $166,092.67 |
| Location #5 | $175,000 | 6/1/2005 | – | – | – | – | $25,007.50 | $42,857.50 | $30,607.50 | $21,857.50 | $120,330.00 |
| | $1,033,639 | | $30,723.50 | $85,877.75 | $122,744.07 | $146,399.21 | $160,119.69 | $144,838.46 | $114,871.60 | $88,903.73 | $894,478.01 |
| Rent Amortization | | | | | | $600 | $2,400 | $2,400 | $2,400 | $2,400 | $10,200 |

Depreciation Table

| Year | Percentage |
|---|---|
| Year 1 | 14.29% |
| Year 2 | 24.49% |
| Year 3 | 17.49% |
| Year 4 | 12.49% |
| Year 5 | 8.93% |
| Year 6 | 8.92% |
| Year 7 | 8.93% |
| Year 8 | 4.46% |
| | 100.00% |

## Rent and Compensation for Year 8

| Rent | Prepaid | Square Feet | Rent/sq. ft. | Monthly Rent | Rent for Year | Compensation | |
|---|---|---|---|---|---|---|---|
| | | | | | | Debby | $164,016 |
| Location #1 | | 2,000 | $2.30 | $4,600 | $55,200 | Location #1 | $309,695 |
| Location #2 | | 2,200 | $2.25 | $4,950 | $59,400 | Location #2 | $348,089 |
| Location #3 | | 1,850 | $2.40 | $4,440 | $53,280 | Location #3 | $377,096 |
| Location #4 | | 2,300 | $2.35 | $5,405 | $64,860 | Location #4 | $246,575 |
| Location #5 | $24,000 | 2,250 | $3.80 | $8,550 | $102,600 | Location #5 | $255,000 |
| Total | | | | | $335,340 | Total | $1,700,472 |

## Projected Distributions on 12/31/08

- **4.1(b) amounts are made on 12/31**

| Distributions | UPR | UCC | 4.1(a) | 4.1(b)(i) | 4.1(b)(ii) | 4.1(b)(iii) | 4.1(b)(iv) | Total |
|---|---|---|---|---|---|---|---|---|
| Ella | $86,500 | $865,000 | | | | | | |
| Debby | $0 | $0 | | | | | | |
| Farzan | $0 | $750,000 | | | | | | |
| Ignacio | | | | | | | | |
| Jada | $50,750 | $435,000 | | | | | | |
| Total | | | | | | | | |

**Projected Balance Sheet as of 12/31/08**

| | Assets | | | | Debt & Equity | | |
|---|---|---|---|---|---|---|---|
| | Value | Book | Tax | | Value | Book | Tax |
| Cash | $2,379,658 | $2,379,658 | $2,379,658 | Accounts Payable | ($25,928) | $27,000 | |
| Accounts Receivable | $18,984 | $9,500 | $0 | Long-Term Debt | | | |
| Food Inventory | $93,497 | $93,497 | $93,497 | | | | |
| Furniture & Equipment | $389,441 | $389,441 | $1,033,639 | | | | |
| Accumulated Depr. | | ($135,678) | ($894,478) | Ella's Capital Account | | $865,000 | $1,065,000 |
| Leaseholds | $22,836 | $22,836 | $24,000 | Debby's Capital Account | | $231,478 | $304,059 |
| Accumulated Amort. | | ($7,928) | ($10,200) | Farzan's Capital Account | | $1,675,913 | $1,216,235 |
| Whole Grain Co Stock | $0 | $0 | $0 | Ignacio's Capital Account | | $128,599 | $105,406 |
| Cheez Corp Stock | | $0 | $0 | Jada's Capital Account | | $435,000 | $84,167 |
| Tax-Exempt Bonds | $74,308 | $71,747 | $75,000 | | | | |
| Goodwill | $208,467 | $150,000 | $0 | | | | |
| Accumulated Amort. | | ($16,082) | $0 | | | | |
| ChezeGlaze TM | $491,550 | $435,000 | $150,000 | | | | |
| Accumulated Amort. | | ($29,000) | ($76,250) | | | | |
| | **$3,678,740** | **$3,362,990** | $2,774,866 | | | **$3,362,990** | $2,774,866 |

FOLDER IV

# 11 DUFFIELD DOCUMENTS

# 11 DUFFIELD LLC OPERATING AGREEMENT

**THIS LIMITED LIABILITY COMPANY AGREEMENT** of 11 Duffield LLC, a Delaware limited liability company (the "**Company**"), is effective as of January 1, Year 14 by and among Manage Great Realty LLC, a New York limited liability company (**"The Manager"**), as the Managing Member, and Debby Day, an individual.

WHEREAS, The Manager, as the initial Managing Member, and Debby, as the initial Class A Members, wish to enter into this Limited Liability Company Agreement of the Company dated as of January 1, Year 14, to acquire and own real property known as 11 Duffield;

NOW THEREFORE, in consideration of the foregoing, the undersigned, being all of the Members of 11 Duffield LLC, hereby agree as follows:

## ARTICLE I

### General Provisions

**Section 1.1 Organization.** The Company has heretofore been organized as a Delaware limited liability company pursuant to the Act.

**Section 1.2 Name.** The name of the Company is 11 Duffield LLC.

**Section 1.3 Term.** The Company shall have perpetual existence until it is dissolved and its affairs wound up in accordance with this Agreement and the Act.

**Section 1.4 Filing of Certificate.** The Certificate was filed with the Secretary of State pursuant to the Act on December 15, Year 13. The Managing Member is hereby authorized to take all other actions reasonably deemed by the Managing Member to be necessary or appropriate from time to time to comply with all applicable requirements for the formation, operation and, when appropriate, termination of the Company as a limited liability company under the Act, provided such actions are not prohibited by any other provision of this Agreement. If there is any inconsistency between the Act and the terms of this Agreement, the terms of this Agreement shall govern.

**Section 1.5 Registered Agent and Office.** The Company's registered agent for service of process and registered office in the State of Delaware shall be that Person and location reflected in the Certificate. The Managing Member may, from time to time, change the registered agent or office through appropriate filings with the Secretary of State. If the registered agent ceases to act as such for any reason or the registered office shall change, the Managing Member shall promptly designate a replacement registered agent or file a notice of change of address, as the case may be. If the Managing Member fails to designate a replacement registered agent or change of address of the registered office and such failure continues for a period of ten (10) days following notice from any Member, any Member may designate a replacement registered agent or file a notice of change of address, subject to further change by the Managing Member as provided in this Section 1.5.

**Section 1.5 Principal Office.** The Company's principal office shall be located at 75 Clinton Street, 13R, New York, New York 11201. The Managing Member may change the location of the Company's principal office from time to time. The Managing Member shall make any filing and take any other action required by applicable law in connection with the change and shall give notice to all Members of the new location of the Company's principal office promptly after the change becomes effective. The Managing Member may establish and maintain additional offices for the Company.

**Section 1.6 Foreign Qualifications.** The Company shall qualify to do business as a foreign limited liability company in each jurisdiction, if any, in which the nature of its business requires such qualification. The Managing Member may select any Person permitted by applicable law to act as registered agent for the Company in each jurisdiction in which it is qualified to do business, and may replace any such Person from time to time.

**Section 1.7 Matters Governed by Existing Agreement.** Any matters that relate to acts or events that occurred prior to the Effective Date and that affect only those Persons who were Members in the Company prior to the Effective Date shall be governed by the Existing Agreement, including, without limitation, matters relating to Tax Returns filed by the Company for any taxable period ending prior to the Effective Date.

## ARTICLE II

### Definitions

**Section 2.1 Defined Terms.** As used in this Agreement, the following terms shall have the following respective meanings (unless otherwise expressly provided herein):

**"The Manager":** As defined in the Preamble.

**"Act":** The Delaware Limited Liability Company Act in its present form or as amended from time to time.

**"Additional Capital Call Amount":** As defined in Section 4.4.

**"Additional Contribution Notice":** As defined in Section 4.4.

**"Adjusted Basis":** The basis for determining gain or loss for federal income tax purposes from the sale or other disposition of property, as defined in Section 1011 of the Code.

**"Adjusted Capital Account":** As defined in Section 5.7(f).

**"Affiliate":** When used with reference to any Person, (i) any Person that, directly or indirectly through one or more intermediaries Controls, is Controlled by, or is under common Control with, the specified Person, and (ii) in the case of natural person, such Person's Family Members.

**"Aggregate Capital Contributions":** With respect to each Member, the sum of (i) such Member's Initial Capital Amount, plus (ii) any Capital Contributions made by such Member on or after the Effective Date (that are not reflected in the Member's Initial Capital Amount).

**"Agreement":** This Limited Liability Company Agreement in its present form or as amended, supplemented or restated from time to time.

**"Assignee":** A Person to whom a Membership Interest has been Transferred and who has not been admitted as a Member.

**"Available Cash":** For any specified period, an amount equal to the excess of (i) all cash revenues received by the Company or any of its Subsidiaries during the period from any source (including proceeds of rental or business interruption insurance and but excluding funds received as Capital Contributions or Capital Proceeds) over (ii) the sum of (a) cash expenditures by the Company or any of its Subsidiaries during the period and other costs and expenses in connection with the normal conduct of the Company's and its Subsidiaries' business and, if applicable, the costs and expenses of winding up and terminating the Company or any of its Subsidiaries, (b) all payments by the Company or any of its Subsidiaries during the period of principal of and interest on loans and other obligations of the Company or any of its Subsidiaries for borrowed money (other than payments of principal of and interest on Member Loans), (c) all capital expenditures by the Company or any of its Subsidiaries during the period, and (d) reasonable reserves established by the Managing Member, but only to the extent the payments and expenditures described in clauses (ii)(a), (b), (c) and (d) are not made from funds received as Capital Contributions or Capital Proceeds, or from cash reserves of the Company or any of its Subsidiaries that were established during, and deducted in determining Available Cash for, any earlier period.

**"Bank Accounts":** As defined in <u>Section 8.3</u>.

**"Business Day":** Any day other than a Saturday, a Sunday or a day on which national banks in New York, New York, are not open for business or are authorized by law to close.

**"Capital Account":** The capital account of a Member maintained in accordance with <u>Section 4.6</u>.

**"Capital Contribution":** Any property (including money) from time to time contributed by a Member to the Company.

**"Capital Proceeds":** An amount equal to the cash proceeds received by the Company or any of its Subsidiaries from a Capital Transaction (excluding the proceeds of rental or business interruption insurance) after the payment by the Company and its Subsidiaries of all debt and other obligations of the Company and its Subsidiaries (or to which its property is or was subject), which cash proceeds are not used by the Company or any of its Subsidiaries to pay for the costs and expenses incurred in connection with the Capital Transaction or applied by the Managing Member to establish reasonable reserves. Capital Proceeds shall include all payments of principal of, and interest on, any promissory note or other obligations received by the Company or any of its Subsidiaries in connection with a Capital Transaction.

**"Capital Transaction":** A transaction in which the Company or any of its Subsidiaries (i) borrows money, (ii) sells, exchanges or otherwise disposes of all or any part of its property, including a sale or other disposition pursuant to a condemnation, or (iii) receives the proceeds of property damage insurance (that are not used to repair or rebuilt the damaged property); or any other transaction that, in accordance with generally accepted accounting principles, is considered capital in nature.

**"Carrying Value":** With respect to any asset, the Adjusted Basis of the asset, except as follows:

(i) The initial Carrying Value of an asset contributed by a Member to the Company shall be the gross fair market value of the asset, as determined by the Managing Member, subject to Section 6.4, at the time the asset is contributed;

(ii) The Carrying Values of the Company's assets shall be adjusted to equal their respective gross fair market values, as determined by the Managing Member, subject to Section 6.4, as of the following times: (a) the acquisition of an additional interest in the Company by any new or existing Assignee or Member in exchange for more than a de minimis Capital Contribution; (b) the distribution by the Company to a Member or an Assignee of more than a de minimis amount of property as consideration for all or part of a Membership Interest or an Assignee's Economic Rights; and (c) the liquidation of the Company within the meaning of Regulations Section 1.704-1(b)(2)(ii)(g); but adjustments pursuant to clauses (a) and (b) above shall be made only if the Managing Member, subject to Section 6.4, reasonably determines that such adjustments are necessary or appropriate to reflect the relative economic interests of the Members in the Company;

(iii) The Carrying Value of an asset of the Company distributed to a Member shall be adjusted immediately prior to the distribution to equal the gross fair market value of the asset on the date of distribution as determined by the Managing Member, subject to Section 6.4; and

(iv) The Carrying Values of the Company's assets shall be increased (or decreased) to reflect any adjustments to the Adjusted Basis of those assets pursuant to Sections 734(b) or 743(b) of the Code, but only to the extent that those adjustments are taken into account in determining Capital Accounts pursuant to Regulations Section 1.704-1(b)(2)(iv)(m); but the Carrying Values shall not be adjusted pursuant to this clause (iv) to the extent the Managing Member, subject to Section 6.4, determines that an adjustment pursuant to clause (ii) above is necessary or appropriate in connection with a transaction that would otherwise result in an adjustment pursuant to this clause (iv).

If the Carrying Value of an asset is determined or adjusted pursuant to clauses (i) or (ii), such Carrying Value shall thereafter be adjusted by the depreciation taken into account with respect to the asset (as determined pursuant to Section 5.2(f)) for purposes of computing Profit and Loss. For purposes of filing the income tax return of the Company, the assets of any Subsidiary shall be treated as if they were assets of the Company.

**"Certificate":** The Certificate of Formation of the Company filed with the Secretary of State, as amended and restated from time to time in accordance with the Act.

**"Class A Distribution":** As defined in Section 11.7.

**"Class A Members":** Those persons denominated as Class A Members on Schedule 1 hereto, as the same may change from time to time in accordance with the terms of this Agreement.

**"Closing Date":** As defined in Section 11.7.

**"Code":** The Internal Revenue Code of 1986, as in effect and hereafter amended.

**"Company":** As defined in the Preamble.

**"Consent of the Class A Members":** The written consent of the holders of fifty percent (50%) or more of the Percentage Interests of the Class A Members on the date of the consent, which consent shall not be unreasonably withheld or unduly delayed. Whenever the Consent of the Class A Members is required, if any Class A Member fails to respond to a written request of its consent within ten (10) days following receipt of such request, such Class A Member shall be deemed to have consented and such Class A Member who expressly withholds consent shall set forth the reasons therefore within ten (10) days after responding to the request.

**"Control":** The effective power, directly or indirectly, to direct or cause the direction of the management and policies of a Person. Control shall be conclusively presumed in the case of the direct or indirect ownership of 50 percent or more of the equity interests.

**"Deficiency Contribution":** As defined in Section 4.5(a)(i).

**"Deficiency Contribution Notice":** As defined in Section 4.5(a)(i).

**"Deficiency Member":** As defined in Section 4.5(a)(i).

**"Documents":** As defined in Section 7.13.

**"Economic Rights":** With respect to an Assignee, the Assignee's rights to receive allocations of Profits and Losses, distributions pursuant to Section 5.1 or Section 11.3 and a return of capital.

**"Effective Date":** The date hereof.

**"Existing Agreement":** As defined in the Recitals.

**"FFM Notice":** As defined in Section 4.5(a)(i).

**"Financing":** Any loan or other debt secured by a direct or indirect pledge of the Properties.

**"Fiscal Year":** The 12-month period ending on December 31 of any year (or such portion thereof during which the Company is in existence).

**"Family Member":** The spouse, children (including natural and adopted children and stepchildren), grandchildren, parents and descendants of the designated natural person. For this purpose, a designated individual's spouse includes the widow or widower of such individual, and an individual's descendants include biological descendants and persons deriving their status as descendants by adoption.

**"Fully-Funded Member":** As defined in Section 4.5(a)(i).

**"Funding Date":** As defined in Section 4.4.

**"Initial Capital Amount":** With respect to each Member, the Initial Capital Amount set forth next to such Member's name on Schedule 2 hereto.

**"Initial Refinancing":** The first time the Company and its Subsidiaries directly or indirectly refinance their assets.

**"Initial Refinancing Net Proceeds":** The cash proceeds received by the Company or any of its Subsidiaries from the Initial Refinancing after payment of all costs and expenses (including reserves required by the lenders) incurred by the Company and its Subsidiaries in connection with the Initial Refinancing.

**"Lender":** As defined in Section 8.2.

**"Loss":** As defined in Section 5.2.

**"Major Decisions":** As defined in Section 6.4.

**"Management Agreement":** The agreement of even date herewith between MANAGER Realty LLC, an Affiliate of the Managing Member, as managing agent and a Subsidiary of the Company, with respect to the management, operation and leasing of the 11 Duffield LLC.

**"Management Rights":** The rights of a Member, subject to the provisions of this Agreement, to participate in the management of the Company, including the rights to receive information, to inspect and audit the books and records and to vote on, consent to, or approve certain actions of the Company to the extent herein provided.

**"Managing Member":** The Managing Member is The Manager.

**"Member":** Each Person listed on Schedule 1, and each Assignee of such Person who is admitted as a Member pursuant to Article X.

**"Member Loan":** A loan to the Company by any Member pursuant to Section 4.5.

**"Member Loan Rate":** As defined in Section 4.5(b).

**"Membership Interest":** With respect to a Member, the Member's entire ownership interest in the Company, including the Member's (i) rights to receive allocations of Profits and Losses, distributions and a return of capital, and (ii) Management Rights.

**"Mortgage":** A mortgage given by any the Company or any Subsidiary to secure loans or advances on, or the unpaid purchase price of, 11 Duffield LLC.

**"Nonrecourse Deductions":** As defined in Regulations Section 1.704-2(b)(1).

**"Notices":** As defined in Section 13.1.

**"Original Agreement":** As defined in the Recitals.

**"Original Property":** As defined in the Recitals.

**"Percentage Interest":** The percentage interest from time to time of each Member in the Company as set forth in Schedule 1, as the same may be amended from time to time.

**"Permitted Transferee":**

(i) A Family Member of a (x) Member or an Assignee or (y) a member, partner or other equity owner of a Member or an Assignee (a "**Principal**");

(ii) The executor, administrator, trustee or personal representative who succeeds to such Member's (or Assignee's) estate or the estate of a Principal as a result of the Member's (or Assignee's) or such Principal's death and any transferee of such Member's (or Assignee's) or such Principal's Membership Interest or Economic Rights, as the case may be, from such Person;

(iii) A trust, guardianship or custodianship for the primary benefit of an individual or individuals described in (i); and

(iv) Any corporation, partnership, limited liability company or other business organization controlled by, and substantially all of the interests in which are owned directly or indirectly by, one or more individuals or entities described in (i), (ii) or (iii) above or by one or more of the Members; provided that with respect to an entity described in this clause (iv), the owners of substantially all of the interests therein execute an instrument reasonably satisfactory to the Members restricting transferability of the interests in such entity so that such interests may not be transferred to Persons other than Permitted Transferees. The determination as to whether an individual or an entity is a Permitted Transferee shall be made by the Managing Member and shall bind all Persons if made in good faith, provided as to the Managing Member or any entity which is a member of the Managing Member, a Permitted Transferee shall include any entity the which is controlled by Manager Parent.

**"Person":** An individual, corporation, trust, association, unincorporated association, estate, partnership. joint venture, limited liability company or other legal entity, including a governmental entity.

**"Preferred Return":** With respect to each Member, an amount equal to 6.75% per annum on such Member's Unreturned Capital Contributions, compounded quarterly in arrears, commencing on the Effective Date. For the avoidance of doubt, if any Member sells all or any portion of its Class A Membership Interest, a purchaser of such Class A Membership Interest (or portion thereof) shall not begin accruing a Preferred Return on its Unreturned Capital Contributions until the day following the date of the closing of such sale (i.e., the purchaser is not acquiring any of the Preferred Return that accrued on the purchased Class A Membership Interest prior to the date of the sale, unless the agreement of sale specifies that the Member is selling a portion of its Unpaid Preferred Return to such purchaser).

**"Profit":** As defined in Section 5 2.

**"Properties":** Any property held by the Company pursuant to its stated purpose of holding real property.

**"Pro Rata Equity Contribution Amount":** As defined in Section 4.5(a).

**"Purchase Notice":** As defined in Section 11.7.

**"Purchase Right":** As defined in Section 11.7.

**"Regulations":** The permanent and temporary regulations, and all amendments, modifications and supplements thereof, from time to time promulgated by the Department of the Treasury under the Code.

**"Regulatory Allocations":** As defined in Section 5.7(l).

**"MANAGER Entity":** As defined in Section 7.2.

**"MANAGER Parent":** Manager Parent LLC, a New York limited liability company.

**"Secretary of State":** The Secretary of State of the State of Delaware.

**"Spin-Off":** As defined in Section 11.6.

**"Subsidiary":** Any entity Controlled directly or indirectly by the Company.

**"Subsidiary Holding Companies":** Any Subsidiary that owns, either directly or indirectly, one of the Properties.

**"Tax Matters Partner":** As defined in Section 5.8.

**"Tax Returns":** As defined in Section 6.4(b).

**"Transfer and Transferred":** A sale, assignment, transfer or other disposition (voluntarily or by operation of law) of, or the granting or creating of a lien, encumbrance or security interest in, a Membership Interest or a Person that directly or indirectly owns an interest in a Member.

**"Unpaid Preferred Return":** With respect to each Member on any date, an amount equal to (i) such Member's Preferred Return, minus (ii) the aggregate amounts previously distributed to such Member pursuant to Section 5.1(a)(i).

**"Unreturned Capital Contributions":** With respect to each Member on any date, an amount equal to (i) such Member's Aggregate Capital Contributions, minus (ii) the aggregate amounts previously distributed to such Member pursuant to Sections 5.1(a)(ii).

## ARTICLE III

### Business, Purposes, and Powers

**Section 3.1 Business and Purposes.** The business and purposes of the Company are, directly or indirectly through any one or more Subsidiaries, acquire, own, hold, renovate, remodel, rent, operate, manage, maintain, improve, repair, sell, finance and refinance the 11 Duffield (or any replacement properties acquired by the Company or any of its Subsidiaries in a transaction intended to qualify under Section 1031 of the Code or a similar Code provision), for the production of income; and (ii) to carry on any and all activities reasonably related thereto (but not including the acquisition of additional assets not related to the ownership, management, operation or maintenance of the Properties or any such replacement properties).

**Section 3.2 Powers.** The Company shall have all powers of a limited liability company under the Act and the power to do or cause any Subsidiary to do all things necessary or convenient to operate the Company's business and accomplish its purposes as described in, and limited by, Section 3.1 and the Certificate, including the following:

(a) to purchase or otherwise acquire the Properties;

(b) to hold, operate, manage, and exercise rights with respect to the Properties (or any replacement properties acquired by the Company or any of its Subsidiaries in a transaction intended to qualify under Section 1031 of the Code or a similar Code provision);

(c) to sell, transfer, assign, convey, lease, mortgage, encumber, pledge, or otherwise dispose of or deal with all or any part of the Properties or 100% of the interest in any Subsidiary;

(d) to incur expenses and to enter into and carry out contracts, agreements, and guaranties necessary to accomplish the business and purposes of the Company;

(e) to raise and provide such funds as may be necessary to further the business and purposes of the Company or any Subsidiary, as applicable, and to borrow money, incur liabilities, and issue promissory notes and other evidences of indebtedness, and to secure the same by security instrument, security interest, pledge, or other lien on all or any part of the Properties or 100% of the interest in any Subsidiary;

(f) to employ or retain on behalf of the Company or any Subsidiary, as applicable, such Persons as the Managing Member deems advisable in the operation and management of the business of the Company or any Subsidiary, as applicable, including (i) the managing agent and leasing agent contemplated in the Management Agreement, and (ii) subject to Section 6.4, such accountants, attorneys, placement agents, and experts as the Managing Member deems appropriate on such terms and at such compensation as the Managing Member shall determine, but subject to the terms of this Agreement;

(g) to hire and appoint employees and agents of the Company or any Subsidiary, as applicable, to define their duties, and to establish their compensation;

(h) to collect, receive, and deposit all sums due or to become due to the Company or any Subsidiary, as applicable;

(i) to pay any and all taxes, charges, and assessments that may be levied, assessed, or imposed upon any property of the Company or Subsidiary, as applicable;

(j) to demand, sue for, collect, recover, and receive, all goods, claims, debts, moneys, interest, and demands whatsoever now due or that may hereafter become due or belong to the Company or any Subsidiary, as applicable, including the right to institute any action, suit, or other legal proceedings for the recovery of any land, building, other real and/or personal property, or any part or parts thereof, to the possession of which the Company or any Subsidiary, as applicable, may be entitled, and to make, execute, and deliver receipts, releases, and other discharges therefor under seal or otherwise;

(k) to make, execute, endorse, accept, collect, and deliver any and all bills of exchange, checks, drafts, and notes of the Company or any Subsidiary, as applicable;

(l) to defend, settle, adjust, compound, submit to arbitration, and compromise all actions, suits, accounts, reckonings, claims, and demands whatsoever that now are or hereafter shall be pending between the Company or any Subsidiary, as applicable, and any Person (other than disputes between or among Members), at law or in equity;

(m) to secure and maintain insurance against liability and property damage with respect to the activities of the Company or any Subsidiary, as applicable; and

(n) to do and perform all acts and things necessary, appropriate, proper, advisable, incidental to, or convenient for, the furtherance and accomplishment of the business and purposes of the Company or any Subsidiary set forth in, and limited by, Section 3.1 and the Certificate.

**Section 3.3** ***Limitations on Scope of Business.*** Except as described in this Article III, the Company is not authorized to carry on any business or activity.

## ARTICLE IV

### Members and Capital Contributions

**Section 4.1 Identity of Members; Percentage Interests.** The Members of the Company and their initial Percentage Interests shall be as set forth on Schedule 1. Any changes in the Members or in the Percentage Interests of a Member shall be reflected in an amendment to Schedule 1 of this Agreement. If the Managing Member acquires a Class A Membership Interest, the Managing Member may, from time to time, be both a Class A Member and the Managing Member.

**Section 4.2 No Partition.** No Member shall seek, institute or maintain any action or proceeding for the partition of any asset owned by the Company or any Subsidiary, and such remedy is hereby waived by the Members.

**Section 4.3 Revaluation of Capital Accounts.** The Capital Accounts of the Members shall be "booked up" as of the Effective Date and, as of the Effective Date, are as set forth on Schedule 3.

**Section 4.4 No Additional Capital Contributions.** No Member shall be required to contribute any additional capital to the Company or to make any loans to the Company. If the Managing Member determines that additional capital is necessary for the operations of the Company, the Managing Member shall so notify the Class A Members pursuant to a written notice (an "**Additional Contribution Notice**") specifying: (a) the total amount of additional Capital Contributions then being requested (the "**Additional Capital Call Amount**"); (b) the amount of each Member's share of such Additional Capital Call Amount, which share shall equal the Member's Percentage Interest multiplied by the Additional Capital Call Amount; and (c) the intended use of such Additional Capital Call Amount; (d) the date on which funds are to be provided (which date shall be no less than ten (10) days after the date of the Additional Contribution Notice except in the case of funds required for emergency expenditures (the "**Funding Date**"); and (e) the account of the Company to which such funds are to be transmitted. Each Member shall be entitled to contribute its share of such Additional Capital Call Amount. All Additional Capital Contributions shall be denominated and payable in U.S. dollars, in cash or immediately available funds.

**Section 4.5 Loans.**

**(a) Member Loans.**

(i) In the event any Member (a "**Deficiency Member**") shall fail to fund its full Percentage Interest of an Additional Capital Call Amount (as to each member its "**Pro Rata Equity Contribution Amount**") requested pursuant to an Additional Contribution Notice (such unfunded contribution or portion thereof, a "**Deficiency Contribution**") by 5:00 p.m. New York time of the Funding Date, then (i) Managing Member shall deliver a notice (a "**Deficiency Contribution Notice**") to each Member that has funded its Pro Rata Equity Contribution Amount (a "**Fully-Funded Member**") advising the Fully-Funded Member(s) of the identity of the Deficiency Member(s) and the amount of Deficiency Contribution(s), and (ii) each Fully-Funded Members Pro Rata Equity Contribution Amount shall be treated as a Member Loan. Each Fully-Funded Member shall have the right, but not the obligation, to elect to fund all or any portion of the Deficiency Contribution(s) by notice to the other Members, delivered within ten (10) days after delivery of the Deficiency Contribution Notice, specifying the portion of the Deficiency Contribution(s) such Fully-Funded Member has elected to fund. Within ten (10) days after delivery by Managing Member of a Deficiency Contribution Notice to the Fully-Funded Member(s), the Managing Member shall deliver a notice (an **"FFM Notice"**) to the Fully-Funded Member(s) specifying (i) which Fully-Funded Member(s) shall have elected to fund the Deficiency Contribution(s), (ii) the amount each Fully-Funded Member shall have elected to fund, as a Member Loan, and (iii) in the case that the aggregate amount of the Deficiency Contribution that the Fully-Funded Members have elected to fund exceeds 100% of the actual Deficiency Contribution, the amount that each Fully-Funded Member shall fund. The Fully-Funded Members shall be obligated to fund that portion of the Deficiency Contribution(s) they elected to fund in their notice, or such lesser sum as otherwise specified by the FFM Notice, to the Managing Member within five (5) days after receipt of such FFM Notice from Managing Member. If more than one (1) Fully-Funded Member shall have elected to fund a Deficiency Contribution and the aggregate amount of the Deficiency Contribution that the Fully-Funded Members have elected to fund exceeds 100% of the actual Deficiency Contribution, then unless otherwise agreed to by the Fully-Funded Members, each Fully-Funded Member shall only have the right to fund, as a Member Loan, such portion of the Deficiency Contribution equal to the product of the Deficiency Contribution and a fraction, the numerator of which is the Percentage Interest of such Fully-Funded Member and the denominator of which is the sum of the Percentage Interests of all the Fully-Funded Members that have elected to make a Deficiency Contribution.

(b) Each Member Loan: (i) shall not be included in the calculation of the Member's respective Percentage Interests; (ii) shall bear interest at the Member Loan Rate; and (iii) shall be entitled to the distributions on account of Member Loans as provided for in Article V and Article XI.

(c) ***Terms of Member Loan.*** The Member Loan shall bear interest at a rate of 12% per annum, compounded quarterly (the "**Member Loan Rate**"), determined on the basis of a 365 or 366 day year, as the case may be, for the actual number of days until the Member Loan and any accrued and unpaid interest thereon shall be paid. Any Available Cash and Capital Proceeds shall first be applied to reduce the principal amount of the Member Loan and any accrued interest thereon. All payments shall be applied first to accrued but unpaid interest and then to principal.

(d) ***Third-Party Loans.*** The Managing Member may, from time to time or at any time, cause the Company to borrow funds or cause the Company to cause any Subsidiary to borrow funds on such terms as the Managing Member, in its sole but good faith judgment deems commercially reasonable terms, and to grant a Mortgage or other lien on the Properties as security for the loan and on the Company's membership interest or other equity interest in any Subsidiary. In addition, if necessary to obtain any Financing permitted by this Agreement, the Members shall be obligated to pledge their Membership Interests in the Company on an absolutely nonrecourse basis, without any guaranty or carve-outs whatsoever. If the Managing Member, the MANAGER Parent, the principals of the MANAGER Parent or any of their Affiliates (other than the Company or any of its Subsidiaries) guaranty any Financing permitted by this Agreement, then each Member shall severally indemnify the guarantors from any action taken by such Member, without the authorization of the Company, to file any petition by such Member to declare either the Company or any Subsidiary bankrupt in an involuntary bankruptcy or similar proceeding.

**Section 4.6 Capital Accounts.**

(a) The Company shall establish and maintain a Capital Account for each Member in accordance with the provisions of Section 704(b) of the Code and the Regulations thereunder.

(b) Each Member's Capital Account shall be maintained in accordance with the following provisions:

(1) Each Member's Capital Account shall be credited with the amounts of such Member's subsequent Capital Contributions, such Member's distributive share of Profits and any items in the nature of income or gain which are specially allocated to the Member pursuant to Article V, and the amount of any liabilities of the Company assumed by such Member or which are secured by any property distributed by the Company to such Member;

(2) Each Member's Capital Account shall be charged with the amounts of cash and the Carrying Value of any property distributed by the Company to such Member pursuant to any provision of this Agreement, such Member's distributive share of Losses and any items in the nature of expenses or losses which are specially allocated to the Member pursuant to Article V, and the amount of any liabilities of such Member assumed by the Company or which are secured by any property contributed by such Member to the Company;

(3) If all or a portion of a Member's Membership Interest is Transferred in accordance with the terms of this Agreement, the transferee shall succeed to the Capital Account of the transferor to the extent it relates to the Transferred Membership Interest; and

(4) In determining the amount of any liability for purposes of this Section 4.6(b), Section 752(c) of the Code and any other applicable provisions of the Code and Regulations shall be taken into account.

This Section 4.6(b) and other provisions of this Agreement relating to the maintenance of Capital Accounts are intended to comply with Regulations Section 1.704-1(b), and shall be interpreted and applied in a manner consistent with such Regulations. If the Managing Member determines that it is prudent to modify the manner in which the Capital Accounts, or any charges or credits thereto (including charges or credits relating to liabilities which are secured by contributions or distributed property or which are assumed by the Company or by Members), are computed in order to comply with such Regulations, the Managing Member may make such modification. Subject to Section 6.4, the Managing Member also may (i) make any adjustments to Capital Accounts that may be necessary or appropriate to maintain equality between the Capital Accounts of the Members and the amount of capital reflected on the Company's balance sheet, as computed for book purposes, in accordance with Regulations Section 1.704-1(b)(2)(iv)(q), and (ii) make any appropriate modifications in the event unanticipated events might otherwise cause this Agreement not to comply with Regulations Section 1.704-1(b). All of the foregoing determinations by the Managing Member shall be subject to Section 6.4.

**Section 4.6 Return of Capital Contributions.** No Member or Assignee shall be entitled to demand the return of the Member's Capital Account or Capital Contribution at any particular time, except upon dissolution of the Company. No Member or Assignee shall be entitled at any time to demand or receive property other than cash. Unless otherwise provided by law, no Member or Assignee shall be personally liable for the return or repayment of all or any part of any other Member's Capital Account or Capital Contribution, it being expressly agreed that any such return of capital pursuant to this Agreement shall be made solely from the assets (which shall not include any right of contribution from a Member or Assignee) of the Company.

**Section 4.7 No Third Party Beneficiary Rights.** The provisions of this Article IV are not intended to be for the benefit of any creditor or any other Person (other than a Member in its, his or her capacity as such) whom to any debts, liabilities or obligations are owed by (or who otherwise has any claim against) the Company or any of the Members; and no such creditor or other Person shall obtain any right under any of such provisions or shall by reason of any of such provisions make any claim in respect of any debt, liability or obligation (or otherwise) against the Company or any of the Members.

## ARTICLE V

### Allocations and Distributions

**Section 5.1 Distributions.**

**(a)** ***General Rule.*** After payment of accrued but unpaid interest and principal of any Member Loans (pro rata based on their outstanding principal balance and accrued and unpaid interest), remaining Available Cash and Capital

Proceeds shall be distributed from time to time to the Members in the following order of priority:

(i) first, to the Members, pro rata in accordance with their respective Unpaid Preferred Return, until each Member's Unpaid Preferred Return is reduced to $0;

(ii) second, to the Members, pro rata in accordance with their respective Unreturned Capital Contributions, until each Member's Unreturned Capital Contributions is reduced to $0;

(iii) thereafter, 50% to the Class A Members, pro rata, in proportion to their respective Percentage Interests, and 50% to the Managing Member.

**Section 5.2 Determination of Profits and Losses.** For purposes of this Agreement, the profit ("**Profit**") or loss ("**Loss**") of the Company for each Fiscal Year shall be the net income or net loss of the Company for such Fiscal Year as determined for federal income tax purposes, but computed with the following adjustments:

(a) without regard to any adjustment to basis pursuant to Section 743 of the Code;

(b) by including as an item of gross income any tax-exempt income received by the Company;

(c) by treating as a deductible expense any expenditure of the Company described in Section 705(a)(2)(B) of the Code;

(d) In the event that any asset of the Company is distributed in kind to a Member or there is a liquidation of the Company pursuant to Article XI, the difference between (i) an amount equal to the Carrying Value of such asset on the date of such distribution and (ii) the fair market value of such asset on that date shall be taken into account as a gain or loss for purposes of computing Profits or Losses;

(e) Gain or loss resulting from any disposition of an asset by the Company from which gain or loss is recognized for federal income tax purposes shall be computed with reference to the Carrying Value of the asset (after adjustment for depreciation (or amortization) determined under subsection (f) below), notwithstanding that the adjusted basis for federal income tax purposes of such asset differs from its Carrying Value;

(f) Depreciation (or amortization) shall be determined based upon the Carrying Value of assets as provided in Regulations Section 1.704-1(b)(2)(iv)(g); and

(g) after making the special allocations (if any) required by Section 5.7.

The amounts of the items of income, gain, loss or deduction of the Company to be specially allocated pursuant to Section 5.7 shall be determined by applying rules analogous to those set forth in subsections (a) through (f).

**Section 5.3 Allocation of Profits and Losses.** Profits and Losses for any taxable year, or portion thereof, shall be allocated among the Members in a manner such that the Capital Account of each Member, immediately after making such allocation, and after taking into account actual distributions made during such taxable year, or portion thereof, is, as nearly as possible, equal (proportionately) to (i) the distributions that would be made to such Member pursuant to Section 11.3 if the Company were dissolved, its affairs wound up and its assets sold for cash equal to their Carrying Value, all Company liabilities, including the Company's share of any liability of any entity treated as a partnership for U.S. federal income tax purposes in which the Company is a partner, were satisfied (limited with respect to each nonrecourse liability to the Carrying Value of the assets securing such liability) and the net assets of the Company were distributed in accordance with Section 11.3 to the Members immediately after making such allocation, minus (ii) such Member's share of Company minimum gain and Member nonrecourse debt minimum gain determined pursuant to Regulations Sections 1.704-2(g)(1) and 1.704-2(i)(5), computed immediately prior to the hypothetical sale of assets. Subject to the other provisions of this Article V, an allocation to a Member of a share of Profit or Loss shall be treated as an allocation of the same share of each item of income, gain, loss or deduction that is taken into account in computing Profit or Loss.

**Section 5.4 Income Tax Elections.** In the event of a Transfer of all or part of a Membership Interest (or of the interest of a partner in a partnership (or of a member in a limited liability company that is treated as a partnership for federal income tax purposes) which is a Member) because of death or sale, the Company shall, if requested by the transferee, make the election described in Section 754 of the Code.

**Section 5.5 Income Tax Allocations.**

(a) Except as otherwise provided herein, the Company's income, gains, deductions and losses for federal income tax purposes, and each item of income, gain, loss or deduction entering into the computation thereof, shall be allocated among the Members in the same proportions as the corresponding "book" items are allocated pursuant to this Article.

(b) In accordance with Section 704(c) of the Code and the Regulations promulgated thereunder, income, gain, loss and deduction with respect to any property contributed to the capital of the Company and any revalued property of the Company shall, solely for tax purposes, be allocated among the Members so as to take account of any variation between the Adjusted Basis of such property to the Company for federal income tax purposes and its Carrying Value. Allocations shall be made using the "traditional method" set forth in Regulations Section 1.704-3(b).

(c) If any portion of the Profit from a Capital Transaction allocated among the Members pursuant to Section 5.5(a) is characterized as ordinary income under the recapture provisions of the Code or is subject to a different rate of tax under the Code, each Member's distributive share of taxable gain from the sale of the property that gave rise to such Profit (to the extent possible) shall include a proportionate share of the recapture income or income that is subject to a different rate of tax equal to that Member's share of prior cumulative depreciation deductions with respect to the property that give rise to the recapture income or the income that is subject to a different rate of tax.

**Section 5.6 Transfers During Fiscal Year.** In the event of the Transfer of all or any part of a Membership Interest (in accordance with the provisions of this Agreement) at any time other than the end of a Fiscal Year, the share of Profit or Loss (in respect of the Membership Interest so Transferred) shall be allocated between the transferor and the transferee in the same ratio as the number of days in the Fiscal Year before and after such Transfer. The preceding sentence shall not apply to Profit or Loss from Capital Transactions or to other extraordinary nonrecurring items. Profit and Loss from Capital Transactions shall be allocated on the basis of the Members' Percentage Interests on the date of closing of the sale and extraordinary or nonrecurring items of gain or loss shall be allocated on the basis of the Members' Percentage Interests on the date the gain is realized or the loss incurred, as the case may be.

**Section 5.7 Special Allocations to Comply with Section 704 Regulations.**

(a) ***General Rule.*** Notwithstanding the provisions of Section 5.3, if the allocation of a Loss to a Member for any Fiscal Year pursuant to Section 5.3 would cause or increase a negative balance in the Member's Adjusted Capital Account (as defined in Section 5.7(f)) on the last day of the Fiscal Year, then the portion of the Loss that would have such effect shall instead be specially allocated among the Members who have positive balances in their Adjusted Capital Accounts on the last day of the Fiscal Year. The Loss to be specially allocated pursuant to the preceding sentence shall be allocated among the Members referred to in the preceding sentence, pro rata, in proportion to their respective Adjusted Capital Accounts.

(b) ***Gross Income Allocation/Qualified Income Offset.*** If, at the end of any Fiscal Year, one or more Members would otherwise have a negative balance in their Adjusted Capital Accounts, then income and gain for such Fiscal Year (and, if necessary, subsequent Fiscal Years) shall be allocated as quickly as possible among all Members who have such negative balances in their Adjusted Capital Accounts, pro rata, in proportion to their respective negative balances to the extent necessary to eliminate such negative balances as of the end of such Fiscal Year; provided that an allocation pursuant to this Section 5.7(b) shall be made only if and to the extent that such Member would have such a negative balance in the Member's Adjusted Capital Account after all other allocations provided for in this Article V have been tentatively made as if this Section 5.7(b) were not a part of this Agreement. The allocations referred to in this paragraph shall be interpreted and applied, inter alia, to satisfy the requirements of Regulations Section 1.704-1(b)(2)(ii)(d)(3).

(c) ***Minimum Gain Chargeback—Nonrecourse Liability.*** If there is a net decrease in the Minimum Gain on Nonrecourse Liability (as defined in Section 5.7(g)) during any Fiscal Year, the Members shall be allocated items of income and gain for the Fiscal Year, before any other allocation of Company items described in Code Section 704(b) is made for the Fiscal Year (and, if necessary subsequent Fiscal Years), in the amounts and in the proportions required by Regulations Sections 1.704-2(f) and 1.704-2(j)(2)(i). The allocations referred to in this paragraph shall be interpreted and applied to satisfy the requirements of Regulations Section 1.704-2(f).

(d) ***Minimum Gain Chargeback—Member Nonrecourse Debt.*** If there is a decrease in the Minimum Gain on Member Nonrecourse Debt during a Fiscal Year, then any Member who has a share of the Minimum Gain on Member Nonrecourse Debt at the beginning of the Fiscal Year shall be allocated items of income and gain for the Fiscal Year, before any other allocation of Company items described in Code Section 704(b) is made for the Fiscal Year (and, if necessary, subsequent Fiscal Years), in the amounts and in the proportions required by Regulations Sections 1.704-2(i)(4) and 1.704-2(j)(2)(ii).

The allocations referred to in this paragraph shall be interpreted and applied to satisfy the requirements of Regulations Section 1.704-2(i)(4).

(e) ***Member Nonrecourse Debt Deductions.*** Member Nonrecourse Deductions with respect to Member Nonrecourse Debt shall be specially allocated among the Member or Members who bear the economic risk of loss with respect to such Member Nonrecourse Debt in the amounts and in the proportions required by Regulations Section 1.704-2(i)(1). The allocations referred to in this subsection shall be interpreted and applied to satisfy the requirements of Regulations Section 1.704-2(i).

(f) ***Adjusted Capital Account.*** The term "**Adjusted Capital Account**" shall mean the amount of a Member's Capital Account (determined before the special allocation to be made pursuant to this subsection, but after making all other adjustments to Capital Account for the Fiscal Year with respect to contributions, allocations and distributions), whether positive or negative, reduced by reasonably expected adjustments described in Regulations Section 1.704-1(b)(2)(ii)(d)(4) and by reasonably expected allocations of loss and deduction described in Regulations Section 1.704-1(b)(2)(ii)(d)(5) and reasonably expected distributions described in Regulations Section 1.704-1 (b)(2)(ii)(d)(6), and increased by the Member's share of Minimum Gain on Nonrecourse Liability (as defined in Section 5.7(g)), and the Member's share of Minimum Gain on Member Nonrecourse Debt (as defined in Section 5.7(h)) as of the last day of the Fiscal Year and the amount of the Member's "risk of loss" (as defined in Regulations Section 1.752-2(b)) with respect to the recourse liabilities of the Company.

(g) ***Minimum Gain on Nonrecourse Liability.*** The term "**Minimum Gain on Nonrecourse Liability**" shall mean the aggregate amount of gain, if any, that would be realized by the Company if, in a taxable transaction, it disposed of all Company property subject to Nonrecourse Liabilities of the Company (as defined in Regulations Section 1.704-2(b)(3)) in full satisfaction thereof (and for no other consideration). The Members intend that Minimum Gain on Nonrecourse Liability shall be determined in accordance with the provisions of Regulations Section 1.704-2(d)(1).

(h) ***Minimum Gain on Member Nonrecourse Debt.*** The term "**Minimum Gain on Member Nonrecourse Debt**" shall mean the aggregate amount of gain if any, that would be realized by the Company if, in a taxable transaction, it disposed of all Company property encumbered by Mortgages securing Member Nonrecourse Debt of the Company (i.e., a nonrecourse debt for which one or more of the Members bears the economic risk of loss, and defined in Regulations Section 1.704-2(b)(4)), in full satisfaction thereof (and for no other consideration). The Members intend that Minimum Gain on Member Nonrecourse Debt shall be determined in accordance with the provisions of Regulations Section 1.704-2(i)(3).

(i) ***Nonrecourse Deductions.*** Nonrecourse Deductions for any Fiscal Year shall be specially allocated among the Members (i) pro rata in accordance with their respective Percentage Interests, until such time as there is no Unpaid Preferred Return and Unreturned Capital Contributions, and (ii) thereafter, 50% to the Managing Member, and 50% to the Class A Members pro rata in accordance with their respective Percentage Interests.

(j) ***Excess Nonrecourse Liabilities.*** Excess nonrecourse liabilities (as defined in Regulations Section 1.752-3(a)(3)) shall be allocated among the Members (i) first, pro rata in accordance with their excess Section 704(c) gain (i.e., Section 704(c) gain that exceeds the Section 704(c) gain described in Regulations Section 1.752-3(a)(2)), (ii) second, pro rata in accordance with their respective Percentage Interests, until such time as there is no Unpaid Preferred Return and Unreturned Capital Contributions, and (iii) thereafter, 50% to the Managing Member, and 50% to the Class A Members pro rata in accordance with their respective Percentage Interests.

(k) ***Section 754 Adjustments.*** In any case where an adjustment to the Adjusted Basis of any Company asset pursuant to Sections 734(b) or 743(b) of the Code is required (pursuant to Regulations Section 1.704-l(b)(2)(iv)(m)(2) or Regulations 1.704-1(b)(2)(iv)(m)(4)), to be taken into account in determining Capital Accounts because of a distribution to a Member in complete liquidation of the Member's interest in the Company, the amount of such adjustment to Capital Accounts shall be treated as an item of gain (if the adjustment increases the basis of the asset) or loss (if the adjustment decreases such basis), and such gain or loss shall be specially allocated (i) among the Members in accordance with their interests in the Company in the event that Regulations Section 1.704-1(b)(2)(iv)(m)(2) applies, or (ii) among the Members to whom such distribution was made in the event that Regulations Section 1.704-1(b)(2)(iv)(m)(4) applies.

(l) ***Curative Allocations.*** The term "**Regulatory Allocations**" shall mean the allocations set forth in <u>Section 5.7(a)</u> through <u>Section 5.7(e)</u> and <u>Section 5.7(i)</u> through <u>Section 5.7(j)</u>. Offsetting special allocations of Company income, gain, loss or deduction shall be made so that, after such offsetting allocations are made, each Member's Capital Account is, to the extent possible, equal to the Capital Account such Member would have had if the Regulatory Allocations were not included in this Agreement. For this purpose, future Regulatory Allocations under <u>Section 5.7(c)</u> and <u>Section 5.7(d)</u> that are likely to offset current Regulatory Allocations under Section 5.7(e) and Section 5.7(i) shall be taken into account.

(m) ***Winding Up.*** If, upon the winding up of the Company, the amount of the Distribution to a Member pursuant to Section 11.3 does not equal its Capital Account immediately before such Distribution (after the tentative allocation of Profit or Loss and special allocations of income, gain, deduction or loss for such Fiscal Year), then, subject to Section 6.4, the Managing Member shall make such special allocations of income, gain, deduction or loss necessary to maintain equality between the Capital Account of the Member and the amount of the Distribution to him. The Managing Member may otherwise make such special allocations of income, gain, deduction or loss for any Fiscal Year necessary to maintain equality between the Capital Account of a Member and the amount that would be distributed to such Member if the Company were dissolved, its affairs wound up and its assets distributed to the Members immediately after making such allocation. For purposes of making allocations for any Fiscal Year pursuant to this Section 5.7(m) prior to the dissolution of the Company pursuant to Article XI, the Managing Member may, in his discretion, treat each of the assets held by the Company as having a fair market value equal to its Carrying Value as of the end of such Fiscal Year. All allocations made pursuant to this Section 5.7(m) shall be made in good faith by the Managing Member.

**Section 5.8 Tax Matters Partner.** The Managing Member shall initially be the "tax matters partner" of the Company pursuant to Section 6231(a)(7) of the Code (the **"Tax Matters Partner"**). If The Manager ceases for any reason to be the Managing Member, then its successor managing member shall become the Tax Matters Partner. The Tax Matters Partner shall be authorized and required to represent the Company (at the expense of the Company) in connection with all examinations of the affairs of the Company by any federal, state or local tax authorities, including any resulting administrative and judicial proceedings, and to expend funds of the Company for professional services and costs associated therewith. The Tax Matters Partner shall take all actions necessary to preserve the rights of the Members with respect to audits and shall provide all Members with notices of all such proceedings and other information as required by law. The Tax Matters Partner shall obtain the prior written consent of each Member before settling, compromising or otherwise altering the defense of any proceeding before the Internal Revenue Service if such Member or any of its constituent partners or members could be materially and adversely affected thereby (such consent not to be unreasonably withheld or delayed; and if such consent is not granted or withheld by notice within ten (10) days following receipt of the request, such consent shall be deemed to be given). The Tax Matters Partner shall keep the Members timely informed of his or her activities under this Section 5.8. The Tax Matters Partner may prepare and file protests or other appropriate responses to such audits. The Tax Matters Partner shall select counsel to represent the Company in connection with any audit conducted by the Internal Revenue Service or by any state or local authority. All costs incurred in connection with the foregoing activities, including legal and accounting costs, shall be borne by the Company. Each Member agrees to cooperate with the Tax Matters Partner and to do or refrain from doing any or all things reasonably required by the Tax Matters Partner in connection with the conduct of all such proceedings.

**Section 5.9 Election to be Taxed as Association.** The Company shall be treated as a partnership for federal income tax purposes. No Member shall cause the Company to elect to be treated other than as a partnership (or shall cause any Subsidiary to be treated as other than a disregarded entity) for federal income tax purposes in accordance with Regulations Section 301.7701-3(c) unless such election is approved in writing by all Members.

**Section 5.10 Assignees Treated as Members.** For all purposes of this Article V and Section 11.3, but for no other purpose, an Assignee shall be treated as a Member and each reference in this Article V and Section 11.3 to the Members shall be deemed to include Assignees.

**Section 5.11 Tax Distributions.** In the event that the Company is required to deposit or pay any tax on behalf of a Member with respect to the taxable income of the Company allocable to such Member for any Fiscal Year, such deposit or payment shall be treated as an advance recoverable from future distributions of Available Cash to the Member. To the extent that such advances to a Member for a Fiscal Year exceed the Available Cash distributable to the Member for such Fiscal Year, and have not been recovered from any other distributions of Available Cash, such advances shall be repaid by the Member to the Company within sixty (60) days of the end of the Fiscal Year.

## ARTICLE VI

### Rights and Duties of Members

**Section 6.1 Management Rights.** All Members shall be entitled to vote on any matter submitted to a vote of the Members. A court-appointed custodian for an individual Member declared to be incompetent or an attorney-in-fact duly appointed by a Member, shall have the right to act on behalf of such Member.

**Section 6.2 Liability of Members.** No Member shall be obligated to make Capital Contributions to the Company. No Member shall have any personal liability with respect to the liabilities or obligations of the Company. The failure of the Company to observe any formalities or requirements relating to the exercise of its powers or the management of its business or affairs under this Agreement or the Act shall not be grounds for imposing personal liability on the Members for liabilities or obligations of the Company.

**Section 6.3 Indemnification.** Subject to the terms of the Certificate and this Agreement, to the fullest extent permitted by the laws of the State of Delaware, each Member shall be entitled to indemnity from the Company (but not from any other Member) for any act performed by such Member within the scope of the authority conferred on such Member by this Agreement except for acts of fraud, gross negligence, misrepresentation, breach of fiduciary duty or willful misconduct.

**Section 6.4 Major Decisions.** None of the following decisions involving the conduct of the business and affairs of the Company shall be made by the Managing Member unless the Consent of the Class A Members is first obtained:

(i) selecting or changing the Company's certified public accountants pursuant to Section 8.4 if such certified public accountants will not be Dewey Long PC;

(ii) amending the Management Agreement to increase the management fee to an amount in excess of 3% of gross revenues, or to increase any other fees, including construction management or leasing fees, to an amount in excess of the then market rate, as determined in good faith by the Managing Member; and

(iii) if the Management Agreement terminates, entering into or causing any Subsidiary to enter into an agreement with another Person for the management of the Properties for a management fee in excess of 3% of gross receipts or for other services at fees in excess of those set forth in the Management Agreement.

(a) The Managing Member shall prepare and file or cause to be filed all federal, state and local income tax returns (the "**Tax Returns**") for the Company. The Class A Members shall have the right to review all Tax Returns prior to filing. Upon written request of any Class A Member, the Managing Member shall promptly provide such returns to such Class A Member for its review. With the Consent of the Class A Members, a Class A Member shall have the right to contest promptly the proposed treatment of any item in a Tax Return, provided that such proposed treatment would have a material adverse effect on one or more of the Class A Members and that such Class A Member has a more likely than not basis for such Class A Member's alternative proposed treatment for such item.

(b) The decisions covered by this Section 6.4 shall be referred to as the "**Major Decisions**").

**Section 6.5 Intentionally Omitted.**

**Section 6.6 Intentionally Omitted.**

**Section 6.7 Delegation of Authority to the Managing Member.** A majority-in-interest (based on Percentage Interest) of the Class A Members may from time to time delegate to the Managing Member any of the powers and authority reserved to the Members in Section 6.4.

**Section 6.8 Outside Activities.** Except as otherwise provided in Section 7.9, each Member and any Person who is an Affiliate of a Member may engage or hold interests in other business ventures of every kind and description for the Member's or the Affiliate's own account, whether or not such business ventures are in direct or indirect competition with the business of the Company and whether or not the Company has any interest therein. Neither the Company nor any of the Members shall have any rights by virtue of this Agreement in such independent business ventures or to the income or profits derived therefrom.

**Section 6.9 Limitations on Powers of Members.** Except as expressly authorized by this Agreement and subject to the terms of the Certificate, no Member shall, directly or indirectly, (i) resign, retire or withdraw from the Company,

(ii) dissolve, terminate or liquidate the Company, (iii) petition a court for the dissolution, termination or liquidation of the Company, or (iv) cause any property of the Company to be subject to the authority of any court, trustee or receiver (including suits for partition and bankruptcy, insolvency and similar proceedings).

## ARTICLE VII

### Rights, Powers, and Duties of the Managing Member

**Section 7.1 Management and Control of Business; Authority of the Managing Member.**

(a) Subject to the provisions of this Agreement, the business and affairs of the Company shall be managed under the direction of the Managing Member, who may exercise all powers of the Company and perform or authorize the performance of all lawful acts which are not by the Act or this Agreement directed or required to be exercised or performed by the Members. The Managing Member shall also be responsible for the implementation of Major Decisions approved as provided in Section 6.4. All acts of the Managing Member within the scope of the Managing Member's authority shall bind the Company. At any time when more than two Persons are serving as the Managing Member, the Managing Member shall act by the vote of a majority (in number) of them.

(b) In furtherance of and not in limitation of the power and authority of the Managing Member, the Managing Member shall have the power and authority to appoint officers to manage the business and affairs of the Company. The officers of the Company are set forth on Schedule 4 hereof, as amended from time to time by the Managing Member. The duties of the officers of the Company shall be as follows:

(i) President. The President shall be the chief executive officer of the Company and, subject to the provisions of this Agreement, shall be responsible for the general management of the business and affairs of the Company, may take any and all action on behalf of the Company and shall have full power and authority to execute and deliver any and all documents on behalf of the Company.

(ii) Vice President(s). The Vice President (if any) or, if there shall be more than one, the Vice Presidents, in order of their seniority or in any other order determined by the President, shall perform, in the absence or disability of the President, the duties and exercise the powers of the President, and, subject to the provisions of this Agreement, shall have such other powers and duties as the President assigns to him or them.

**Section 7.2 Selection of the Managing Member; Number; Tenure.** The Managing Member of the Company shall be The Manager; provided, however, that at any time, and at the sole discretion of The Manager, and without the consent of the Class A Members, any entity that is Controlled by Manager Parent (a **"MANAGER Entity"**) may be appointed as the Managing Member provided that, at the time of such appointment, Manager Parent shall either, together or individually, Control such MANAGER Entity. The Managing Member shall hold office until its dissolution, incapacity, resignation, or removal (in accordance with the provisions of this Agreement). For the avoidance of doubt, neither The Manager nor any such MANAGER Entity shall become a Class A Member solely as a result of it being appointed as the Managing Member, but shall be a Class A Member with respect to any Class A Membership Interest that it has acquired or thereafter acquires.

**Section 7.3 Vacancies.** A vacancy in the position of the Managing Member shall be filled by a vote of a majority-in-interest (based on Percentage Interest) of the Members.

**Section 7.4 Removal and Resignation of the Managing Member.** The Managing Member may be removed only for Cause by the majority-in-interest (based on Percentage Interest) of the Class A Members. For purposes of this Agreement, "Cause" shall include:

(a) the Managing Member's failure to account for or deposit funds belonging to the Company in a Bank Account, or the Managing Member's commission of any material act of fraud (unless due to the act of an employee of the Managing Member, provided that the Managing Member reimburses the Company for any losses suffered by the Company), or material willful misconduct which is not cured within ten (10) Business Days following written notice;

(b) the Managing Member's knowing willful and gross neglect of its duties hereunder which materially adversely affects the operation of the Properties, provided that the Managing Member must first be given notice by a majority-in-interest of the Class A Members of such alleged knowing, willful and gross negligence and a period of sixty (60) days in which to cure said alleged negligence. If it cannot reasonably be cured within such sixty (60) day period, such period shall be extended for such time as is reasonably necessary to cure such default, provided the Managing Member commences such cure within such sixty (60) day period and diligently prosecutes such cure to completion; or

(c) the bankruptcy or insolvency of the Managing Member or the Managing Member's conviction of a felony.

The Managing Member may resign at any time by giving written notice to the Class A Members. Unless otherwise specified in such written notice, a resignation shall take effect upon its delivery to the Class A Members. A resignation need not be accepted in order for it to be effective.

In the event that the Managing Member is removed or resigns, its interest in the Company shall be converted to that of a Class A Member. From and after the effective date of such removal or resignation, a majority-in-interest (based on Percentage Interest) of the Members shall control and manage the Company and shall have the power to appoint a new Managing Member or a committee of Members to manage the Company in place of the resigning or terminated Managing Member.

**Section 7.5 Limitations on the Managing Member's Authority.** The Managing Member shall not take any action, expend any sum, make any decision or incur any obligation with respect to any Major Decision, unless the Major Decision is approved by the Class A Members in the manner required by Section 6.4.

**Section 7.6 The Managing Member's Compensation.** Except pursuant to the Management Agreement, which has been entered into with an Affiliate of the Managing Member, the Managing Member shall not be compensated, as such, for its services as Managing Member. However, the Managing Member shall be reimbursed by the Company for all reasonable out-of-pocket expenses paid or incurred by the Managing Member in the performance of the Managing Member's duties under this Agreement.

**Section 7.7 Signing of Documents.** Subject to Section 6.4, the Managing Member is authorized, in the name and on behalf of the Company, to sign and deliver all contracts, agreements, leases, notes, mortgages and other documents and instruments which are necessary, appropriate or convenient for the conduct of the Company's day-to-day business and the furtherance of its purposes or which are necessary, appropriate or convenient to carry out Major Decisions approved by the Members pursuant to Section 6.4.

**Section 7.8 Dealing with Related Persons.** Subject to Section 6.4, the Managing Member, on behalf of the Company, may employ or cause any Subsidiary to employ a Member or an Affiliate of a Member to render or perform a service; may contract to buy property from, or sell property to, any such Member or Affiliate; or may otherwise deal with any such Member or Affiliate; provided that any such transaction shall be fully disclosed to all Members, shall be on terms that are fair and equitable to the Company or any Subsidiary, as applicable, and no less favorable to the Company or any Subsidiary, as applicable, than the terms, if any, available from unrelated Persons. The Members acknowledge that an Affiliate of the Managing Member is a party to the Management Agreement and the terms thereof are approved in all respects.

**Section 7.9 Outside Activities.** The Managing Member shall devote such time and attention to the business and affairs of the Company as may be reasonably necessary for the proper performance of its duties. The Managing Member, and any Person who is an Affiliate of the Managing Member, may engage in or hold interests in other business ventures of every kind and description for its own account, whether or not such business ventures are in direct or indirect competition with the business of the Company, and whether or not the Company also has an interest therein. Neither the Company nor any of the Members shall have any rights by virtue of this Agreement in such permitted business ventures or to the income or profits derived therefrom.

**Section 7.10 Indemnification of the Managing Member.** Subject to the terms of the Certificate, the Company (but not any Member) shall, to the fullest extent permitted by the laws of the State of Delaware, indemnify, defend and hold the Managing Member harmless from and against any and all liability for any act performed by such Managing Member within the scope of the authority conferred on it by this Agreement, except for acts of fraud or gross, willful or intentional misconduct, breach of fiduciary duty of the Managing Member or willful misconduct which are determined by the final unappealable order of a court of competent jurisdiction.

**Section 7.11 Liability of the Managing Member to Members.** The Managing Member shall not be liable, responsible or accountable in damages or otherwise to the Company or any Member for any loss suffered by the Company which arises out of any action or inaction of the Managing Member if the Managing Member acted in good faith and in a manner the Managing Member reasonably believed to be in, or not opposed to, the best interests of the Company and such course of conduct did not constitute actual material fraud, material willful misconduct. gross negligence or a breach of fiduciary duty on the part of the Managing Member.

**Section 7.12 The Managing Member's Standard of Care.** The Managing Member's duty of care in the discharge of the Managing Member's duties to the Company and the Members is limited to refraining from engaging in grossly negligent or reckless conduct, intentional misconduct, or conduct that involves a breach of fiduciary duty. In discharging its duties, the Managing Member shall be fully protected in relying in good faith upon the records maintained by the Company in the ordinary course of its business and upon such information, opinions, reports or statements by any of the Members or agents of the Company, or by any other Persons, whom the Managing Member reasonably believes have been selected with reasonable care by or on behalf of the Company and as to matters the Managing Member reasonably believes are within such agent's or other Person's professional or expert competence, including information, opinions, reports or statements as to the value and amount of the assets, liabilities, profits or losses of the Company or any other facts pertinent to the existence and amount of assets from which distributions to Members might properly be paid.

**Section 7.13 Right to Rely on Authority of the Managing Member.** No Person dealing with the Managing Member shall be required to determine the Managing Member's authority to make any undertaking on behalf of the Company, or to determine any fact or circumstance bearing upon the existence of the Managing Member's authority. Every contract, agreement, lease, promissory note, deed, Mortgage or other instrument or document (collectively, **"Documents"**) executed by the Managing Member, shall be conclusive evidence in favor of every Person relying thereon or claiming thereunder that:

(a) at the time of the execution or delivery of the Document, the Company was in existence and this Agreement was in full force and effect;

(b) the Document was duly approved by the Managing Member or the Members in accordance with this Agreement and is binding upon the Company; and

(c) the Managing Member was duly authorized and empowered to execute and deliver the Document for and on behalf of the Company.

## ARITCLE VIII

### Books of Account and Reports; Access to Records

**Section 8.1 Books and Records.** The Managing Member shall keep, or cause to be kept, at the principal place of business of the Company (or at such other place of business or office as the Managing Member may designate) true and correct books of account, in which shall be entered fully and accurately each and every transaction of the Company. Each Member or its, his or her designated agent shall have access at the Company's office to the Company's books of account and all other information concerning the Company required by the Act to be made available to Members at reasonable times on Business Days, and may make copies thereof. A Member must give the Company written notice of its, his or her desire to exercise rights under the preceding sentence at least ten (10) Business Days in advance. The Company's books shall be kept on a method of accounting in accordance with accepted federal income tax accounting principles, consistently applied, selected by the Managing Member and for a fiscal period which is the calendar year. Any Member shall have the right to a private audit of the books and records of the Company, provided such audit is made at the office of the Company at which such books and records are located and at the expense of the Member desiring it and is made at reasonable times on Business Days, after written notice given to the Company at least ten (10) Business Days in advance.

**Section 8.2 Reports to Members.** The Managing Member shall cause the Company to prepare and deliver to each Member the following financial reports with respect to the Company and any Subsidiary: (i) within thirty (30) days after the end of each calendar month, a cash flow statement, a statement of collections and expenses, a rent roll and a statement of accounts receivable and accounts payable, (ii) concurrently with the delivery to the lender at the Initial Refinancing (the **"Lender"**) and any future holder of a mortgage encumbering the Properties, a copy of all financial statements and other reports delivered by the Company or any Subsidiary to the Lender or such future holder excluding financial information with respect to the Managing Member, its affiliates or principals, and (iii) within one hundred twenty (120) days after the end of each Fiscal Year, compiled financial statements (prepared on an income tax basis) certified by an independent public accountant, including a balance sheet, a statement of income and expense and a statement of source and application of funds, and the information necessary to enable the Member to complete his/her federal and state income Tax Returns for such Fiscal Year.

**Section 8.3 Banking.** All funds of the Company shall be deposited in its name in such commercial bank or invested in such federally-insured savings and loan account or accounts, in such U.S. Treasury obligations, or in such bank certificates of deposit, as the Managing Member may determine (the **"Bank Accounts"**). All withdrawals from any such Bank Account shall be made upon a check or order signed by the Managing Member or by any other individual(s) designated by the Managing Member from time to time; but the Managing Member may restrict the amounts that can be withdrawn by any such individual. All such withdrawn funds shall only be used for Company purposes as provided in this Agreement and in accordance with the terms hereof. No other funds shall be deposited into the Company Bank Accounts or commingled with Company investments.

**Section 8.4 Accountants.** Subject to Section 6.4, the Managing Member shall cause the Company to retain a firm of certified public accountants to prepare and file the Company's federal and state income Tax Returns and to provide other outside accounting services from time to time required by the Company. Subject to Section 6.4, the Managing Member may from time to time retain a different firm of certified public accountants to be the accountants for the Company.

## ARTICLE IX

### Transfers of Membership Interests and Economic Rights

**Section 9.1 Member's or Assignee's Right to Transfer.** Except as otherwise provided in this Section 9.1, a Member may not Transfer all or any part of the Member's Membership Interest and an Assignee may not Transfer all or any part of the Assignee's Economic Rights unless the Managing Member's prior written consent is obtained for each such Transfer. The Managing Member may grant or withhold its approval of a Transfer in its sole and absolute discretion. Notwithstanding the foregoing, a Member may Transfer the Member's Membership Interest (or an interest in such Member) and an Assignee may Transfer the Assignee's Economic Rights (or an interest in such Assignee) to another Member or a Permitted Transferee without the approval of the Managing Member, but only if the conditions in Section 9.2 are satisfied. An owner of an interest in the Managing Member (or of an interest in an entity which owns an interest in the Managing Member) may transfer such interest, subject to the conditions of Section 9.2.

**Section 9.2 Conditions of Transfer.** No Membership Interest, Economic Rights, or interest in a Member or Assignee (or interest in a Person which directly or indirectly owns an interest in a Member or Assignee) shall be Transferred:

(a) if the Transfer is prohibited by, or would cause a default under, any Mortgage encumbering the Properties or under any loan agreement to which the Company or any Subsidiary is a party;

(b) in the case of a Transfer of a direct interest in the Company to a Person who is not a Member or a Permitted Transferee, unless the Company receives an opinion of counsel satisfactory to the Members that such Transfer is exempt from the registration requirements of any applicable federal or state securities laws;

(c) in the case of a Transfer of a direct interest in the Company to a Person who is not a Member, unless the Company receives from the Person to whom the Membership Interest or the Economic Rights are Transferred, such Person's taxpayer identification number and any other documents or information reasonably requested by the Members; or

(d) if as a result of such Transfer, Manager Parent shall either, together or individually, cease to maintain Control of the Managing Member (which includes any MANAGER Entity that becomes the Managing Member).

**Section 9.3 Transfer as Security Prohibited.** Neither a Member nor any of its Assignees shall Transfer all or any part of its, his or her Membership Interest or any of its, his or her Assignee's Economic Rights as security for a debt or other obligation, except as specifically provided herein. Notwithstanding the foregoing, the Managing Member (and any direct or indirect members of the Managing Member) shall have the right to pledge its (or their) direct or indirect Membership Interest to any lender in connection with any Financing relating to the Properties or the Company's interest in any Subsidiary, including, without limitation, any pledge given to secure a guaranty of all or any portion of the borrower's obligations with respect to such financing.

**Section 9.4 Non-Complying Transfers Void.** Any attempted Transfer of all or any part of a Member's Membership Interest or an Assignee's Economic Rights that does not comply with the provisions of Section 9.1 and Section 9.2 shall be null and void and of no legal effect.

## ARTICLE X

### Admission of Assignees

**Section 10.1 Rights of Assignees.** The Assignee of a Membership Interest has no Management Rights and, unless the Assignee is a Permitted Transferee, no right to become a Member. The Assignee's only rights are the Economic Rights allocable to the Transferred Membership Interest.

**Section 10.2 Admission of Assignee as a Member.** An Assignee shall be admitted as a Member with all rights of the Member who initially Transferred the Membership Interest to the Assignee, but only if (i) the Member who initially Transferred the Membership Interest so provides in the instrument of Transfer, (ii) the Assignee agrees in writing to be bound by the provisions of this Agreement, and (iii) unless Section 10.3 applies, the Managing Member, with the Consent of the Class A Members, consents in writing to the admission of the Assignee as a Member. Each Member shall have the right to give or withhold its, his or her consent to the admission of the Assignee as a Member in the Member's sole and absolute discretion. An Assignee who is admitted as a Member shall have all the rights and powers and be subject to all the restrictions and liabilities of the Member who originally Transferred the Membership Interest. The admission of the Assignee as a Member, without more, shall not release the Member who originally Transferred the Membership Interest from any liability to the Company that exists before such admission.

**Section 10.3 Admission of Certain Permitted Transferees.** A Permitted Transferee to whom a Membership Interest is Transferred shall be admitted as a Member, without the necessity of obtaining the written consent of the Managing

Member or the other Members, only if (i) the Transfer complied with the conditions in Section 9.2, and (ii) the conditions described in clauses (i) and (ii) of Section 10.2 are satisfied.

## ARTICLE XI

### Dissolution of Company

**Section 11.1 Events Causing Dissolution.** Subject to Section 11.7, the Company shall be dissolved and its affairs wound up upon the sale, exchange, or other disposition (including condemnation) by the Company of all or substantially all of its assets; provided, however, that if, in connection with such sale or other disposition, the Company receives a promissory note or notes evidencing all or a part of the purchase price of such property, the Company shall not be dissolved until such promissory note(s) is (are) satisfied, sold or otherwise disposed of. The Company shall not be dissolved by the resignation, withdrawal, bankruptcy or dissolution of it a member.

**Section 11.2 Winding Up.** If the Company is dissolved, then the Managing Member shall proceed with dispatch and without any unnecessary delay to sell or otherwise liquidate all property of the Company. Any act or event (including the passage of time) causing a dissolution of the Company shall in no way affect the validity of, or shorten the term of, any lease, deed of trust, mortgage, contract or other obligation entered into by or on behalf of the Company. The full rights, powers and authorities of the Managing Member shall continue so long as appropriate and necessary to complete the process of winding up the business and affairs of the Company.

**Section 11.3 Application of Assets in Winding Up.** In winding up the Company, after paying or making provision for payment of all of its liabilities, the remaining net proceeds and liquid assets shall be distributed among the Members in the manner specified in Section 5.1(a).

**Section 11.4 Negative Capital Accounts.** If, after the allocation of the Profit or Loss pursuant to Article V from a sale of any Subsidiary or of the Properties and the distribution of the remaining net proceeds and liquid assets among the Members and upon final liquidation of the Company, the Capital Account of any Member is negative, the Member shall not be obligated to restore the negative balance in its Capital Account.

**Section 11.5 Termination.** The Company shall terminate, except for the purpose of suits, other proceedings, and appropriate action as provided in the Act, when all of its property shall have been disposed of and the net proceeds and liquid assets, after satisfaction of liabilities to Company creditors, shall have been distributed among the Members. As soon as practicable after the termination of the Company, the Managing Member shall cause a certificate of cancellation to be filed with the Secretary of State. The Managing Member shall have authority to distribute any Company property discovered after dissolution, convey real estate, and take such other action as may be necessary on behalf of and in the name of the Company

**Section 11.6 Division of the Company.** At any time following the second anniversary of the Effective Date (provided that at such time there is no outstanding Refinancing Shortfall or outstanding Refinancing Shortfall Return), the Managing Member may, in its sole and absolute discretion, cause the Company to distribute to the Members, in one or more transactions, pro rata in accordance with their then Membership Interests in the Company, 100% of the membership interests in any or all of the Subsidiary Holding Companies (a **"Spin-Off"**). If a Spin-Off occurs, the limited liability company agreement of each Subsidiary Holding Company shall be amended to have the same terms as this Agreement, with such changes as are necessary to account for the fact that each Subsidiary Holding Company owns only one of the Properties. The Capital Account, Aggregate Capital Contribution amount, Unpaid Preferred Return (if any), Unreturned Capital Contributions (if any), Refinancing Shortfall (if any) Refinancing Shortfall Return (if any), Member Loan (if any) of each Member at the time of the Spin-Off, and any other similar item that is appropriately allocated among the Subsidiary Holding Companies, shall be allocated among the membership interests in each of the Subsidiary Holding Companies received by such Member, in the proportion that (i) the aggregate price the Company paid under the Sales Contract for the Property held by each Subsidiary Holding Company, bears to (ii) the aggregate price the Company paid for all the Properties it acquired under the Sales Contract. For example, if the aggregate price the Company paid for a particular property under the Sales Contract represents 25% of the aggregate price the Company paid for all the properties it acquired under the Sales Contract, then 25% of each Member's Capital Account, Aggregate Capital Contribution amount, Unpaid Preferred Return (if any), Unreturned Capital Contributions (if any), Refinancing Shortfall (if any) Refinancing Shortfall Return (if any), Member Loan (if any) (and any other similar item that is appropriately allocated among the Subsidiary Holding Companies) at the time of the Spin-Off shall be allocated to such Member's membership interest in the Subsidiary Holding Company that owns such property. The Percentage Interest of each Member in each Subsidiary Holding Company immediately following the Spin-Off shall be the same as each Member's Percentage Interest in the Company immediately before the Spin-Off.

## ARTICLE XII

### Amendments

**Section 12.1 Procedure.** This Agreement may only be amended by the written consent of the Managing Member and the holders of sixty five percent (65%) or more of the Percentage Interests of all the Class A Members, provided, however, that (i) no amendment that would treat any Class A Member differently (in an adverse manner) than all the other Class A Members may be made without the written consent of such Class A Member, and (ii) the Managing Member may amend this Agreement without the consent of any of the Class A Members if such amendment is ministerial in nature.

## ARTICLE XIII

### Miscellaneous Provisions

**Section 13.1 Notices.** All notices, demands, consents, approvals or other communications (collectively, a **"Notice"**) provided for in this Agreement or required by law shall be in writing and shall be delivered personally by overnight delivery service (e.g., Federal Express or DHL) or private courier service or sent by certified or registered mail, return receipt requested, first class postage prepaid, and shall be addressed (i) if to the Managing Member, at the address for Notices set forth opposite or beneath such Member's signature at the foot of this Agreement, with a further copy (not constituting notice) to:

Manage Great Realty LLC
75 Clinton Street, 13R
Brooklyn, NY 11201

and (ii) if to a Class A Member, at the address for Notices set forth opposite or beneath such Member's signature at the foot of this Agreement, with a further copy (not constituting notice) to:

Manage Great Realty LLC
75 Clinton Street, 13R
Brooklyn, NY 11201
Debby Day
13 Adams Street, Apt. 7C
Brooklyn, NY 11201

and (iii) if to a Person who becomes a Member after the Effective Date, at the address for Notices furnished by such Person to the Company at the time of his admission. The Members may change their address for Notices by providing notice to the Company and all Members pursuant to the provisions of this Section. Notices shall be deemed given on the date of receipt or first refusal of a Notice delivered by hand. Notices given by counsel for any Member shall be deemed valid Notices if addressed and sent in accordance with the provisions of this Section.

**Section 13.2 Integration.** This Agreement and the Management Agreement set forth all (and are intended by all parties hereto to be an integration of all) of the promises, agreements, conditions, understandings, warranties and representations among the parties hereto with respect to the Company, the Company business and the property of the Company, and there are no promises, agreements, conditions, understandings, warranties, or representations, oral or written, express or implied, among them other than as set forth herein.

**Section 13.3 Governing Law.** It is the intention of the parties that all questions with respect to the construction of this Agreement and the rights and liabilities of the parties hereto shall be determined in accordance with the laws of the State of Delaware.

**Section 13.4 Binding Effect.** This Agreement shall be binding upon, and inure to the benefit of, the parties hereto and their respective spouses, heirs, executors, administrators, personal and legal representatives, successors and assigns.

**Section 13.5 Waiver of Trial by Jury.** It is mutually agreed by the parties hereto that the respective parties hereto shall, and they hereby do, waive trial by jury in any action, proceeding or counterclaim brought by either of the parties hereto against the other on any matters whatsoever arising out of or in any way connected with this Agreement.

**Section 13.6 Counterparts.** This Agreement may be executed in any number of counterparts, each of which will for all purposes be deemed an original instrument, and all such counterparts together will constitute but one and the same Agreement.

**Section 13.7 Further Assurances.** Each of the Members agrees to execute, acknowledge, deliver, file, record and publish such further certificates, instruments, agreements and other documents and to take all such further action as may be required by law or deemed by the Managing Member to he necessary or useful in furtherance of the Company's purposes and the objectives and intentions underlying this Agreement and not inconsistent with the terms hereof.

**Section 13.8 Representations and Warranties/Covenants.** In order to induce the other Members to enter into this Agreement, Manager Parent represents and warrant that, as of the date hereof, it Controls the Managing Member. Manager Parent hereby covenants that it will not permit an interest in a Person which directly or indirectly owns an interest in the Managing Member to be Transferred in contravention of the provisions of <u>Section 9.2</u>.

IN WITNESS WHEREOF, the undersigned parties have signed this Agreement as of the day and year first above written.

<u>Darwin Lee</u>

Name: Darwin Lee

Title: Manager of Manage Great Realty LLC

<u>Debby Day</u>

Name: Debby Day

# SCHEDULE 1

## Names, Addresses, and Percentage Interests of Members

| Name and Address | Percentage Interest |
|---|---|
| Managing Member: | |
| Manage Great Realty LLC<br>75 Clinton Street, 13R<br>Brooklyn, NY 11201 | 4% |
| Class A Members: | |
| Debby Day<br>13 Adams Street, Apt. 7C<br>Brooklyn, NY 11201 | 96% |

# SCHEDULE 2

## Initial Capital Amount of Each Member

| Member | Initial Capital Amount |
|---|---|
| Manage Great Realty LLC | $120,000 |
| Debby Day | $3,150,000 |

# SCHEDULE 3

## Capital Accounts of Members as of Effective Time

| Member | Initial Capital Account |
|---|---|

# SCHEDULE 4

## Executive Officers of the Company

## 11 DUFFIELD MORTGAGE NOTE

| | |
|---|---|
| Date of Note: | January 1, Year 14 |
| Principal Amount: | $12,175,000.00 |
| Maturity Date: | January 1, Year 44 |

**Interest Rate:** An interest rate equal at all times to five and three-tenths (5.3%) percent per annum. Interest shall be computed on a 360-day basis (i.e., interest for each day during which the Principal Amount, or any part thereof, is outstanding shall be computed at Interest Rate divided by 360).

**Business Day:** Business Day means a day (other than Saturday, Sunday, federal holiday, or a day on which commercial banks in New York are required or permitted to close) on which the Bank is open and conducting its customary banking transactions.

**State:** Shall mean the State of New York.

**FOR VALUE RECEIVED,** 11 DUFFIELD LLC, a Delaware limited liability company (the **"Borrower"),** having an address as indicated below, **HEREBY PROMISES TO PAY** to the order of NATIONAL BANK, N.A., a national banking association, (hereinafter, together with its successors and assigns, referred to as the **"Lender")** in immediately available federal funds, the Principal Amount. The Borrower shall pay thirty (30) consecutive annual installments comprised of principal as specified in the amortization schedule attached hereto as Schedule A (based upon a thirty (30) year amortization schedule), together with accrued interest on the Principal Amount. The said payments shall be due on the first (1st) day of each year commencing on January 1, Year 15. Notwithstanding anything to the contrary herein, payment dates shall be subject to adjustment in accordance with the Following Business Day Convention which means that any payment due date that would otherwise fall on a day that is not a Business Day shall be extended to the first following day that is a Business Day. Such extension of time will not be included in the calculation of interest due.

Borrower hereby authorizes Lender to charge checking account number 110-220-335 at Local Bank, N.A. (or such other account maintained by Borrower at Parkside Bank, N.A. as Borrower shall designate by written notice to Lender) (the **"Deposit Account")** to satisfy the scheduled payments of principal and/or interest due and payable to Lender hereunder on the first (1st) day of each month (each, a **"Charge Date")** and Lender is hereby authorized to charge the Deposit Account on each Charge Date or, if any Charge Date shall fall on a Saturday, Sunday or legal holiday, then the Lender reserves the right to charge the Deposit Account on either on the first (1st) Business Day immediately preceding or on the first (1st) Business Day immediately following any such Charge Date until the Note shall be paid in full.

Borrower agrees to maintain sufficient funds in the Deposit Account to satisfy the payment due Lender under the Note on each Charge Date during the term of this Note. If sufficient funds are not available in the Deposit Account on any

Charge Date to pay the amounts then due and payable under this Note, Lender, in its sole discretion, is authorized to: (a) charge the Deposit Account for such lesser amount as shall then be available; and/or (b) charge the Deposit Account on such later date or dates that funds shall be available in the Deposit Account to satisfy the payment then due (or balance of such payment then due). Notwithstanding the foregoing, Borrower shall only be entitled to receive credit in respect of any payments of principal and interest due under the Note for funds actually received by Lender as a result of any such charges to the Deposit Account. Borrower shall be liable to Lender for any late fees or interest at the Default Rate on any payments not made on a timely basis by Borrower because of insufficient funds in the Deposit Account on any Charge Date. In the event the Deposit Account continues to contain insufficient funds to fully satisfy the payments due Lender under the Note, Borrower shall be responsible for making all such payments from another source and in no event shall the obligations of Borrower under the Note be affected or diminished as a result of any shortages in the Deposit Account, it being understood and agreed that Borrower shall at all times remain liable for payment in full of all indebtedness under the Note.

Lender may, at Lender's sole discretion, discontinue charging the Deposit Account at any time on not less than ten (10) days' written notice to the Borrower, in which event, Borrower shall thereafter be responsible for making all payments hereunder to Lender at the address set forth in Lender's notice.

Borrower shall pay a late payment charge of six cents ($.06) for each dollar ($1.00) of each payment that is made more than fifteen (15) days after the due date thereof, which charge shall be due and payable with each such late payment.

If any present or future law, governmental rule, regulation, policy, guideline, directive or similar requirement (whether or not having the force of law) imposes, modifies, or deems applicable any capital adequacy, capital maintenance or similar requirement which affects the manner in which Lender allocates capital resources to its commitments (including any commitments hereunder), and as a result thereof, in the opinion of Lender, the rate of return on Lender's capital with regard to the loan evidenced by this Note is reduced to a level below that which Lender could have achieved but for such circumstances, then in such case and upon notice from Lender to Borrower, from time to time, Borrower shall pay Lender such additional amount or amounts as shall compensate Lender for such reduction in Lender's rate of return. Such notice shall contain the statement of Lender with regard to any such amount or amounts which shall, in the absence of manifest error, be binding upon Borrower. In determining such amount, Lender may use any reasonable method of averaging and attribution that it deems applicable. For the avoidance of doubt, the foregoing provisions shall apply to all requests, rules, guidelines or directives concerning capital adequacy issued in connection with the Dodd-Frank Wall Street Reform and Consumer Protection Act and all requests, rules, regulations, guidelines or directives concerning capital adequacy promulgated by the Bank for International Settlements, the Basel Committee on Banking Regulations and Supervisory Practices (or any successor or similar authority) or the United States financial regulatory authorities, regardless of the date adopted, issued, promulgated or implemented

This Note is secured by, and the parties hereto are entitled to the benefits and security of, that certain Mortgage and Security Agreement (the **"Mortgage")**, dated the date hereof, from Borrower, as mortgagor, to Lender, as mortgagee, encumbering, among other things, certain real property and improvements described in the Mortgage all of the covenants, conditions and agreements of the Mortgage being made a part of this Note by this reference.

Except as may be otherwise provided in the Mortgage, all monthly payments received by Lender hereunder shall be applied first, to the payment of accrued interest on the Principal Amount, second, to the reduction of the Principal Amount of this Note, and finally, the balance, if any, to the payment of any fees, costs, expenses or charges then payable by Borrower to Lender hereunder, under the Mortgage or under any other document executed and delivered by Borrower in connection with the loan evidenced by this Note.

Borrower agrees that if it fails to timely make any payment due under this Note or upon the happening of any **"Event of Default"** under the Mortgage, (as defined in the Mortgage), the outstanding Principal Amount, together with accrued interest and all other expenses, including, reasonable attorneys' fees, shall immediately become due and payable at the option of the holder of this Note, notwithstanding the Maturity Date. For purposes hereof, attorneys' fees shall include, without limitation, fees and disbursements for legal services incurred by the holder hereof in collecting or enforcing payment hereof whether or not suit is brought, and if suit is brought, then through all appellate actions. From and after any **"Event of Default"** under the Mortgage, the interest rate of this Note shall be the **"Default Rate"** (as defined in the Mortgage).

In no event shall the total of all charges payable under this Note, the Mortgage and any other documents executed and delivered in connection herewith and therewith that are or could be held to be in the nature of interest exceed the maximum rate permitted to be charged by applicable law. Should Lender receive any payment that is or would be in excess of that permitted to be charged under any such applicable law, such payment shall have been, and shall be deemed to have been, made in error and shall thereupon be applied to reduce the principal balance outstanding on this Note.

Borrower waives demand, presentment for payment, notice of dishonor, protest and notice of protest of this Note.

Any notice, demand or request relating to any matter set forth in this Note shall be given in the manner provided for in the Mortgage. Time is of the essence as to all dates set forth herein.

This Note may not be waived, changed, modified, terminated or discharged orally, but only by an agreement in writing signed by the party against whom enforcement of any such waiver, change, modification, termination or discharge is sought.

This Note may be prepaid, in whole or in part without a prepayment premium, so long as (i) Lender is given not less than thirty (30) days' notice of such prepayment, (ii) each prepayment is accompanied by the payment of accrued and unpaid interest on the principal amount prepaid together with all late charges and other losses, costs and expenses attributable to such prepayment, (iii) each prepayment is made on a Charge Date, and (iv) each prepayment is made in immediately available federal funds. All partial prepayments shall be applied to the installments of principal due hereunder in the inverse order of their maturity.

Borrower shall indemnify Lender, and hold Lender harmless from any loss, damages, liability, or expense which Lender may sustain or incur as a consequence of the making of a prepayment, whether by voluntary prepayment, acceleration or otherwise, on a day which is not the last day of a LIBOR Interest Period with respect thereto. With respect to such prepayment, such indemnification shall equal the excess, if any, of (i) the amount of interest which would have accrued on the amount so prepaid for the period from the date of such prepayment at the applicable rate of interest provided for herein over (ii) the amount of interest (as reasonably determined by Lender) which would have accrued to Lender on such amount by placing such amount on deposit for a comparable period with leading banks in the London interbank Eurodollar market. This covenant shall survive the termination of this Note, and the payment of the entire outstanding Principal Amount, all other unpaid indebtedness secured by the Mortgage.

BORROWER, AND BY ITS ACCEPTANCE HEREOF, LENDER, EACH HEREBY AGREES NOT TO ELECT A TRIAL BY JURY OF ANY ISSUE TRIABLE OF RIGHT BY JURY, AND WAIVE ANY RIGHT TO TRIAL BY JURY FULLY TO THE EXTENT THAT ANY SUCH RIGHT SHALL NOW OR HEREAFTER EXIST WITH REGARD TO THIS NOTE, OR ANY CLAIM, COUNTERCLAI M OR OTHER ACTION ARISING IN CONNECTION THEREWITH. THIS WAIVER OF RIGHT TO TRIAL BY JURY IS GIVEN KNOWINGLY AND VOLUNTARI LY BY BORROWER AND LENDER, AND IS INTENDED TO ENCOMPASS INDIVIDUALLY EACH INSTANCE AND EACH ISSUE AS TO WHICH THE RIGHT TO A TRIAL BY JURY WOULD OTHERWISE ACCRUE. BORROWER AND LENDER ARE EACH HEREBY AUTHORIZED TO FILE A COPY OF THIS PARAGRAPH IN ANY PROCEEDING AS CONCLUSIVE EVIDENCE OF THIS WAIVER.

BORROWER HEREBY EXPRESSLY AND UNCONDITIONALLY WAIVES, IN CONNECTION WITH ANY SUIT, ACTION OR PROCEEDING BROUGHT BY OR ON BEHALF OF LENDER ON THIS NOTE, ANY AND EVERY RIGHT BORROWER MAY HAVE TO (I) INJUNCTIVE RELIEF, (II) INTERPOSE ANY COUNTERCLAI M THEREIN (OTHER THAN COMPULSORY COUNTERCLAIMS), AND (Ill) HAVE THE SAME CONSOLIDATED WITH ANY OTHER OR SEPARATE SUIT, ACTION OR PROCEEDING. NOTHING HEREIN CONTAINED SHALL PREVENT OR PROHIBIT BORROWER FROM INSTITUTING OR MAINTAINING A SEPARATE ACTION AGAINST LENDER WITH RESPECT TO ANY ASSERTED CLAIM.

This Note and the rights and obligations of the parties hereunder shall in all respects be governed by, and construed and enforced in accordance with, the laws of the State (without giving effect to the State's principles of conflicts of law). Borrower hereby irrevocably submits to the nonexclusive jurisdiction of any state or federal court in the State sitting in the Counties of over any suit, action or proceeding arising out of or relating to this Note, and Borrower hereby agrees and consents that, in addition to any methods of service of process provided for under applicable law, all service of process in any such suit, action or proceeding in any state or federal court in the State sitting in the County of Kings may be made by certified or registered mail, return receipt requested, directed to the Borrower at the address indicated below, and service so made shall be complete five (5) days after the same shall have been so mailed.

Borrower may hedge the floating interest expense of the Loan for the full term of the Loan by maintaining one or more interest rate hedging transactions with Lender (or with another financial institution satisfactory to Lender, as evidenced in writing) in an aggregate notional amount equal to 100% of the outstanding principal balance of the Loan originally scheduled to be outstanding over such term when the hedge is executed and providing for a fixed rate acceptable to Lender, with Borrower making fixed rate payments and receiving floating rate payments to offset changes in the variable interest expense of the Loan, all upon terms and subject to such conditions as shall be acceptable to Lender (or if such transaction is with another financial institution, all upon terms and subject to such conditions satisfactory to Lender, as evidenced in writing). The indebtedness evidenced by this Note shall include any "Additional Interest" (as defined in the Mortgage) due pursuant to any such interest rate hedging transactions. Any prepayment, acceleration, reduction, increase or any change in the terms of Lender will not alter the notional amount of any such interest rate swap transactions or otherwise affect the Borrower's obligations to continue to make payments under any such interest rate swap transactions, which will remain in force and effect notwithstanding any such prepayment, acceleration, reduction, increase or change, subject to the terms of such interest rate swap transactions.

**IN WITNESS WHEREOF,** the Borrower has executed and delivered this Note on the Date of Note.

| Address: | Borrower: |
|---|---|
| 75 Clinton Street, 13R<br>Brooklyn, NY 11201 | 11 DUFFIELD LLC |
| | By: <u>Darwin Lee</u><br>Name: Darwin Lee<br>Title: Manager of Manage Great Realty LLC, Manager of 11 Duffield LLC |

# Schedule A
## Loan Amortization Schedule (11 Duffield)

| Loan Information | |
|---|---|
| Loan amount | $121,75,000 |
| Annual interest rate | 5.30 % |
| Loan period in years | 30 |
| Number of payments per year | 1 |
| Start date of loan | 1-1-14 |
| Optional extra payments | $ - |

| Loan summary | |
|---|---|
| Scheduled payment | $8,19,290 |
| Scheduled number of payments | 30 |
| Actual number of payments | 30 |
| Total early payments | 0 |
| Total interest | $124,03,697 |

| Pmt. No. | Payment Date | Beginning Balance | Scheduled Payment | Extra Payment | Total Payment | Principal | Interest | Ending Balance | Cumulative Interest |
|---|---|---|---|---|---|---|---|---|---|
| 1 | 1/1/15 | $12,175,000 | $819,290 | $0 | $819,290 | $174,015 | $645,275 | $12,000,985 | $645,275 |
| 2 | 1/1/16 | $12,000,985 | $819,290 | | $819,290 | $183,238 | $636,052 | $11,817,747 | $1,281,327 |
| 3 | 1/1/17 | $11,817,747 | $819,290 | $0 | $819,290 | $192,949 | $626,341 | $11,624,798 | $1,907,668 |
| 4 | 1/1/18 | $11,624,798 | $819,290 | $0 | $819,290 | $203,176 | $616,114 | $11,421,622 | $2,523,782 |
| 5 | 1/1/19 | $11,421,622 | $819,290 | $0 | $819,290 | $213,944 | $605,346 | $11,207,679 | $3,129,128 |
| 6 | 1/1/20 | $11,207,679 | $819,290 | $0 | $819,290 | $225,283 | $594,007 | $10,982,396 | $3,723,135 |
| 7 | 1/1/21 | $10,982,396 | $819,290 | $0 | $819,290 | $237,223 | $582,067 | $10,745,173 | $4,305,202 |
| 8 | 1/1/22 | $10,745,173 | $819,290 | $0 | $819,290 | $249,796 | $569,494 | $10,495,377 | $4,874,696 |
| 9 | 1/1/23 | $10,495,377 | $819,290 | $0 | $819,290 | $263,035 | $556,255 | $10,232,342 | $5,430,951 |
| 10 | 1/1/24 | $10,232,342 | $819,290 | $0 | $819,290 | $276,976 | $542,314 | $9,955,366 | $5,973,265 |
| 11 | 1/1/25 | $9,955,366 | $819,290 | $0 | $819,290 | $291,656 | $527,634 | $9,663,711 | $6,500,900 |
| 12 | 1/1/26 | $9,663,711 | $819,290 | $0 | $819,290 | $307,113 | $512,177 | $9,356,597 | $7,013,076 |
| 13 | 1/1/27 | $9,356,597 | $819,290 | $0 | $819,290 | $323,390 | $495,900 | $9,033,207 | $7,508,976 |
| 14 | 1/1/28 | $9,033,207 | $819,290 | $0 | $819,290 | $340,530 | $478,760 | $8,692,677 | $7,987,736 |
| 15 | 1/1/29 | $8,692,677 | $819,290 | $0 | $819,290 | $358,578 | $460,712 | $8,334,099 | $8,448,448 |
| 16 | 1/1/30 | $8,334,099 | $819,290 | $0 | $819,290 | $377,583 | $441,707 | $7,956,516 | $8,890,155 |
| 17 | 1/1/31 | $7,956,516 | $819,290 | $0 | $819,290 | $397,595 | $421,695 | $7,558,922 | $9,311,851 |
| 18 | 1/1/32 | $7,558,922 | $819,290 | $0 | $819,290 | $418,667 | $400,623 | $7,140,255 | $9,712,473 |
| 19 | 1/1/33 | $7,140,255 | $819,290 | $0 | $819,290 | $440,856 | $378,434 | $6,699,399 | $10,090,907 |
| 20 | 1/1/34 | $6,699,399 | $819,290 | $0 | $819,290 | $464,222 | $355,068 | $6,235,177 | $10,445,975 |
| 21 | 1/1/35 | $6,235,177 | $819,290 | $0 | $819,290 | $488,826 | $330,464 | $5,746,351 | $10,776,439 |
| 22 | 1/1/36 | $5,746,351 | $819,290 | $0 | $819,290 | $514,733 | $304,557 | $5,231,618 | $11,080,996 |
| 23 | 1/1/37 | $5,231,618 | $819,290 | $0 | $819,290 | $542,014 | $277,276 | $4,689,604 | $11,358,272 |
| 24 | 1/1/38 | $4,689,604 | $819,290 | $0 | $819,290 | $570,741 | $248,549 | $4,118,863 | $11,606,821 |
| 25 | 1/1/39 | $4,118,863 | $819,290 | $0 | $819,290 | $600,990 | $218,300 | $3,517,873 | $11,825,120 |
| 26 | 1/1/40 | $3,517,873 | $819,290 | $0 | $819,290 | $632,843 | $186,447 | $2,885,030 | $12,011,568 |
| 27 | 1/1/41 | $2,885,030 | $819,290 | $0 | $819,290 | $666,383 | $152,907 | $2,218,647 | $12,164,474 |
| 28 | 1/1/42 | $2,218,647 | $819,290 | $0 | $819,290 | $701,702 | $117,588 | $1,516,945 | $12,282,063 |
| 29 | 1/1/43 | $1,516,945 | $819,290 | $0 | $819,290 | $738,892 | $80,398 | $778,053 | $12,362,461 |
| 30 | 1/1/44 | $778,053 | $819,290 | $0 | $778,053 | $736,816 | $41,237 | $0 | $12,403,697 |

## 11 DUFFIELD MORTGAGE AND SECURITY AGREEMENT

Dated: January 1, Year 14
the amount of $12,175,000.00

from

11 DUFFIELD LLC, Mortgagor
a Delaware limited liability company, having an office at:
75 Clinton Street, 13R
Brooklyn, NY 11201

to

NATIONAL BANK, N.A., Mortgagee
a national banking association, having an office at:
1 Broad Street
New York, New York, 10038

LOCATION OF PREMISES:

| | |
|---|---|
| **Street:** | **11 Duffield** |
| **Town of:** | **Brooklyn** |
| **County of:** | **Kings** |
| **State of:** | **New York** |
| **Section:** | **3742** |
| **Block:** | **97** |
| **Lot:** | **23** |

After recording, please return to:

National Bank
1 Broad Street
New York, New York 10038

**MORTGAGE AND SECURITY AGREEMENT** (the **"Mortgage"**), made as January 1, Year 14, given by 11 DUFFIELD LLC, a Delaware limited liability company, having an address at 75 Clinton Street, 13R, Brooklyn, New York 11201 (**"Morgagor"**), in favor of NATIONAL BANK, N.A., a national banking association, having an office at 1 Broad Street, New York, New York 10038 (**"Mortgagee"**).

### WITNESSETH

**WHEREAS,** Mortgagor is the owner.of, that certain parcel of real property known as 11 Duffield as more particularly described in Schedule A attached hereto and made a part hereof;

**WHEREAS,** concurrently herewith, Mortgagor is borrowing from Mortgagee the principal sum of $12,175,000.00 (the **"Mortgage Amount")** and in connection therewith, Mortgagor has executed and delivered to Mortgagee that certain Mortgage Loan Note, dated of even date herewith, made by Mortgagor, as borrower, in favor of Mortgagee, as lender, in the original principal amount of $12,175,000.00 (such Mortgage Loan Note, as the same may be hereafter amended, modified or extended, being hereinafter called the **"Note")** evidencing the indebtedness of Mortgagor to Mortgagee; and

**WHEREAS,** to secure the payment of the indebtedness under the Note in the Mortgage Amount, together with interest thereon at the interest rate or rates set forth in the Note, and together with any other sums that may become due and payable hereunder or under the Note, the Hedging Contracts (as hereinafter defined) or the other Loan Documents (as hereinafter defined), and to secure the performance by Mortgagor of its obligations hereunder, under the Note, the Hedging Contracts and the other Loan Documents, Mortgagor has agreed to execute and deliver to Mortgagee this Mortgage.

## Certain Definitions

As used in this Mortgage, unless the context otherwise specifies or requires, the following terms shall have the meanings herein specified, such definitions to be applicable equally to the singular and to the plural forms of such terms.

**"Additional Interest"** shall mean any and all amounts which may become due and payable and payable by Mortgagor under the terms and provisions of any Hedging Contract, including, without limitation, any and all breakage costs, liquidated damages or other amounts payable by Mortgagor pursuant to any Hedging Contract upon the occurrence of a default under such Hedging Contract (it being agreed, however, that any Hedging Contract is a separate legal obligation separate from the Loan).

**"Affiliate"** means with respect to any Person, (a) any Person which, directly or indirectly through one or more intermediaries controls, or is controlled by, or is under common control with such Person, or (b) any Person who is a director or officer (i) of such Person, (ii) of any subsidiary of such Person, or (iii) of any Person described in clause (a) above. For purposes of this definition, control of a Person means the power, direct or indirect, (x) to vote 5% or more of the Capital Stock having ordinary voting power for the election of directors (or comparable equivalent) of such Person, or (y) to direct or cause the direction of the management and policies of such Person whether by contract or otherwise. Control may be by ownership, contract, or otherwise.

**"Affiliate Counterparty"** means a Person who is an Affiliate of the Mortgagee at the time such Person entered into any Hedging Contract.

**"Agreements"** shall mean all agreements, contracts, certificates, instruments, franchises, permits, licenses, plans, specifications, warranties, guarantees, and other documents, now or hereafter entered into, and all rights therein and thereto, respecting or pertaining to the use, occupation, construction, management or operation of the Land and any part thereof and any Improvements or respecting any business or activity conducted at the Premises or any part thereof, or relating to any of the Chattels, and all right, title and interest of Mortgagor therein and thereunder, including, without limitation, the right, upon the happening of an Event of Default hereunder, to receive and collect any sums payable to Mortgagor thereunder.

**"Capital Stock"** means any and all shares, interests, participations or other equivalents (however designated) of capital stock of a corporation, any and all other ownership interests in a Person (other than a corporation) and any and all warrants or options to purchase any of the foregoing.

**"Chattels"** shall mean the Equipment, the Fixtures and the Personal Property.

**"Claim"** shall mean any action, claim, counterclaim, cross-claim, cause of action, suit, liability, demand, loss, expense, penalty, fine, judgment or other cost of any kind or nature whatsoever, including, without limitation, all fees, costs and expenses incurred in connection therewith of attorneys, consultants, contractors and experts.

**"CMLTD"** shall mean the current scheduled principal or capital lease payments required to be paid during the following four quarters.

**"Code"** shall mean the Uniform Commercial Code in effect in the State, as amended from time to time.

**"Commodity Exchange Act"** means the Commodity Exchange Act (7
U.S.C Section 1 et seq.) as amended from time to time and any successor statute.

**"Default Rate"** shall mean the Interest Rate provided in the Note plus four (4%) percent per annum, but in no event to exceed the maximum rate allowed by law.

**"Distributions"** shall mean all cash dividends to shareholders, and all cash distributions to shareholders of Subchapter S corporations, to partners of partnerships, to members of limited liability companies or to beneficiaries of trusts.

**"Earnings"** shall mean earnings as defined under GAAP.

**"Easements"** shall mean all easements, rights-of-way or use, rights, strips and gores of land, streets, ways, alleys, passages, sewer rights, water, water courses, water rights and powers, air rights, mineral rights and development rights, and all estates, rights, titles, interests, privileges, liberties, servitudes, tenements, hereditaments and appurtenances of any nature whatsoever, in any way now or hereafter belonging, relating or pertaining to the Land and/or the Improvements and the reversion and reversions, remainder and remainders, and all land lying in the bed of any street, road or avenue, opened or proposed, in front of or adjoining the Land, to the center line thereof and all the estates, rights, titles, interest, dower and rights of dower, curtesy and rights of curtesy, property, possession, claim and demand whatsoever, both at law and in equity, of Mortgagor of, in and to the Land and/or the Improvements and every part and parcel thereof, with the appurtenances thereto.

**"EBITDA"** shall mean, for any period, Earnings from continuing operations before payment of federal, state and local income taxes, plus Interest Expense, depreciation and amortization, in each case for such period, computed and calculated in accordance with GAAP.

**"Equipment"** shall mean all **"equipment,"** as such term is defined in Article 9 of the Code, now owned or hereafter acquired by Mortgagor, which is used at or in connection with the Improvements or the Land or is located thereon or therein (including, but not limited to, all machinery, equipment, furnishing, and electronic data-processing and other office equipment now owned or hereafter acquired by the Mortgagor and any and all additions, substitutions and replacements of any of the foregoing), together with all attachments, components, parts, equipment and accessories installed thereon or affixed thereto. Notwithstanding the foregoing, Equipment shall not include any property belonging to tenants under leases at the Premises, except to the extent that the Mortgagor shall have any rights or interest therein.

**"Events of Default"** shall mean the events and circumstances described as such in Section 2.01 hereof.

**"Expenses"** shall mean all out-of-pocket fees, charges, costs and expenses of any nature whatsoever incurred at any time and from time to time (whether before or after an Event of Default) by Mortgagee in making, funding, administering or modifying the Loan, in negotiating or entering into any "workout" of the Loan, or in exercising or enforcing any rights, powers and remedies provided in this Mortgage, any of the other Loan Documents or any Hedging Contract, including, without limitation, reasonable attorneys' fees and expenses, court costs, receiver's fees, management fees and costs incurred in the repair, maintenance and operation of, or taking possession of, or selling, all or any part of the Mortgaged Property.

**"Fixtures"** shall mean all Equipment now owned, or the ownership of which is hereafter acquired, by Mortgagor which is so related to the Land and/or Improvements that it is deemed fixtures or real property under the law of the particular state in which the Equipment is located, including, without limitation, all building or construction materials intended for construction, reconstruction, alteration or repair of or installation at the Premises, construction equipment, appliances, machinery, plant equipment, fittings, apparatuses, fixtures and other items now or hereafter attached to, installed in or used in connection with (temporarily or permanently) any of the Premises, including, but not limited to, engines, devices for the operation of pumps, pipes, plumbing, cleaning, call and sprinkler systems, fire extinguishing apparatuses and equipment, heating, ventilating, plumbing, laundry, incinerating, electrical, air conditioning and air cooling equipment and systems, gas and electric machinery, appurtenances and equipment, pollution control equipment, security systems, disposals, dishwashers, refrigerators and ranges, recreational equipment and facilities of all kinds, and water, gas, electrical, storm and sanitary sewer facilities, utility lines and equipment (whether owned individually or jointly with others, and, if owned jointly, to the extent of the Mortgagor's interest therein) and all other utilities whether or not situated in Easements, all water tanks, water supply, water power sites, fuel stations, fuel tanks, fuel supply, and all other structures, together with all accessions, appurtenances, additions, replacements, betterments and substitutions for any of the foregoing and the proceeds thereof. Notwithstanding the foregoing, "Fixtures" shall not include any property which tenants are entitled to remove pursuant to leases at the Premises, except to the extent that Mortgagor shall have any right or interest therein.

**"GAAP"** shall mean Generally Accepted Accounting Principles in effect from time to time in the United States.

**"Guarantor"** shall mean, collectively, Manage Great Realty LLC, a New York limited liability company, Debby Day, an individual.

**"Hedging Contract"** means each ISDA Master Agreement and schedules and related confirmation and/or any other documents, instruments, or agreements executed to further evidence or secure the Hedging Obligations as the same may be hereafter amended, restated, renewed, replaced, supplemented or otherwise modified from time to time.

**"Hedging Obligations"** means all obligations under any agreement, contract or transaction that constitutes a "swap" within the meaning of Section 1a(47) of the Commodity Exchange Act and shall include without limitation, any interest rate swap transactions, basis swaps, forward rate transactions, commodity swaps, commodity options, equity or equity index swaps, equity or equity index options, bond options, interest rate options, foreign exchange transactions, cap transactions, floor transactions, collar transactions, forward transactions, currency swap transactions, cross-currency rate swap transactions, currency options or similar agreements including, without limitation, the Hedging Contracts.

**"Improvements"** shall mean all structures, buildings, additions, extensions, modifications and all other improvements of any kind whatsoever, and replacements of any of the foregoing, now or hereafter located at or upon the Land.

**"Indebtedness"** shall have the meaning accorded such term in the Granting Clause of this Mortgage.

**"Intangibles"** shall mean all **"general intangibles"** (as such quoted term is defined in the Code) in any way relating to the Premises, or any part thereof, and that Mortgagor owns, including, without limitation, all intellectual property, goodwill and books and records relating to the business operated or to be operated on the Premises or any part thereof, together with all unearned premiums, accrued, accruing or to accrue under all insurance policies now or hereafter obtained by Mortgagor insuring the Mortgaged Property and all rights and interest of Mortgagor thereunder.

**"Interest Expense"** shall mean, for any period, ordinary, regular, recurring and continuing expenses for interest on all borrowed money.

**"Interest Rate"** shall have the meaning accorded such term in the Note.

**"Land"** shall mean the real property described in Schedule A attached hereto and by this reference, made a part hereof, including, without limitation, all of the air space, easements, rights, privileges, royalties and appurtenances thereunto belonging or in anywise appertaining thereto, and all of the estate, right, title, interest, claim or demand whatsoever of Mortgagor therein and in the streets, alleys and ways adjacent thereto, either at law or in equity, in possession or expectancy, now or hereafter acquired.

**"Loan"** shall mean the loan from Mortgagee to Mortgagor evidenced by the Note, which is being secured by, among other things, this Mortgage.

**"Loan Documents"** shall mean this Mortgage, the Note, that certain ADA and Environmental Indemnity Agreement, dated of even date herewith, executed and delivered by Mortgagor among others, that certain Assignment of Leases and Rents, dated of even date herewith, executed and delivered by Mortgagor in favor of Mortgagee, for itself and as agent for any Affiliate Counterparty or any other Affiliate of Mortgagee, that certain Guaranty of Payment, dated of even date herewith, executed and delivered by each Guarantor in favor of Mortgagee and any Affiliate Counterparty, that certain Shareholder Debt Subordination Agreement, dated of even date herewith, executed and delivered by Mortgagor among others, all Uniform Commercial Code financing statements in respect of the Mortgaged Property and all other documents, agreements, instruments, certificates, title policies and the like securing and/or evidencing the Mortgage Amount and other Indebtedness and/or executed and/or delivered by or on behalf of the Mortgagor in connection with the closing of the Loan or at any time thereafter.

**"Mortgaged Property"** shall have the meaning accorded such term in the Granting Clause of this Mortgage.

**"Person"** shall mean an individual, a corporation, a partnership, a joint venture, a limited liability company, a trust, an unincorporated association, any governmental authority or any other entity.

**"Personal Property"** shall mean all furniture, furnishings, objects of art, machinery, goods, tools, supplies, appliances, contract rights, accounts, including, without limitation, all bank accounts maintained by or on behalf of Mortgagor, the Impound Account (as hereafter defined), if any, and any other accounts established pursuant to any of the Loan Documents or any Hedging Contract, accounts receivable, franchises, licenses, certificates and permits, and all other personal property of any kind or character whatsoever (as defined in and subject to the provisions of the Code), other than Fixtures, which are now or hereafter owned by Mortgagor and which are located within or about the Premises, together with all accessories, replacements and substitutions thereto or therefor and the proceeds thereof, and the right, title and interest of Mortgagor in and to any of the Personal Property which may be subject to the lien of any security interest, as defined in the Code, superior to tho lion of this Mortgage, and all proceeds and products of the foregoing.

**"Power of Sale"** shall mean, in addition to any right to process with a judicial foreclosure and sale, the right, power and authority of Mortgagee to sell or cause the sale of the Mortgaged Property and/or a part or parts thereof, at a public sale or auction, after any Event of Default in accordance with and pursuant to the laws of the State now in effect and/or hereafter enacted, which provide for and/or enable the property encumbered by a mortgage to be sold by a mortgagee and/or its agents and/or representatives in a public and/or private non-judicial sale.

**"Premises"** shall mean, collectively, the Land and the Improvements.

**"State"** shall mean the State of New York.

All terms of this Mortgage not defined above shall have the respective meanings accorded such terms in this Mortgage.

## Granting Clause

NOW, THEREFORE, Mortgagor, in consideration of the premises and in order to secure payment of (a) the principal of the Note and the interest and any and all other sums payable on the Note, under this Mortgage or the other Loan Documents as well as, without limitation, all other loans, advances, indebtedness, notes, and liabilities, (b) all Hedging Obligations owing to Mortgagee or any Affiliate Counterparty (including any Additional Interest due thereunder) and (c) all other amounts, in each case, liquidated or unliquidated, owing by the Mortgagor to the Mortgagee, any Affiliate of Mortgagee or any Affiliate Counterparty at any time, of each and every kind, nature and description, whether arising under this Mortgage or otherwise, and whether secured or unsecured, direct or indirect (that is, whether the same are due directly by the Mortgagor to the Mortgagee or any Affiliate Counterparty or other Affiliate thereof; or are due indirectly by the Mortgagor to the Mortgagee or any Affiliate Counterparty or other Affiliate thereof as endorser, guarantor or other surety, or as borrower of obligations due third Persons which have been endorsed or assigned to the Mortgagee or any Affiliate Counterparty or other Affiliate thereof, or otherwise), absolute or contingent, due or to become due, now existing or hereafter arising or contracted, including, without limitation, payment when due of all amounts outstanding respecting any of the Loan Documents or any Hedging Contract (all of such obligations are hereinafter referred to, collectively, as the **"Indebtedness"),** and the performance and observance of all the other provisions hereof, of the Note, the other Loan Documents or any Hedging Contract with Mortgagee, any Affiliate Counterparty or any other Affiliate, hereby gives, grants, mortgages, bargains, sells, warrants, aliens, remises, releases, conveys, assigns, transfers, hypothecates, deposits, pledges, sets over and confirms unto Mortgagee, for itself and as agent for any Affiliate Counterparty or any other Affiliate of Mortgagee with respect to or otherwise holding any of the Indebtedness, all its estate, right, title and interest in, to and under any and all of the following described property (collectively, the **"Mortgaged Property"),** whether now owned or held or hereafter acquired:

(a) the Land;

(b) the Improvements;

(c) the Easements;

(d) the Chattels;

(e) the Intangibles;

(f) the Agreements;

(g) all awards or payments, including interest thereon, which may heretofore and hereafter be made with respect to the Premises, whether from the exercise of the right of eminent domain or condemnation (including but not limited to any transfer made in lieu of or in anticipation of the exercise of the right), or for a change of grade, or for any other injury to or decrease in the value of the Premises;

(h) all proceeds in respect of the Mortgaged Property under any insurance policies covering the Mortgaged Property, including, without limitation, the right to receive and apply the proceeds of any insurance, judgments, or settlements made in lieu thereof, for damage to the Mortgaged Property;

(i) all refunds, rebates or credits in connection with reduction in real estate taxes and assessments charged against the Premises as a result of tax certiorari or any applications or proceedings for reduction or otherwise;

(j) all leases and other agreements affecting the use, enjoyment or occupancy of the Premises or any part thereof heretofore or hereafter entered into (collectively, the **"Leases")** and all right, title and interest of Mortgagor therein and thereunder, including, without limitation, cash, letters of credit or securities deposited thereunder to secure the performance by the lessees of their obligations thereunder and all rents, additional rents, revenues, income, issues and profits (including all oil and gas or other mineral royalties and bonuses) from the Land and the Improvements (collectively, the **"Rents")** and all proceeds from the sale or other disposition of the Leases;

(k) the right, in the name and on behalf of Mortgagor, to appear in and defend any action or proceeding brought with respect to the Mortgaged Property and to commence any action or proceeding to protect the interest of the Mortgagee in the Mortgaged Property; and

(l) all proceeds of any of the foregoing converted into cash, property, claims or otherwise.

**TO HAVE AND TO HOLD** unto Mortgagee and its successors and assigns, forever to its and their own proper use and behoof; and Mortgagor also does for itself, its successors and assigns, covenant with the Mortgagee, and its successors and assigns, that at and until the ensealing of these presents, it is well seized of the Premises in fee simple, and has good right to mortgage, bargain and sell the same and that the same are free from all encumbrances whatsoever except for those permitted encumbrances and other matters set forth on Schedule B of the title insurance policy insuring the lien of this Mortgage (collectively, the **"Permitted Encumbrances").**

## ARTICLE I.

### Particular Covenants of Mortgagor

Mortgagor represents, warrants, covenants and agrees as follows:

SECTION 1.01 Mortgagor represents and warrants that it has a good and marketable title to an indefeasible fee estate in the Premises subject to no lien, charge or encumbrance, other than the Permitted Encumbrances; that it will own the Chattels free and clear of liens and claims; that this Mortgage is and will remain a valid and enforceable first lien on the Mortgaged Property subject only to the exceptions referred to above or in Schedule A; that the execution and delivery of this Mortgage, the Note, the other Loan Documents and the Hedging Contracts has been duly authorized by Mortgagor and that there is no provision in any document relating to Mortgagor that evidences or establishes the existence of Mortgagor requiring further consent for such action by any other entity or person;

that it is duly organized, validly existing and is in good standing under the Jaws of the state of its organization; that it has (i) all necessary licenses, authorizations, registrations, permits and/or approvals and (ii) full power and authority to own its properties and carry on its business as presently conducted and the execution and delivery by it of and performance of its obligations under this Mortgage, the Note, the other Loan Documents or any Hedging Contract will not result in Mortgagor being in default under any provisions of any document that evidences or establishes the existence of Mortgagor or of any mortgage, credit or other agreement to which Mortgagor is a party or by which it is bound or that affects Mortgagor or the Premises, or any part thereof; that it will preserve such title, and will forever warrant and defend the same unto Mortgagee and its successors and assigns, and will forever warrant and defend the validity and priority of such lien hereof against the claims of all persons and parties whomsoever, subject only to the Permitted Encumbrances.

SECTION 1.02 (a) Mortgagor will, at the sole cost and expense of Mortgagor, and without expense to Mortgagee, do, execute, acknowledge and deliver all and every such further acts, deeds, conveyances, mortgages, deeds of trust, assignments, notices of assignment, transfers and assurances as Mortgagee shall from time to time reasonably require, for the better assuring, conveying, mortgaging, assigning, transferring and confirming unto Mortgagee the property and rights hereby conveyed, mortgaged or assigned or intended now or hereafter so to be, or that Mortgagor may be or may hereafter become bound to convey, mortgage or assign to Mortgagee, or for more effectively carrying out the intention or facilitating the performance of the terms of this Mortgage, or for recording this Mortgage and, on demand, will execute and deliver and hereby authorizes Mortgagee to execute and record in the name of Mortgagor to the extent it may be lawful to do so, chattel mortgages or comparable security instruments to evidence more effectively the lien hereof upon the Mortgaged Property or any part thereof. Mortgagor will also, at Mortgagee's request, sign any affidavits or other documents or instruments which may be necessary to maintain the priority of the lien of this Mortgage with respect to the Mortgaged Property or any part thereof, or to release or enforce such lien, including but not limited to any amendments, corrections, deletions or additions to this Mortgage. Notwithstanding the foregoing, in no event, however, shall Mortgagor be obligated to execute any document and/or undertake any obligation which would materially and adversely increase Mortgagor's obligations under the Loan Documents.

(b) Mortgagor expressly agrees, intending that Mortgagee rely thereon, that this Mortgage shall also constitute a **"security agreement,"** as such term is defined in the Code with respect to the Chattels, Intangibles and other Mortgaged Property. Mortgagor further expressly agrees, intending that Mortgagee rely thereon, that this Mortgage, to the extent permitted by law, shall also constitute a **"financing statement,"** as such term is defined in the Code with respect to the Fixtures. By its execution of this Mortgage, Mortgagor hereby authorizes Mortgagee to file and/or record this Mortgage as a security instrument and fixture filing with respect to the Mortgaged Property or any part thereof, and authorizes Mortgagee to file one or more financing statements, amendments, fixture filings, renewals or continuation statements with respect to the Mortgaged Property or any part thereof, and authorizes Mortgagee to file any other document or instrument as may from time to time be permitted under the Code or which Mortgagee may otherwise deem desirable in connection with the Mortgaged Property or any part thereof. If requested by Mortgagee, Mortgagor agrees to sign all such financing statements, amendments, renewal or continuation statements and other instruments and documents or, at Mortgagee's option, Mortgagee is hereby authorized by Mortgagor to sign all such financing statements, amendments, renewals continuation statements, documents and instruments in Mortgagor' s name as Mortgagor' s attorney-in-fact.

SECTION 1.03 (a) Mortgagor forthwith upon the execution and delivery of this Mortgage, and thereafter from time to time, will cause this Mortgage, and any security instrument creating a lien or evidencing the lien hereof upon the Chattels and/or the Intangibles and each instrument of further assurance to be filed, registered and/or recorded in such manner and in such places as may be required by any present or future law in order to publish notice of and fully to protect the lien hereof upon, and the interest of Mortgagee in, the Mortgaged Property. Notwithstanding the foregoing, in no event, however, shall Mortgagor be obligated to execute any document and/or undertake any obligation which would materially and adversely increase Mortgagor's obligations under the Loan Documents.

(b) Mortgagor will pay all filing, registration or recording fees, taxes and other charges, and all costs and expenses incident to the execution, acknowledgment, delivery and recording and/or filing of this Mortgage, the other Loan Documents, any mortgage supplemental hereto, any other security instrument with respect to the Chattels or the Intangibles, and any instrument of further assurance, and all Federal, state, county and municipal stamp taxes and other taxes, duties, impositions, assessments and charges arising out of or in connection with the execution and delivery of the Note, this Mortgage or any mortgage supplemental hereto, any security instrument with respect to the Chattels and/or the Intangibles, any other Loan Document or any instrument of further assurance.

(c) Upon Mortgagor's full satisfaction of the Indebtedness and all of Mortgagor's other obligations under the Note, this Mortgage, the other Loan Documents and any Hedging Contract, at Mortgagor's request and at Mortgagor's sole cost and expense (including, without limitation, the payment of all reasonable legal fees and disbursements), Mortgagee shall execute and deliver to Mortgagor a release of the lien of this Mortgage and termination statements as to any Uniform Commercial Code financing statements filed by Mortgagee in respect of the Mortgaged Property. Mortgagor shall be responsible for the recordation and filing of such release and termination statements, and the cost thereof.

SECTION 1.04 Mortgagor will punctually pay the principal and interest and all other sums to become due in respect of the Note and any Hedging Contract at the time and place and in the manner specified in the Note and any Hedging Contract, according to the true intent and meaning thereof, all in any coin or currency of the United States of America that at the time of such payment shall be legal tender for the payment of public and private debts, and all such principal and interest due in respect of the Note and amounts due under any Hedging Contract are hereby deemed an obligation due under this Mortgage.

SECTION 1.05 Mortgagor will, so long as it is the owner of the Mortgaged Property or any part thereof, do all things necessary to preserve and keep in full force and effect its existence, franchises, rights and privileges as a business or entity under the laws of the state of its organization and will comply with all regulations, rules, ordinances, statutes, orders and decrees of any governmental authority or court applicable to Mortgagor or to the Mortgaged Property or any part thereof.

SECTION 1.06 All right, title and interest of Mortgagor in and to all extensions, improvements, betterments, renewals, substitutes and replacements of, and all additions and appurtenances to, the Mortgaged Property hereafter acquired by, or released to, Mortgagor, or constructed, assembled or placed by Mortgagor on the Premises or any part thereof, and all conversions of the security constituted thereby, immediately upon such acquisition, release, construction, assembling, placement or conversion, as the case may be, and in each such case, without any further mortgage, conveyance, assignment or other act by Mortgagor, shall become subject to the lien of this Mortgage as fully and completely, and with the same effect, as though now owned by Mortgagor and specifically described in the Granting Clause hereof, but at any and all times Mortgagor will execute and deliver to Mortgagee any and all such further assurances, mortgages, conveyances or assignments thereof as the Mortgagee may require for the purpose of expressly and specifically subjecting the same to the lien of this Mortgage. Notwithstanding the foregoing, in no event, however, shall Mortgagor be obligated to execute any document and/or undertake any obligation which would materially and adversely increase Mo1igagor's obligations under the Loan Documents.

SECTION 1.07 (a) Mortgagor, from time to time when the same shall become due and payable, will pay and discharge all taxes of every kind and nature, all general and special assessments, levies, permits, inspection and license fees, all water and sewer rents and charges, and all other public charges whether of a like or different nature, imposed upon or assessed against the Mortgaged Property, or any part thereof, or upon the revenues, rents, issues, income and profits of the Mortgaged Property, or any part thereof, or arising in respect of the occupancy, use or possession thereof (collectively, the **"Impositions")**. Mortgagor will, upon the request of Mortgagee, deliver to Mortgagee receipts evidencing the payment of all such Impositions, or any part thereof, or the revenues, rents, issues, income or profits thereof.

(b) Mortgagor will pay, from time to time when the same shall become due, all lawful claims and demands of mechanics, materialmen, laborers and others, which claims and demands, if unpaid, might result in, or permit the creation of, a lien on the Mortgaged Property or any part thereof, or on the revenues, rents, issues, income and profits arising therefrom and in general will do or cause to be done everything necessary so that the lien of this Mortgage shall be fully preserved, at the sole cost and expense of Mortgagor, without expense to Mortgagee.

(c) Nothing in this Section 1.07 shall require the payment or discharge of any obligation imposed upon Mortgagor by this Section so long as Mortgagor shall in good faith and at its own cost and expense contest the same or the validity thereof by appropriate legal proceedings that shall operate to prevent the collection thereof or other realization thereon and the sale or forfeiture of the Premises or any part thereof to satisfy the same; provided that during such contest Mortgagor shall, at the option of Mortgagee, provide security satisfactory to Mortgagee, assuring the discharge of Mortgagor's obligation hereunder and of any additional charge, penalty or expense arising from or incurred as a result of such contest; and provided further that if, at any time, payment of any obligation imposed upon Mortgagor by subsection (a) of this Section shall become necessary to prevent the delivery of a tax deed, or its equivalent, conveying the Premises or any other part of the Mortgaged Property, or any part thereof, because of non payment, then Mortgagor shall pay the same in sufficient time to prevent the delivery of such tax deed or its equivalent.

SECTION 1.08 Mortgagor will pay any and all taxes, charges, fees and/or levies by reason of Mortgagee's ownership of and interest in the Note, this Mortgage, the other Loan Documents or any Hedging Contract and/or resulting from the exercise by Mortgagee of any of its rights and/or remedies provided for under this Mortgage, except for income taxes. The obligations assumed by Mortgagor pursuant to this Section 1.08 shall survive the exercise by Mortgagee of any of its rights and/or remedies under this Mortgage.

SECTION 1.09 (a) Mortgagor shall keep the Premises and Chattels insured against such perils and hazards, and in such amounts and with such limits, as Mortgagee may from time to time require, and in any event will continuously maintain, at Mortgagor's sole cost and expense, the following described policies of insurance (collectively, the **"Insurance Policies")**:

(i) Property insurance insuring the Improvements and Chattels against loss and damage by fire and other hazards on an "all risk" policy form, covering insurance risks covered by a standard extended coverage insurance policy, and covering such other risks as Mortgagee may reasonably require, in amounts equal to the full replacement cost of the Improvements and Chattels, including, without limitation, fixtures and equipment, Mortgagor's interest **in** any leasehold improvements, and the cost of debris removal, with an agreed amount endorsement and inflation guard endorsement;

(ii) Commercial general liability insurance with respect to the Premises, including death, bodily injury and broad form property damage coverage with a combined single limit **in** an amount not less than One Million Dollars

($1,000,000) per occurrence and Two Million Dollars ($2,000,000) in the aggregate, as well as One Million Dollars ($1,000,000) in property damage, for any policy year;

(iii) If the Premises, or any part thereof, are located in an area that has been identified by the Federal Emergency Management Agency as being located in a special flood hazard area, Mortgagor will keep, for as long as any Indebtedness remains unpaid, the Improvements covered by flood insurance in an amount equal to the lesser of (A) the full replacement cost of the Premises or (B) the maximum limit of coverage available for the Premises under the National Flood Insurance Act of 1968 and the Flood Disaster Protection Act of 1973, as the same may have been or may hereafter be amended or modified (and any successor act thereto); and

(iv) Such other types and amounts of insurance coverage (including, without limitation, risks of war, terrorist acts and nuclear explosion) as are reasonably requested by Mortgagee and are customarily (A) maintained by owners or operators of properties similarly situated to the Premises, or (B) required by institutional lenders in like transactions.

Each of the Insurance Policies shall be endorsed to name the Mortgagee and its successors and assigns as mortgagee or lender loss payee, with loss payable to the Mortgagee and its successors and assigns, without contribution or assessment, pursuant to a standard first mortgage endorsement in the form of, or substantially equivalent to, the New York standard mortgagee endorsement, provided that with respect to liability insurance or other policies of insurance required hereunder where a mortgagee or lender loss payee endorsement is not available, Mortgagee shall, to the fullest extent available, be named as an additional insured in any such Insurance Policies. All Insurance Policies and endorsements required pursuant *to* this Section 1.09 shall be fully paid for, nonassessable and contain such provisions and expiration dates and be in such form and amounts as indicated above and shall be issued by an insurance company licensed *to* sell insurance in the State, and having an AA+ Best Company rating. Without limiting the foregoing, each policy shall specifically provide that (A) such policy may not be cancelled except upon thirty (30) days' prior written notice *to* the Mortgagee and that no act or thing done by the Mortgagor shall invalidate the policy as against the Mortgagee and (B) any and all insurance proceeds will be paid to the Mortgagee so long as Mortgagee certifies *to* the insurer that the unpaid Indebtedness exceeds the proceeds of insurance. Mortgagor shall assign and deliver the Insurance Policies *to* the Mortgagee and Mortgagee shall have and hold said Insurance Policies as collateral and further security for the payment of the Indebtedness until the full payment of the Indebtedness. In addition, from time *to* time, upon occurrence of any change in the use, operation or value of the Premises, or in the availability of insurance in the area in which the Premises are located, Mortgagor shall, within five (5) days after demand by Mortgagee, take out such additional amounts and/or such other kinds of insurance as Mortgagee may require.

(b) Mortgagor shall not take out separate insurance concurrent in form or contributing in the event of loss with that required to be maintained under this Section 1.09, unless Mortgagee is included thereon as a named insured with loss payable to Mortgagee under the standard mortgage endorsement of the character above described. Mortgagor shall immediately notify Mortgagee whenever any such separate insurance is taken out and shall promptly deliver to Mortgagee the policy or policies of such insurance.

(c) Upon the request of Mortgagee, Mortgagor shall establish and maintain at all times while this Mortgage continues in effect an impound account (the **"Impound Account")** with Mortgagee for payment of real estate taxes and assessments and insurance on the Mortgaged Property and as additional security for the Indebtedness. Upon the request of Mortgagee, Mortgagor shall deposit in the Impound Account an amount determined by Mortgagee to be necessary to ensure that there will be on deposit with Mortgagee an amount which, when added to the monthly payments subsequently required to be deposited with Mortgagee hereunder on account of real estate taxes, assessments and insurance premiums, will result in there being on deposit with Mortgagee in the Impound Account an amount sufficient to pay the next due annual installment of real estate taxes and assessments on the Mortgaged Property at least one (1) month prior to the delinquency date thereof (if paid in one installment) and the next due annual insurance premiums with respect to the Mortgaged Property at least one (1) month prior to the delinquency date thereof (if paid in one installment). Commencing on the next monthly payment date under the Note and continuing thereafter on each monthly payment date under the Note, Mortgagor shall pay to Mortgagee, concurrently with and in addition to the monthly payment due under the Note and until the Indebtedness is fully paid and performed, deposits in an amount equal to one-twelfth (1/12) of the amount of the annual real estate taxes and assessments that will next become due and payable on the Mortgaged Property, plus one-twelfth (1/12) of the amount of the annual premiums that will next become due and payable on insurance policies which Mortgagor is required to maintain hereunder, each as estimated and determined by Mortgagee. So long as no default hereunder has occurred and is continuing, all sums in the Impound Account shall be held by Mortgagee in the Impound Account to pay said taxes, assessments and insurance premiums in one installment before the same become delinquent. Mortgagor shall be responsible for ensuring the receipt by Mortgagee, at least thirty (30) days prior to the respective due date for payment thereof, of all bills, invoices and statements for all taxes, assessments and insurance premiums to be paid from the Impound Account, and so long as no default hereunder has occurred and is continuing, Mortgagee shall pay the governmental authority or other party entitled thereto directly to the extent funds are available for such purpose in the Impound Account. In making any payment from the Impound Account, Mortgagee shall be entitled to rely on any bill, statement or estimate procured from the appropriate public office or insurance company or agent without any inquiry into the accuracy of such bill, statement or estimate and without any inquiry into the accuracy, validity, enforceability or contestability of any tax, assessment, valuation, sale, forfeiture, tax lien or title or claim thereof.

The Impound Account shall not, unless otherwise explicitly required by applicable law, be or be deemed to be escrow or trust funds, but, at Mortgagee's option and in Mortgagee's discretion, may either be held in a separate account or be commingled by Mortgagee with the general funds of Mortgagee. No interest on funds contained in the Impound Account, if any, shall be paid by Mortgagee to Mortgagor. The Impound Account is solely for the protection of Mortgagee and entails no responsibility on Mortgagee's part beyond the payment of taxes, assessments and insurance premiums following receipt of bills, invoices or statements therefor in accordance with the terms hereof and beyond the allowing of due credit for the sums actually received. Upon assignment of this Mortgage by Mortgagee, any funds in the Impound Account shall be turned over to assignee and any responsibility of Mortgagee, as assignor, with respect thereto shall terminate. If the total funds in the Impound Account shall exceed the amount of payments actually applied by Mortgagee for the purposes of the Impound Account, such excess may be credited by Mortgagee on subsequent payments to be made hereunder or, at the option of Mortgagee, refunded to Mortgagor. If, however, the Impound Account shall not contain sufficient funds to pay the sums required when the same shall become due and payable, Mortgagor shall, within (10) days after receipt of written notice therefor, deposit with Mortgagee the full amount of any such deficiency. If Mortgagor shall fail to deposit with Mortgagee the full amount of such deficiency as provided above, Mortgagee shall have the option, but not the obligation, to make such deposit, and all amounts so deposited by Mortgagee, together with interest thereon at the applicable Default Rate from the date so deposited by Mortgagee, until actually paid by Mortgagor, shall be immediately paid by Mortgagor on demand and shall be secured by this Mortgage. If there is a default under this Mortgage which is not cured within any applicable grace or cure period, Mortgagee may, but shall not be obligated to, apply at any time the balance then remaining in the Impound Account against the Indebtedness in whatever order Mortgagee shall subjectively determine. No such application of the Impound Account shall be deemed to cure any default hereunder. Upon full payment of the Indebtedness in accordance with its terms or at such earlier time as Mortgagee may elect, the balance of the Impound Account then in Mortgagee's possession shall be paid over to Mortgagor and no other party shall have any right or claim thereto.

(d) Mortgagor shall give Mortgagee prompt written notice of any damage to, or destruction of, the Improvements, or any part thereof, or of any other casualty or loss at or affecting the Premises or the Chattels, and Mortgagee shall have the right to join Mortgagor in adjusting any insurance claim in respect of any such damage, destruction, casualty or loss in excess of $50,000. Notwithstanding anything to the contrary contained herein or in Section 254 of the Real Property Law of the State of New York or any other provision of applicable law, the proceeds of any insurance coming into the possession of Mortgagee in respect of any damage, destruction, casualty or loss shall not be deemed trust funds, and Mortgagee shall have the option, in its sole discretion, to apply any insurance proceeds it may receive pursuant hereto or otherwise to the payment of the Indebtedness, or to allow all or a portion of such proceeds to be used for the restoration of the Mortgaged Property. In the event any such insurance proceeds shall be used to reduce the Indebtedness, the same shall be applied by Mortgagee, after the deduction therefrom and repayment to Mortgagee of any and all costs incurred by Mortgagee in the recovery thereof (including reasonable attorneys' fees and disbursements), in any manner it shall designate, including but not limited to, the application of such proceeds to the then unpaid installments of the principal balance due under the Note in the inverse order of their maturity, such that the regular payments, if any, under the Note shall not be reduced or altered in any manner. Any prepayment of the Note from the proceeds of insurance shall be without prepayment premium. Notwithstanding the foregoing, if the Improvements have been damaged or destroyed, Mortgagee shall allow Mortgagor to use any such insurance proceeds for the restoration of the Improvements, provided that Mortgagee shall reasonably determine that the restoration of the Improvements can be completed prior to the Maturity Date (as defined in the Note) of the Note, and that insurance proceeds shall be sufficient to complete the restoration, or if the amount of such insurance proceeds shall be insufficient to complete such restoration, Mortgagor deposits with Mortgagee an amount equal to the difference between Mortgagee's estimated cost of such restoration and the insurance proceeds received.

(e) Unless the Indebtedness is paid in full to Mortgagee and any Affiliate Counterparty or other Affiliate of Mortgagee within thirty (30) days of the date of any damage, destruction, loss or other casualty to the Improvements, and provided that casualty insurance proceeds are made available to Mortgagor, Mortgagor shall promptly commence and diligently continue to perform the repairs, restoration and rebuilding of the portion of the Improvements so damaged or destroyed (hereinafter the **"Work")** so as to restore the Improvements and Chattels in full compliance with all legal requirements and so that the Mortgaged Property shall be at least equal in value and general utility as they were prior to such damage or destruction, and if such damage or destruction, in the reasonable judgment of Mortgagee, shall exceed Fifty Thousand ($50,000) Dollars (hereinafter, collectively **"Major Work"),** Mortgagor shall, prior to the commencement of the Major Work, furnish to Mortgagee for its approval: (1) complete plans and specifications for the Major Work, with satisfactory evidence of the approval thereof (i) by all governmental authorities whose approval is required and (ii) by Mortgagee's inspector or an architect satisfactory to Mortgagee (hereinafter, the **"Architect")** and which shall be accompanied by the Architect's signed estimate, bearing the Architect's seal, of the entire cost of completing the Major Work; (2) certified or photostatic copies of all permits and approvals required by law in connection with the commencement and conduct ot the Major Work; and (3) a surety bond or guaranty of the payment for and completion of the Major Work, which bond or guaranty shall be in form satisfactory to Mortgagee and shall be signed by surety or sureties, or guarantor or guarantors, as the case may be, who are acceptable to Mortgagee, and in an amount not less than the Architect's estimate of the entire cost of completing the Major Work, less the amount of insurance proceeds and Mortgagor deposits, if any, then held by Mortgagee for application toward the cost of the Major Work. Mortgagor shall not commence any of the Major Work until Mortgagor shall have complied with applicable requirements referred to in this subsection (e), and after commencing the Major Work, Mortgagor shall perform the Major Work diligently and in good faith in accordance with the plans and specifications referred to in this subsection (e), if applicable.

(f) During any period that Work is being performed at the Premises, Mortgagor, at its sole cost and expense, shall maintain in full force and effect a builder's "all risk" insurance policy insuring the Improvements against such risks on a replacement cost basis (including, without limitation, fire and extended coverage and collapse of the Improvements to agreed limits) as Mortgagee may request Such policy shall be deemed an Insurance Policy hereunder for all purposes and shall fully comply with the provisions of Section 1.09(a) hereof.

(g) If the insurance proceeds, less the cost, if any, to Mortgagee of such recovery and of paying out such proceeds (including reasonable attorneys' fees and costs allocable to inspecting the Work and the plans and specifications therefor) should be paid towards restoration of the Improvements and Chattels or if such insurance proceeds are applied toward such restoration, then such insurance proceeds shall be applied by Mortgagee to the payment of the cost of the Work and shall be paid out from time to time to Mortgagor and/or, at Mortgagee's option, directly to the contractor, subcontractors, materialmen, laborers, engineers, architects and other persons rendering services or materials for the Work, as said Work progresses except as otherwise hereinafter provided, but subject to the following conditions, any of which Mortgagee may freely waive, at Mortgagee's sole discretion:

(i) If the Work to be done is Major Work, as determined by Mortgagee, the Architect shall be in charge of such Major Work;

(ii) Each request for payment shall be made on five (5) days prior notice to Mortgagee and shall be accompanied by a certificate of the Mortgagees inspector or the Architect if one is required under subsection (e) above, otherwise by a certificate of an officer of Mortgagor, stating (A) that all of the Work completed has been done in compliance with the approved plans and specifications, if any be required under said subsection (e) above, and in accordance with all provisions of law; (B) the sum requested is justly required to reimburse Mortgagor for payments by Mortgagor to, or is justly due to, the contractor, subcontractor, materialmen, laborers, engineers, architects or other persons rendering services or materials for the Work (giving a brief description of such services and materials), and that when added to all sums, if any, previously paid out by Mortgagee does not exceed the value of the Work done to date of such certificate, and (C) that the amount of such proceeds and other deposits remaining in the hands of Mortgagee will be sufficient on completion of the Work to pay for the same in full (giving in such reasonable detail as Mortgagee may require an estimate of the cost of such completion);

(iii) Each request shall be accompanied by waivers of liens satisfactory to Mortgagee covering that part of the Work previously paid for, if any, and by a search prepared by the title company which insured the lien of the Mortgage or by other evidence satisfactory to Mortgagee, that there has not been filed with respect to the Premises or any part thereof any mechanic's lien or other lien or instrument for the retention of title in respect of any part of the Work not discharged of record and that there exist no encumbrances on or affecting the Premises or any part thereof or any part of the other Mortgaged Property, other than the Permitted Encumbrances, if any;

(iv) The request for any payment after the Work has been completed shall be accompanied by a copy of all certificates, permits, licenses, waivers and/or other documents required by law to render occupancy of the Premises legal; and

(v) Upon completion of the Work and payment in full therefor, or upon failure on the part of Mortgagor to commence, as provided in Section 1.09(e) above, or diligently to continue the Work, or at any time upon request by Mortgagor, Mortgagee may apply the amount of any such proceeds then or thereafter in the hands of Mortgagee to the payment of the Indebtedness; provided, however, that nothing herein contained shall prevent Mortgagee from applying at any time the whole or any part of such proceeds to the curing of any default after expiration of applicable notice and cure periods under this Mortgage, the Note, any other Loan Documents or any Hedging Contract.

SECTION 1.10 If Mortgagor shall fail to perform any of the covenants contained in Sections 1.01, 1.03, 1.05, 1.07, 1.08, 1.09, 1.12 or 1.21 hereof, Mortgagee may make advances to perform the same on its behalf upon ten (10) days' prior written notice to Mortgagor, and all sums so advanced shall be a lien upon the Mortgaged Property and shall be secured hereby. Mortgagor will repay on demand all sums so advanced on its behalf with interest at the Default Rate. The provisions of this Section shall not prevent any default in the observance of any covenant contained in said Sections 1.01, 1.03, 1.05, 1.07, 1.08, 1.09, 1.12 or 1.21 from constituting an Event of Default.

SECTION 1.11 (a) Mortgagor will keep adequate records and books of account in accordance with generally accepted accounting principles **("GAAP")** and will permit Mortgagee, by its agents, accountants and attorneys, to visit and inspect the Premises and examine its records and books of account and to discuss its affairs, finances and accounts with the officers of Mortgagor upon reasonable notice to Mortgagor, at such reasonable times as may be requested by Mortgagee.

(b) Mortgagor will deliver to Mortgagee, with reasonable promptness but in no event more than two hundred seventy (270) days after the end of each calendar year, copies of its Federal and state tax returns for the preceding calendar year. Throughout the term of this Mortgage, Mortgagor, with reasonable promptness, will deliver to Mortgagee such other information with respect to Mortgagor as Mortgagee may reasonably request from time to time.

(c) Mortgagor, within five (5) business days upon request in person, or within seven (7) business days upon request by mail, will furnish a written statement duly acknowledged of the amount due whether for principal or interest on the Note and whether any offsets, counterclaims or defenses exist against Mortgagee, or the Indebtedness, or any part thereof.

SECTION 1.12 Mortgagor will not commit any waste on the Mortgaged Property, or any part thereof, or make any change in the use of the Mortgaged Property, or any part thereof, that will in any way decrease the value of the Mortgaged Property or increase the risk of fire or other hazard or casualty arising out of construction or operation. Mortgagor will, at all times, maintain the Improvements in good operating order and condition and will promptly make, from time to time, all repairs, renewals, replacements, additions and improvements in connection therewith which are necessary or desirable to such end. The Improvements shall not be demolished or substantially altered, nor shall any Chattels be removed without the prior written consent of Mortgagee, except where appropriate replacements free of superior title, liens and claims are immediately made having value at least equal to the value of the removed Chattels.

SECTION 1.13 Mortgagor, immediately upon obtaining knowledge of the institution of any proceedings for the condemnation of the Premises or any part thereof, will notify Mortgagee of the pendency of such proceedings. Mortgagee may participate in any such proceedings and Mortgagor from time to time will deliver to Mortgagee all instruments requested by it to permit such participation. In the event of such condemnation proceedings, the award or compensation payable is hereby assigned to and shall be paid to Mortgagee. Mortgagee shall be under no obligation to question or challenge the amount of any such award or compensation and may accept the same in the amount in which the same shall be paid. In any such condemnation proceedings, Mortgagee may be represented by counsel selected by Mortgagee. The proceeds of any award or compensation so received shall at the option of Mortgagee, either be applied toward the payment of the Indebtedness notwithstanding the fact that the Indebtedness may not then be due and payable, and/or to the restoration of the Improvements (in the case of a partial condemnation that affects the Improvements in such a way that restoration is required to such Improvements). In the event that any portion of the condemnation awards or compensation shall be used to reduce the Indebtedness, same shall be applied by Mortgagee in any manner it shall designate, including, but not limited to, the application of such award or compensation to the then unpaid installments of the principal balance due under the Note in the inverse order of their maturity such that the regular payments under the Note shall not be reduced or altered in any manner. Notwithstanding the foregoing, if restoration of the Improvements is required as a result of a condemnation, Mortgagee shall allow Mortgagor to use a portion of the condemnation awards or compensation (prorated to reflect the portion of the Improvements which have been taken) for the restoration of the Improvements, provided that Mortgagee shall reasonably determine that the restoration of the Improvements can be completed prior to the Maturity Date (as defined in the Note) of the Note, and that the condemnation awards or compensation shall be sufficient to complete the restoration, or if the amount of such condemnation awards or compensation shall be insufficient to complete such restoration, Mortgagor deposits with Mortgagee an amount equal to the difference between Mortgagee's estimated cost of such restoration and the condemnation awards or compensation received. Mortgagor, upon request by Mortgagee, shall make, execute and deliver any and all instruments requested for the purpose of confirming the assignment of the aforesaid awards and compensation to Mortgagee free and clear of any liens, charges or encumbrances of any kind or nature whatsoever. Mortgagee shall not be limited to the interest paid on the proceeds of any award or compensation, but shall be entitled to the payment by Mortgagor of interest at the applicable rate provided for in the Note.

SECTION 1.14 (a) The Mortgagor will not (i) execute an assignment of any Leases affecting the Premises or any part thereon, or the Rents, or any part thereof, from the Premises, except in favor of Mortgagee, or (ii) except where the lessee under any Lease is in default thereunder, terminate or consent to the cancellation or surrender of any such Lease, now existing or hereafter entered into, having an unexpired term of one (1) year or more, except that any Lease may be cancelled provided that promptly after the cancellation or surrender thereof a new Lease is entered into with a new lessee having a credit standing, in the reasonable judgment of the Mortgagee, at least equivalent to that of the lessee whose lease was cancelled, on substantially the same or better terms as the terminated or cancelled Lease, or (iii) modify any such Lease so as to shorten the unexpired term thereof or so as to decrease the amount of the Rents payable thereunder, or (iv) accept prepayments of any installments of Rents to become due under such Leases, except prepayments in the nature of security for the performance of the lessees thereunder, or (v) in any other manner materially impair the value of the Mortgaged Property or the security of this Mortgage in the reasonable judgment of the Mortgagee.

(b) Mortgagor will not execute any Lease of all or a substantial portion of the Premises except for actual occupancy by the lessee thereunder, and will at all times promptly and faithfully perform, or cause to be performed promptly, all of the covenants, conditions and agreements contained in all Leases of the Premises, or any part thereof, now or hereafter existing, on the part of the lessor thereunder to be kept and performed and will at all times do all things necessary to compel performance by the lessee under each Lease of all obligations, covenants and agreements by such lessee to be performed thereunder. If any of such Leases provide for the giving by the lessee of an estoppel certificate with respect to the status of any such Leases, Mortgagor shall exercise its right to request such certificates within ten (10) days of any demand therefor by Mortgagee.

(c) Mortgagor shall furnish to Mortgagee, within ninety (90) days after the end of each fiscal year, a written statement containing the names of all lessees of the Improvements and Premises or any part thereof, the terms of their respective leases, the space occupied and the rentals payable thereunder.

SECTION 1.15 Unless otherwise prohibited by applicable law, each Lease of the Premises, or of any part thereof, shall provide that, in the event of the enforcement by Mortgagee of the remedies provided for by law or by this Mortgage, the lessee thereunder will, upon request of any person succeeding to the interest of Mortgagor as a result of such enforcement, automatically become the lessee of said successor in interest, without change in the terms or other provisions of such Lease; provided, however, that said successor in interest shall not be bound by (i) any payment of rent or additional rent for more than one (1) month in advance, except prepayments in the nature of security for the performance by said lessee of its obligations under said Lease, or (ii) any material amendment or modification of the Lease made without the consent of Mortgagee or such successor in interest. Reference is hereby made to Section 291-f of the Real Property Law of the State of New York, for purposes of obtaining for Mortgagee the benefit of Section 291-f in connection with this Mortgage. Each such Lease shall provide that upon request by such successor in interest, such lessee shall execute and deliver an instrument or instruments confirming such attornment.

SECTION 1.16 Mortgagor hereby agrees that if in connection with the closing of the Loan (a) any of the Loan Documents or Hedging Contracts executed by Mortgagor misstates or inaccurately reflects the true and correct terms and provisions of the Loan or the Hedging Obligations, or (b) Mortgagor failed to execute any documents or instruments that should have been executed by Mortgagor (regardless of whether said misstatement, inaccuracy or failure was due to the unilateral mistake of Mortgagee, the mutual mistake of Mortgagor and Mortgagee, or clerical error), then in such event, Mortgagor shall, within ten (10) days of Mortgagee's request, and in order to correct any such misstatement, inaccuracy or failure, execute such new Loan Documents and/or Hedging Contracts as Mortgagee or any Affiliate Counterparty or any other Affiliate of Mortgagee may deem necessary or desirable to remedy said inaccuracy, mistake or failure.

SECTION 1.17 In the event any payment provided for herein or in the Note shall become overdue for a period in excess of fifteen (15) days, a late charge of six cents ($.06) for each dollar ($1.00) so overdue shall become immediately due to Mortgagee for the purpose of defraying the expenses incidental to handling such delinquent payment, and such charge shall be deemed to be part of the Indebtedness and secured by the lien of this Mortgage. Late charges shall be payable with the next installment of principal and/or interest due under the Note.

SECTION 1.18 Mortgagor, in compliance with Section 13 of the Lien Law of the State, will receive the advances secured by this Mortgage, and will hold the right to receive such advances, as a trust fund to be applied first for the purpose of paying the cost of Improvements to the Premises and will apply the same first to the payment of the cost of any such Improvements to the Premises before using any part of the total of the same for any other purpose.

SECTION 1.19 Mortgagor agrees that it shall indemnify and hold Mortgagee, its Affiliate Counterparties and any other of its Affiliates and their respective successors and assigns harmless against any loss or liability, cost or expense, including without limitation, any judgments, reasonable attorneys' fees, costs of appeal bonds and printing costs, arising out of or relating to any proceedings instituted by any claimant alleging priority over the lien of this Mortgage by any claimant alleging a violation by Mortgagor or Mortgagee of any section of Article 3-A of the Lien Law of the State of New York.

SECTION 1.20 Mortgagor shall execute and deliver to the appropriate governmental authority any affidavit, instrument, document and/or filing required pursuant to any applicable statute, ordinance, rule and/or regulation in connection with the Premises, the Note, other Loan Documents and any Hedging Contracts and/or the business and affairs of Mortgagor.

SECTION 1.21 Mortgagor expressly covenants and agrees to pay in full the reasonable fees and expenses of Mortgagee's counsel, promptly upon the receipt of a statement therefor, which are incurred prior to and after the date hereof and which fees and expenses arise in connection with any matter incidental to the loan that is evidenced by the Note and secured by this Mortgage and those fees and expenses that are incurred after the date hereof which fees and expenses arise in connection with the enforcement of any document executed in connection with the loan.

SECTION 1.22 (a) Mortgagor represents and warrants that, except as set forth in that certain Phase I Environmental Assessment, dated June Year 14, prepared by Environmental Control Consultants, to the best of Mortgagor's knowledge, after due inquiry and investigation, the Premises are not now and have never been used to generate, manufacture, refine, transport, treat, store, handle, dispose, transfer, produce, process or in any manner deal with, except in accordance with applicable laws, Hazardous Materials (as hereinafter defined), and that no Hazardous Materials have ever been installed, placed, or in any manner dealt with on the Premises, and that no owner of the Premises or any tenant, subtenant, occupant, prior tenant, prior subtenant or prior occupant has received any notice or advice from any governmental agency or any tenant, subtenant or occupant with regard to Hazardous Materials on, from or affecting the Premises. Mortgagor covenants that the Premises shall be kept free of Hazardous Materials, and shall not be used to generate, manufacture, refine, transport, treat, store, handle, dispose, transfer, produce, process or in any manner deal with, Hazardous Materials, and Mortgagor shall not cause or permit, as a result of any intentional or unintentional act or omission on the part of Mortgagor or any tenant or subtenant or occupant, the installation of Hazardous Materials at the Premises or onto any other property or affecting any "natural resources" (as such term is defined in CERCLA (as hereafter defined)) or suffer the presence of Hazardous Materials on the Premises. Mortgagor agrees to comply with and ensure compliance by all tenants, subtenants and occupants with all applicable Federal, state and local laws, ordinances, rules and regulations with respect to Hazardous Materials (collectively, "Environmental Laws"), and shall keep the Premises and the other Mortgaged Property free and clear of any liens or assessments imposed pursuant to such Environmental Laws. Mortgagor shall conduct and complete all investigations, studies, sampling, and testing, and all remedial, removal, and other actions necessary to clean up and remove all Hazardous Materials on, from or affecting the Mortgaged Property or any part thereof in accordance with all applicable

Environmental Laws and to the satisfaction of Mortgagee. For these purposes, **"Hazardous Materials"** shall include, without limitation, any flammable explosives, radioactive materials, hazardous wastes, hazardous or toxic substances, or related or similar materials, asbestos or any material containing asbestos, or any other substance or material as defined by any Federal, state or local Environmental Law including, without limitation, the Comprehensive Environmental Response, Compensation, and Liability Act of 1980, 42 U.S.C. Sections 9601, et seq., as amended, including, without limitation, the Superfund Amendments and Reauthorization Act of 1986 **("CERCLA"),** the Hazardous Materials Transportation Act, as amended, 49 U.S.C. Section 1801, et seq., the Resource Conservation and Recovery Act, as amended, 42 U.S.C. Sections 6901, et seq., and in the regulations adopted and publications promulgated pursuant thereto. These obligations and liabilities of Mortgagor shall survive any foreclosure involving the Mortgaged Property or the delivery of a deed in lieu of foreclosure.

(b) Mortgagor shall protect, indemnify and save harmless Mortgagee, its Affiliate Counterparties and its other Affiliates and their respective successors and assigns from and against all liabilities, obligations, claims, assessments, damages, penalties, causes of action, costs and expenses (including without limitation reasonable attorneys' fees and expenses), imposed upon or incurred by or asserted against Mortgagee, its Affiliate Counterparties or any other of its Affiliates or their respective successors and assigns by reason of (i) the presence, disposal, escape, seepage, leakage, spillage, discharge, emission, release, or threatened release of any Hazardous Materials in, on, above, under, from or affecting the Premises or any other property or natural resources; (ii) any personal injury (including wrongful death) or property damage (real or personal) arising out of or related to such Hazardous Materials; (iii) any lawsuit brought or threatened, settlement reached, or government order relating to such Hazardous Materials; or (iv) any violation of laws, orders, regulations, requirements, or demands of government authorities, or any policies or requirements of Mortgagee which are based upon or in any way related to such Hazardous Materials including, without limitation, attorneys' or consultants' fees, investigation and laboratory fees, court costs, litigation expenses, and diminution in value, and (v) any violation of any Environmental Laws.

(c) Mortgagor shall, to the extent it has notice or knowledge, give prompt written notice to Mortgagee of: (i) any proceeding or inquiry by any governmental authority with respect to the presence of any Hazardous Materials on the Mortgaged Property or the migration thereof from or to other property; (ii) all claims made or threatened by any party against Mortgagor or the Mortgaged Property relating to any loss or injury resulting from any Hazardous Materials; (iii) the storage, production, release, discharge or disposal of any Hazardous Materials at the Premises other than in accordance with all applicable Environmental Laws; and/or (iv) Mortgagor's discovery of any occurrence or condition that could cause the Mortgaged Property or any part thereof to be subject to any restrictions on the ownership, occupancy, transferability or use of the Mortgaged Property under any Environmental Law.

(d) Mortgagor shall promptly provide to Mortgagee copies of all written notices or other communications received by Mortgagor from any governmental agency, tenant, subtenant or occupant with respect to Hazardous Materials at, in, on, under or otherwise affecting the Mortgaged Property or any part thereof, including without limitation, any notices or other communication relating to any actual or threatened inquiry, investigation, claim, proceeding or action concerning Hazardous Materials or other environmental conditions affecting the Premises.

(e) Mortgagor shall keep Mortgagee apprised of the status of any governmental inquiry or investigation relating to environmental matters at the Premises, any enforcement, clean-up, removal, remediation or other governmental proceedings or actions threatened, instituted or completed or pursuant to any Environmental Laws with respect to the Mortgaged Property or any part thereof, as well as any other claims, actions or proceedings with respect to the Premises relating to environmental matters. Mortgagor shall not enter into any settlement, agreement, consent decree, deed notice or other arrangement or compromise with respect to any governmental inquiry, investigation, proceeding or action, or other claim, action or proceeding relating to Hazardous Materials and/or the clean-up or remediation of the Premises without Mortgagee's prior written consent. Mortgagee may, but shall not be required to, participate in any inquiry, investigation, or proceeding or action with respect to the Premises in connection with any Environmental Law or Hazardous Materials, and Mortgagor shall pay all attorneys' fees and disbursements incurred by Mortgagee in connection therewith.

SECTION 1.23 Mortgagor has not and shall not:

(a) engage in any business activity other than the ownership, operation and maintenance of the Premises, and those business activities in which Mortgagor is currently engaged, and activities incidental thereto;

(b) acquire or own any material assets other than (i) the Premises, and (ii) such incidental Chattels and Intangibles as may be necessary for the operation of the Premises and those business activities in which Mortgagor is currently engaged;

(c) merge into or consolidate with any person or entity or dissolve, terminate or liquidate in whole or in part, transfer or otherwise dispose of all or substantially all of its assets or change its legal structure;

(d) fail to preserve its existence as an entity duly organized, validly existing and in good standing (if applicable) under the laws of the jurisdiction of its organization or formation, or without the prior written consent of Mortgagee, amend, modify, terminate or fail to comply with the provisions of Mortgagor's Operating Agreement, Articles or Certificate of Incorporation or Formation and By-Laws, or certificate of partnership or limited partnership, partnership or trust agreement or any other similar or analogous organizational documents of Mortgagor, as the case may be, as same may be further amended or supplemented, if such amendment, modification, termination or failure to comply would adversely affect the ability of Mortgagor to perform its obligations hereunder or under the Note and/or other Loan Documents.

(e) own any subsidiary or make any investment in, any person or entity without the consent of Mortgagee;

(f) commingle its assets with the assets of any of its members, stockholders, directors, officers, partners, trustees, Affiliates, principals or of any other person or entity;

(g) incur any debt, secured or unsecured, direct or contingent, including guaranteeing any obligation, other than Mortgagor's obligations under the Note, the other Loan Documents or any Hedging Contract in respect of the Indebtedness, except in the ordinary course of its business, provided that such debt is paid when due and is not a debt for borrowed money or evidenced by a promissory note;

(h) become insolvent or fail to pay its debts and liabilities from its assets as the same shall become due;

(i) fail to maintain its records, books of account and bank accounts separate and apart from those of the members, stockholders, directors, officers, partners, trustees, principals and affiliates of Mortgagor, the Affiliates of any member, stockholder, director, officer or partner of Mortgagor, and any other person or entity;

(j) enter into any contract or agreement with any member, stockholder, director, officer, general partner, trustee, principal or Affiliate of Mortgagor, except upon terms and conditions that are intrinsically fair and substantially similar to those that would be available on an arms-length basis with third parties other than any member, shareholder, director, officer, partner, trustee, principal or Affiliate of Mortgagor;

(k) seek the dissolution or winding up in whole, or in part, of Mortgagor;

(l) maintain its assets in such a manner that it will be costly or difficult to segregate, ascertain or identify its individual assets from those of any member, stockholder, director, officer, partner, trustee, principal or Affiliate of Mortgagor, or of any member, stockholder, director, officer, partner, trustee, principal or Affiliate thereof or of any other person or entity;

(m) hold itself out to be responsible for the debts of another person or

(n) make any loans or advances to any third party, including any member, stockholder, director, officer, partner, trustee, principal or Affiliate of Mortgagor, or to any member, stockholder, director, officer, partner, trustee, principal or Affiliate thereof or of any other person or entity;

(o) fail to file its own tax returns;

(p) fail either to hold itself out to the public as a legal entity separate and distinct from any other entity or person or to conduct its business solely in its own name in order not (i) to mislead others as to the identity with which such other party is transacting business, or (ii) to suggest that Mortgagor is responsible for the debts of any third party (including any member, stockholder, director, officer, partner, trustee, principal or Affiliate thereof);

(q) fail to maintain adequate capital for the normal obligations reasonably foreseeable in a business of its size and character and in light of its contemplated business operations; or

(r) file or consent to the filing of any petition, either voluntary or involuntary, to take advantage of any applicable insolvency, bankruptcy, liquidation or reorganization statute, or make an assignment for the benefit of creditors.

SECTION 1.24 Mortgagor agrees as follows:

(a) Mortgagor agrees that the Premises shall at all times comply to the extent applicable with the requirements of the Americans with Disabilities Act of 1990, as amended from time to time, the Fair Housing Amendments Act of 1988, as amended from time to time, all state and local laws and ordinances related to handicapped access and all rules, regulations, and orders issued pursuant thereto including, without limitation, the Americans with Disabilities Act Accessibility Guidelines for Buildings and Facilities, as amended from time to time (collectively, **"Access Laws").**

(b) Notwithstanding any provisions set forth herein or in any other documents regarding Mortgagee's approval or alterations of the Premises, Mortgagor shall not alter the Premises in any manner that would increase Mortgagor's responsibilities for compliance with the applicable Access Laws without the prior written approval of Mortgagee. The foregoing shall apply to tenant improvements constructed by Mortgagor or by any of its tenants. Mortgagee may condition any such approval upon receipt of a certificate of Access Laws compliance from an architect, engineer, or other person reasonably acceptable to Mortgagee.

(c) Mortgagor agrees to give prompt notice to Mortgagee of the receipt by Mortgagor of any complaints related to violations of any Access Laws and of commencement of any proceedings or investigations related to compliance with applicable Access Laws.

SECTION 1.25 Mortgagor acknowledges that Mortgagee has relied upon as the sole Members and Managers of Mortgagor and their experience in owning, managing, and/or operating properties similar to the Premises in connection with the closing of the Loan. Accordingly, except as expressly hereafter provided, Mortgagor shall not sell, convey, dispose of, alienate, hypothecate, lease (except to space tenants in accordance with the provisions of Section 1.14 hereof), assign, pledge, mortgage, encumber or otherwise transfer (each a **"Transfer"** and, collectively, **"Transfers")** the Premises, or any part thereof or interest therein, in any manner or way, whether voluntarily or involuntarily, and any such Transfer shall constitute an Event of Default hereunder giving Mortgagee the right, at its sole option, to declare any or all of the Indebtedness secured hereby immediately due and payable and to otherwise exercise any of its other rights and remedies contained in Article II hereof; and if such acceleration occurs during any period when a prepayment fee is payable pursuant to the provisions set forth in the Note, then, in addition, such prepayment fee shall then be immediately due and payable to the same extent as though Mortgagor were prepaying the entire Indebtedness secured hereby on the date of such acceleration. For the purposes of this Section 1.25, each of the following events shall be deemed to be a Transfer by Mortgagor: (i) if Mortgagor shall enter into any installment sales agreement pursuant to which Mortgagor agrees to sell the Premises, or any part thereof or any interest therein; (ii) if Mortgagor shall lease or sublease all or a substantial part of the Premises to any person or entity for other than actual occupancy by such person or entity; (iii) if Mortgagor, or any of its direct or indirect members, shareholders, general or limited partners, or other beneficial or equity owners (and including, without limitation, the beneficiary of any trust that may hold a direct or indirect ownership interest in Mortgagor) (all such direct or indirect members, shareholders, general or limited partners or other beneficial or equity owners, individually, a **"Mortgagor Equity Owner"** and, collectively, **"Mortgagor Equity Owners"),** shall be an entity, the Transfer, either voluntarily or involuntarily, of any of the ownership interest of Mortgagor; (iv) any other Transfer of any direct or indirect ownership interest in Mortgagor; (v) the occurrence of any transaction pursuant to which any person or entity is granted an option to purchase all or any part of the Premises, or any direct, indirect or beneficial ownership interest in Mortgagor, or (vi) any transaction, agreement or arrangement occurs or is entered into pursuant to which any person or entity is given any right to control, direct or veto any material actions or decisions by Mortgagor, directly or indirectly, whether through an equity ownership interest, contract right or otherwise. Notwithstanding the foregoing, however, any involuntary Transfer of any direct or indirect equity interest in Mortgagor caused by the death, incompetency or dissolution of (x) any shareholder, member, or general or limited partner, (y) the beneficiary of a trust having an equity interest in Mortgagor, or (z) any other equity owner of Mortgagor, shall not be a default under this Mortgage or result in an Event of Default hereunder so long as Mortgagor shall be reconstituted, if required for the continued valid existence of Mortgagor following any such death, incompetency or dissolution, and so long as those persons responsible for the management of the Mortgagor on the date hereof remain unchanged after such death, incompetency or dissolution, or any substitute or replacement management of the Mortgagor following any such death, incompetency or dissolution shall be approved by Mortgagee, in its sole discretion. Notwithstanding the foregoing, so long as the individual Guarantors maintain complete management and control of Mortgagor, transfers of ownership interest in the Mortgagor by, to and among, the direct and indirect members of the Mortgagor (for purposes herein, the "Members"), to immediate family members of Members, as applicable, to entities controlled by the Members or the immediate family members of Members, to trust established for the benefit of the Members or the immediate family members of Members, shall be permitted, so long as such transfers do not exceed an aggregate of 49% of the ownership interests in the Mortgagor; provided, however, that in the event any such Transfer results in an individual or entity obtaining more than a ten (10%) percent interest in Mortgagor, then such individual or entity must execute and deliver to Lender a certain Guaranty of Payment and ADA and Environmental Indemnity Agreement in form and substance executed by the Guarantors simultaneously with the date of this Mortgage. In no event shall the addition of any individual or entity as a guarantor hereunder affect or impair the existing Guaranty of Payment and ADA and Environmental Indemnity Agreement executed simultaneously with the date of this Mortgage and, at the written request of Mortgagee, the Guarantors shall reaffirm the effectiveness of same by a written agreement in form and substance satisfactory to Mortgagee. No such sale, conveyance, transfer or other vesting shall change the direct or indirect control or management of Mortgagor. Copies of any and all documents evidencing any such sale, conveyance, transfer or other vesting must be provided to Mortgagee within thirty (30) days after the occurrence of said action including, without limitation, a statement detailing the action and a listing of reallocations and percentages of ownership interest in Mortgagor. As used herein, "immediate family members" shall mean a spouse, a parent, a grandparent, a sibling, a child or a grandchild, of a Member, as applicable. For purposes hereof, an indirect member is a member who owns his, her or its membership entity through an entity that is a direct member of Mortgagor.

SECTION 1.26 Mortgagor shall maintain a loan to value ratio of 70% which means that the outstanding principal balance due, together with all unpaid interest which shall have accrued thereon, shall not exceed 70% of the fair market value of the Premises at the time of any such determination. Fair market value shall be determined by Mortgagee from time to time by reference to acceptable guides and indices and/or appraisals or such other means as Mortgagee, in its discretion, deems appropriate. In the event that Mortgagee shall at any time determine that the loan to value ratio is greater than 70%, Mortgagor shall within ten (10) days of notice and demand by Mortgagee, either reduce the loan amount or pledge such additional collateral as may be acceptable to Mortgagee in order to maintain the required loan to value ratio. Mortgagor's failure to either reduce the loan balance as necessary or satisfy Mortgagee's demand for additional collateral acceptable to it within ten (10) days of notice having been given by Mortgagee as required by Section 3.02, shall be considered a default hereunder.

SECTION 1.27 During the term of the Loan and so long as any part of the Indebtedness is outstanding, Mortgagor shall maintain its primary banking relationship with Mortgagee, including, but not limited to, the maintenance with Mortgagee of all operating accounts of Mortgagor, as well as all tenant security, escrow, contract deposits and other accounts with respect to the Improvements.

SECTION 1.28 So long as any Indebtedness shall remain outstanding, Mortgagor, on a combined and combining basis with all entity Guarantors, shall maintain a debt service coverage ratio of not less than 1.20:1.0 for each fiscal year. As used herein, debt service coverage ratio shall mean the ratio of Mortgagor's EBITDA, minus taxes paid in cash and Distributions to Interest Expense plus CMLTD (and shall not include any gains or losses from the sale of assets outside the normal course of business or any other extraordinary accounting adjustments or non-recurring items of income or loss except as determined by Mortgagee). The debt service coverage ratio shall be tested annually commencing as of December 31, 2015.

SECTION 1.29 If at any time Mortgagee shall deem it necessary to obtain a current appraisal of the Premises, Mortgagee may, at Mortgagor's sole cost and expense, engage the services of an appraiser to provide a current appraisal of the

Premises and Mortgagor shall timely pay to such appraiser all fees and expenses charged for such appraisal or if Mortgagee shall have paid for such appraisal, Mortgagor shall reimburse Mortgagee for same within ten (10) days of demand.

SECTION 1.30 Mortgagor represents, warrants, and covenants as follows:

(a) Neither Mortgagor, nor Mortgagor's principals, constituents, investors or Affiliates is in violation of any legal requirements relating to terrorism or money laundering, including Executive Order No. 13224 on Terrorist Financing (effective September 24, 2001, (the **"Executive Order")** and the Uniting and Strengthening America by Providing Appropriate Tools Required to Intercept and Obstruct Terrorism Act of 2001 (Public Law 107-56, the **"Patriot Act").**

(b) Neither Mortgagor, nor Mortgagor's principals, constituents, investors or Affiliates is a **"Prohibited Person"** which is defined as follows:

(i) a person or entity that is listed in the annex to, or is otherwise subject to the provisions of, the Executive Order;

(ii) a person or entity owned or controlled by, or acting for or on behalf of, any person or entity that is listed in the annex to, or is otherwise subject to the provisions of, the Executive Order;

(iii) a person or entity with whom Mortgagor is prohibited from dealing or otherwise engaging in any transaction by any terrorism or money laundering legal requirements, including the Executive Order and the Patriot Act;

(iv) a person or entity who commits, threatens or conspires to commit or supports "terrorism" as defined in the Executive Order;

(v) a person or entity that is named as a "specially designated national and blocked person" on the most current list published by the U.S. Treasury Department Office of Foreign Assets Control; or

(vi) a person or entity who is affiliated with a person or entity listed above.

(c) Neither Mortgagor, nor Mortgagor's principals, constituents, investors or Affiliates will (i) conduct any business or engage in any transaction or dealing with any Prohibited Person, including the making or receiving of any contribution of funds, goods or services to or for the benefit of any Prohibited Person, (ii) deal in, or otherwise engage in any transaction relating to, any property or interests in property blocked pursuant to the Executive Order; or (iii) engage in or conspire to engage in any transaction that evades or avoids, or has the purposes of evading or avoiding, or attempts to violate, any of the prohibitions set forth in the Executive Order or the Patriot Act.

(d) Mortgagee is subject to the requirements of the Patriot Act and hereby notifies the Mortgagor that pursuant to the requirements of the Patriot Act, it is required to obtain, verify and record information that identifies the Mortgagor, which information includes the name and address of the Mortgagor and other information that will allow Mortgagee to identify the Mortgagor in accordance with the Patriot Act.

SECTION 1.31 The parties hereto agree that all sums that may or shall become due and payable by the Mortgagor to the Mortgagee (or any Affiliate Counterparty or other Affiliate of Mortgagee) in accordance with any Hedging Contract, whether or not such Hedging Contract is directly between the Mortgagor and the

Mortgagee or between the Mortgagor and Mortgagee's Affiliate Counterparty or any other Affiliate, or any of their respective Affiliates, assignors or assignees, shall be secured by this Mortgage as Additional Interest only and shall constitute part of the Indebtedness. The lien of this Mortgage insofar as it secures payment of sums that may or shall become due and payable by the Mortgagor to the Mortgagee (or any Affiliate Counterparty or other of Mortgagee's Affiliates) in accordance with Hedging Contracts is and shall continue to be equal in priority to the lien of this Mortgage insofar as it secures payment of the principal balance of any other Indebtedness. The parties hereto agree that, if the Note shall be declared to be immediately due and payable as the result of an occurrence of an Event of Default or if the Note is not paid in full at maturity, then all sums that become available to the Mortgagee as a result of the foreclosure of this Mortgage shall be applied as provided in Section 2.02 herein.

(End of Article I)

## ARTICLE II.

### Events of Default and Remedies

SECTION 2.01 Each of the following shall constitute an Event of Default:

(a) if (i) Mortgagor shall default in making any payment of any principal, interest or other amount due under any Indebtedness when and as the same shall become due and payable, or (ii) Mortgagor shall default in timely making any payment of any tax required by Section 1.08 hereof to be paid; or

(b) if Mortgagor shall default in the due observance or performance of any covenant, term or agreement on the part of Mortgagor contained in Section 1.01, 1.03, 1.07, 1.09 or 1.26 hereof and such default shall have continued for a period of fifteen (15) days after written notice has been given to Mortgagor by Mortgagee specifying such default; or

(c) if any representation or warranty of Mortgagor made in Section 1.01 or in any Hedging Contract shall now or hereafter be false; or

(d) if Mortgagor shall default in the due observance or performance of any other covenant or condition on the part of Mortgagor in the Note, or in this Mortgage, or any other documents evidencing any Indebtedness and Mortgagor shall fail to remedy such default within a commercially reasonable time, not to exceed twenty (20) days, after notice by Mortgagee to Mortgagor of such default; provided, however, that if any such default cannot be cured within such twenty (20) day period, Mortgagor shall be afforded up to an additional forty-five (45) days to cure such default so long as such time to cure does not require an extension of the Maturity Date of the Note and provided Mortgagor shall have commenced such cure within such initial twenty (20) day period and shall thereafter diligently continue to cure such default; or

(e) if by the order of a court of competent jurisdiction, a trustee, receiver or liquidator of the Mortgaged Property, or any part thereof, or of Mortgagor shall be appointed and such order shall not be discharged or dismissed within forty-five (45) days after such appointment; or

(f) if Mortgagor shall: (i) commence a voluntary case under any applicable bankruptcy, insolvency or other similar law now or hereafter in effect, (ii) consent to the entry of an order for relief in an involuntary case under any such law or to the appointment of or taking possession by a receiver, liquidator, assignee, trustee, custodian, sequestrator (or other similar official) of Mortgagor or of any substantial part of its property, (iii) make any general assignment for the benefit of creditors, (iv) fail generally to pay its debts as such debts become due, or (v) take any action in furtherance of any of the foregoing; or

(g) if any of the creditors of Mortgagor shall commence against Mortgagor an involuntary case under any applicable bankruptcy, insolvency or other similar law now or hereafter in effect and if such case shall not be discharged or dismissed within sixty (60) days after the date on which such case was commenced, or

(h) if final judgment for the payment of money in excess of $25,000.00 shall be rendered against Mortgagor and Mortgagor shall not discharge the same or cause it to be discharged within forty-five (45) days from the entry thereof, or shall not appeal therefrom or from the order, decree or process upon which or pursuant to which said judgment was granted, based or entered, and secure a stay of execution pending such appeal; or

(i) any of the events enumerated in clauses (e) through (h) of this Section 2.01 shall happen to any Guarantor or any of their property, provided that with respect to the events enumerated in clauses (e) through (h) of this Section 2.01 happening to Guarantor's property, such an event shall constitute an Event of Default only **if,** individually or in the aggregate, it (they) has a material adverse affect on the financial condition of such Guarantor; or

(j) if any Transfer prohibited by Section 1.25 hereof shall occur; or

(k) if a default by Mortgagor shall occur under any mortgage or deed of trust that is prior or subordinate to the lien of this Mortgage, or the mortgagee under any prior or subordinate mortgage or the trustee under any prior or subordinate deed of trust commences a foreclosure action in connection with said mortgage or deed of trust; it being further agreed by Mortgagor that an Event of Default hereunder shall constitute an Event of Default under any such other mortgage or deed of trust held by Mortgagee; or

(I) if any Guarantor or principal of any Guarantor dies, defaults under or attempts to withdraw, cancel or disclaim liability under any guaranty issued to Mortgagee, provided, however that in the event of a death of any individual Guarantor, Mortgagor shall have sixty (60) days following such death to designate a replacement Guarantor acceptable to Mortgagee and execute any documentation required by Mortgagee in connection with such replacement before such death constitutes an Event of Default; or

(m) if Mortgagor or any Guarantor terminates, revokes or attempts to terminate, or revoke any guaranty of indebtedness, or defaults under any other agreement with Mortgagee or any Affiliate Counterparty or other Affiliate of Mortgagee; or

(n) if it shall be illegal for Mortgagor to pay any tax referred to in Section 1.08 hereof or if the payment of such tax by Mortgagor would result in the violation of the usury laws of the State; or

(o) if any person or entity having or claiming an interest in Mortgagor or the Mortgaged Property, or any part thereof, commences an action or proceeding against Mortgagor, the Mortgaged Property, or any part thereof, or any person or entity having or claiming an interest in Mortgagor or the Mortgaged Property, or any part thereof; or

(p) Mortgagor breaches or violates the terms of, or if a default (and expiration of any applicable cure period), or an "Event of Default" or "Termination Event", occurs under, any Hedging Contract or any other existing or future agreement (related or unrelated) between Mortgagor and Mortgagee and/or any Affiliate Counterparty or other Affiliate of Mortgagee; or

(q) the existence or occurrence at any time of one or more conditions or events, which, in the sole opinion of Mortgagee, has resulted, or is reasonably likely to result in a material adverse change in the assets or financial condition of Mortgagor.

Upon the occurrence of an Event of Default:

I. <u>Acceleration of the Indebtedness.</u> During the continuance of any such Event of Default, Mortgagee, by written notice given to Mortgagor, may declare the entire principal of the Note then outstanding (if not then due and payable), and all accrued and unpaid interest thereon, together with all other Indebtedness, to be due and payable immediately, notwithstanding anything to the contrary herein or in the Note or the other Loan Documents or any Hedging Contract;

II. <u>Possession of the Mortgaged Property.</u> During the continuance of any such Event of Default, with or without the appointment of a receiver, or an application therefor, Mortgagee personally, or by its agents or attorneys, may enter into and upon all or any part of the Premises, and each and every part thereof, and may exclude Mortgagor, its agents and servants wholly therefrom; and having and holding the same, may use, operate, manage and control the Premises and conduct the business thereof, either personally or by its superintendents, managers, agents, servants, attorneys or receivers; and upon every such entry, Mortgagee, at the expense of the Mortgagor, from time to time, either by purchase, repairs or construction, may maintain and restore the Mortgaged Property, whereof it shall become possessed as aforesaid, may complete the construction of any of the Improvements and in the course of such completion may make such changes in the contemplated Improvements as it may deem desirable and may insure the same; and likewise, from time to time, at the expense of Mortgagor, Mortgagee may procure title reports, title insurance, surveys, appraisals and such other reports as Mortgagee, in its sole discretion, shall deem necessary, and make all necessary or proper repairs, renewals and such useful alterations, additions, betterments and improvements thereto and thereon as to it may deem advisable; and in every such case

Mortgagee shall have the right to manage and operate the Premises and to carry on the business thereof and exercise all rights and powers of Mortgagor with respect thereto either in the name of Mortgagor or otherwise as it shall deem best; and Mortgagee shall be entitled to collect and receive all earnings, revenues, rents, issues, profits and income of the Premises and every part thereof, all of which shall for all purposes constitute property of Mortgagor; and in furtherance of such right Mortgagee may collect the Rents payable under all Leases of the Premises directly from the lessees thereunder upon notice to each such lessee that an Event of Default exists hereunder accompanied by a demand on such lessee for the payment to Mortgagee of all Rents due and to become due under its Lease, and Mortgagor, for the benefit of Mortgagee and each such lessee hereby covenants and agrees that the lessee shall be under no duty to question the accuracy of Mortgagee's statement of default and shall unequivocally be authorized to pay said Rents to Mortgagee without regard to the truth of Mortgagee's statement of default and notwithstanding notices from Mortgagor disputing the existence of an Event of Default such that the payment of Rent by the lessee to Mortgagee pursuant to such a demand shall constitute performance in full of the lessee's obligation under the Lease for the payment of Rents by the lessee to Mortgagor; and after deducting the expenses of conducting the business thereof and of all maintenance, repairs, renewals, replacements, alterations, additions, betterments and improvements and amounts necessary to pay for taxes, assessments, insurance and prior or other proper charges upon the Mortgaged Property, or any part thereof, as well as just and reasonable compensation for the services of Mortgagee and for all attorneys, counsel, agents, clerks, servants and other employees by it properly engaged and employed, Mortgagee shall apply the moneys arising as aforesaid, <u>first</u> to the payment of accrued interest under the Note, <u>second</u> to the payment of the principal of the Note, when and as the same shall become payable, and <u>finally</u> to the payment of any other Indebtedness and sums required to be paid by Mortgagor under this Mortgage, the other Loan Documents or any Hedging Contract.

III. <u>Foreclosure, Etc.</u> Mortgagee, with or without entry, personally or by its agents or attorneys, insofar as applicable, may:

(1) sell (and in the case of any default by any purchaser, resell) the Mortgaged Property, or any part thereof, to the extent permitted and pursuant to the procedures provided by law, and all estate, right, title and interest, claim and demand therein, and right of redemption thereof, at one or more sales as an entirety or in parcels, and at such time and place upon such terms and after such notice thereof as may be determined by Mortgagee or as required or permitted by law; or

(2) institute proceedings for the complete or partial foreclosure of this Mortgage; or

(3) take such steps to protect and enforce its rights whether by action, suit or proceeding in equity or at law for the specific performance of any covenant, condition or agreement in the Note, this Mortgage, the other

Loan Documents or any Hedging Contract, or in aid of the execution of any power herein granted, or for any foreclosure hereunder, or for the enforcement of any other appropriate legal or equitable remedy or otherwise as Mortgagee shall elect.

IV. Power of Sale. To the extent a non-judicial sale is permitted under the laws of the State, Mortgagor hereby unconditionally and irrevocably gives, grants, sets over and confirms unto the Mortgagee the Power of Sale, which may be unconditionally exercised at any time or times after an Event of Default and in connection therewith, Mortgagor hereby (a) consents to any one or more adjournments of the sale date which Mortgagee may grant, consent to and/or schedule, whether or not Mortgagor is notified of such adjournment and (b) waives any and all objections Mortgagor may have to the date of sale, the place of sale, the terms of sale, and any other matter selected by Mortgagee. The sale by Mortgagee of less than the whole of the Mortgaged Property shall not exhaust the right to sell any remainder of the Mortgaged Property, and Mortgagee is specifically empowered to make a successive sale or sales until the whole of the Mortgaged Property shall be sold. If the proceeds of the sale of less than the whole of the Mortgaged Property is less than the aggregate of the Indebtedness and other obligations secured hereby and payable under subsection

(d) of Section 2.02, then this Mortgage and the lien hereof shall remain in full force and effect as to the unsold portion of the Mortgaged Property just as though no sale had been made.

V. Assent to Decree. Mortgagor hereby assents to the passage of a decree for the sale of the Mortgaged Property, or any part thereof, by any court having jurisdiction, without notice to Mortgagor (except as expressly required by applicable law).

VI. Appointment of Receiver. After the happening of any Event of Default and during its continuance, or upon the commencement of any proceedings to foreclose this Mortgage or to enforce the specific performance hereof or in aid thereof or upon the commencement of any other judicial proceeding to enforce any right of Mortgagee, Mortgagee shall be entitled, as a matter of right, if it shall so elect, without the giving of notice to any other party and without regard to the adequacy or inadequacy of any security for the Indebtedness, forthwith either before or after declaring the unpaid principal of the Note to be due and payable, to the appointment of a receiver or receivers in respect of the Premises and/or other Mortgaged Property, and Mortgagor hereby consents to the appointment of such receiver or receivers.

VII. Rights of a Secured Party. Mortgagee shall also have such other rights and/or remedies provided to a mortgagee and/or a secured party by the Code.

SECTION 2.02 (a) Mortgagee may adjourn from time to time any sale by it to be made under or by virtue of this Mortgage by announcement at the time and place appointed for such sale or for such adjourned sale or sales; and, except as otherwise provided by any applicable provision of law, Mortgagee, without further notice or publication, may make such sale at the time and place to which the same shall be so adjourned.

(b) Upon the completion of any sale or sales made by Mortgagee under or by virtue of this Article II, Mortgagee, or an officer of any court empowered to do so, shall execute and deliver to the accepted purchaser or purchasers a good and sufficient instrument, or good and sufficient instruments, conveying, assigning and transferring all estate, right, title and interest in and to the property and rights sold and shall execute and deliver to the appropriate governmental authority any affidavit, instrument, document and/or filing required pursuant to any applicable statute, ordinance, rule and/or regulation, of the State. As long as the Loan and other Indebtedness secured by this Mortgage remains unpaid, Mortgagee is hereby irrevocably appointed the true and lawful attorney of Mortgagor, in its name and stead, to make all necessary conveyances, assignments, transfers and deliveries of the Mortgaged Property and rights so sold and for that purpose Mortgagee may execute all necessary instruments of conveyance, assignment and transfer, including, without limitation, any affidavit, instrument, document or filing required pursuant to any applicable statute, rule or regulation of the State as the same may be amended from time to time, and may substitute one or more persons with like power, Mortgagor hereby ratifying and confirming all that its said attorney or such substitute or substitutes shall lawfully do by virtue hereof. Nevertheless Mortgagor, if so requested by Mortgagee, shall ratify and confirm any such sale or sales by executing and delivering to Mortgagee or to such purchaser or purchasers all such instruments as may be advisable, in the reasonable judgment of Mortgagee, for that purpose, and as may be designated in such request. Any such sale or sales made under or by virtue of this Article II, whether made under or by virtue of judicial proceedings or of a judgment or decree of foreclosure and sale, shall operate to divest all the estate, right, title, interest, claim and demand whatsoever, whether at law or in equity, of Mortgagor in and to the properties and rights so sold, and shall be a perpetual bar both at law and in equity against Mortgagor and against any and all persons claiming or who may claim the same, or any part thereof, from, through or under Mortgagor.

(c) In the event of any sale made under or by virtue of this Article II (whether made under or by virtue of judicial proceedings, a judgment or decree of foreclosure or a Power of Sale), the entire principal of, and interest on, the Note, if not previously due and payable, and all other sums required to be paid by Mortgagor pursuant to this Mortgage or any Hedging Contract, immediately thereupon, shall, anything in the Note or in this Mortgage to the contrary notwithstanding, become due and payable.

(d) The purchase money proceeds or avails of any sale made under or by virtue of this Article II, together with any other sums which then may be held by Mortgagee under this Mortgage, whether under the provisions of this Article II or otherwise, shall be applied as follows:

First To the payment of the costs and expenses of such sale, including, but not limited to, the reasonable compensation to Mortgagee, its agents and counsel, and any sums that may be due under and/or pursuant to any statute, rule, regulation and/or law which imposes any tax, charge, fee and/or levy in connection with and/or arising from the exercise of any right and/or remedy under this Mortgage or the requirement that any sum be paid in order to record and/or file any deed, instrument of transfer or other such document in connection with any such sale and of any judicial proceedings wherein the same may be made, and of all expenses, liabilities and advances made or incurred by Mortgagee under this Mortgage, together with interest at the Default Rate on all advances made by Mortgagee and all taxes or assessments, except any taxes, assessments or other charges subject to which the Mortgaged Property shall have been sold.

Second: To the payment of the whole amount then due, owing or unpaid upon the Note for interest, on the unpaid principal at the Default Rate from and after the happening of any Event of Default described in Section 2.01 from the due date of any such payment of principal until the same is paid.

Third: on a pari passu basis, to the payment of the whole amount then due, owing or unpaid (x) upon the Note for principal, and (y) all Hedging Obligations owing to Mortgagee or any Affiliate Counterparty.

Fourth: To the payment of the whole amount then due, owing or unpaid upon any other note made by Mortgagor held by Mortgagee for principal and interest, with interest on the unpaid principal at the default rate set forth in such other note, if applicable, from and after the happening of any Event of Default described in Section 2.01 from the due date of any such payment of principal until the same is paid.

Fifth: To the payment of any other Indebtedness and any other sums required to be paid by Mortgagor pursuant to any provision of this Mortgage, the Note, the other Loan Documents or any Hedging Contract.

Sixth: To the payment of the surplus, if any, to Mortgagor.

(e) Upon any sale made under or by virtue of this Article II, whether made under or by virtue of judicial proceedings, a judgment or decree of foreclosure and sale, or a Power of Sale, Mortgagee may bid for and acquire the Mortgaged Property or any part thereof and in lieu of paying cash therefor may make settlement for the purchase price by crediting upon the Indebtedness of Mortgagor secured by this Mortgage the net sales price after deducting therefrom the expenses of the sale and the costs of the action and any other sums which Mortgagee is authorized to deduct under this Mortgage.

SECTION 2.03 (a) In case an Event of Default described in Section 2.01 shall have occurred and be continuing, then, upon written demand of Mortgagee, Mortgagor will pay to Mortgagee the whole amount which then shall have become due and payable on the Note, for principal or interest or both, and all amounts due under any Hedging Contract, as the case may be, and after the happening of said Event of Default will also pay to Mortgagee interest at the Default Rate on the then unpaid principal of the Note, and the sums required to be paid by Mortgagor pursuant to any provision of this Mortgage, and in addition thereto such further amount as shall be sufficient to cover the costs and expenses of collection, including reasonable compensation to Mortgagee, its agents, and counsel and any expenses incurred by Mortgagee hereunder. In the event Mortgagor shall fail forthwith to pay such amounts upon such demand, Mortgagee shall be entitled and empowered to institute such action or proceedings at law or in equity as may be advised by its counsel for the collection of the sums so due and unpaid, and may prosecute any such action or proceedings to judgment or final decree, and may enforce any such judgment or final decree against Mortgagor and collect, out of the property of Mortgagor wherever situated, as well as out of the Mortgaged Property, in any manner provided by law, moneys adjudged or decreed to be payable.

(b) Mortgagee shall be entitled to recover judgment as aforesaid either before or after or during the pendency of any proceedings for the enforcement of the provisions of this Mortgage; and the right of Mortgagee to recover such judgment shall not be affected by any entry or sale hereunder, or by the exercise of any other right, power or remedy for the enforcement of the provisions of this Mortgage, or the foreclosure of the lien hereof; and in the event of a sale of the Mortgaged Property, or any part thereof, and of the application of the proceeds of sale, as in this Mortgage provided, to the payment of the debt hereby secured, Mortgagee shall be entitled to enforce payment of, and to receive all amounts then remaining due and unpaid upon the Note, the other Loan Documents and the Hedging Contracts, and to enforce payment of all other charges, payments and costs due under this Mortgage, the other Loan Documents and the Hedging Contracts, and shall be entitled to recover judgment for any portion of the debt remaining unpaid, with interest at the Default Rate. In case of the commencement of any case against Mortgagor under any applicable bankruptcy, insolvency, or other similar law now or hereafter in effect or any proceedings for its reorganization or involving the liquidation of its assets, then Mortgagee shall be entitled to prove the whole amount of principal and interest due upon the Note to the full amount thereof, and all other payments, charges and costs due under this Mortgage along with the amount of any other Indebtedness, without deducting therefrom any proceeds obtained from the sale of the whole or any part of the Mortgaged Property, provided, however, that in no case shall Mortgagee receive a greater amount than such principal and interest and such other payments, charges and costs and other Indebtedness from the aggregate amount of the proceeds of the sale of the Mortgaged Property and the distribution from the estate of Mortgagor.

(c) No recovery of any judgment by Mortgagee and no levy of an execution under any judgment upon the Mortgaged Property or upon any other property of Mortgagor shall affect in any manner or to any extent, the lien of this Mortgage upon the Mortgaged Property, or any part thereof, of any liens, rights, powers or remedies of Mortgagee hereunder, but such liens, rights, powers and remedies of Mortgagee shall continue unimpaired as before.

(d) Any moneys thus collected by Mortgagee under this Section 2.03 shall be applied to the Indebtedness secured hereby by Mortgagee in accordance with the provisions of subsection (d) of Section 2.02.

SECTION 2.04 After the happening of any Event of Default and immediately upon the commencement of any action, suit or other legal proceedings by Mortgagee to obtain judgment for the principal of, or interest on, the Note, and/or all other Indebtedness and/or other sums required to be paid by Mortgagor pursuant to any provision of this Mortgage, or of any other nature in aid of the enforcement of the Note or of this Mortgage, Mortgagor will (a) consent to the service of process as provided in Section 3.11 hereof and enter its voluntary appearance in such action, suit or proceeding, and (b) if required by Mortgagee, consent to the appointment of a receiver or receivers of the Mortgaged Property, or any part thereof, and of all the earnings, revenues, rents, issues, profits and income thereof.

SECTION 2.05 Notwithstanding the appointment of any receiver, liquidator or trustee of Mortgagor, or of any of its property, or of the Mortgaged Property or any part thereof, Mortgagee shall be entitled to retain possession and control of all property now or hereafter held under this Mortgage.

SECTION 2.06 No remedy herein conferred upon or reserved to Mortgagee is intended to be exclusive of any other remedy or remedies, and each and every such remedy shall be cumulative, and shall be in addition to every other remedy given hereunder or now or hereafter existing at law or in equity or by statute. No delay or omission of Mortgagee to exercise any right or power accruing upon any Event of Default shall impair any such right or power, or shall be construed to be a waiver of any such Event of Default or any acquiescence therein; and every power and remedy given by this Mortgage to Mortgagee may be exercised from time to time as often as may be deemed expedient by Mortgagee. Nothing in this Mortgage shall affect the obligation of Mortgagor to pay the principal of, and interest on, the Note in the manner and at the time and place therein respectively expressed.

SECTION 2.07 Mortgagor will not at any time insist upon, or plead, or in any manner whatever claim or take any benefit or advantage of any stay or extension or moratorium law, any exemption from execution or sale of the Mortgaged Property or any part thereof, wherever enacted, now or at any time hereafter in force, which may affect the covenants and terms of performance of this Mortgage, nor claim, take or insist upon any benefit or advantage of any law now or hereafter in force providing for the valuation or appraisal of the Mortgaged Property, or any part thereof, prior to any sale or sales thereof which may be made pursuant to any provision herein, or pursuant to the decree, judgment or order of any court of competent jurisdiction; nor, after any such sale or sales, claim or exercise any right under any statute heretofore or hereafter enacted to redeem the property so sold or any part thereof and Mortgagor hereby expressly waives all benefit or advantage of any such law or laws, and covenants not to hinder, delay or impede the execution of any power herein granted or delegated to Mortgagee, but to suffer and permit the execution of every power as though no such law or laws had been made or enacted. Mortgagor, for itself and all who may claim under it, waives, to the extent that it lawfully may, all right to have the Mortgaged Property, or any part thereof, marshaled upon any foreclosure hereof.

SECTION 2.08 During the continuance of any Event of Default, and pending the exercise by Mortgagee of its right to exclude Mortgagor from all or any part of the Premises, Mortgagor agrees to pay the fair and reasonable rental value for the use and occupancy of the Mortgaged Property, or any part thereof that is in its possession for such period, and upon default of any such payment, will vacate and surrender possession of the Mortgaged Property, or any part thereof, to Mortgagee or to a receiver, if any, and in default thereof may be evicted by any summary action or proceeding for the recovery of possession of the Premises for non payment of rent, however designated.

(End of Article II)

## ARTICLE III.

### Miscellaneous

SECTION 3.01 In the event any one or more of the provisions contained in this Mortgage or in the Note shall for any reason be held to be invalid, illegal or unenforceable in any respect, such invalidity, illegality or unenforceability shall, at the option of Mortgagee, not affect any other provision of this Mortgage, but this Mortgage shall be construed as if such invalid, illegal or unenforceable provision had never been contained herein or therein.

SECTION 3.02 All notices hereunder shall be in writing and shall be deemed to have been sufficiently given or served for all purposes three (3) days after being sent by registered or certified mail, return receipt requested, or one (1) day after being sent by nationally recognized night courier, in the case of Mortgagee, at its address above, and in the case of Mortgagor at its address above stated or at such other address of which any party shall have notified any other party giving such notice in writing as aforesaid.

SECTION 3.03 All covenants hereof shall be construed as affording to Mortgagee rights additional to and not exclusive of the rights conferred under the provisions of Sections 254 and 273 of the Real Property Law of the State of New York, or any other applicable law.

SECTION 3.04 All of the grants, terms, conditions, provisions and covenants of this Mortgage shall run with the land, shall be binding upon Mortgagor and shall inure to the benefit of Mortgagee, for itself and as agent for any Affiliate Counterparty or other Affiliate holding any Indebtedness, subsequent holders of this Mortgage and their respective successors and assigns. For the purpose of this Mortgage, the term "Mortgagor" shall include and refer to the mortgagor named herein, any subsequent owner of the Mortgaged Property, or any part thereof, and their respective heirs, executors, legal representatives, successors and assigns. If there is more than one Mortgagor, all their undertakings hereunder shall be deemed joint and several.

SECTION 3.05 The enforcement of this Mortgage shall be governed, construed and interpreted by the laws of the State (without giving effect to New York' s principles of conflicts of law). Nothing in this Mortgage, the Note or in any other Loan Documents between Mortgagor and Mortgagee shall require Mortgagor to pay, or Mortgagee to accept, interest in an amount which would subject Mortgagee to any penalty or forfeiture under applicable law. In the event that the payment of any charges, fees or other sums due hereunder or under the Note or any other Loan Documents, which are or could be held to be in the nature of interest and which would subject Mortgagee to any penalty or forfeiture under applicable law, then, ipso facto, the obligations of Mortgagor to make such payment shall be reduced to the highest rate authorized under applicable law. Should Mortgagee receive any payment which is or would be in excess of the highest rate authorized under law, such payment shall have been, and shall be deemed to have been, made in error, and shall automatically be applied to reduce the outstanding principal balance of the Indebtedness.

SECTION 3.06

(a) This Mortgage and all of the terms, covenants, provisions, conditions and grants contained in this Mortgage cannot be altered, amended, waived, modified or discharged orally, and no executory agreement shall be effective to modify, waive or discharge, in whole or in part, anything contained in this Mortgage unless it is in writing and signed by the party against whom enforcement of the modification, alteration, amendment, waiver or discharge is sought.

(b) Any amendment, waiver or consent with respect to this Mortgage that (i) amends or modifies this Section 3.06, (ii) except to the extent that Mortgagee is similarly adversely impacted, modifies any other provision of this Mortgage in a manner that adversely impacts the rights of an Affiliate Counterparty: (x) with respect to the priority hereunder of any security for any Hedging Obligations (including, without limitation, the definitions of Affiliate Counterparty, Indebtedness, Hedging Contract and Hedging Obligations and the provisions of Section 2.02(d) hereof), or (y) as an indemnitee hereunder; or (iii) imposes any additional obligations on an Affiliate Counterparty in each case under this Section 3.06(b) shall, in addition to the consent of the Mortgagee, require the consent of any Affiliate Counterparty.

SECTION 3.07 Mortgagor acknowledges that it has received a true copy of this Mortgage.

SECTION 3.08 Time is of the essence as to each of Mortgagor's obligations under this Mortgage.

SECTION 3.09 The information set forth on the cover hereof is hereby incorporated herein.

SECTION 3.10 The Mortgaged Property includes, and shall be deemed to include, inter alia, the Chattels and the Intangibles, regardless of whether they are held or hereafter acquired, by Mortgagor in, to and under the Mortgaged Property. By executing and delivering this Mortgage, Mortgagor has granted, in the same manner and with the same effect described in the Granting Clause hereof, to Mortgagee, for itself and as agent for any Affiliate Counterparty or other Affiliate holding any Indebtedness, as additional security, a security interest in the Chattels and the Intangibles which are subject to the Code. If any Event of Default shall occur, Mortgagee shall have, in addition to any and all other rights and remedies set forth in this Mortgage, and may exercise without demand, any and all rights and remedies granted to a secured party under the Code, including, but not limited to, the right to take possession of the Chattels and the Intangibles, or any part thereof, and the right to advertise and sell the Chattels and the Intangibles, or any part thereof, pursuant to and in accordance with the power of sale provided for in this Mortgage. Mortgagor agrees that any notice of sale or other action intended by Mortgagee with respect to the Chattels and the Intangibles, or any part thereof, shall constitute reasonable notice if it is sent to Mortgagor not less than ten (10) days prior to any such sale or intended action. The proceeds of any such sale of the Chattels and the Intangibles, or any part thereof, shall be applied to the Indebtedness in the manner set forth in Section 2.02 (d) of this Mortgage.

SECTION 3.11 Mortgagor hereby irrevocably submits to the nonexclusive jurisdiction of any New York state or federal court sitting in the Counties of Kings or New York over any suit, action or proceeding arising out of or relating to this Mortgage and any other Loan Documents, and any such legal actions shall be initiated by any methods of service of process provided for under applicable law.

SECTION 3.12 This Mortgage does not cover real property principally improved or to be improved by one or more structures containing in the aggregate not more than six (6) residential dwelling units, each having their own separate cooking facilities.

SECTION 3.13 Mortgagor and Mortgagee shall upon a mutual agreement to do so execute such documents as may be necessary in order to effectuate the modification of this Mortgage, including the execution of substitute mortgages, so as to create two or more coordinate liens on the Mortgaged Property or a portion thereof in such amounts as may be mutually agreed upon but in no event to exceed, in the aggregate, the Mortgage Amount. Mortgagor shall pay all costs in connection with said modification, including, but not limited to, title examination costs, title insurance premiums, charges, and any mortgage recording taxes. Nothing contained herein shall require Mortgagee to execute said documents if the property encumbered by said coordinate mortgages shall be less than the property mortgaged hereby.

SECTION 3.14 MORTGAGOR, AND BY ITS ACCEPTANCE HEREOF, MORTGAGEE, EACH HEREBY AGREES NOT TO ELECT A TRIAL BY JURY OF ANY ISSUE TRIABLE OF RIGHT BY JURY, AND WAIVE ANY RIGHT TO TRIAL BY JURY FULLY TO THE EXTENT THAT ANY SUCH RIGHT SHALL NOW OR HEREAFTER EXIST WITH REGARD TO THE MORTGAGE, OR ANY CLAIM, COUNTERCLAIM OR OTHER ACTION ARISING IN CONNECTION THEREWITH. THIS WAIVER OF RIGHT TO TRIAL BY JURY IS GIVEN KNOWINGLY AND VOLUNTARILY BY MORTGAGOR AND MORTGAGEE, AND IS INTENDED TO ENCOMPASS INDIVIDUALLY EACH INSTANCE AND EACH ISSUE AS TO WHICH THE RIGHT TO A TRIAL BY JURY WOULD OTHERWISE ACCRUE. MORTGAGOR AND MORTGAGEE ARE EACH HEREBY AUTHORIZED TO FILE A COPY OF THIS PARAGRAPH IN ANY PROCEEDING AS CONCLUSIVE EVIDENCE OF THIS WAIVER.

SECTION 3.15 MORTGAGOR HEREBY EXPRESSLY AND UNCONDITIONALLY WAIVES, IN CONNECTION WITH ANY SUIT, ACTION OR PROCEEDING BROUGHT BY OR ON BEHALF OF MORTGAGEE ON THIS MORTGAGE, ANY AND EVERY RIGHT MORTGAGOR MAY HAVE TO (I) INJUNCTIVE RELIEF, (II) INTERPOSE ANY COUNTERCLAIM THEREIN (OTHER THAN COMPULSORY COUNTERCLAIMS), AND (III) HAVE THE SAME CONSOLIDATED WITH ANY OTHER OR SEPARATE SUIT, ACTION OR PROCEEDING. NOTHING HEREIN CONTAINED SHALL PREVENT OR PROHIBIT MORTGAGOR FROM INSTITUTING OR

MAINTAINING A SEPARATE ACTION AGAINST MORTGAGEE WITH RESPECT TO ANY ASSERTED CLAIM.

SECTION 3.16 Mortgagee, in its sole discretion, shall have the right to announce and publicize relevant information with respect to the financing secured by this Mortgage, as it deems appropriate or desirable, by means and media selected by the Mortgagee, including, but not limited to, newspapers, magazines, trade publications and the like. Such publicity may, at Mortgagee's discretion, include all pertinent information relating to the Note, the Mortgage and the Premises including, without limitation, the term, purpose, interest rate, Mortgage Amount, name of Mortgagor and Mortgagee, location of the Premises and the nature of any Improvements. The form and content of the published information shall be in the sole discretion of Mortgagee. All expenses related to such publicity shall be the sole responsibility of Mortgagee.

SECTION 3.17 Mortgagor hereby indemnifies Mortgagee and any Affiliate Counterparty and any other of its Affiliates (including their respective agents and representatives) and holds Mortgagee and any Affiliate Counterparty and any other of its Affiliates (including their respective agents and representatives) harmless from and against any and all Claims and Expenses directly or indirectly arising out of or resulting from any transaction, act, omission, event or circumstance in any way connected with the Loan, other Indebtedness, the Mortgaged Property, the Loan Documents or any Hedging Contract, including, without limitation, any Claim arising out of or resulting from any assertion or allegation that Mortgagee, or any Affiliate Counterparty or any other of its Affiliates is liable for any act or omission of Mortgagor or any other Person in connection with the ownership, development, financing, operation or sale of the Mortgaged Property, or any part thereof; provided, however, that Mortgagor shall not be obligated to indemnify Mortgagee or any Affiliate Counterparty or any other Affiliate of Mortgagee with respect to any Claim that is determined by a final non-appealable order or judgment as arising solely from the gross negligence or willful misconduct of Mortgagee, any Affiliate Counterparty or any other of its Affiliates, or any of their respective agents or representatives. The agreements and indemnifications contained in this Section shall apply to Claims arising both before and after the repayment of the Loan and other Indebtedness and shall survive the repayment of the Loan and any other Indebtedness, any foreclosure or deed in lieu thereof and any other action by Mortgagee, any Affiliate Counterparty or any other of its Affiliates to enforce the rights and remedies of Mortgagee, such Affiliate Counterparty or such other Affiliate hereunder or under the other Loan Documents or under any Hedging Contract.

SECTION 3.18 This Mortgage may be executed in any number of counterparts, and each of such counterparts shall for all purposes be deemed to be an original and all such counterparts shall together constitute but one and the same mortgage.

SECTION 3.19 Mortgagor and Mortgagee acknowledge and agree that an Affiliate Counterparty or other Affiliate of Mortgagee is or may be providing a Hedging Contract as an accommodation to Mortgagor; accordingly, it is intended by the parties that all Hedging Obligations with any Affiliate Counterparty or other Affiliate of Mortgagee shall be secured by this Mortgage and Mortgagee, as agent for such Affiliate Counterparty or other Affiliate, shall collect and pay over to such Affiliate Counterparty or other Affiliate amounts received from Mortgagor and/or the collateral to satisfy the Hedging Obligations in the manner and order set forth in this Mortgage and the other Loan Documents. The parties acknowledge that Mortgagee has the right to acquire a participation or other interest in the Hedging Obligations to facilitate the collateralization of the same.

**IN WITNESS WHEREOF,** this Mortgage has been duly executed by Mortgagor as of the day and year first above written.

MORTGAGOR:

11 DUFFIELD LLC

By: Darwin Lee
Name: Darwin Lee
Title: Manager of Manage Great Realty LLC, Manager of 11 Duffield LLC

# 11 DUFFIELD GUARANTY OF PAYMENT

**THIS GUARANTY OF PAYMENT** (this "**Guaranty**") is made as of the 1st day of January, Year 14, by Manage Great Realty LLC, a New York limited liability company and Debby Day, an individual (jointly and severally, and with any of their successors and assigns, each a "**Guarantor**"), in favor of NATIONAL BANK, N.A., a national banking association, having an office at 1 Broad Street, New York, New York 10038 (the "**Lender**") and the CRB Bank, a Canadian charterd bank ("**Hedging Counterparty**" and together with the Lender, the "**Beneficiaries**").

## RECITALS:

**WHEREAS,** contemporaneously herewith, Lender is making a loan to 11 DUFFILED LLC, a Delaware limited liability company (with its successors and assigns, "**Borrower**") in the principal amount of twelve million one hundred seventy five thousand Dollars ($12,175,000.00) (the "**Loan**"), which Loan is evidenced by that certain Mortgage Loan Note, dated of even date herewith, made by Borrower, as maker, in favor of Lender, as payee (together with all extensions, renewals, modifications, substitutions and amendments thereof, the "**Note**");

**WHEREAS,** the Loan and related obligations are secured by, among other things, that certain Mortgage and Security Agreement (together with all extensions, renewals, modifications, substitutions and amendments thereof, the "**Mortgage**"), dated as of even date herewith, made by Borrower in favor of Lender and granting Lender, for itself and as agent for Hedging Counter art a first priority lien on that certain real property known as 11 Duffield and as more particularly described on Schedule A to the Mortgage (the "**Premises**"), together with the buildings and other improvements located thereon (the "**Improvements**"); and together with the Premises, collectively, the "**Property**");

**WHEREAS,** Lender requires as a condition to the making of the Loan that each Guarantor shall have executed and delivered this Guaranty for the benefit of Lender;

**WHEREAS,** Borrower may from time to time enter into the Hedging Contracts (as hereafter defined) with Hedging Counterparty; and

**WHEREAS,** Hedging Counterparty requires as a condition to the entry into the Hedging Contracts that each Guarantor shall have executed and delivered this Guaranty for the benefit of the Hedging Counterparty.

**NOW, THEREFORE,** in consideration of the premises and other good and valuable consideration, the receipt of which is hereby acknowledged, and in order to induce Lender to make the Loan to Borrower and to induce the Hedging Counterparty to enter into the Hedging Contracts with Borrower, each Guarantor hereby represents, warrants and covenants to the Beneficiaries as follows:

1. <u>Authorization and Enforceability of Loan Documents.</u> The Note, the Mortgage, any indemnification agreement relating to compliance with ADA and any Environmental Law (each, as hereafter defined) (a "**Property**

**Indemnity Agreement"**) and all of the other documents executed and delivered by Borrower in connection with the Loan (collectively, the **"Loan Documents"**) and all agreements and other documents executed and delivered by Borrower in connection with any Hedging Obligations (as defined in the Mortgage) (the **"Hedging Contracts"**) have been duly authorized and executed by Borrower and are legal, valid and binding instruments, enforceable against Borrower in accordance with their respective terms, subject to the effect of bankruptcy, insolvency, reorganization, moratorium or other legal or equitable principles now or hereafter in effect generally affecting creditors' rights and remedies.

2. <u>Obligations Guaranteed.</u> Each Guarantor jointly and severally with all Guarantors, the Borrower and each Other Guarantor (as hereafter defined) unconditionally guarantees to the Beneficiaries all of the following (collectively, the **"Guaranteed Obligations"**):

(a) the prompt and unconditional payment of three million dollars ($3,000,000) of the Loan and the interest thereon, whether now or hereafter advanced, as the same shall become due and payable under the Note, whether at stated maturity, by acceleration or otherwise, and any and all sums of money that, at the time, may have become due and payable under the provisions of the Note, the Mortgage or any other Loan Document, as well as, without limitation, all other loans, advances, indebtedness, notes, and liabilities;

(b) all obligations under any rate swap, basis swap, forward rate transactions, commodity swaps, commodity options, equity or equity index swaps, equity or equity index options, bond options, interest rate options, foreign exchange transactions, cap transactions, floor transactions, collar transactions, forward transactions, currency swap transactions, cross-currency rate swap transactions, currency options between Borrower and Hedging Counterparty, other than Excluded Hedging Obligations (the **"Hedging Obligations")**; for purposes hereof **"Excluded Hedging Obligations"** means any Hedging Obligation if, and to the extent that, all or a portion of the guarantee by such Guarantor of, or the grant by such Guarantor of a security interest to secure, such Hedging Obligation (or any guarantee thereof) is or becomes impermissible under the Commodity Exchange Act (as hereafter defined) by virtue of such Guarantor's failure for any reason to constitute an "eligible contract participant" as defined in the Commodity Exchange Act at the time this Guaranty becomes effective with respect to such Hedging Obligation;

(c) all other amounts, in each case, liquidated or unliquidated, owing by the Borrower to the Beneficiaries (or either of them) any time, of each and every kind, nature and description, whether arising under the Mortgage, any other Loan Document, the Hedging Contracts or otherwise, and whether secured or unsecured, direct or indirect (that is, whether the same are due directly by the Borrower to either Beneficiary; or are due indirectly by the Borrower to either Beneficiary as endorser, guarantor or other surety, or as borrower of obligations due third persons which have been endorsed or assigned to either Beneficiary, or otherwise), absolute or contingent, due or to become due, now existing or hereafter arising or contracted, including, without limitation, payment when due of all amounts outstanding respecting any of the Loan Documents or the Hedging Contracts and the due and prompt performance of all of the terms, agreements, covenants and conditions of the Note, the Mortgage, the other Loan Documents and the Hedging Contracts, but, in any event, with respect to the Hedging Counterparty, excluding any Excluded Hedging Obligation; and

(d) any and all expenses that may be paid or incurred by either Beneficiary in the collection of all or any portion of such Guarantor's obligations hereunder or the exercise or enforcement of any one or more of the other rights, powers, privileges, remedies and interests of the Beneficiaries under the Loan Documents, or the Hedging Contracts, including, without limitation, reasonable attorneys' fees, irrespective of the manner or success of any such collection, exercise or enforcement, and whether or not such expenses constitute part of the Borrower's obligations but, in any event, with respect to the Hedging Counterparty, excluding any Excluded Hedging Obligation.

3. Unconditional Guaranty. This Guaranty is an absolute, unconditional, present and continuing guaranty of payment and performance and not of collection and is in no way conditioned or contingent upon any attempt to enforce any of either Beneficiary's rights against Borrower or to collect from the Borrower or upon any other condition or contingency. Beneficiaries shall have the right to proceed against any Guarantor immediately upon (a) any "Event of Default" under any Loan Document, and (b) any "Event of Default," termination event or similar event under the Hedging Contracts, in each case, without taking any prior action or proceeding to enforce any of the Loan Documents, the Hedging Contracts or any of them, or for the liquidation or foreclosure of any security Beneficiaries at any time hold pursuant thereto. Each Guarantor hereby waives and releases any claim (within the meaning of 11 U.S.C. §101) which such Guarantor may have against Borrower arising from a payment made by such Guarantor under this Guaranty and, except as set forth in Section 8 hereof, agrees not to assert or take advantage of any subrogation rights of such Guarantor or any right of such Guarantor to proceed against Borrower, another Guarantor or any Other Guarantor for reimbursement. It is expressly understood that the waivers and agreements of each Guarantor constitute additional and cumulative benefits given to Beneficiaries for their security and as an inducement for their respective extension of credit to Borrower. Each Beneficiary may at any time and from time to time take any and/or all actions and enforce all rights and remedies available to it hereunder or under applicable law to collect from any Guarantor any amounts then due and payable hereunder by any Guarantor and/or to cause any Guarantor to fulfill his, her or its obligations hereunder. Notwithstanding anything to the contrary in this Guaranty, the Note, any of the Loan Documents or the Hedging Contracts, neither of the Beneficiaries shall be deemed to have waived any right which either of them

may have under Section 506(a), 506(b), 1111(b) or any other provisions of the Bankruptcy Code to file a claim for the full amount of the Indebtedness or to require that all collateral shall. continue to secure all of the Indebtedness owing to either Beneficiary in accordance with the Loan Documents and the Hedging Contracts, as the case may be.

4. Liability Unimpaired. No Guarantor's liability hereunder shall in any way be limited or impaired by, and each Guarantor hereby consents to and agrees to be bound by, any amendment or modification of the provisions of any of the Loan Documents, the Hedging Contracts or any other instrument or agreement made to or with any Beneficiary by Borrower or any Guarantor, or any Person who succeeds Borrower as owner of all or part of the Property prior to foreclosure of the Mortgage or exercise of any power of sale contained therein. In addition, no Guarantor's liability hereunder shall in any way be limited or impaired by (i) any extensions of time for performance required by any of said documents, (ii) any sale, assignment or foreclosure of the Note or Mortgage or any sale or transfer of all or part of the property covered by the Mortgage, (iii) any exculpatory provision in any of said documents limiting either Beneficiary's recourse to the Property or to any other security, or limiting either Beneficiary's rights to a deficiency judgment against Borrower, (iv) the release of Borrower, any Guarantor, any Other Guarantor or any other Person from performance or observance of any of the agreements, covenants, terms or conditions contained in any of said documents for any reason, including by the applicable Beneficiary's election, by operation of law (including, but not limited to the Commodity Exchange Act) or otherwise, (v) the release or substitution in whole or in part of any security for the Loan or Hedging Obligations, (vi) either Beneficiary's failure to record the Mortgage or file any UCC financing statements (or the improper recording or filing of any thereof) or to otherwise perfect, protect, secure or insure any security interest or lien given as security for the Loan or Hedging Obligations, (vii) the invalidity, irregularity or unenforceability, in whole or in part, of any of the Loan Documents, the Hedging Contracts, this Guaranty or any other instrument or agreement executed or delivered to either Beneficiary in connection with the Loan or the Hedging Contracts, except to the extent that there is a final adjudication by a court of competent jurisdiction of a valid defense to Borrower's obligations under the Loan Documents or the Hedging Contracts to payment of the Indebtedness, (viii) the inaccuracy of any of the representations and warranties made by Borrower in the Mortgage, the other Loan Documents or Hedging Contracts, or (ix) any other action or circumstance whatsoever that constitutes, or might be construed to constitute, a legal or equitable discharge or defense (except full payment and satisfaction) of Borrower for its obligations under any of the Loan Documents or the Hedging Contracts or of any Guarantor under this Guaranty; and, in any such case, whether with or without notice to any Guarantor and with or without consideration.

5. Defined Terms. As used herein, the following terms shall have the meanings ascribed thereto below:

(a) **"ADA"** shall mean the Americans with Disabilities Act of 1990, as amended and supplemented from time to time.

(b) **"Affiliate"** shall mean with respect to any Person, (a) any Person which, directly or indirectly through one or more intermediaries controls, or is controlled by, or is under common control with such Person, or (b) any Person who is a director or officer (i) of such Person, (ii) of any Subsidiary of such Person, or (iii) any person described in clause (a) above. For purposes of this definition, control of a Person means the power, direct or indirect, (x) to vote 5% or more of the ownership interests having ordinary voting power for the election of directors (or comparable equivalent) of such Person, or (y) to direct or cause the direction of the management and policies of such Person whether by contract or otherwise; control may be by ownership, contract, or otherwise.

(c) **"Commodity Exchange Act"** shall mean the Commodity Exchange Act (7 U.S.C. §1 et seq.), as amended or supplemented from time to time, and any successor statute or any other rule, regulation or order of the Commodity Futures Trading Commission (or the application or official interpretation of any thereof).

(d) **"Enforcement Costs"** shall mean any and all expenses that may be paid or incurred by either Beneficiary in the collection of all or any portion of any Guarantor's obligations hereunder or the exercise or enforcement of any one or more of the other rights, powers, privileges, remedies and interests of the Beneficiaries under the Loan Documents, the Hedging Contracts or under this Guaranty, including, without limitation, reasonable attorneys' fees, irrespective of the manner or success of any such collection, exercise or enforcement, and whether or not such expenses constitute part of the Borrower's obligations.

(e) **"Environmental Law"** shall mean any present and future federal, state and local laws, statutes, ordinances, rules, regulations and the like, as well as common law, relating to the safety, welfare and protection of human health or the environment or any natural resource, relating to any Hazardous Materials (as defined in the Mortgage), relating to liability for or costs of other actual or threatened danger to the safety, welfare or human health or the environment or any natural resource and includes, but is not limited to, the following statutes, as amended, any successor thereto, and any regulations promulgated pursuant thereto, and any state or local statutes, ordinances, rules, regulations and the like addressing similar issues: the Comprehensive Environmental Response, Compensation and Liability Act of 1980, as amended (as amended, including, without limitation, the Superfund Amendments and Reauthorization Act of 1986, **"CERCLA"),** 42 U.S.C. §9601 et seq.; the Emergency Planning and Community Right-to-Know Act of 1986; the Hazardous Substances Transportation Act; the Resource Conservation and Recovery Act (including but not limited to Subtitle I relating to underground storage tanks); the Solid Waste Disposal Act; the Clean Water Act; the Clean Air Act; the Toxic Substances Control

Act; the Safe Drinking Water Act; the Occupational Safety and Health Act; the Federal Water Pollution Control Act; the Federal Insecticide, Fungicide and Rodenticide Act; the Endangered Species Act; the National Environmental Policy Act; and the River and Harbors Appropriation Act. The term **"Environmental Law"** also includes, but is not limited to, any present and future federal, state and local laws, statutes ordinances, rules, regulations and the like, as well as common law conditioning transfer of property upon a negative declaration or other approval of a governmental authority of the environmental condition of the Property; requiring notification or disclosure of releases of Hazardous Materials or other environmental condition of the Property to any governmental authority or other Person, whether or not in connection with transfer of title to or interest in property; imposing conditions or requirements in connection with permits or other authorization for lawful activity; relating to nuisance, trespass or other causes of action related to the Property; and relating to wrongful death, personal injury, or property or other damage in connection with any physical condition or use of the Property.

(f) **"Other Guarantor"** shall mean any Person executing a guaranty (other than this Guaranty) in favor of either Beneficiary.

(g) **"Person"** shall mean any individual, corporation, partnership, limited liability company, joint venture, estate, trust, unincorporated association, any other entity, any federal, state, county or municipal government or any bureau, department or agency thereof, and any fiduciary acting in such capacity on behalf of any of the foregoing.

(h) **"State"** shall mean the State of New York.

6. Preservation of Loan Documents and Hedging Contracts. Each Guarantor will cause Borrower to maintain and preserve the enforceability of the Loan Documents and Hedging Contracts as the same may be modified and will not permit Borrower to take or to fail to take actions of any kind which might be the basis for a claim that such Guarantor has a defense to such Guarantor's obligations hereunder.

7. Security; Guarantor's Events of Default.

(a) As security for any and all of the obligations of each Guarantor under this Guaranty, now existing or hereafter arising hereunder or otherwise, each Guarantor hereby grants to the Lender for itself and as agent for the Hedging Counterparty a lien upon and a security interest in any and all moneys or other property (i.e., goods and merchandise, as well as any and all documents relative thereto; funds, securities, choses in action and any and all other forms of property whether real, personal or mixed, and any right, title or interest of the Guarantor therein or thereto), and the proceeds thereof, which have been, or may hereafter be, deposited or delivered to the Lender (or with any third party acting on either Beneficiary's behalf) by or for the account or credit of such Guarantor whether for safekeeping, custody, pledge, deposit, transmission, collection or otherwise. All remittances and property shall be deemed delivered to the Lender as soon as put in transit to the Lender by mail or carrier.

(b) Upon the occurrence of any of the following events with respect to any Guarantor (each a **"Guarantor's Event of Default"**): (i) such Guarantor defaults under this Guaranty or any other agreement with either Beneficiary to which such Guarantor is a party; (ii) any representation or warranty made by such Guarantor herein or in any other agreement with either Beneficiary to which such Guarantor is a party is false or untrue as of the date such representation or warranty is made; (iii) such Guarantor commences any case, proceeding, or other action under any law of any jurisdiction relating to bankruptcy, insolvency, reorganization, or relief of debtors or seeks to have an order for relief entered with respect to such Guarantor or seeks to be adjudicated a bankrupt or insolvent, or seeks reorganization, arrangement, adjustment, liquidation, dissolution, composition or other relief with respect to such Guarantor or such Guarantor's debts, or seeks the appointment of a receiver, trustee, custodian, or other similar official for such Guarantor or for all or any substantial part of such Guarantor's property; (iv) such Guarantor makes a general assignment for the benefit of creditors; (v) there is commenced against such Guarantor, any case, proceeding or other action of the type referred to in clause (iii) above or seeking the issuance of a warrant of attachment, execution, distraint, or similar process against all or any substantial part of such Guarantor's property, which case, proceeding or other action results in an entry of an order for relief or is not dismissed, discharged or bonded within fifteen (15) days of the commencement thereof; (vi) such Guarantor takes any action indicating such Guarantor's consent to, approval of, or acquiescence in or in furtherance of, any of the acts set forth in clauses (iii) and (v) above; (vii) the death or incapacity of such Guarantor, if an individual; (viii) such Guarantor admits in writing such Guarantor's inability to pay such Guarantor's debts as they mature; (ix) such Guarantor terminates or dissolves or suspends such Guarantor's usual business activities or conveys, sells, leases, transfers or otherwise disposes of all or a substantial part of such Guarantor's property, business or assets other than in the ordinary course of business; or (x) the existence or occurrence at any time of one or more conditions or events that, in the sole opinion of either Beneficiary, has resulted or is reasonably likely to result in a material adverse change in the business, properties or financial condition of such Guarantor; then, in any such case, and irrespective of whether there is any "Event of Default" under any Loan Document or the Hedging Contracts, any or all of the obligations of such Guarantor shall, at the applicable Beneficiary's option become (for the purpose of this Guaranty) immediately due and payable by such Guarantor, without demand or notice. In addition, upon the occurrence of any Guarantor's Event of Default, the Beneficiaries shall have all of the rights and remedies provided to a secured party by the Uniform Commercial Code as in effect in the State at that time. Each Guarantor agrees that, in the event that notice is necessary, written notice mailed to such Guarantor at the address given below five (5) days prior to the date of public sale of the property subject to the lien and security interest created herein or prior to the date after which private sale or any other disposition of said property will be made shall constitute reasonable notice, but notice given in any other reasonable manner or at any other reasonable time shall be sufficient.

8. Indemnification; Payments; Certain Waivers. Each Guarantor (i) waives any right or claim of right to cause a marshalling of Borrower's assets or to cause either Beneficiary to proceed against any of the security for the Indebtedness, including, without limitation, the Loan, the Hedging Obligations or the other obligations guaranteed hereby before proceeding against such Guarantor, (ii) agrees that any payments required to be made by such Guarantor hereunder shall become due on demand in accordance with the terms of Section 2 (and if applicable Section 3) hereof and without presentment to Borrower or such Guarantor, demand for payment or protest, or notice of non-payment or protest, and (iii) except as hereinafter provided, expressly waives and relinquishes all rights and remedies accorded by applicable law to guarantors. Without limiting the generality of the foregoing, each Guarantor hereby waives all rights (x) to participate in any claim or remedy either Beneficiary may now or hereafter have against Borrower or in any collateral which any Beneficiary, now has or hereafter may acquire for the obligations guaranteed hereby and (y) except as provided below, to contribution, indemnification, set-off, exoneration or reimbursement, whether from Borrower, another Guarantor, any Other Guarantor, or any other Person now or hereafter primarily or secondarily liable for any of Borrower's obligations to either Beneficiary, and whether arising by contract or operation of law or otherwise by reason of such Guarantor's execution, delivery or performance of this Guaranty. No Guarantor waives and each Guarantor hereby retains all rights of subrogation, contribution, indemnification, set-off or reimbursement against Borrower or another Guarantor or any Other Guarantor that such Guarantor may have (the **"Undersigned's Rights"**); provided however that (i) this Guaranty shall neither be contingent upon the existence of the Undersigned's Rights nor subject to any claims or defenses whatsoever which may be asserted in connection with the enforcement or attempted enforcement of the Undersigned's Rights including, without limitation, any claim that the Undersigned's Rights were abrogated by any acts of either Beneficiary, and (ii) until the Indebtedness and all other amounts guaranteed hereunder (including, without limitation, the Loan and Hedging Obligations) shall have been paid in full, each Guarantor hereby postpones and subordinates (A) the exercise of any and all of the Undersigned's Rights to each Beneficiary's rights against such Guarantor under this Guaranty, against Borrower under any of the Loan Documents and the Hedging Contracts, as the case may be, or any Other Guarantor and (B) any of the Undersigned's Rights to any collateral securing the Indebtedness, including, without limitation, the Loan and the Hedging Obligations.

9. Reinstatement. This Guaranty shall continue to be effective, or be reinstated automatically, as the case may be, if at any time payment, in whole or

in part, of any of the obligations guaranteed hereby is rescinded or otherwise must be restored or returned by either Beneficiary (whether as a preference, fraudulent conveyance or otherwise) upon or in connection with the insolvency, bankruptcy, dissolution, liquidation or reorganization of Borrower, another Guarantor, any Other Guarantor or any other Person, or upon or as a result of the appointment of a receiver, intervenor or conservator of, or trustee or similar officer for, Borrower, another Guarantor, any Other Guarantor or any other Person or for a substantial part of Borrower's, another Guarantor's, any Other Guarantor's or any of such other Person's property, as the case may be, or otherwise, all as though such payment had not been made. Each Guarantor further agrees that in the event any such payment is rescinded or must be restored or returned, all costs and reasonable expenses (including, without limitation, reasonable legal fees and expenses) incurred by or on behalf of either Beneficiary in defending or enforcing such continuance or reinstatement, as the case may be, shall constitute Enforcement Costs, the payment of which is guaranteed by such Guarantor pursuant to Section 2 above and covered by such Guarantor's indemnity pursuant to Section 8 above.

10. Litigation Compliance with Judgments. Each Guarantor represents and warrants with respect to itself that there are no actions, suits or proceedings pending or threatened against or affecting such Guarantor, at law, in equity or before or by any governmental authorities that would have a material effect on such Guarantor's ability to perform its obligations hereunder; to the best of such Guarantor's knowledge, such Guarantor is not in default with respect to any order, writ, injunction, decree or demand of any court or governmental authorities.

11. Authorization and Enforceability; No Conflicts. Each Guarantor represents and warrants that it has the full power and authority to enter into and perform its obligations under this Guaranty and this Guaranty is a legal, valid and binding instrument, enforceable against such Guarantor in accordance with its terms. Each Guarantor that is not an individual hereby represents and warrants that the execution, delivery and performance of this Guaranty has been authorized by all proper and necessary actions of such Guarantor. Each Guarantor represents and warrants with respect to itself that the consummation of the transactions contemplated hereby and the performance of this Guaranty has not resulted and will not result in any breach of, or constitute a default under, any mortgage, deed of trust, lease, bank loan or credit agreement, corporate charter, by-laws, partnership agreement or other instrument to which such Guarantor is a party or by which such Guarantor may be bound or affected.

12. Compliance with Laws. Each Guarantor represents and warrants with respect to itself that such Guarantor is in compliance with, and the transactions contemplated by the Loan Documents or the Hedging Contracts and this Guaranty do not and will not violate any provision of, or require any filing, registration, consent or approval under, any federal, state or local law, rule, regulation, ordinance, order, writ, judgment, injunction, decree, determination or award, including the Commodity Exchange Act, the ADA and any Environmental

Law presently in effect having applicability to such Guarantor (collectively, the **"Laws"**), and agrees that such Guarantor will comply promptly with all Laws now or hereafter in effect having applicability to such Guarantor.

13. Accuracy of Information; Full Disclosure. Each Guarantor represents and warrants with respect to itself that neither this Guaranty nor any documents, financial statements, reports, notices, schedules, certificates, statements or other writings furnished by or on behalf of such Guarantor to either Beneficiary in connection with the negotiation of this Guaranty, the Loan Documents or the Hedging Contracts or the consummation of the transactions contemplated thereby, or required herein or by the other Loan Documents or the Hedging Contracts to be furnished by or on behalf of such Guarantor, contains any untrue or misleading statement of a material fact; there is no fact which such Guarantor has not disclosed to the Beneficiaries in writing which materially affects adversely any of the property covered by the Mortgage or the business affairs or financial condition of such Guarantor, or the ability of such Guarantor to perform this Guaranty.

14. Financial Statements. Each Guarantor represents, warrants and covenants with respect to itself as follows:

(a) The most recent financial statements heretofore delivered by such Guarantor, if any, to either Beneficiary are true and correct in all respects, have been prepared in accordance with sound accounting principles consistently applied and fairly present such Guarantor's financial condition as of the date thereof, and no material adverse change has occurred in the financial condition reflected therein since the date thereof.

(b) If such Guarantor is other than an individual, such Guarantor shall deliver to the Beneficiaries:

(i) annually, as soon as available, but in any event within two hundred seventy (270) days after the last day of each calendar year, copies of its Federal and state tax returns from the prior calendar year; and

(ii) promptly after written request by Lender therefor, company-prepared interim financial statements and gallon reports, in each case as may be acceptable to Lender from time to time.

(c) If such Guarantor is an individual,

(i) such Guarantor shall deliver to the Beneficiaries annually, as soon as available, but in any event within two hundred seventy (270) days after the last day of each calendar year, (x) the signed, personal financial statement of such Guarantor, on Lender's standard form or such other form as may be acceptable to the Lender from time to time, together with supporting documentation acceptable to Lender verifying such Guarantor's liquidity as set forth therein and (y) the Federal and state tax returns from the prior calendar year; and

(ii) promptly after written request by Lender therefor, a Schedule K-1 with respect to each entity owned by such Guarantor.

(d) Promptly after a written request therefor, such Guarantor shall deliver to the Beneficiaries such other financial data or information as either Beneficiary may reasonably request from time to time.

(e) Each Guarantor authorizes the Lender to make or have made any credit, employment or investigation inquiry that the Lender determines appropriate for the extension of credit, periodic evaluation of the Indebtedness or the collection of amounts owed to the Lender (and if applicable any Affiliate Counterparty) on the Indebtedness, or for any other legitimate purposes associated with the Indebtedness, including without limitation, obtaining one or more business or consumer credit reports. This authorization will also apply to the Lender's agents, affiliates, successors, and assigns.

15. Eligible Contract Participant Status. Each Guarantor, in its own capacity and in its capacity as guarantor for and on behalf of Borrower, represents and warrants to the Beneficiaries that, on and as of the date hereof and on each date on which a "Swap Transaction Event" (as defined in the ISDA August 2012 OF Supplement, as published on August 13, 2012) occurs between Hedging Counterparty and Borrower, it is an "eligible contract participant" within the meaning of Section 1a(18) of the Commodity Exchange Act as amended from time to time, and applicable regulations thereunder.

16. Non-Waiver Remedies Cumulative. No failure or delay on either Beneficiary's part in exercising any right, power or privilege under any of the Loan Documents, the Hedging Contracts, this Guaranty or any other document made to or with either Beneficiary in connection with the Loan or the Hedging Obligations, shall operate as a waiver of any such privilege, power or right or shall be deemed to constitute either Beneficiary's acquiescence in any default by Borrower or Guarantor under any of said documents. A waiver by either Beneficiary of any right or remedy under any of the Loan Documents, this Guaranty or the Hedging Contracts, on any one occasion shall not be construed as a bar to any right or remedy which either Beneficiary otherwise would have on any future occasion, and any such waiver by one Beneficiary shall not be deemed to be a waiver by the other Beneficiary. The rights and remedies provided in said documents are cumulative, may be exercised singly or concurrently and are not exclusive of any rights or remedies provided by law.

17. Transfers of Interests in Loan. Each Guarantor acknowledges that Lender, at Lender's sole discretion, may sell, assign or transfer interests in the Loan, this Guaranty and the other Loan Documents to one or more participants, purchasers and/or assignees (collectively, **"Participants"**) and agrees in connection therewith, all Loan Documents and other documentation, financial statements, appraisals and other data, or copies thereof, relevant to Borrower, each Guarantor, the Premises, the Improvements or the Mortgage, may be provided to and retained by any such participant, purchaser or assignee or prospective participant, purchaser or assignee. Each Guarantor agrees that Lender shall have no obligation to give any Guarantor written notice of any sale, assignment or transfer of any interest or participation in the Loan or any part thereof.

18. Separate Indemnity. Each Guarantor acknowledges and agrees that the Beneficiaries' respective rights (and such Guarantor's obligations) under this Guaranty shall be in addition to all of such Beneficiary's rights (and all of such

Guarantor's obligations) under any indemnity agreement executed and delivered to such Beneficiary by Borrower and/or such Guarantor in connection with the Loan or the Hedging Obligations, and payments by such Guarantor under this Guaranty shall not reduce any of such Guarantor's obligations and liabilities under any such indemnity agreement.

19. Severability. Any provision of this Guaranty, or the application thereof to any Person or circumstance (including any invalidation of any Guarantor's or Other Guarantor's obligations under or in connection with the Commodity Exchange Act), that, for any reason, in whole or in part, is prohibited or unenforceable in any jurisdiction shall, as to such jurisdiction, be ineffective to the extent of such prohibition or unenforceability without invalidating the remaining provisions of this Guaranty (or the remaining portions of such provision) or the application thereof to any other person or circumstance, and any such prohibition or unenforceability in any jurisdiction shall not invalidate or render unenforceable such provision (or portion thereof) or the application thereof to any person or circumstance in any other jurisdiction.

20. Entire Agreement; Amendments. This Guaranty contains the entire agreement of the parties with respect to the subject matter hereof and supersedes all prior oral or written agreements or statements relating to such subject matter, and none of the terms and provisions hereof may be waived, amended or terminated except by a written instrument signed by the Person against whom enforcement of the waiver, amendment or termination is sought.

21. Successors and Assigns. This Guaranty shall be binding upon and shall inure to the benefit of the Beneficiaries and each Guarantor and their respective heirs, personal representatives, successors and assigns. This Guaranty may be assigned by either Beneficiary with respect to all or any portion of the obligations guaranteed hereby, and when so assigned each Guarantor shall be liable under this Guaranty to the assignee(s) of the portion(s) of the obligations guaranteed hereby so assigned without in any manner affecting the liability of any Guarantor hereunder to the Beneficiaries with respect to any portion of the obligations guaranteed hereby retained by the Beneficiaries.

22. WAIVER OF TRIAL BY JURY. EACH GUARANTOR, AND BY ITS ACCEPTANCE HEREOF, LENDER AND HEDGING COUNTERPARTY, EACH HEREBY KNOWINGLY, VOLUNTARI LY AND INTENTIONALLY WAIVES THE RIGHT TO A TRIAL BY JURY TO THE EXTENT THAT ANY SUCH RIGHT SHALL NOW OR HEREAFTER EXIST IN RESPECT OF ANY LITIGATION BASED ON THIS GUARANTY, ARISING OUT OF, UNDER OR IN CONNECTION WITH THIS GUARANTY OR ANY OTHER LOAN DOCUMENTS CONTEMPLATED TO BE EXECUTED IN CONNECTION HEREWITH, OR ANY HEDGING CONTRACTS, OR ANY COURSE OF CONDUCT, COURSE OF DEALINGS, STATEMENTS (WHETHER VERBAL OR WRITTEN) OR ACTIONS OF ANY PARTY. THIS WAIVER IS INTENDED TO ENCOMPASS INDIVIDUALLY EACH INSTANCE AND EACH ISSUE AS TO WHICH THE RIGHT TO A TRIAL BY JURY WOULD OTHERWISE

ACCRUE AND CONSTITUTES A MATERIAL INDUCEMENT FOR BORROWER AND LENDER AND HEDGING COUNTERPARTY TO ENTER INTO THE TRANSACTIONS CONTEMPLATED HEREBY. LENDER AND HEDGING COUNTERPARTY ARE EACH HEREBY AUTHORIZED TO FILE A COPY OF THIS PARAGRAPH IN ANY PROCEEDING AS CONCLUSIVE EVIDENCE OF THIS WAIVER.

23. ADDITIONAL WAIVERS IN THE EVENT OF ENFORCEMENT/ CONSENT TO JURISDICTION AND VENUE. EACH GUARANTOR HEREBY EXPRESSLY AND UNCONDITIONALLY WAIVES, IN CONNECTION WITH ANY SUIT, ACTION OR PROCEEDING BROUGHT BY OR ON BEHALF OF LENDER OR HEDGING COUNTERPARTY ON THIS GUARANTY, ANY AND EVERY RIGHT SUCH GUARANTOR MAY HAVE: (I) TO OBJECT TO THE JURISDICTION OR VENUE OF ANY STATE COURT SITTING IN KINGS OR NEW YORK COUNTY OR ANY FEDERAL COURT LOCATED IN THE STATE, (II) TO INJUNCTIVE RELIEF, (III) TO INTERPOSE ANY COUNTERCLAIM THEREIN (OTHER THAN COMPULSORY COUNTERCLAIMS), AND (IV) TO HAVE THE SAME CONSOLIDATED WITH ANY OTHER OR SEPARATE SUIT, ACTION OR PROCEEDING. EACH GUARANTOR HEREBY AGREES AND CONSENTS TO, IN ADDITION TO ANY METHODS OF SERVICE OF PROCESS PROVIDED FOR UNDER APPLICABLE LAW, SERVICE OF PROCESS IN ANY SUCH SUIT BEING MADE UPON SUCH GUARANTOR BY MAIL AT THE ADDRESS SET FORTH HEREIN AND SERVICE SO MADE SHALL BE COMPLETE FIVE (5) DAYS AFTER THE SAME SHALL HAVE BEEN SO MAILED. THE FOREGOING WAIVERS ARE GIVEN KNOWINGLY AND VOLUNTARILY BY EACH GUARANTOR. LENDER AND HEDGING COUNTERPARTY ARE EACH HEREBY AUTHORIZED TO FILE A COPY OF THIS PARAGRAPH IN ANY PROCEEDING AS CONCLUSIVE EVIDENCE OF ANY OR ALL OF THE FOREGOING WAIVERS.

24. Governing Law. This Guaranty and the rights and obligations of the parties hereunder shall in all respects be governed by, and construed and enforced in accordance with, the laws of the State without regard to the State's principles of conflicts of law.

25. Section Headings. Any section headings and captions in this Guaranty are for convenience only and shall not affect the interpretation or construction hereof.

26. Liability Unaffected by Release. Any Guarantor or other Person liable upon or in respect of any obligation hereby guaranteed may be released without affecting the liability of any other Guarantor hereunder.

27. Joint and Several Obligations. If more than one Person comprises Guarantor, then each such Person's obligations and liability under this Guaranty shall be joint and several.

28. Notices. Notices shall be given in the manner provided in the Mortgage and with respect to each Guarantor at the address set forth below.

29. Principles of Construction. All references to sections, paragraphs, schedules and exhibits are to sections, schedules and exhibits in or to this Guaranty unless otherwise specified. Unless otherwise specified, the words "hereof," "herein" and "hereunder" and words of similar import when used in this Guaranty shall refer to this Guaranty as a whole and not to any particular provision of this Guaranty. The recitals to this Guaranty shall be deemed a part hereof and all exhibits and schedules attached hereto, if any, are incorporated herein by reference for all purposes. Unless otherwise specified, all meanings attributed to defined terms herein shall be equally applicable to both the singular and plural forms of the terms so defined and "including" means including without limitation. Whenever the context requires, each gender shall include all other genders.

30. Patriot Act Notice. Lender is subject to the requirements of the USA Patriot Act (Title Ill of Pub. L. 107-56) (signed into law October 26, 2001)) (the "Act") and hereby notifies the Guarantor that pursuant to the requirements of the Act, it is required to obtain, verify and record information that identifies the Guarantor, which information includes the name and address of the Guarantor and other information that will allow Lender to identify the Guarantor in accordance with the Act.

31. Counterparts. This Guaranty may be executed in any number of counterparts, each of which shall be an original and all of which shall constitute together but one and the same agreement. Any signature delivered by a party by facsimile or email transmission shall be deemed to be an original signature hereto.

**IN WITNESS WHEREOF,** each Guarantor has executed or caused this Guaranty to be duly executed and delivered by its duly authorized official as of the date first above stated.

Debby Day

Debby Day, Individually

Address of Guarantor:
13 Adams Street, Apt. 7C
Brooklyn, New York 11201

Manage Great Realty LLC

By: Darwin Lee
Name: Darwin Lee
Title: Manager

# 11 DUFFIELD ADA AND ENVIRONMENTAL INDEMNITY AGREEMENT

**ADA AND ENVIRONMENTAL INDEMNITY AGREEMENT** (this "**Agreement**") made jointly and severally as of January 1, Year 14, by 11 Duffield LLC, a Delaware limited liability company, having an office at 75 Clinton Street, Brooklyn, New York 11201 ("**Borrower**"), and Managing Great Realty, LLC, a New York limited liability company, and Debby Day, an individual (collectively, "**Obligors**"; and together with Borrower, jointly and severally, "**Indemnitor**"), in favor of NATIONAL BANK, N.A., a national banking association, having an office at 1 Broad Street, New York, New York 10038 ("**Lender**") for itself and as agent for any Affiliate Counterparty or any other Affiliate holding any Indebtedness together with Lender and their respective officers, employees and agents, each an "**Indemnitee**") and the other Indemnified Parties (as such term is defined below).

## RECITALS:

**WHEREAS,** concurrently herewith, Lender is extending credit to Borrower in the initial principal sum of $12,175,000 (the **"Loan")** and, in connection therewith, Borrower has executed and delivered to Lender that certain Mortgage Loan Note, dated of even date herewith, made by Borrower as mortgagor, in favor of Lender as mortgagee, in the original principal amount of $12,175,000 (such Mortgage Loan Note, as the same may be hereafter amended, modified, restated, renewed, replaced, supplemented or extended, being hereinafter called the **"Note"),** which Note evidences the Indebtedness of Borrower to Lender; and which is secured pursuant to that certain Mortgage and Security Agreement dated as of even date hereof (the **"Mortgage"** and together with the Note and related loan and security documents (the **"Loan Documents"**),

**WHEREAS,** to further induce Lender to make the Loan, and it is a condition of making the Loan that Borrower shall have executed and delivered this Agreement for the benefit of Lender;

**WHEREAS,** Borrower may from time to time enter into one or more Hedging Contracts with an Affiliate Counterparty;

**WHEREAS,** Affiliate Counterparty requires as a condition to the entry into any Hedging Contracts that Borrower shall have executed and delivered this Agreement for the benefit of such Affiliate Counterparty; and

**WHEREAS,** all capitalized terms used in this Agreement but not defined herein, shall have the respective meanings accorded such terms in the Mortgage.

**NOW THEREFORE,** in consideration of the making of the Loan and the entry into any Hedging Obligations, and the covenants, agreements, representations and warranties set forth in this Agreement, the parties hereto hereby agree as follows:

1. <u>Representations and Warranties.</u>

Indemnitor hereby represents and warrants to Indemnitee that, (a) to the best knowledge of Indemnitor, there are no Hazardous Substances (as defined below) or underground storage tanks at, on, or under the Property, except those that in compliance with all Environmental Laws (as defined below) and for which all required permits pursuant to any applicable Environmental Law have been issued and all such permits, if any, are in full force and effect; (b) to the best knowledge of Indemnitor, there are no past, present or threatened Releases (as defined below) of Hazardous Substances at, in, on, under, above or from the Property which have not been fully remediated in accordance with all applicable Environmental Laws; (c) to the best knowledge of Indemnitor, there is no threat of any Release of Hazardous Substances migrating to the Property; (d) to the best knowledge of Indemnitor, there is no past or present non-compliance with Environmental Laws, or with permits issued pursuant thereto, in connection with the Property which has not been fully remediated in accordance with all applicable Environmental Laws; (e) Indemnitor has no knowledge of, and has not received, any written or oral notice or other communication from any Person (including but not limited to a governmental entity) relating to Hazardous Substances or Remediation (as defined below) thereof, or possible liability of any Person pursuant to any Environmental Law, other environmental conditions in connection with the Property, assessments relating to damage to any "natural resources" (as defined in CERCLA (as hereafter defined)), or any actual or potential administrative or judicial proceedings in connection with any of the foregoing; and (f) Indemnitor has truthfully and fully provided to Indemnitee, in writing, any and all information relating to conditions at, in, on, under, above or from the Property that is known to Indemnitor and that is contained in files and records of Indemnitor, including but not limited to any reports relating to Hazardous Substances in, on, under or from the Property and/or to the environmental condition of the Property.

2. Covenants.

(a) Indemnitor covenants and agrees that: (i) all uses and operations on or of the Property, whether by Indemnitor or any other Person, shall be in compliance with all Environmental Laws and permits issued pursuant thereto; (ii) there shall be no Releases of Hazardous Substances at, in, on, under, above or from the Property; (iii) there shall be no Hazardous Substances at, in, on, under, above or emanating from the Property or affecting any natural resources, except those that are both (A) in compliance with all Environmental Laws and with permits required thereunder issued pursuant thereto and (B) fully disclosed to Indemnitee in writing; (iv) Indemnitor shall keep the Property free and clear of all liens and other encumbrances imposed pursuant to any Environmental Law, whether due to any act or omission of Indemnitor or any other Person (the **"Environmental Liens"**); (v) Indemnitor shall, at its sole cost and expense, fully and expeditiously cooperate in all activities pursuant to Paragraph 3 of this Agreement, including but not limited to providing all relevant information and making knowledgeable Persons available for interviews; (vi) Indemnitor shall, at its sole cost and expense, perform any environmental site assessment or other investigation of environmental conditions in connection with the Property, pursuant to any reasonable written request of Indemnitee (including but not limited to sampling, testing and analysis of soil, water, air, building materials, and other materials and substances whether solid, liquid or gas), and share with Indemnitee the reports and other results thereof, and Indemnitee shall be entitled to rely on such reports and other results thereof; (vii) Indemnitor shall, at its sole cost and expense, comply with all reasonable written requests of Indemnitee to (A) effectuate Remediation of any condition (including but not limited to a Release of a Hazardous Substance) at, in, on, under, above or from the Property; (B) comply with any Environmental Law; (C) comply with any directive from any governmental authority; and (D) take any other reasonable action necessary or appropriate for the safety, welfare and protection of human health or the environment (including any natural resources); (viii) Indemnitor shall not do or allow any tenant or other user of the Property to do any act that materially increases the dangers to human health or the environment (including any natural resources), poses an unreasonable risk of harm to any Person (whether on or off the Property), impairs or may impair the value of the Property, is contrary to any requirement of any insurer, constitutes a public or private nuisance, constitutes waste, or violates any covenant, condition, agreement or easement applicable to the Property; and (ix) Indemnitor shall immediately notify Indemnitee in writing of (A) any presence or Releases or threatened Releases of Hazardous Substances at, in, on, under, above, from or migrating towards the Property; (B) any non-compliance with any Environmental Laws related in any way to the Property; (C) any actual or potential Environmental Lien; (D) any required or proposed Remediation of environmental conditions relating to the Property; and (E) any written or oral notice or other communication of which any Indemnitor becomes aware from any source whatsoever (including but not limited to a governmental entity) relating in any way to Hazardous Substances or Remediation thereof, possible liability of any Person pursuant to any Environmental Law, other environmental conditions in connection with the Property, or any actual or potential administrative or judicial proceedings in connection with anything referred to in this Agreement.

(b) Indemnitor covenants and agrees that (i) the Property shall at all times comply with all requirements of the ADA, (ii) Indemnitor shall, at its sole cost and expense, comply with all reasonable written requests of Indemnitee to (A) effectuate compliance with the ADA and (B) comply with any directive from any governmental authority relating to ADA compliance and (iii) Indemnitor shall immediately notify Indemnitee in writing of (A) any non-compliance with the ADA related in any way to the Property and (B) any written or oral notice or other communication of which Indemnitor becomes aware from any source whatsoever (including but not limited to a governmental entity) relating in any way to the ADA or compliance therewith, possible liability of any Person pursuant to the ADA, or any actual or potential administrative or judicial proceedings in connection with anything referred to in this Agreement.

3. Indemnified Rights/Cooperation and Access.

(a) In the event the Indemnified Parties have a reasonable basis to believe that an environmental hazard exists at, in, on, under, above or emanating from the Property that, in the reasonable discretion of the Indemnified Parties, endangers any tenants or other occupants of the Property or their guests or the general public or any natural resources or materially and adversely affects the value of the Property, upon reasonable notice from the Indemnitee, Indemnitor shall, at Indemnitor's expense, promptly cause an engineer or consultant reasonably satisfactory to the Indemnified Parties to conduct an environmental assessment or audit (the scope of which shall be determined in the sole and absolute discretion of the Indemnified Parties exercising commercially reasonable judgment) and take any samples of soil, groundwater or other water, air, or building materials or any other invasive testing reasonably requested by Indemnitee and promptly deliver the results of any such assessment, audit, sampling or other testing; provided, however, if such results are not delivered to the Indemnified Parties within a reasonable period or if the Indemnified Parties have a reasonable basis to believe that an environmental hazard exists at, in, on, under, above or emanating from the Property that, in the reasonable judgment of the Indemnified Parties, endangers any tenant or other occupant of the Property or their guests or the general public or any natural resources or may materially and adversely affect the value of the Property, upon reasonable notice to Indemnitor, the Indemnified Parties and any other Person designated by the Indemnified Parties, including but not limited to any receiver, any representative of a governmental entity, and any environmental consultant, shall have the right, but not the obligation, to enter upon the Property at all reasonable times to assess any and all aspects of the environmental condition of the Property and its use, including but not limited to conducting any environmental assessment or audit (the scope of which shall be determined in the sole and absolute discretion of the Indemnified Parties exercising commercially reasonable judgment) and taking samples of soil, groundwater or other water, air, or building materials, and reasonably conducting other invasive testing. Indemnitor shall cooperate with and provide the Indemnified Parties and any Person designated by the Indemnified Parties with access to the Property in connection with the exercise by the Indemnified Parties of their rights under this Agreement.

(b) In the event the Indemnified Parties have a reasonable basis to believe that the Property is not in compliance with the ADA, upon reasonable notice from the Indemnitee, Indemnitor shall, at Indemnitor's expense, promptly cause an engineer or consultant reasonably satisfactory to the Indemnified Parties to conduct any ADA assessment reasonably required by Indemnitee (the scope of which shall be determined in the sole and absolute discretion of the Indemnified Parties exercising commercially reasonable judgment) and promptly deliver the results of any such assessment to the Indemnified Parties. Indemnitor shall cooperate with and provide the Indemnified Parties and any Person designated by the Indemnified Parties with access to the Property to determine if the Property is in compliance with the ADA.

4. Indemnification. Indemnitor covenants and agrees, at its sole cost and expense, to protect, defend, indemnify, release and hold Indemnified Parties harmless from and against any and all Losses (defined below) imposed upon or incurred by or asserted against any Indemnified Parties and directly or indirectly arising out of or in any way relating to any one or more of the following: (a) any presence of any Hazardous Substances at, in, on, under, above or emanating from the Property or affecting any natural resources; (b) any past, present or threatened Release of Hazardous Substances at, in, on, under, above or emanating from the Property or affecting any natural resource; (c) any activity by Indemnitor, any Person affiliated with Indemnitor, and any tenant or other user of the Property in connection with any actual, proposed or threatened use, treatment, storage, holding, existence, disposition or other Release, generation, production, manufacturing, processing, refining, control, management, abatement, removal, handling, transfer or transportation to or from the Property of any Hazardous Substances at any time located at, in, on, under, or above the Property; (d) any activity by Indemnitor, any Person affiliated with Indemnitor, and any tenant or other user of the Property in connection with any actual or proposed Remediation of any Hazardous Substances at any time located at, in, on, under, or above the Property, whether or not such Remediation is voluntary or pursuant to court or administrative order, including but not limited to any removal, remedial or corrective action; (e) any past, present or threatened non-compliance or violations of any Environmental Laws (or permits issued pursuant to any Environmental Law) in connection with the Property or operations thereon, including but not limited to any failure by Indemnitor, any Person affiliated with Indemnitor, and any tenant or other user of the Property to comply with any order of any governmental authority in connection with any Environmental Laws; (f) the imposition, recording or filing or the threatened imposition, recording or filing of any Environmental Lien encumbering the Property; (g) any administrative processes or proceedings or judicial proceedings in any way connected with any matter addressed in this Agreement; (h) any past, present or threatened injury to, destruction of or loss of natural resources in any way connected with the Property, including but not limited to costs to investigate and assess such injury, destruction or loss; (i) any acts of Indemnitor, any Person affiliated with Indemnitor, and any tenant or other user of the Property in arranging for disposal or treatment, or arranging with a transporter for transport for disposal or treatment, of Hazardous Substances at any facility or incineration vessel containing such or similar Hazardous Substances; U) any acts of Indemnitor, any Person affiliated with any Indemnitor, and any tenant or other user of the Property in accepting any Hazardous Substances for transport to disposal or treatment facilities, incineration vessels or sites from which there is a Release, or a threatened Release of any Hazardous Substance which

causes the incurrence of costs for Remediation; (k) any personal injury, wrongful death, or property or other damage arising under any statutory or common law or tort law theory, including but not limited to damages assessed for private or public nuisance or for the conducting of an abnormally dangerous activity on or near the Property; (I) any past, present or future non compliance with the ADA; and (m) misrepresentation or inaccuracy in any material representation or warranty or material breach or failure to perform any covenants or other obligations pursuant to this Agreement or the Mortgage; provided, however, that nothing contained in this Section 4 shall impose liability upon Indemnitor with respect to conditions or circumstances which did not exist prior to, and arise solely out of actions, conditions or events occurring after, any sale of the Property by foreclosure of the Mortgage or deed-in-lieu thereof.

5. Duty to Defend and Attorneys' and Other Fees and Expenses. Upon written request by any Indemnified Party, Indemnitor shall defend same (if requested by any Indemnified Party, in the name of the Indemnified Party) by attorneys and other professionals reasonably approved by the Indemnified Parties. Notwithstanding the foregoing, any Indemnified Parties may, in their sole discretion, engage their own attorneys and other professionals to defend or assist them, and, at the option of any such Indemnified Parties, their attorneys shall control the resolution of any claim, counterclaim, action or proceeding, providing that no compromise or settlement shall be entered into by any such Indemnified Party without Indemnitor's prior consent, which consent shall not be unreasonably withheld. Upon demand, Indemnitor shall pay or, in the sole and absolute discretion of the Indemnified Parties, reimburse, the Indemnified Parties for the payment of reasonable fees and disbursements of attorneys, engineers, environmental consultants, laboratories and other professionals in connection therewith.

6. Definitions. As used in this Agreement, the following terms shall have the following meanings:

**"ADA"** means the Americans with Disabilities Act of 1990, as amended and supplemented from time to time.

**"Environmental Law"** means any present and future federal, state and local laws, statutes, ordinances, rules, regulations and the like, as well as common law, relating to the safety, welfare and protection of human health or the environment or any natural resource, relating to any Hazardous Substances, relating to liability for or costs of other actual or threatened danger to the safety, welfare or human health or the environment or any natural resource and includes, but is not limited to, the following statutes, as amended, any successor thereto, and any regulations promulgated pursuant thereto, and any state or local statutes, ordinances, rules, regulations and the like addressing similar issues: the Comprehensive Environmental Response, Compensation and Liability Act of 1980, as amended (as amended, including, without limitation, the Superfund Amendments and Reauthorization Act of 1986, **"CERCLA")**, 42 U.S.C. §9601 et seq; the Emergency Planning and Community Right-to-Know Act of 1986; the Hazardous Substances Transportation Act; the Resource Conservation and

Recovery Act (including but not limited to Subtitle I relating to underground storage tanks); the Solid Waste Disposal Act; the Clean Water Act; the Clean Air Act; the Toxic Substances Control Act; the Safe Drinking Water Act; the Occupational Safety and Health Act; the Federal Water Pollution Control Act; the Federal Insecticide, Fungicide and Rodenticide Act; the Endangered Species Act; the National Environmental Policy Act; and the River and Harbors Appropriation Act. The term **"Environmental Law"** also includes, but is not limited to, any present and future federal, state and local laws, statutes ordinances, rules, regulations and the like, as well as common law conditioning transfer of property upon a negative declaration or other approval of a governmental authority of the environmental condition of the Property; requiring notification or disclosure of Releases of Hazardous Substances or other environmental condition of the Property to any Governmental Authority or other Person, whether or not in connection with transfer of title to or interest in property; imposing conditions or requirements in connection with permits or other authorization for lawful activity; relating to nuisance, trespass or other causes of action related to the Property; and relating to wrongful death, personal injury, or property or other damage in connection with any physical condition or use of the Property.

**"Hazardous Substances"** means any and all substances (whether solid, liquid or gas) defined, listed, or otherwise classified as toxic or hazardous substances, materials, wastes, pollutants or contaminants or words of similar meaning or regulatory effect under any present or future Environmental Laws or that may have a negative impact on human health, welfare or safety, the environment or any natural resources, including but not limited to, petroleum and petroleum products, asbestos and asbestos-containing materials, polychlorinated biphenyls, lead, Lead Based Paint, radon, radioactive materials, Mold, flammables and explosives, infectious substances or any other substances or materials now or hereafter regulated by any Environmental Law, but excluding substances of kinds and in amounts ordinarily and customarily used or stored in similar properties for the purposes of cleaning or other maintenance or operations and otherwise in compliance with all Environmental Laws.

**"Indemnified Parties"** includes Indemnitee, any Person who is or will have been involved in the origination of the Loan, any Person who is or will have been involved with the servicing of the Loan, any Person in whose name the encumbrance created by the Mortgage is or will have been recorded, Persons who may hold or acquire or will have held a full or partial interest in the Loan or Hedging Obligations as well as their respective directors, officers, shareholders, partners, members, employees, agents, servants, representatives, contractors, subcontractors, affiliates, subsidiaries, participants, successors and assigns of any and all of the foregoing (including but not limited to any other Person who holds or acquires or will have held a participation or other full or partial interest in the Loan or Hedging Obligations or the Property, whether during the term of the Loan or as a part of or following a foreclosure of the Mortgage and including, but not limited to, any successors by merger, consolidation or acquisition of all or a substantial portion of Indemnitee's assets and business); provided that Indemnified Parties shall not include any Person at or after a foreclosure sale of the Property or conveyance of the Property by deed-in-lieu of foreclosure other than Indemnitee or its affiliated designee.

**"Legal Action"** means any claim, counterclaim, action, suit or proceeding, whether administrative or judicial in nature.

**"Lead Based Paint"** means any paint, stain or similar product or surface coating that contains more than 1.0 milligram of lead per square centimeter and/or 0.5% of lead by weight.

**"Losses"** includes any losses, damages (excluding consequential damages), costs, fees, expenses, claims, suits, judgments, awards, liabilities (including but not limited to strict liabilities), obligations, debts, diminutions in value, fines, penalties, charges, costs of Remediation (whether or not performed voluntarily), amounts paid in settlement, litigation costs, attorneys' fees, engineers' fees, environmental consultants' fees, and investigation costs (including but not limited to costs for sampling, testing and analysis of soil, water, air, building materials, and other materials and substances whether solid, liquid or gas), of whatever kind or nature, and whether or not incurred in connection with any judicial or administrative proceedings, actions, claims, suits, judgments or awards.

**"Mold"** means any fungi that reproduce through the release of spores or the splitting of cells or other means, including but not limited to, mold, mildew, fungi, fungal spores, hyphae, fragments and metabolites such as mycotoxins and microbial volatile organic compounds.

**"Person"** includes an individual, corporation, limited liability company, partnership, trust, unincorporated association, government, governmental authority, and any other entity.

**"Release"** with respect to any Hazardous Substance includes but is not limited to any release, deposit, discharge, emission, leaking, leaching, spilling, seeping, migrating, injecting, pumping, pouring, emptying, escaping, dumping, disposing or other movement of Hazardous Substances.

**"Remediation"** includes but is not limited to any response, remedial, removal, or corrective action; any activity to clean up, detoxify, decontaminate, contain or otherwise remediate any Hazardous Substance; any actions to prevent, cure or mitigate any Release of any Hazardous Substance; any action to comply with any Environmental Laws or with any permits issued pursuant thereto; any inspection, investigation, study, monitoring, assessment, audit, sampling and testing, laboratory or other analysis, or evaluation relating to any Hazardous Substances or to anything referred to herein.

**"Property"** means the real property described on Schedule A attached hereto, together with all buildings and other improvements located thereon.

7. Unimpaired Liability. The liability of Indemnitor under this Agreement shall in no way be limited or impaired by, and Indemnitor hereby consents to and agrees to be bound by, any amendment or modification of the provisions of the Note, the Mortgage, any other Loan Documents or any Hedging Contracts to or with Indemnitee by Indemnitor or any Person who succeeds Indemnitor

or any Person as owner of the Property. In addition, the liability of Indemnitor under this Agreement shall in no way be limited or impaired by (i) any extensions of time for performance by Borrower required by the Note, the Mortgage, any of the other Loan Documents or any Hedging Contracts, (ii) any sale or transfer of all or part of the Property, (iii) any exculpatory provision in the Note, the Mortgage, any of the other Loan Documents or any Hedging Contracts limiting Indemnitee's recourse to the Property or to any other security for the Indebtedness, or limiting Indemnitee's rights to a deficiency judgment against Borrower or any Obligor, (iv) the accuracy or inaccuracy of the representations and warranties made by any Indemnitor under the Note, the Mortgage, any of the other Loan Documents or any Hedging Contract or herein, (v) the release of Indemnitor or any other Person from performance or observance of any of the agreements, covenants, terms or condition contained in the Note, the Mortgage, any of the other Loan Documents or any Hedging Contracts, whether by operation of law, Indemnitee's voluntary act, or otherwise, (vi) the release or substitution in whole or in part of any security for the Indebtedness, or (vii) Indemnitee's failure to record the Mortgage or file any UCC financing statements (or the improper recording or filing of any thereof) or the failure to otherwise perfect, protect, secure or insure any security interest or lien given as security for the Indebtedness; and, in any such case, whether with or without notice to Indemnitor and with or without consideration. Nothing contained herein shall be construed to obligate Indemnitor to indemnify, defend and hold harmless any Indemnified Party from and against any Losses incurred by such Indemnified Party by reason of such Indemnified Party's own willful misconduct or gross negligence.

8. Enforcement. Indemnified Parties may enforce the obligations of Indemnitor without first resorting to or exhausting any security or collateral or without first having recourse to the Note, the Mortgage, any other Loan Documents or any Hedging Contracts, or the Property or any part thereof, through foreclosure proceedings or otherwise; provided, however, that nothing herein shall inhibit or prevent Indemnitee from suing on the Note, foreclosing or exercising any power of sale under the Mortgage, or exercising any other rights and remedies thereunder or under any Hedging Contracts. This Agreement is not collateral or security for the debt of Indemnitor pursuant to the Loan or any Hedging Obligations, unless the applicable Indemnitee expressly elects in writing to make this Agreement additional collateral or security for the debt of Indemnitor pursuant to the Loan or any Hedging Obligations, which Indemnitee is entitled to do in its sole and absolute discretion. It is not necessary for an Event of Default to have occurred pursuant to and as defined in the Mortgage or any Hedging Contract for Indemnified Parties to exercise their rights pursuant to this Agreement. Indemnitor is fully and personally liable for their obligations pursuant to this Agreement and such liability is not limited to the original or amortized principal balance of the Loan, amount of Hedging Obligations or the value of the Property.

9. Survival. The obligations and liabilities of Indemnitor under this Agreement shall fully survive indefinitely notwithstanding any termination, satisfaction, assignment, entry of a judgment of foreclosure, exercise of any power of sale, or delivery of a deed in lieu of foreclosure of the Mortgage; provided, however, that nothing in this Section 9 shall impose liability upon Indemnitor with respect to conditions or circumstances which did not exist prior to, and arise solely out of actions, conditions or events occurring after, any sale or conveyance of the Property by foreclosure of the Mortgage or deed-in-lieu thereof. Notwithstanding the foregoing, the obligations and liabilities of Indemnitor under this Agreement shall not inure to the benefit of any purchaser or transferee of the Property upon and after a sale of the Property by foreclosure of the Mortgage or deed-in-lieu thereof unless such purchaser or transferee is the holder of the Mortgage at the time of such foreclosure or deed-in-lieu thereof or is an affiliate or nominee of such holder.

10. Interest. Any amounts payable to any Indemnified Parties under this Agreement shall become immediately due and payable on demand and, if not paid within five (5) days of such demand therefor, shall bear interest at the Default Rate.

11. Waivers.

a. EACH INDEMNITOR HEREBY EXPRESSLY AND UNCONDITIONALLY WAIVES, IN CONNECTION WITH ANY SUIT, ACTION OR PROCEEDING BROUGHT BY OR ON BEHALF OF ANY INDEMNIFIED PARTY ON THIS AGREEMENT, ANY AND EVERY RIGHT SUCH INDEMNITOR MAY HAVE: (I) TO OBJECT TO THE JURISDICTION OR VENUE OF ANY STATE COURT SITTING IN KINGS OR NEW YORK COUNTY OR ANY FEDERAL COURT LOCATED IN THE STATE, (II) TO INJUNCTIVE RELIEF, (Ill) TO INTERPOSE ANY COUNTERCLAI M THEREIN (OTHER THAN COMPULSORY COUNTERCLAIMS), AND (IV) TO HAVE THE SAME CONSOLIDATED WITH ANY OTHER OR SEPARATE SUIT, ACTION OR PROCEEDING. EACH INDEMNITOR HEREBY AGREES AND CONSENTS TO, IN ADDITION TO ANY METHODS OF SERVICE OF PROCESS PROVIDED FOR UNDER APPLICABLE LAW, SERVICE OF PROCESS IN ANY SUCH SUIT BEING MADE UPON SUCH INDEMNITOR BY MAIL AT THE ADDRESS SET FORTH HEREIN AND SERVICE SO MADE SHALL BE COMPLETE FIVE (5) DAYS AFTER THE SAME SHALL HAVE BEEN SO MAILED. THE FOREGOING WAIVERS ARE GIVEN KNOWINGLY AND VOLUNTARI LY BY EACH INDEMNITOR. AND ANY AFFILIATE COUNTERPARTY THE INDEMNIFIED PARTIES ARE HEREBY AUTHORIZED TO FILE A COPY OF THIS PARAGRAPH IN ANY PROCEEDING AS CONCLUSIVE EVIDENCE OF ANY OR ALL OF THE FOREGOING WAIVERS.

b. INDEMNITOR HEREBY KNOWINGLY, VOLUNTARI LY AND INTENTIONALLY WAIVES THE RIGHT TO A TRIAL BY JURY TO THE EXTENT THAT ANY SUCH RIGHT SHALL NOW OR HEREAFTER EXIST IN RESPECT OF ANY LITIGATION BASED ON THIS AGREEMENT, ARISING OUT OF, UNDER OR IN CONNECTION WITH THIS AGREEMENT, ANY OTHER LOAN DOCUMENTS OR HEDGING CONTRACTS CONTEMPLATED TO BE EXECUTED IN CONNECTION HEREWITH, OR ANY COURSE OF CONDUCT, COURSE OF DEALINGS, STATEMENTS (WHETHER VERBAL OR WRITTEN) OR ACTIONS OF ANY PARTY. THIS WAIVER IS INTENDED TO ENCOMPASS INDIVIDUALLY EACH INSTANCE AND EACH ISSUE AS TO WHICH THE RIGHT TO A TRIAL BY JURY WOULD OTHERWISE ACCRUE CONSTITUTES A MATERIAL INDUCEMENT FOR BORROWER, LENDER AND AFFILIATE COUNTERPARTY TO ENTER INTO THE TRANSACTIONS CONTEMPLATED HEREBY. EACH INDEMNITOR IS HEREBY AUTHORIZED TO FILE A COPY OF THIS PARAGRAPH IN ANY PROCEEDING AS CONCLUSIVE EVIDENCE OF THIS WAIVER.

12. Subrogation. Indemnitor shall take any and all reasonable actions, including institution of legal action against third parties, necessary or appropriate to obtain reimbursement, payment or compensation from such Persons responsible for the presence of any Hazardous Substances at, in, on, under, above or in the vicinity of the Property and any remediation, disposal or cleanup in connection therewith or otherwise obligated by law to pay any costs and expenses in connection with same. Indemnified Parties shall be and hereby are subrogated to all of Indemnitor's rights now or hereafter in such claims.

13. Indemnitor's Representations and Warranties. Indemnitor represents and warrants to Indemnitee that:

(a) It has the full power and authority to execute and deliver this Agreement and to perform its obligations hereunder; the execution, delivery and performance of this Agreement by Indemnitor has been duly and validly authorized; and all requisite action has been taken by Indemnitor to make this Agreement valid and binding upon Indemnitor, enforceable in accordance with its terms;

(b) Its execution of, and compliance with, this Agreement will not result in the breach of any term or provision of the charter, by-laws, partnership or trust agreement, or other governing instrument of Indemnitor or result in the breach of any term or provision of, or conflict with or constitute a default under, or result in the acceleration of any obligation under, any agreement, indenture or loan or credit agreement or other instrument to which Indemnitor or the Property is subject, or result in the violation of any law, rule, regulation, order, judgment or decree to which Indemnitor or the Property is subject;

(c) To the best of Indemnitor's knowledge, there is no action, suit, proceeding or investigation pending or threatened against it which, either in any one instance or in the aggregate, may result in any material adverse change in the business, operations, financial condition, properties or assets of Indemnitor, or in any material impairment of the right or ability of Indemnitor to carry on its business substantially as now conducted, or in any material liability on the part of Indemnitor, or which would draw into question the validity of this Agreement or of any action taken or to be taken in connection with the obligations of Indemnitor contemplated herein, or which would be likely to impair materially the ability of Indemnitor to perform under the terms of this Agreement;

(d) It does not believe, nor does it have any reason or cause to believe, that it cannot perform each and every covenant contained in this Agreement;

(e) To the best of Indemnitor's knowledge, no approval, authorization, order, license or consent of, or registration or filing with, any governmental authority or other person, and no approval, authorization or consent of any other party is required in connection with this Agreement which has not been obtained; and

(f) This Agreement constitutes a valid, legal and binding obligation of Indemnitor, enforceable against it in accordance with the terms hereof.

14. <u>No Waiver.</u> No delay by any Indemnified Parties in exercising any right, power or privilege under this Agreement shall operate as a waiver of any such privilege, power or right.

15. <u>Notice of Legal Actions.</u> Each party hereto shall, within five (5) business days of receipt thereof, give written notice to the other party hereto of (i) any notice, advice or other communication from any governmental entity or any source whatsoever with respect to Hazardous Substances or the ADA on, from or affecting the Property, and (ii) any legal action brought against such party or related to the Property, with respect to which Indemnitor may have liability under this Agreement. Such notice shall comply with the provisions of Section 18 hereof.

16. <u>Examination of Books and Records.</u> Indemnified Parties and their accountants shall have the right to examine the records, books, management and other papers of Indemnitor which reflect upon its financial condition, at the Property or at the office regularly maintained by Indemnitor where the books and records are located. Indemnified Parties and their accountants shall have the right to make copies and extracts from the foregoing records and other papers. In addition, at reasonable times and upon reasonable notice, Indemnified Parties and their accountants shall have the right to examine and audit the books and records of Indemnitor pertaining to the income, expenses and operation of the Property during reasonable business hours at the office of Indemnitor where the books and records are located.

17. <u>Taxes.</u> Indemnitor has filed all federal, state, county, municipal, and city income and other tax returns required to have been filed by it and has paid all taxes and related liabilities which have become due pursuant to such returns

or pursuant to any assessments received by it. Indemnitor has no knowledge of ny basis for any additional assessment in respect of any such taxes and related liabilities for prior years.

18. Notices. All notices or other written communications hereunder shall be made in accordance with the notice provisions of the Mortgage.

19. Duplicate Originals; Counterparts. This Agreement may be executed in any number of duplicate originals and each duplicate original shall be deemed to be an original. This Agreement may be executed in several counterparts, each of which counterparts shall be deemed an original instrument and all of which together shall constitute a single Agreement. The failure of any party hereto to execute this Agreement, or any counterpart hereof, shall not relieve the other signatories from their obligations hereunder.

20. No Oral Change. This Agreement, and any provisions hereof, may not be modified, amended, waived, extended, changed, discharged or terminated orally or by any act or failure to act on the part of Indemnitor or any Indemnified Party, but only by an agreement in writing signed by the party against whom enforcement of any modification, amendment, waiver, extension, change, discharge or termination is sought.

21. Headinqs, Etc. The headings and captions of various paragraphs of this Agreement are for convenience of reference only and are not to be construed as defining or limiting, in any way, the scope or intent of the provisions hereof.

22. Number and Gender/Successors and Assigns. All pronouns and any variations thereof shall be deemed to refer to the masculine, feminine, neuter, singular or plural as the identity of the Person or Persons referred to may require. Without limiting the effect of specific references in any provision of this Agreement, the term **"Indemnitor"** shall be deemed to refer to each and every Person comprising an Indemnitor from time to time, as the sense of a particular provision may require, and to include the heirs, executors, administrators, legal representatives, successors and assigns of Indemnitor, all of whom shall be bound by the provisions of this Agreement, provided that no obligation of Indemnitor may be assigned except with the written consent of Indemnitee. Each reference herein to Indemnitee shall be deemed to include its successors and assigns. This Agreement shall inure to the benefit of Indemnified Parties and their respective successors and assigns forever.

23. Release of Liability. Any one or more parties liable upon or in respect of this Agreement may be released without affecting the liability of any party not so released.

24. Rights Cumulative. The rights and remedies herein provided are cumulative and not exclusive of any rights or remedies which Indemnitee has under the Note, the Mortgage, the other Loan Documents or any Hedging Contract or would otherwise have at law or in equity.

25. Inapplicable Provisions. If any term, condition or covenant of this Agreement shall be held to be invalid, illegal or unenforceable in any respect, this Agreement shall be construed without such provision.

26. Governing Law. This Guaranty and the rights and obligations of the parties hereunder shall in all respects be governed by, and construed and enforced in accordance with, the laws of the State without regard to the State's principles of conflicts of law.

27. Joint and Several Liability. The Persons comprising Indemnitor shall be jointly and severally liable under this Agreement for all obligations, liabilities, representations, warranties, covenants and agreements of Indemnitor hereunder.

28. Miscellaneous.

(a) Wherever pursuant to this Agreement (i) Indemnitee has the right to approve or disapprove any request, action or matter, or consent or withhold its consent with respect to any request, action or matter, (ii) any arrangement, term or matter is to be satisfactory to Indemnitee, or (iii) any other decision or determination is to be made by Indemnitee, the decision or determination of Indemnitee with respect to same shall be in the sole and absolute discretion of Indemnitee and shall be final and conclusive, except as may be otherwise expressly provided herein.

(b) Wherever pursuant to this Agreement it is provided that Indemnitor pay any costs and expenses, such costs and expenses shall include, but not be limited to, reasonable attorneys' fees and disbursements of Indemnitee and the other Indemnified Parties.

**IN WITNESS WHEREOF,** this Agreement has been executed by Indemnitor and is effective as of the day and year first above written.

INDEMNITOR BORROWER:

11 Duffield LLC

By Darwin Lee__________________
Name: Darwin Lee
Title: Manager, Manage Great Real Estate LLC,
Manager of 11 Duffield LLC

OBLIGORS;

Manage Great Real Estate LLC

By: Darwin Lee__________________
Name: Darwin Lee
Title: Manager

Debby Day__________________
Debby Day, Individually

# 11 DUFFIELD ASSIGNMENT OF LEASES AND RENTS

Dated: January 1, Year 14

From **11 DUFFIELD LLC,** as assignor,
a Delaware limited liability company

to

**NATIONAL BANK, N.A.,** as assignee,
a national banking association

LOCATION OF PREMISES:

| | |
|---|---|
| Street: | 11 Duffield |
| Town of: | Brooklyn |
| County of: | Kings |
| State of: | New York |
| Section: | 3742 |
| Block: | 97 |
| Lot: | 23 |

After recording, please return to:

National Bank
1 Broad Street
New York, New York 1003

**THIS ASSIGNMENT OF LEASES AND RENTS** (this **"Assignment"**) made as of January 1, Year 14, by 11 Duffield LLC, a Delaware limited liability company its principal place of business at 75 Clinton Street, 13R, Brooklyn, New York 11201 **"Borrower"** to NATIONAL BANK, N.A., a national banking association, having an office at 1 Broad Street, New York, New York 10038 (**"Lender"**) for itself and as agent for any Affiliate Counterparty or any other Affiliate holding any Indebtedness (together with Lender, each an **"Assignee"** and collectively **"Assignees"**).

## RECITALS:

**WHEREAS,** concurrently herewith, Lender is extending credit to Borrower in the initial principal sum of $12,750,000 (the **"Loan"**) and, in connection therewith, Borrower has executed and delivered to Lender that certain Mortgage Loan Note, dated of even date herewith, made by Borrower as mortgagor, in favor of Lender as mortgagee, in the original principal amount of $12,750,000 (such Mortgage Loan Note, as the same may be hereafter amended, modified, restated, renewed, replaced, supplemented or extended, being hereinafter called the **"Note"**), which Note evidences the Indebtedness of Borrower to Lender; and which is secured pursuant to that certain Mortgage and Security Agreement dated as of even date hereof (the **"Mortgage"** and together with the Note and related loan and security documents, the **"Loan Documents"**),

**WHEREAS,** to further induce Lender to make the Loan, and it is a condition of making the Loan that Borrower shall have executed and delivered this Assignment for the benefit of Lender;

**WHEREAS,** Borrower may from time to time enter into one or more Hedging Contracts with Affiliate Counterparty;

**WHEREAS,** Affiliate Counterparty requires as a condition to the entry into any Hedging Contracts that Borrower shall have executed and delivered this Assignment for the benefit of such Affiliate Counterparty; and

**WHEREAS,** all capitalized terms used in this Assignment, but not defined herein, shall have the respective meanings accorded such terms in the Mortgage.

**NOW THEREFORE,** in consideration of the making of the Loan and the entry into any Hedging Obligations, and the covenants, agreements, representations and warranties set forth in this Assignment, the parties hereto hereby agree as follows:

## Article 1—Assignment

Section 1.1 PROPERTY ASSIGNED. Borrower hereby absolutely, irrevocably and unconditionally transfers, assigns, sets over and grants to Lender for itself and as agent for any Affiliate Counterparty or any other Affiliate holding any Indebtedness the following property, rights, interests and estates, now owned, or hereafter acquired by Borrower:

(a) Leases. All existing and future **"leases"** and **"lease provisions"** (as described in Exhibit B annexed hereto and made a part hereof) affecting the use, enjoyment, or occupancy of all or any part of that certain lot or piece of land, more particularly described in Exhibit A annexed hereto and made a part hereof, or all or any part of the buildings, structures, fixtures, additions, enlargements, extensions, modifications, repairs, replacements and improvements now or hereafter located thereon (collectively, the **"Property"**) and the right, title and interest of Borrower, its successors and assigns, therein and thereunder.

(b) Other Leases and Agreements. All other leases and other agreements, whether or not in writing, affecting the use, enjoyment or occupancy of the Property or any portion thereof now or hereafter made, whether made before or after the filing by or against Borrower of any petition for relief under 11 U.S.C. §101 et seq., as the same may be amended from time to time (the **"Bankruptcy Code"**), together with any extension, renewal or replacement of the same, this Assignment of other present and future leases and present and future agreements being effective without further or supplemental assignment. The **"leases"** and the **"lease provisions"** described in Subsection 1.1(a) and the leases and other agreements described in this Subsection 1.1(b) are collectively referred to as the **"Leases"**.

(c) Rents. All **"rents"** (as described in Exhibit B annexed hereto and made a part hereof) whether paid or accruing before or after the filing by or against Borrower of any petition for relief under the Bankruptcy Code (collectively, the **"Rents"**).

(d) Bankruptcy Claims. All of Borrower's claims and rights (the **"Bankruptcy Claims"**) to the payment of damages arising from any rejection by a lessee of any Lease under the Bankruptcy Code.

(e) Lease Guaranties. All of Borrower's right, title and interest in and claims under any and all lease guaranties, letters of credit and any other credit support (individually, a **"Lease Guaranty"**, and collectively, the **"Lease Guaranties"**) given by any guarantor in connection with any of the Leases or leasing commissions (individually, a **"Lease Guarantor"**, and collectively, the **"Lease Guarantors"**) to Borrower.

(f) Proceeds. All proceeds from the sale or other disposition of the Leases, the Rents, the Lease Guaranties and the Bankruptcy Claims.

(g) Other. All rights, powers, privileges, options and other benefits of Borrower as lessor under the Leases and beneficiary under the Lease Guaranties, including without limitation the immediate and continuing right to make claim for, receive, collect and receipt for all Rents payable or receivable under the Leases and all sums payable under the Lease Guaranties or pursuant thereto (and to apply the same to the payment of the Indebtedness), and to do all other things which Borrower or any lessor is or may become entitled to do under the Leases or the Lease Guaranties.

(h) Entry. The right, at Lender's option, upon revocation of the license granted herein, to enter upon the Property in person, by Lender or by court-appointed receiver, to collect the Rents.

(i) Power of Attorney. Borrower's irrevocable power of attorney, coupled with an interest, to take any and all of the actions set forth in Section 3.1 of this Assignment and any or all other actions designated by Lender for the proper management and preservation of the Property.

(j) Other Rights and Agreements. Any and all other rights of Borrower in and to the items set forth in subsections (a) through (i) above, and all amendments, modifications, replacements, renewals and substitutions thereof.

## Article 2—Terms of Assignment

Section 2.1 Present Assignment and License Back. Borrower intends that this Assignment constitute a present, absolute assignment of the Leases, Rents, Lease Guaranties and Bankruptcy Claims, and not an assignment for additional security only. Nevertheless, subject to the terms of this Section 2.1 and Section 3.1 hereof, Lender grants to Borrower a revocable license to collect and receive the Rents, as well as other sums due under the Lease Guaranties. Borrower shall hold the Rents, as well as all sums received pursuant to any Lease Guaranty, or a portion thereof sufficient to discharge all current sums due on the Indebtedness, in trust for the benefit of Lender, for itself and as agent for any Affiliate Counterparty, for use in the payment of such sums.

Section 2.2 Notice to Lessees. Borrower hereby authorizes and directs the lessees named in the Leases or any other future lessees or occupants of the Property and all Lease Guarantors to pay over to Lender or to such other party as Lender directs all Rents and all sums due under any Lease Guaranties upon receipt from Lender of written notice to the effect that Lender is then the holder of this Assignment and that an Event of Default (as defined in the Mortgage) exists, and to continue so to do until otherwise notified by Lender.

Section 2.3 Incorporation by Reference. All representations, warranties, covenants, conditions and agreements contained in the Mortgage, the other Loan Documents and any Hedging Contract, as same may be modified, renewed, substituted or extended are hereby made a part of this Assignment to the same extent and with the same force as if fully set forth herein.

Section 2.4 Representations and Warranties of Borrower. Borrower hereby represents and warrants as follows:

(a) Borrower is the sole and absolute owner of the entire landlord's or lessor's interest in the Leases and said rents, issues and profits;

(b) Borrower has made no prior assignment of any of the Leases or with respect to any of said rents, issues or profits;

(c) Borrower has neither done any act nor omitted to do any act which might prevent Lender from, or limit Lender in, acting under any of the provisions of this Assignment;

(d) Neither the execution and delivery of this Assignment or any of the Leases, the performance of each and every covenant of Borrower under this Assignment and the Leases, nor the meeting of each and every condition contained in this Assignment, conflicts with, or constitutes a breach or default under, any agreement, indenture or other instrument to which Borrower is a party, or any law, ordinance, administrative regulation or court decree which is applicable to Borrower;

(e) No action has been brought or, so far as is known to Borrower, is threatened, which would interfere in any way with the right of Borrower to execute this Assignment and perform all of Borrower's obligations contained in this Assignment and in the Leases;

(f) Borrower has delivered to Lender correct and complete copies of all Leases existing as of the date of this Assignment, and all amendments, exhibits, addenda and schedules thereto;

(g) Borrower has delivered to Lender a rent roll as of the date hereof with respect to all Leases existing as of the date of this Assignment (hereinafter referred to as the "Rent Roll"). There are no occupancies, rights, privileges or licenses in or to the Property other than pursuant to the Leases reflected on the Rent Roll. Except as set forth in the Rent Roll, the Leases were duly executed and delivered, pursuant to authority legally adequate therefor, are now in full force and effect, and are the legal, valid and binding obligations of the parties thereto, enforceable in accordance with their terms. The Rent Roll accurately and completely sets forth all rents payable by and security, if any, deposited by tenants, with no tenant having paid more than one (1) month's rent in advance;

(h) All tenant improvements or work to be done, furnished or paid for by Borrower, or credited or allowed to a tenant, for, or in connection with, the Property pursuant to any Lease has been completed and paid for or provided for in a manner satisfactory to Lender. No leasing, brokerage or like commissions, fees or payments are due from Borrower in respect of the Leases; and

(i) No default exists on the part of Borrower in the fulfillment, performance or observance of any of the terms, conditions or covenants of landlord or lessor contained in any of the Leases, and (i) no payment default or any other material default exists on the part of any tenant in the fulfillment, performance or observance of any of the terms, conditions or covenants of tenant or lessee contained in any of the Leases, (ii) to the best of Borrower's knowledge, there any no defenses, counterclaims, offsets, concessions or rebates available to any tenant thereunder, (iii) Borrower has not given or made, or received, any notice of default, or any claim, which remains uncured or unsatisfied, with respect to any of the Leases and (iv) to the best of Borrower's knowledge, there is no basis for any such claim or notice of default by any tenant

## Article 3—Remedies

Section 3.1 Remedies of Lender. Upon the occurrence of an Event of Default, the license granted to Borrower in Section 2.1 of this Assignment shall automatically be revoked, and Lender shall immediately be entitled to possession of all Rents and sums due under any Lease Guaranties, whether or not Lender enters upon or takes control of the Property. In addition, Lender may, at its option, without waiving such Event of Default, without regard to the adequacy of the security for the Indebtedness, either in person or by Lender's nominee or attorney, with or without bringing any action or proceeding, or by a receiver appointed by a court, (i) dispossess Borrower and its agents and servants from the Property, without liability for trespass, damages or otherwise, and exclude Borrower and its agents or servants wholly therefrom, (ii) take possession of the Property and all books, records and accounts relating thereto, (iii) hold, manage, lease and operate the Property on such terms and for such period of time as Lender may deem proper, (iv) either with or without taking possession of the Property, in its own name, demand, sue for or otherwise collect and receive all Rents and sums due under all Lease Guaranties, including those past due and unpaid, and (v) make from time to time all such alterations, renovations, repairs or replacements to the Property as Lender may deem proper. Lender may apply the Rents collected and sums received under any Lease Guaranties pursuant hereto to the payment of the following in such order and proportion as Lender in its sole discretion may determine, any law, custom or use to the contrary notwithstanding: (a) all expenses of managing and securing the Property, including, without limitation, the salaries, fees and wages of a managing agent, attorneys and such other employees or agents as Lender may reasonably deem necessary or desirable and all reasonable expenses of operating and maintaining the Property, including, without limitation, all taxes, charges, claims, assessments, water charges, sewer rents and any other liens, and premiums for all insurance which Lender may reasonably deem necessary or desirable, and the reasonable cost of all alterations, renovations, repairs or replacements, and all expenses incidental to taking and retaining possession of the Property, and (b) all other Indebtedness, including, without limitation, all costs and expenses, including reasonable attorneys' fees, incurred in the collection of any of all of the Indebtedness, including all costs, expenses and attorneys' fees incurred in seeking to realize on or to protect or preserve Lender's interest in any other collateral securing any or all of the Indebtedness. In addition, upon the occurrence of an Event of Default, Lender, at its option, may (1) complete any construction on the Property in such manner and form as Lender deems advisable, (2) exercise all rights and powers of Borrower, including, without limitation, the right to negotiate, execute, cancel, enforce or modify Leases, obtain and evict tenants, and demand, sue for, collect and receive all Rents from the Property and all sums due under any Lease Guaranties, (3) either require Borrower to pay monthly in advance to Lender, or any receiver appointed to collect the Rents, the fair and reasonable rental value for the use and occupancy of such part of the Property as may be in possession of Borrower or (4) require Borrower to vacate and surrender possession of the Property to Lender or to such receiver and, in default thereof, Borrower may be evicted by summary proceedings or otherwise.

Section 3.2 Other Remedies. Nothing contained in this Assignment and no act done or omitted by Lender pursuant to the power and rights granted to Lender hereunder shall be deemed to be a waiver by either Assignee of its rights and remedies under the Mortgage, the Note, the other Loan Documents or any Hedging Contract and this Assignment is made and accepted without prejudice to any of the rights and remedies possessed by Assignees under the terms thereof. The right of each Assignee to collect the Indebtedness, and to enforce any other security therefor held by it may be exercised by such Assignee either prior to, simultaneously with, or subsequent to any action taken by Lender hereunder. Borrower hereby absolutely, unconditionally and irrevocably waives any and all rights to assert any setoff, counterclaim or crossclaim of any nature whatsoever with respect to the obligations of Borrower under this Assignment, the Mortgage, the Note, the other Loan Documents, any Hedging Contract or otherwise with respect to the Loan or any Hedging Obligations in any action or proceeding brought by either Assignee to collect same, or any portion thereof, or to enforce and realize upon the lien and security interest created by this Assignment, the Mortgage, the Note, any of the other Loan Documents or any Hedging Contract (provided, however, that the foregoing shall not be deemed a waiver of Borrower's right to assert any compulsory counterclaim if such counterclaim is compelled under local law or rule of procedure, nor shall the foregoing be deemed a waiver of Borrower's right to assert any claim which would constitute a defense, setoff, counterclaim or crossclaim of any nature whatsoever against either Assignee in any separate action or proceeding).

Section 3.3 <u>Other Security.</u> Assignees may take or release other security for the payment of the Indebtedness, may release any party primarily or secondarily liable therefor and may apply any other security held by either of them to the reduction or satisfaction of the Indebtedness, without prejudice to any of its rights under this Assignment.

Section 3.4 <u>Non-Waiver.</u> The exercise by Lender of the option granted it in <u>Section 3.1</u> of this Assignment and the collection of the Rents and sums due under the Lease Guaranties and the application thereof as herein provided shall not be considered a waiver of any default by Borrower under the Note, the Mortgage, the Leases, this Assignment, the other Loan Documents or any Hedging Contract. The failure of Lender to insist upon strict performance of any term hereof shall not be deemed to be a waiver of any term of this Assignment. Borrower shall not be relieved of Borrower's obligations hereunder by reason of (a) the failure of either Assignee to comply with any request of Borrower or any other party to take any action to enforce any of the provisions hereof or of the Mortgage, the Note, the other Loan Documents or any Hedging Contract, (b) the release regardless of consideration, of the whole or any part of the Property, or (c) any agreement or stipulation by either Assignee extending the time of payment or otherwise modifying or supplementing the terms of this Assignment, the Mortgage, the Note, the other Loan Documents or any Hedging Contract. Each Assignee may resort for the payment of the Indebtedness to any other security held by it in such order and manner as set forth in the Mortgage. Each Assignee may take any action to recover the Indebtedness, or any portion thereof, or, in the case of Lender, to enforce any covenant hereof without prejudice to the right of Lender thereafter to enforce its rights under this Assignment. The rights of Lender under this Assignment shall be separate, distinct and cumulative and none shall be given effect to the exclusion of the others. No act of Lender shall be construed as an election to proceed under any one provision herein to the exclusion of any other provision.

Section 3.5 Bankruptcy. (a) Upon or at any time after the occurrence of an Event of Default, Lender, for itself and as agent for any Affiliate Counterparty, shall have the right to proceed in its own name or in the name of Borrower in respect of any claim, suit, action or proceeding relating to the rejection of any Lease, including, without limitation, the right to file and prosecute, to the exclusion of Borrower, any proofs of claim, complaints, motions, applications, notices and other documents, in any case in respect of the lessee under such Lease under the Bankruptcy Code.

(b) If there shall be filed by or against Borrower a petition under the Bankruptcy Code, and Borrower, as lessor under any Lease, shall determine to reject such Lease pursuant to Section 365(a) of the Bankruptcy Code, then Borrower shall give Lender not less than ten (10) days' prior notice of the date on which Borrower shall apply to the bankruptcy court for authority to reject the Lease. Lender shall have the right, but not the obligation, to serve upon Borrower within such ten-day period a notice stating that (i) Lender demands that Borrower assume and assign the Lease to Lender pursuant to Section 365 of the Bankruptcy Code and (ii) Lender covenants to cure or provide adequate assurance of future performance under the Lease. If Lender serves upon Borrower the notice described in the preceding sentence, Borrower shall not seek to reject the Lease and shall comply with the demand provided for in clause (i) of the preceding sentence within thirty (30) days after the notice shall have been given, subject to the performance by Lender of the covenant provided for in clause (ii) of the preceding sentence.

## Article 4—No Liability, Further Assurances

Section 4.1 No Liability of Lender. This Assignment shall not be construed to bind Lender to the performance of any of the covenants, conditions or provisions contained in any Lease or Lease Guaranty or otherwise impose any obligation upon Lender. Lender shall not be liable for any loss sustained by Borrower resulting from Lender's failure to let the Property after an Event of Default or from any other act or omission of Lender in managing the Property after an Event of Default unless such loss is caused by the willful misconduct or bad faith of Lender. Lender shall not be obligated to perform or discharge any obligation, duty or liability under the Leases or any Lease Guaranties or under or by reason of this Assignment, and Borrower shall indemnify Lender, any Affiliate Counterparty and its other Affiliates for, and hold Lender, any Affiliate Counterparty and its other Affiliates harmless from, any and all liability, loss or damage that may or might be incurred under the Leases, any Lease Guaranties or under or by reason of this Assignment and from any and all claims and demands whatsoever, including the defense of any such claims or demands that may be asserted against Lender, any Affiliate Counterparty or any of its other Affiliates by reason of any alleged obligations and undertakings on its part to perform or discharge any of the terms, covenants or agreements contained in the Leases or any Lease Guaranties. Should Lender, any Affiliate Counterparty or its other Affiliates incur any such liability, the amount thereof, including costs, expenses and reasonable attorneys' fees, shall be secured by this Assignment and by the Mortgage and the other Loan Documents and Borrower shall reimburse Lender, any Affiliate Counterparty and its other Affiliates therefor immediately upon demand and upon the failure of Borrower to do so, Lender may, at its option, declare all sums secured by this Assignment and by the Mortgage, the other Loan Documents and any Hedging Contract immediately due and payable. This Assignment shall not operate to place any obligation or liability for the control, care, management or repair of the Property upon Lender, any Affiliate Counterparty or any of its other Affiliates, nor for the carrying out of any of the terms and conditions of the Leases or any Lease Guaranties; nor shall it operate to make Lender, any Affiliate Counterparty or its other Affiliates responsible or liable for any waste committed on the Property by the tenants or any other parties, or for any dangerous or defective condition of the Property including, without limitation, the presence of any Hazardous Substances (as defined in the Mortgage), or for any negligence in the management, upkeep, repair or control of the Property resulting in loss or injury or death to any tenant, licensee, employee or stranger.

Section 4.2 No Mortqaqee in Possession. Nothing herein contained shall be construed as establishing Lender as a "mortgagee in possession" in the absence of the taking of actual possession of the Property by Lender. In the exercise of the powers herein granted Lender, no liability shall be asserted or enforced against Lender, all such liability being expressly waived and released by Borrower.

Section 4.3 Further Assurances. Borrower will, at the cost of Borrower, and without expense to Lender, do, execute, acknowledge and deliver all and every such further acts, conveyances, assignments, notices of assignments, transfers and assurances as Lender shall, from time to time, reasonably require for the better assuring, conveying, assigning, transferring and confirming unto Lender the property and rights hereby assigned or intended now or hereafter so to be, or which Borrower may be or may hereafter become bound to convey or assign to Lender, or for carrying out the intention or facilitating the performance of the terms of this Assignment or for filing, registering or recording this Assignment and, on demand, will execute and deliver and hereby authorizes Lender to execute in the name of Borrower to the extent Lender may lawfully do so, one or more financing statements, chattel mortgages or comparable security instruments, to evidence more effectively the lien and security interest hereof in and upon the Leases.

## Article 5—Miscellaneous Provisions

Section 5.1 Conflict of Terms. In case of any conflict between the terms of this Assignment and the terms of the Mortgage, the terms of the Mortgage shall prevail.

Section 5.2 No Oral Change. This Assignment and any provisions hereof may not be modified, amended, waived, extended, changed, discharged or terminated orally, or by any act or failure to act on the part of Borrower, but only by an agreement in writing signed by the party against whom the enforcement of any modification, amendment, waiver, extension, change, discharge or termination is sought including, if required pursuant to the Mortgage, any Affiliate Counterparty.

Section 5.3 General Definitions. All capitalized terms not defined herein shall have the respective meanings set forth in the Mortgage. Unless the context clearly indicates a contrary intent or unless otherwise specifically provided herein, words used in this Assignment may be used interchangeably in singular or plural form and the word "Borrower" shall mean "each Borrower and any subsequent owner or owners of the Property or any part thereof or interest therein," the word "Lender" shall mean "each Lender and any subsequent holder of the Note or any part thereof', the word "Affiliate Counterparty" shall mean "each Affiliate Counterparty and any subsequent party to any Hedging Contract relating to the Mortgage and the Note with Borrower", the word "Note" shall mean "the Note and any other evidence of Indebtedness secured by the Mortgage or other Loan Documents," the word "Hedging Contract" shall mean "any Hedging Contract and any other evidence of Indebtedness secured by the Mortgage or other Loan Documents," the word "Property" shall include any portion of the Property and any interest therein, the phrases "attorneys' fees", "legal fees" and "counsel fees" shall include any and all attorney, paralegal and law clerk fees and disbursements, including, but not limited to, fees and disbursements at the pre-trial, trial and appellate levels incurred or paid by Lender in protecting its interest in the Property, the Leases and the Rents and enforcing its rights hereunder; whenever the context may require, any pronouns used herein shall include the corresponding masculine, feminine or neuter forms, and the singular form of nouns and pronouns shall include the plural and vice versa.

Section 5.4 Inapplicable Provisions. If any term, covenant or condition of this Assignment is held to be invalid, illegal or unenforceable in any respect, this Assignment shall be construed without such provision.

Section 5.5 Governing Law and Venue.

(a) The enforcement of this Assignment shall be governed, construed and interpreted by the laws of the State (without giving effect to the State's principles of conflicts of law).

(b)BORROWERHEREBYEXPRESSLYANDUNCONDITIONALLY WAIVES, IN CONNECTION WITH ANY SUIT, ACTION OR PROCEEDING BROUGHT BY OR ON BEHALF OF ASSIGNEE ON THIS ASSIGNMENT, ANY AND EVERY RIGHT BORROWER MAY HAVE (I) TO OBJECT TO THE JURISDICTION OR VENUE OF ANY STATE COURT IN KINGS OR NEW YORK COUNTY OR ANY FEDERAL COURT LOCATED IN THE STATE, (II) TO INJUNCTIVE RELIEF, (Ill) TO INTERPOSE ANY COUNTERCLAIM THEREIN (OTHER THAN COMPULSORY COUNTERCLAIMS), AND (IV) TO HAVE THE SAME CONSOLIDATED WITH ANY OTHER OR SEPARATE SUIT, ACTION OR PROCEEDING. THE FOREGOING WAIVERS ARE GIVEN KNOWINGLY AND VOLUNTARILY BY BORROWER. ASSIGNEE IS HEREBY AUTHORIZED TO FILE A COPY OF THIS PARAGRAPH IN ANY PROCEEDING AS

CONCLUSIVE EVIDENCE OF ANY OR ALL OF THE FOREGOING WAIVERS.

Section 5.6 <u>Notices.</u> All notices or other written communications hereunder shall be delivered in accordance with the terms of the Mortgage.

Section 5.7 Waiver of Trial by Jury. BORROWER HEREBY KNOWINGLY, VOLUNTARILY AND INTENTIONALLY WAIVES THE RIGHT TO A TRIAL BY JURY TO THE EXTENT THAT ANY SUCH RIGHT SHALL NOW OR HEREAFTER EXIST IN RESPECT OF ANY LITIGATION BASED ON THIS ASSIGNMENT, ARISING OUT OF, UNDER OR IN CONNECTION WITH THIS ASSIGNMENT, ANY OTHER LOAN DOCUMENTS OR HEDGING CONTRACTS CONTEMPLATED TO BE EXECUTED IN CONNECTION HEREWITH, OR ANY COURSE OF CONDUCT, COURSE OF DEALINGS, STATEMENTS (WHETHER VERBAL OR WRITTEN) OR ACTIONS OF ANY PARTY. THIS WAIVER IS INTENDED TO ENCOMPASS INDIVIDUALLY EACH INSTANCE AND EACH ISSUE AS TO WHICH THE RIGHT TO A TRIAL BY JURY WOULD OTHERWISE ACCRUE AND CONSTITUTES A MATERIAL INDUCEMENT FOR BORROWER AND LENDER AND ANY AFFILIATE COUNTERPARTY TO ENTER INTO THE TRANSACTIONS CONTEMPLATED HEREBY. LENDER AND ANY AFFILIATE COUNTERPARTY ARE EACH HEREBY AUTHORIZED TO FILE A COPY OF THIS PARAGRAPH IN ANY PROCEEDING AS CONCLUSIVE EVIDENCE OF THIS WAIVER.

Section 5.8 <u>Successors and Assigns.</u> This Assignment shall be binding upon and inure to the benefit of Borrower and Lender and their respective successors and assigns forever.

Section 5.9 <u>Headinqs, Etc.</u> The headings and captions of various paragraphs of this Assignment are for convenience of reference only and are not to be construed as defining or limiting, in any way, the scope or intent of the provisions hereof.

Section 5.10 <u>Additional Borrower Covenants.</u> Borrower hereby covenants and agrees

(a) that Borrower shall not, without the consent of Lender, (i) amend, modify or waive the provisions of any Lease or terminate, reduce rents under or shorten the term of any Lease, except pursuant to and in accordance with the provisions of the this Assignment, the Mortgage and the other Loan Documents; (ii) collect any Rents (exclusive of security deposits) more than thirty (30) days in advance of the time when the same shall become due; (iii) waive or release any tenant from the performance or observation by such tenant of any obligation or condition of any of the Leases; (iv) give any consent to any assignment or sublease by the tenant under any of the Leases; (v) agree to subordinate any of the Leases to any mortgage or other encumbrance; or (vi) modify the terms of any guaranty of any of the Leases, or terminate any such guaranty. Borrower shall (unless such notice is contained in a Lease) deliver notice of this Assignment in form and substance acceptable to Lender, to all present and future holders of any interest in any Lease, by assignment or otherwise. Borrower shall request the recipient of any such notice to acknowledge the receipt thereof.

(b) Borrower shall not execute any Lease of all or a substantial portion of the Property except for actual occupancy by the lessee thereunder, and will at all times promptly and faithfully perform, or cause to be performed promptly, all of the covenants, conditions and agreements contained in all Leases of the Property, or any part thereof, now or hereafter existing, on the part of the lessor thereunder to be kept and performed and will at all times do all things necessary to compel performance by the lessee under each Lease of all obligations, covenants and agreements by such lessee to be performed thereunder; and appear in and defend any action arising out of, or in any manner connected with, any of the Leases, or the obligations or liabilities of Borrower as the landlord or lessor thereunder, or of the tenant or any guarantor thereunder. If any of such Leases provide for the giving by the lessee of an estoppel certificate with respect to the status of any such Leases, Mortgagor shall exercise its right to request such certificates within ten (10) days of any demand therefor by Mortgagee.

(c) Borrower shall submit a proposed standard form of lease to be used by Borrower in connection with the Property for approval by Lender (hereinafter, as approved by Lender, referred to as the "Standard Form Lease") prior to its submission to any proposed tenant, and Borrower will make such amendments, modifications or additions thereto as may be required by Lender.

(d) Borrower shall not execute an assignment of any Leases affecting the Property or any part thereon, or the Rents, or any part thereof, from the Property, except in favor of Lender.

(e) Borrower shall not, without the prior written consent of Lender, enter into any new Lease.

Section 5.11 Counterparts. This Assignment may be executed in any number of counterparts, each of which shall be an original, but all of which together shall constitute one instrument.

**IN WITNESS WHEREOF,** Borrower has executed this Assignment the day and year first above written.

BORROWER:

11 DUFFIELD LLC

By: Darwin Lee
Name: Darwin Lee
Title: Manager, Manage Great Realty LLC,
Manager of 11 Duffield LLC

## EXHIBIT A
## DESCRIPTION OF PROPERTY

That property located at 11 Duffield, Brooklyn, Kings County, New York. Section 3742, Block 97, Lot 23, and all improvements thereon.

# EXHIBIT B
# DESCRIPTION OF LEASES AND RENTS

As used in Subsection 1.1(a), the term **"leases"** shall mean all leases, subleases, licenses, franchises, concessions or grants of other possessory interests, tenancies, and any other agreements affecting the use, possession or occupancy of the Property or any part thereof (including, without limitation, guest rooms, restaurants, bars, conference and meeting rooms, and banquet halls and other public facilities), whether now or hereafter existing or entered into (including, without limitation, any use or occupancy arrangements created pursuant to Section 365(d) of the Bankruptcy Code or otherwise in connection with the commencement or continuance of any bankruptcy, reorganization, arrangement, insolvency, dissolution, receivership or similar proceedings, or any assignment for the benefit of creditors, in respect of any tenant or occupant of any portion of the Property) and all amendments, modifications, supplements, extensions or renewals thereof, whether now or hereafter existing and all amendments, modifications, supplements, extensions or renewals thereof. As used in Subsection 1.1(a) the term **"lease provisions"** shall mean the right to enforce, whether at law or in equity or by any other means, all terms, covenants and provisions of the Leases.

As used in Subsection 1.1(c), the term **"rents"** shall mean all rents, issues, profits, royalties (including all oil and gas or other hydrocarbon substances), earnings, receipts, revenues, accounts, account receivable, security deposits and other deposits (subject to the prior right of the tenants making such deposits) and income, including, without limitation, fixed, additional and percentage rents, and all operating expense reimbursements, reimbursements for increases in taxes, sums paid by tenants to Borrower to reimburse Borrower for amounts originally paid or to be paid by Borrower or any of Borrower's affiliates for which such tenants were liable, as, or example, tenant improvements costs in excess of any work letter, lease takeover costs, moving expenses and tax and operating expense pass-throughs for which a tenant is solely liable, parking, maintenance, common area, tax, insurance, utility and service charges and contributions, proceeds of sale of electricity, gas, heating, air-conditioning and other utilities and services, deficiency rents and liquidated damages, and other benefits now or hereafter derived from any portion of the Property or otherwise due and payable or to become due and payable as a result of any ownership, use, possession, occupancy or operation thereof and/or services rendered, goods provided and business conducted in connection therewith (including any payments received pursuant to Section 502(b) of the Bankruptcy Code or otherwise in arrangement, insolvency, dissolution, receivership or similar proceedings, or any assignment for the benefit of creditors, in respect of any tenant or other occupants of any portion of the Property and all claims as a creditor in connection with any of the foregoing) and all cash or security deposits, advance rentals, and all deposits or payments of a similar nature relating thereto, now or hereafter, including during any period of redemption, derived from the Property or any portion thereof and all proceeds from the cancellation, surrender, sale or other disposition of the Leases.

# 11 DUFFIELD FINANCIALS

An electronic version of these financial statements is available on the Aspen Publishing product page for *Taxation and Business Planning for Partnerships and LLCs, 2020-2021 Client File* by Bradley Borden under the Student Resources tab.

## Summary of 11 Duffield LLC's Cash Flows

| | Year 14 | Year 15 | Year 16 | Year 17 | Year 18 | Year 19 | Year 20 |
|---|---|---|---|---|---|---|---|
| **Cash Flows from Operations** | | | | | | | |
| Rent Revenue | $723,475 | $1,176,392 | $1,237,691 | $1,326,978 | $1,559,738 | $1,797,645 | $1,916,001 |
| Operating Expenses | ($675,000) | ($682,213) | ($713,461) | ($758,612) | ($774,028) | ($774,637) | ($789,343) |
| Interest | $0 | ($645,275) | ($636,052) | ($626,341) | ($616,114) | ($605,346) | ($594,007) |
| Management Fees | | | | | | | |
| **Net Cash from Operations** | $48,475 | ($151,096) | ($111,822) | ($57,975) | $169,596 | $417,662 | $532,651 |
| **Cash Flows from Investment** | | | | | | | |
| Sale or Disposition of Property | | | | | | | |
| Purchase of Property | ($14,600,000) | | | | | | |
| Capital Improvements | | | | | | | |
| Purchase of Investments | | | | | | | |
| **Net Cash from Investment** | ($14,600,000) | $0 | $0 | $0 | $0 | $0 | $0 |
| **Cash Flows from Financing** | | | | | | | |
| Member Contributions | | | | | | | |
| Debby | $3,150,000 | | | | | | |
| MGR | $120,000 | | | | | | |
| Loan Proceeds | $12,175,000 | | | | | | |
| Loan Repayment | ($174,015) | ($183,238) | ($192,949) | ($203,176) | ($213,944) | ($225,283) | ($237,223) |
| Line of Credit (LOC) | $0 | $0 | $0 | $190,796 | $44,348 | $0 | $0 |
| LOC Repayment | | $0 | $0 | $0 | $0 | ($192,379) | ($42,765) |
| Distributions | | | | | | | |
| Debby | $0 | $0 | $0 | $0 | $0 | $0 | $0 |
| MGR | $0 | $0 | $0 | $0 | $0 | $0 | $0 |

| | | | | | | | |
|---|---|---|---|---|---|---|---|
| **Net Cash from Financing** | $15,270,985 | ($183,238) | ($192,949) | ($12,380) | ($169,596) | ($417,662) | ($279,988) |
| **Net Cash Flows** | $719,460 | ($334,334) | ($304,771) | ($70,355) | $0 | $0 | $252,663 |
| **Year End Cash Balance** | $719,460 | $385,126 | $80,355 | $10,000 | $10,000 | $10,000 | $262,663 |
| **Reserves** | $719,460 | $385,126 | $80,355 | $10,000 | $10,000 | $10,000 | $262,663 |
| **Available Cash** | $0 | $0 | $0 | $0 | $0 | $0 | $0 |

**Summary of 11 Duffield LLC's Taxable Income**

| | Year 14 | Year 15 | Year 16 | Year 17 | Year 18 | Year 19 | Year 20 |
|---|---|---|---|---|---|---|---|
| **Items of Gross Income** | | | | | | | |
| Rent | $723,475 | $1,176,392 | $1,237,691 | $1,326,978 | $1,559,738 | $1,797,645 | $1,916,001 |
| **Total Gross Income** | $723,475 | $1,176,392 | $1,237,691 | $1,326,978 | $1,559,738 | $1,797,645 | $1,916,001 |
| | | | | | | | |
| **Deductions** | | | | | | | |
| Operating Expenses | ($675,000) | ($682,213) | ($713,461) | ($758,612) | ($774,028) | ($774,637) | ($789,343) |
| Interest | $0 | ($645,275) | ($636,052) | ($626,341) | ($616,114) | ($605,346) | ($594,007) |
| Depreciation (11 Duffield) | ($418,161) | ($544,102) | ($465,352) | ($409,102) | ($369,052) | ($368,940) | ($369,052) |
| Depreciation (Amarillo) | | | | | | | |
| **Total Deductions** | ($1,093,161) | ($1,871,590) | ($1,814,865) | ($1,794,055) | ($1,759,194) | ($1,748,922) | ($1,752,403) |
| | | | | | | | |
| **Taxable Income** | ($369,686) | ($695,198) | ($577,174) | ($467,077) | ($199,456) | $48,722 | $163,599 |

| Undistributed Contributions and Preferred Returns (Year End) | | | | | | | | |
|---|---|---|---|---|---|---|---|---|
| | | Year 14 | Year 15 | Year 16 | Year 17 | Year 18 | Year 19 | Year 20 |
| **UCC** | | | | | | | | |
| Debby | | $3,150,000 | $3,150,000 | $3,150,000 | $3,150,000 | $3,150,000 | $3,150,000 | $3,150,000 |
| MGR | | $120,000 | $120,000 | $120,000 | $120,000 | $120,000 | $120,000 | $120,000 |
| **UPR** | 6.75% | | | | | | | |
| Debby | | $62,016 | $274,641 | $487,266 | $699,891 | $912,516 | $1,125,141 | $1,337,766 |
| MGR | | $2,363 | $10,463 | $18,563 | $26,663 | $34,763 | $42,863 | $50,963 |

| Member Capital Accounts | | | | | | | |
|---|---|---|---|---|---|---|---|
| | Year 14 | Year 15 | Year 16 | Year 17 | Year 18 | Year 19 | Year 20 |
| **Debby** | | | | | | | |
| Contributions | $3,150,000 | $0 | $0 | $0 | $0 | $0 | $0 |
| Distributions | $0 | $0 | $0 | $0 | $0 | $0 | $0 |
| Pre-Tax Balance | $3,150,000 | $2,793,880 | $2,124,194 | $1,568,201 | $1,118,264 | $926,127 | $973,061 |
| 5.3(i) Income (Loss) | ($356,120) | ($669,687) | ($555,993) | ($449,937) | ($192,137) | $46,934 | $157,595 |
| Year-End Balance | $2,793,880 | $2,124,194 | $1,568,201 | $1,118,264 | $926,127 | $973,061 | $1,130,656 |
| **MGR** | | | | | | | |
| Contributions | $120,000 | $0 | $0 | $0 | $0 | $0 | $0 |
| Distributions | $0 | $0 | $0 | $0 | $0 | $0 | $0 |
| Pre-Tax Balance | $120,000 | $106,434 | $80,922 | $59,741 | $42,601 | $35,281 | $37,069 |
| 5.3(i) Income (Loss) | ($13,566) | ($25,512) | ($21,181) | ($17,140) | ($7,320) | $1,788 | $6,004 |
| Year-End Balance | $106,434 | $80,922 | $59,741 | $42,601 | $35,281 | $37,069 | $43,073 |

| Member Outside Bases | | | | | | | |
|---|---|---|---|---|---|---|---|
| | Year 14 | Year 15 | Year 16 | Year 17 | Year 18 | Year 19 | Year 20 |
| **Debby** | | | | | | | |
| Contributions | $3,150,000 | $0 | $0 | $0 | $0 | $0 | $0 |
| 5.3 Income (Loss) | ($356,120) | ($669,687) | ($555,993) | ($449,937) | ($192,137) | $46,934 | $157,595 |
| Distributions | $0 | $0 | $0 | $0 | $0 | $0 | $0 |
| 752 Amount | | | | | | | |
| Year-End Basis | | | | | | | |
| **MGR** | | | | | | | |
| Contributions | $120,000 | $0 | $0 | $0 | $0 | $0 | $0 |
| 5.3 Income (Loss) | ($13,566) | ($25,512) | ($21,181) | ($17,140) | ($7,320) | $1,788 | $6,004 |
| Distributions | $0 | $0 | $0 | $0 | $0 | $0 | $0 |
| 752 Amount | | | | | | | |
| Year-End Basis | | | | | | | |

| 5.3(i) Hypo Liquidation | | | | | | | |
|---|---|---|---|---|---|---|---|
| | Year 14 | Year 15 | Year 16 | Year 17 | Year 18 | Year 19 | Year 20 |
| Assets | | | | | | | |
| Year-End Cash | $719,460 | $385,126 | $80,355 | $10,000 | $10,000 | $10,000 | $262,663 |
| 11 Duffield | $14,600,000 | $14,600,000 | $14,600,000 | $14,600,000 | $14,600,000 | $14,600,000 | $14,600,000 |
| Accum. Depr. | ($418,161) | ($962,263) | ($1,427,615) | ($1,836,718) | ($2,205,770) | ($2,574,710) | ($2,943,762) |
| Liability | ($12,000,985) | ($11,817,747) | ($11,624,798) | ($11,421,622) | ($11,207,679) | ($10,982,396) | ($10,745,173) |
| Amarillo (book) | | | | | | | |
| Accum. Depr. (book) | | | | | | | |
| Liability | | | | | | | |
| Line of Credit | $0 | $0 | $0 | ($190,796) | ($235,144) | ($42,765) | $0 |
| Cash for Liquidation | $2,900,314 | $2,205,116 | $1,627,942 | $1,160,864 | $961,408 | $1,010,130 | $1,173,729 |

## 5.3 Hypo Carrying-Value Distribution

| | Year 14 | Year 15 | Year 16 | Year 17 | Year 18 | Year 19 | Year 20 |
|---|---|---|---|---|---|---|---|
| **Hypo Distribution to Debby** | | | | | | | |
| 5.1(a)(i) | $62,016 | $274,641 | $487,266 | $699,891 | $912,516 | $973,061 | $1,130,656 |
| 5.1(a)(ii) | $2,731,865 | $1,849,553 | $1,080,935 | $418,373 | $13,611 | ($0) | ($0) |
| 5.1(a)(iii) | $0 | $0 | $0 | $0 | $0 | $0 | $0 |
| Total to Debby | $2,793,880 | $2,124,194 | $1,568,201 | $1,118,264 | $926,127 | $973,061 | $1,130,656 |
| 5.3(ii) Minimum 75% Gain | $0 | $0 | $0 | $0 | $0 | $0 | $0 |
| Net Carrying-Value Distribution | $2,793,880 | $2,124,194 | $1,568,201 | $1,118,264 | $926,127 | $973,061 | $1,130,656 |
| % of Total | 96% | 96% | 96% | 96% | 96% | 96% | 96% |
| **Hypo Distribution to MGR** | | | | | | | |
| 5.1(a)(i) | $2,363 | $10,463 | $18,563 | $26,663 | $34,763 | $37,069 | $43,073 |
| 5.1(a)(ii) | $104,071 | $70,459 | $41,178 | $15,938 | $519 | ($0) | ($0) |
| 5.1(a)(iii) | $0 | $0 | $0 | $0 | $0 | $0 | $0 |
| Total to MGR | $106,434 | $80,922 | $59,741 | $42,601 | $35,281 | $37,069 | $43,073 |
| 5.3(ii) Minimum Gain 25% | $0 | $0 | $0 | $0 | $0 | $0 | $0 |
| Net Carrying-Value Distribution | $106,434 | $80,922 | $59,741 | $42,601 | $35,281 | $37,069 | $43,073 |
| % of Total | 4% | 4% | 4% | 4% | 4% | 4% | 4% |

FOLDER VI

# THE AMARILLO DOCUMENTS

# THE AMARILLO MORTGAGE NOTE

Date of Note: January 1, Year 17
Principal Amount: $3,830,000.00
Maturity Date: July 1, Year 41

**Interest Rate:** An interest rate equal at all times to five and three-tenths (6.5%) percent per annum. Interest shall be computed on a 360-day basis (i.e., interest for each day during which the Principal Amount, or any part thereof, is outstanding shall be computed at Interest Rate divided by 360).

**Business Day:** Business Day means a day (other than Saturday, Sunday, federal holiday, or a day on which commercial banks in New York are required or permitted to close) on which the Bank is open and conducting its customary banking transactions.

**State:** Shall mean the State of New York.

**FOR VALUE RECEIVED,** MULTIPLE REAL ESTATE HOLDINGS, LP, a New York limited partnership (the **"Borrower"**), having an address as indicated below, **HEREBY PROMISES TO PAY** to the order of RBB BANK, N.A., a national banking association, (hereinafter, together with its successors and assigns, referred to as the **"Lender"**) in immediately available federal funds, the Principal Amount. The Borrower shall pay thirty (30) consecutive semiannual installments comprised of interest only until January 1, Year 22, at which point Borrow shall pay principal as specified in the amortization schedule attached hereto as Schedule A (based upon a twenty (20) year amortization schedule), together with accrued interest on the Principal Amount. The said payments shall be due on the first (1st) day of January and the first day of July commencing on July 1, Year 17. Notwithstanding anything to the contrary herein, payment dates shall be subject to adjustment in accordance with the Following Business Day Convention which means that any payment due date that would otherwise fall on a day that is not a Business Day shall be extended to the first following day that is a Business Day. Such extension of time will not be included in the calculation of interest due.



Borrower hereby authorizes Lender to charge checking account number 776-6680-3435 at Local Bank, N.A. (or such other account maintained by Borrower at Parkside Bank, N.A. as Borrower shall designate by written notice to Lender) (the **"Deposit Account"**) to satisfy the scheduled payments of principal and/or interest due and payable to Lender hereunder on the first (1st) day of each month (each, a **"Charge Date"**) and Lender is hereby authorized to charge the Deposit Account on each Charge Date or, if any Charge Date shall fall on a Saturday, Sunday or legal holiday, then the Lender reserves the right to charge the Deposit Account on either on the first (1st) Business Day immediately preceding or on the first (1st) Business Day immediately following any such Charge Date until the Note shall be paid in full.

Borrower agrees to maintain sufficient funds in the Deposit Account to satisfy the payment due Lender under the Note on each Charge Date during the term of this Note. If sufficient funds are not available in the Deposit Account on any

Charge Date to pay the amounts then due and payable under this Note, Lender, in its sole discretion, is authorized to: (a) charge the Deposit Account for such lesser amount as shall then be available; and/or (b) charge the Deposit Account on such later date or dates that funds shall be available in the Deposit Account to satisfy the payment then due (or balance of such payment then due). Notwithstanding the foregoing, Borrower shall only be entitled to receive credit in respect of any payments of principal and interest due under the Note for funds actually received by Lender as a result of any such charges to the Deposit Account. Borrower shall be liable to Lender for any late fees or interest at the Default Rate on any payments not made on a timely basis by Borrower because of insufficient funds in the Deposit Account on any Charge Date. In the event the Deposit Account continues to contain insufficient funds to fully satisfy the payments due Lender under the Note, Borrower shall be responsible for making all such payments from another source and in no event shall the obligations of Borrower under the Note be affected or diminished as a result of any shortages in the Deposit Account, it being understood and agreed that Borrower shall at all times remain liable for payment in full of all indebtedness under the Note.

Lender may, at Lender's sole discretion, discontinue charging the Deposit Account at any time on not less than ten (10) days' written notice to the Borrower, in which event, Borrower shall thereafter be responsible for making all payments hereunder to Lender at the address set forth in Lender's notice.

Borrower shall pay a late payment charge of nine cents ($.09) for each dollar ($1.00) of each payment that is made more than fifteen (15) days after the due date thereof, which charge shall be due and payable with each such late payment.

If any present or future law, governmental rule, regulation, policy, guideline, directive or similar requirement (whether or not having the force of law) imposes, modifies, or deems applicable any capital adequacy, capital maintenance or similar requirement which affects the manner in which Lender allocates capital resources to its commitments (including any commitments hereunder), and as a result thereof, in the opinion of Lender, the rate of return on Lender's capital with regard to the loan evidenced by this Note is reduced to a level below that which Lender could have achieved but for such circumstances, then in such case and upon notice from Lender to Borrower, from time to time, Borrower shall pay Lender such additional amount or amounts as shall compensate Lender for such reduction in Lender's rate of return. Such notice shall contain the statement of Lender with regard to any such amount or amounts which shall, in the absence of manifest error, be binding upon Borrower. In determining such amount, Lender may use any reasonable method of averaging and attribution that it deems applicable. For the avoidance of doubt, the foregoing provisions shall apply to all requests, rules, guidelines or directives concerning capital adequacy issued in connection with the Dodd-Frank Wall Street Reform and Consumer Protection Act and all requests, rules, regulations, guidelines or directives concerning capital adequacy promulgated by the Bank for International Settlements, the Basel Committee on Banking Regulations and Supervisory Practices (or any successor or similar authority) or the United States financial regulatory authorities, regardless of the date adopted, issued, promulgated or implemented

This Note is secured by, and the parties hereto are entitled to the benefits and security of, that certain Mortgage and Security Agreement (the **"Mortgage")**, dated the date hereof, from Borrower, as mortgagor, to Lender, as mortgagee, encumbering, among other things, certain real property and improvements described in the Mortgage all of the covenants, conditions and agreements of the Mortgage being made a part of this Note by this reference.

Except as may be otherwise provided in the Mortgage, all monthly payments received by Lender hereunder shall be applied first, to the payment of accrued interest on the Principal Amount, second, to the reduction of the Principal Amount of this Note, and finally, the balance, if any, to the payment of any fees, costs, expenses or charges then payable by Borrower to Lender hereunder, under the Mortgage or under any other document executed and delivered by Borrower in connection with the loan evidenced by this Note.

Borrower agrees that if it fails to timely make any payment due under this Note or upon the happening of any **"Event of Default"** under the Mortgage, (as defined in the Mortgage), the outstanding Principal Amount, together with accrued interest and all other expenses, including, reasonable attorneys' fees, shall immediately become due and payable at the option of the holder of this Note, notwithstanding the Maturity Date. For purposes hereof, attorneys' fees shall include, without limitation, fees and disbursements for legal services incurred by the holder hereof in collecting or enforcing payment hereof whether or not suit is brought, and if suit is brought, then through all appellate actions. From and after any **"Event of Default"** under the Mortgage, the interest rate of this Note shall be the **"Default Rate"** (as defined in the Mortgage).

In no event shall the total of all charges payable under this Note, the Mortgage and any other documents executed and delivered in connection herewith and therewith that are or could be held to be in the nature of interest exceed the maximum rate permitted to be charged by applicable law. Should Lender receive any payment that is or would be in excess of that permitted to be charged under any such applicable law, such payment shall have been, and shall be deemed to have been, made in error and shall thereupon be applied to reduce the principal balance outstanding on this Note.

Borrower waives demand, presentment for payment, notice of dishonor, protest and notice of protest of this Note.

Any notice, demand or request relating to any matter set forth in this Note shall be given in the manner provided for in the Mortgage. Time is of the essence as to all dates set forth herein.

This Note may not be waived, changed, modified, terminated or discharged orally, but only by an agreement in writing signed by the party against whom enforcement of any such waiver, change, modification, termination or discharge is sought.

This Note may be prepaid, in whole or in part without a prepayment premium, so long as (i) Lender is given not less than thirty (30) days' notice of such prepayment, (ii) each prepayment is accompanied by the payment of accrued and unpaid interest on the principal amount prepaid together with all late charges and other losses, costs and expenses attributable to such prepayment, (iii) each prepayment is made on a Charge Date, and (iv) each prepayment is made in immediately available federal funds. All partial prepayments shall be applied to the installments of principal due hereunder in the inverse order of their maturity.

Borrower shall indemnify Lender, and hold Lender harmless from any loss, damages, liability, or expense which Lender may sustain or incur as a consequence of the making of a prepayment, whether by voluntary prepayment, acceleration or otherwise, on a day which is not the last day of a LIBOR Interest Period with respect thereto. With respect to such prepayment, such indemnification shall equal the excess, if any, of (i) the amount of interest which would have accrued on the amount so prepaid for the period from the date of such prepayment at the applicable rate of interest provided for herein over (ii) the amount of interest (as reasonably determined by Lender) which would have accrued to Lender on such amount by placing such amount on deposit for a comparable period with leading banks in the London interbank Eurodollar market. This covenant shall survive the termination of this Note, and the payment of the entire outstanding Principal Amount, all other unpaid indebtedness secured by the Mortgage.

BORROWER, AND BY ITS ACCEPTANCE HEREOF, LENDER, EACH HEREBY AGREES NOT TO ELECT A TRIAL BY JURY OF ANY ISSUE TRIABLE OF RIGHT BY JURY, AND WAIVE ANY RIGHT TO TRIAL BY JURY FULLY TO THE EXTENT THAT ANY SUCH RIGHT SHALL NOW OR HEREAFTER EXIST WITH REGARD TO THIS NOTE, OR ANY CLAIM, COUNTERCLAI M OR OTHER ACTION ARISING IN CONNECTION THEREWITH. THIS WAIVER OF RIGHT TO TRIAL BY JURY IS GIVEN KNOWINGLY AND VOLUNTARI LY BY BORROWER AND LENDER, AND IS INTENDED TO ENCOMPASS INDIVIDUALLY EACH INSTANCE AND EACH ISSUE AS TO WHICH THE RIGHT TO A TRIAL BY JURY WOULD OTHERWISE ACCRUE. BORROWER AND LENDER ARE EACH HEREBY AUTHORIZED TO FILE A COPY OF THIS PARAGRAPH IN ANY PROCEEDING AS CONCLUSIVE EVIDENCE OF THIS WAIVER.

BORROWER HEREBY EXPRESSLY AND UNCONDITIONALLY WAIVES, IN CONNECTION WITH ANY SUIT, ACTION OR PROCEEDING BROUGHT BY OR ON BEHALF OF LENDER ON THIS NOTE, ANY AND EVERY RIGHT BORROWER MAY HAVE TO (I) INJUNCTIVE RELIEF, (II) INTERPOSE ANY COUNTERCLAI M THEREIN (OTHER THAN COMPULSORY COUNTERCLAIMS), AND (Ill) HAVE THE SAME CONSOLIDATED WITH ANY OTHER OR SEPARATE SUIT, ACTION OR PROCEEDING. NOTHING HEREIN CONTAINED SHALL PREVENT OR PROHIBIT BORROWER FROM INSTITUTING OR MAINTAINING A SEPARATE ACTION AGAINST LENDER WITH RESPECT TO ANY ASSERTED CLAIM.

This Note and the rights and obligations of the parties hereunder shall in all respects be governed by, and construed and enforced in accordance with, the laws of the State (without giving effect to the State's principles of conflicts of law). Borrower hereby irrevocably submits to the nonexclusive jurisdiction of any state or federal court in the State sitting in the Counties of over any suit, action or proceeding arising out of or relating to this Note, and Borrower hereby agrees and consents that, in addition to any methods of service of process provided for under applicable law, all service of process in any such suit, action or proceeding in any state or federal court in the State sitting in the County of Kings may be made by certified or registered mail, return receipt requested, directed to the Borrower at the address indicated below, and service so made shall be complete five (5) days after the same shall have been so mailed.

Borrower may hedge the floating interest expense of the Loan for the full term of the Loan by maintaining one or more interest rate hedging transactions with Lender (or with another financial institution satisfactory to Lender, as evidenced in writing) in an aggregate notional amount equal to 100% of the outstanding principal balance of the Loan originally scheduled to be outstanding over such term when the hedge is executed and providing for a fixed rate acceptable to Lender, with Borrower making fixed rate payments and receiving floating rate payments to offset changes in the variable interest expense of the Loan, all upon terms and subject to such conditions as shall be acceptable to Lender (or if such transaction is with another financial institution, all upon terms and subject to such conditions satisfactory to Lender, as evidenced in writing). The indebtedness evidenced by this Note shall include any "Additional Interest" (as defined in the Mortgage) due pursuant to any such interest rate hedging transactions. Any prepayment, acceleration, reduction, increase or any change in the terms of Lender will not alter the notional amount of any such interest rate swap transactions or otherwise affect the Borrower's obligations to continue to make payments under any such interest rate swap transactions, which will remain in force and effect notwithstanding any such prepayment, acceleration, reduction, increase or change, subject to the terms of such interest rate swap transactions.



**IN WITNESS WHEREOF,** the Borrower has executed and delivered this Note on the Date of Note.

Address:

147 Evans Street, 17M
Brooklyn, NY 11201

Borrower:

Multiple Real Estate Holdings, LP

By: *Jasmine Hsia*
Name: Jasmine Hsia
Title: Manager of MREH LLC, General Partner of Multiple Real Estate Holdings, LP

# Schedule A
# Loan Amortization Schedule (Amarillo)

| Loan Information | |
|---|---|
| Loan amount | $ 3830000 |
| Annual interest rate | 6.50 % |
| Loan period in years | 20 |
| Number of payments per year | 2 |
| Start date of loan | 1-1-17 |
| Optional extra payments | $ - |

| Loan summary | |
|---|---|
| Scheduled payment | $ 1,72,457 |
| Scheduled number of payments | 40 |
| Actual number of payments | 49 |
| Total early payments | – |
| Total interest | $ 41,88,555 |

| Pmt. No. | Payment Date | Beginning Balance | Scheduled Payment | Extra Payment | Total Payment | Principal | Interest | Ending Balance | Cumulative Interest |
|---|---|---|---|---|---|---|---|---|---|
| 1 | 7/1/17 | $ 3,830,000 | $ 124,475 | $ - | $ 124,475 | $ - | $ 124,475 | $ 3,830,000 | $ 124,475 |
| 2 | 1/1/18 | $ 3,830,000 | $ 124,475 | | $ 124,475 | $ - | $ 124,475 | $ 3,830,000 | $ 248,950 |
| 3 | 7/1/18 | $ 3,830,000 | $ 124,475 | $ - | $ 124,475 | $ - | $ 124,475 | $ 3,830,000 | $ 373,425 |
| 4 | 1/1/19 | $ 3,830,000 | $ 124,475 | $ - | $ 124,475 | $ - | $ 124,475 | $ 3,830,000 | $ 497,900 |
| 5 | 7/1/19 | $ 3,830,000 | $ 124,475 | $ - | $ 124,475 | $ - | $ 124,475 | $ 3,830,000 | $ 622,375 |
| 6 | 1/1/20 | $ 3,830,000 | $ 124,475 | $ - | $ 124,475 | $ - | $ 124,475 | $ 3,830,000 | $ 746,850 |
| 7 | 7/1/20 | $ 3,830,000 | $ 124,475 | $ - | $ 124,475 | $ - | $ 124,475 | $ 3,830,000 | $ 871,325 |
| 8 | 1/1/21 | $ 3,830,000 | $ 172,457 | $ - | $ 172,457 | $ - | $ 124,475 | $ 3,830,000 | $ 995,800 |
| 9 | 7/1/21 | $ 3,830,000 | $ 172,457 | $ - | $ 172,457 | $ - | $ 124,475 | $ 3,830,000 | $ 1,120,275 |
| 10 | 1/1/22 | $ 3,830,000 | $ 172,457 | $ - | $ 172,457 | $ 47,982 | $ 124,475 | $ 3,782,018 | $ 1,244,750 |
| 11 | 7/1/22 | $ 3,782,018 | $ 172,457 | $ - | $ 172,457 | $ 49,541 | $ 122,916 | $ 3,732,477 | $ 1,367,666 |
| 12 | 1/1/23 | $ 3,732,477 | $ 172,457 | $ - | $ 172,457 | $ 51,152 | $ 121,305 | $ 3,681,325 | $ 1,488,971 |
| 13 | 7/1/23 | $ 3,681,325 | $ 172,457 | $ - | $ 172,457 | $ 52,814 | $ 119,643 | $ 3,628,511 | $ 1,608,614 |
| 14 | 1/1/24 | $ 3,628,511 | $ 172,457 | $ - | $ 172,457 | $ 54,530 | $ 117,927 | $ 3,573,981 | $ 1,726,541 |
| 15 | 7/1/24 | $ 3,573,981 | $ 172,457 | $ - | $ 172,457 | $ 56,303 | $ 116,154 | $ 3,517,678 | $ 1,842,695 |
| 16 | 1/1/25 | $ 3,517,678 | $ 172,457 | $ - | $ 172,457 | $ 58,132 | $ 114,325 | $ 3,459,546 | $ 1,957,020 |
| 17 | 7/1/25 | $ 3,459,546 | $ 172,457 | $ - | $ 172,457 | $ 60,022 | $ 112,435 | $ 3,399,524 | $ 2,069,455 |
| 18 | 1/1/26 | $ 3,399,524 | $ 172,457 | $ - | $ 172,457 | $ 61,972 | $ 110,485 | $ 3,337,551 | $ 2,179,939 |
| 19 | 7/1/26 | $ 3,337,551 | $ 172,457 | $ - | $ 172,457 | $ 63,987 | $ 108,470 | $ 3,273,565 | $ 2,288,410 |
| 20 | 1/1/27 | $ 3,273,565 | $ 172,457 | $ - | $ 172,457 | $ 66,066 | $ 106,391 | $ 3,207,499 | $ 2,394,801 |
| 21 | 7/1/27 | $ 3,207,499 | $ 172,457 | $ - | $ 172,457 | $ 68,213 | $ 104,244 | $ 3,139,285 | $ 2,499,044 |
| 22 | 1/1/28 | $ 3,139,285 | $ 172,457 | $ - | $ 172,457 | $ 70,430 | $ 102,027 | $ 3,068,855 | $ 2,601,071 |
| 23 | 7/1/28 | $ 3,068,855 | $ 172,457 | $ - | $ 172,457 | $ 72,719 | $ 99,738 | $ 2,996,136 | $ 2,700,809 |
| 24 | 1/1/29 | $ 2,996,136 | $ 172,457 | $ - | $ 172,457 | $ 75,083 | $ 97,374 | $ 2,921,053 | $ 2,798,183 |
| 25 | 7/1/29 | $ 2,921,053 | $ 172,457 | $ - | $ 172,457 | $ 77,523 | $ 94,934 | $ 2,843,530 | $ 2,893,118 |
| 26 | 1/1/30 | $ 2,843,530 | $ 172,457 | $ - | $ 172,457 | $ 80,042 | $ 92,415 | $ 2,763,488 | $ 2,985,532 |
| 27 | 7/1/30 | $ 2,763,488 | $ 172,457 | $ - | $ 172,457 | $ 82,644 | $ 89,813 | $ 2,680,845 | $ 3,075,346 |
| 28 | 1/1/31 | $ 2,680,845 | $ 172,457 | $ - | $ 172,457 | $ 85,330 | $ 87,127 | $ 2,595,515 | $ 3,162,473 |
| 29 | 7/1/31 | $ 2,595,515 | $ 172,457 | $ - | $ 172,457 | $ 88,103 | $ 84,354 | $ 2,507,412 | $ 3,246,827 |

| Pmt. No. | Payment Date | Beginning Balance | Scheduled Payment | Extra Payment | Total Payment | Principal | Interest | Ending Balance | Cumulative Interest |
|---|---|---|---|---|---|---|---|---|---|
| 30 | 1/1/32 | $ 2,507,412 | $ 172,457 | $ - | $ 172,457 | $ 90,966 | $ 81,491 | $ 2,416,446 | $ 3,328,318 |
| 31 | 7/1/32 | $ 2,416,446 | $ 172,457 | $ - | $ 172,457 | $ 93,923 | $ 78,534 | $ 2,322,524 | $ 3,406,853 |
| 32 | 1/1/33 | $ 2,322,524 | $ 172,457 | $ - | $ 172,457 | $ 96,975 | $ 75,482 | $ 2,225,549 | $ 3,482,335 |
| 33 | 7/1/33 | $ 2,225,549 | $ 172,457 | $ - | $ 172,457 | $ 100,127 | $ 72,330 | $ 2,125,422 | $ 3,554,665 |
| 34 | 1/1/34 | $ 2,125,422 | $ 172,457 | $ - | $ 172,457 | $ 103,381 | $ 69,076 | $ 2,022,041 | $ 3,623,741 |
| 35 | 7/1/34 | $ 2,022,041 | $ 172,457 | $ - | $ 172,457 | $ 106,741 | $ 65,716 | $ 1,915,300 | $ 3,689,458 |
| 36 | 1/1/35 | $ 1,915,300 | $ 172,457 | $ - | $ 172,457 | $ 110,210 | $ 62,247 | $ 1,805,091 | $ 3,751,705 |
| 37 | 7/1/35 | $ 1,805,091 | $ 172,457 | $ - | $ 172,457 | $ 113,792 | $ 58,665 | $ 1,691,299 | $ 3,810,370 |
| 38 | 1/1/36 | $ 1,691,299 | $ 172,457 | $ - | $ 172,457 | $ 117,490 | $ 54,967 | $ 1,573,809 | $ 3,865,338 |
| 39 | 7/1/36 | $ 1,573,809 | $ 172,457 | $ - | $ 172,457 | $ 121,308 | $ 51,149 | $ 1,452,501 | $ 3,916,486 |
| 40 | 1/1/37 | $ 1,452,501 | $ 172,457 | $ - | $ 172,457 | $ 125,251 | $ 47,206 | $ 1,327,250 | $ 3,963,693 |
| 41 | 7/1/37 | $ 1,327,250 | $ 172,457 | $ - | $ 172,457 | $ 129,321 | $ 43,136 | $ 1,197,929 | $ 4,006,828 |
| 42 | 1/1/38 | $ 1,197,929 | $ 172,457 | $ - | $ 172,457 | $ 133,524 | $ 38,933 | $ 1,064,405 | $ 4,045,761 |
| 43 | 7/1/38 | $ 1,064,405 | $ 172,457 | $ - | $ 172,457 | $ 137,864 | $ 34,593 | $ 926,541 | $ 4,080,354 |
| 44 | 1/1/39 | $ 926,541 | $ 172,457 | $ - | $ 172,457 | $ 142,344 | $ 30,113 | $ 784,196 | $ 4,110,467 |
| 45 | 7/1/39 | $ 784,196 | $ 172,457 | $ - | $ 172,457 | $ 146,971 | $ 25,486 | $ 637,226 | $ 4,135,953 |
| 46 | 1/1/40 | $ 637,226 | $ 172,457 | $ - | $ 172,457 | $ 151,747 | $ 20,710 | $ 485,479 | $ 4,156,663 |
| 47 | 7/1/40 | $ 485,479 | $ 172,457 | $ - | $ 172,457 | $ 156,679 | $ 15,778 | $ 328,800 | $ 4,172,441 |
| 48 | 1/1/41 | $ 328,800 | $ 172,457 | $ - | $ 172,457 | $ 161,771 | $ 10,686 | $ 167,029 | $ 4,183,127 |
| 49 | 7/1/41 | $ 167,029 | $ 172,457 | $ - | $ 167,029 | $ 161,600 | $ 5,428 | $ - | $ 4,188,555 |

## THE AMARILLO GUARANTY OF PAYMENT

**THIS GUARANTY OF PAYMENT** (this "**Guaranty**") is made as of the 1st day of January, Year 14, by Debby Day, an individual (jointly and severally, and with any of their successors and assigns, each a "**Guarantor**"), in favor of RBB BANK, N.A., a national banking association, having an office at 15 Wall Drive, New York, New York 15069 (the "**Lender**") and the CRB Bank, a Canadian charterd bank ("**Hedging Counterparty**" and together with the Lender, the "**Beneficiaries**").

## RECITALS:

**WHEREAS,** contemporaneously herewith, Lender is making a loan to Multiple Real Estate Holdings, LP, a New York limited partnership (with its successors and assigns, **"Borrower")** in the principal amount of Three Million Eight Hundred Thirty Dollars ($3,83,000.00) (the **"Loan"),** which Loan is evidenced by that certain Mortgage Loan Note, dated of even date herewith, made by Borrower, as maker, in favor of Lender, as payee (together with all extensions, renewals, modifications, substitutions and amendments thereof, the **"Note"**);

**WHEREAS,** the Loan and related obligations are secured by, among other things, that certain Mortgage and Security Agreement (together with all extensions, renewals, modifications, substitutions and amendments thereof, the **"Mortgage"**), dated as of even date herewith, made by Borrower in favor of Lender and granting Lender, for itself and as agent for Hedging Counter art a first priority lien on that certain real property known as 11 Duffield and as more particularly described on Schedule A to the Mortgage (the **"Premises"**), together with the buildings and other improvements located thereon (the **"Improvements"**); and together with the Premises, collectively, the **"Property"**);

**WHEREAS,** Lender requires as a condition to the making of the Loan that each Guarantor shall have executed and delivered this Guaranty for the benefit of Lender;

**WHEREAS,** Borrower may from time to time enter into the Hedging Contracts (as hereafter defined) with Hedging Counterparty; and

**WHEREAS,** Hedging Counterparty requires as a condition to the entry into the Hedging Contracts that each Guarantor shall have executed and delivered this Guaranty for the benefit of the Hedging Counterparty.

**NOW, THEREFORE,** in consideration of the premises and other good and valuable consideration, the receipt of which is hereby acknowledged, and in order to induce Lender to make the Loan to Borrower and to induce the Hedging Counterparty to enter into the Hedging Contracts with Borrower, each Guarantor hereby represents, warrants and covenants to the Beneficiaries as follows:

1. Authorization and Enforceability of Loan Documents. The Note, the Mortgage, any indemnification agreement relating to compliance with ADA and any Environmental Law (each, as hereafter defined) (a **"Property Indemnity Agreement"**) and all of the other documents executed and delivered by Borrower in connection with the Loan (collectively, the **"Loan Documents"**)

and all agreements and other documents executed and delivered by Borrower in connection with any Hedging Obligations (as defined in the Mortgage) (the **"Hedging Contracts"**) have been duly authorized and executed by Borrower and are legal, valid and binding instruments, enforceable against Borrower in accordance with their respective terms, subject to the effect of bankruptcy, insolvency, reorganization, moratorium or other legal or equitable principles now or hereafter in effect generally affecting creditors' rights and remedies.

2. Obligations Guaranteed. Each Guarantor jointly and severally with all Guarantors, the Borrower and each Other Guarantor (as hereafter defined) unconditionally guarantees to the Beneficiaries all of the following (collectively, the **"Guaranteed Obligations"**):

a. the prompt and unconditional payment of up to Eight Hundred dollars ($800,000) of the Loan and the interest thereon, whether now or hereafter advanced, as the same shall become due and payable under the Note to the extent the assets of the Borrower are insufficient to pay the guaranteed amount, whether at stated maturity, by acceleration or otherwise, and any and all sums of money that, at the time, may have become due and payable under the provisions of the Note, the Mortgage or any other Loan Document, as well as, without limitation, all other loans, advances, indebtedness, notes, and liabilities;

b. all obligations under any rate swap, basis swap, forward rate transactions, commodity swaps, commodity options, equity or equity index swaps, equity or equity index options, bond options, interest rate options, foreign exchange transactions, cap transactions, floor transactions, collar transactions, forward transactions, currency swap transactions, cross-currency rate swap transactions, currency options between Borrower and Hedging Counterparty, other than Excluded Hedging Obligations (the **"Hedging Obligations"**); for purposes hereof **"Excluded Hedging Obligations"** means any Hedging Obligation if, and to the extent that, all or a portion of the guarantee by such Guarantor of, or the grant by such Guarantor of a security interest to secure, such Hedging Obligation (or any guarantee thereof) is or becomes impermissible under the Commodity Exchange Act (as hereafter defined) by virtue of such Guarantor's failure for any reason to constitute an "eligible contract participant" as defined in the Commodity Exchange Act at the time this Guaranty becomes effective with respect to such Hedging Obligation;

c. all other amounts, in each case, liquidated or unliquidated, owing by the Borrower to the Beneficiaries (or either of them) any time, of each and every kind, nature and description, whether arising under the Mortgage, any other Loan Document, the Hedging Contracts or otherwise, and whether secured or unsecured, direct or indirect (that is, whether the same are due directly by the Borrower to either Beneficiary; or are due indirectly by the Borrower to either Beneficiary as endorser, guarantor or other surety, or as borrower of obligations due third persons which have been endorsed or assigned to either Beneficiary, or otherwise), absolute or contingent, due or to become due, now existing or hereafter arising or contracted, including, without limitation, payment when due of all amounts outstanding respecting any of the Loan Documents or the Hedging Contracts and the due and prompt performance of all of the terms, agreements, covenants and conditions of the Note, the Mortgage, the other Loan Documents and the Hedging Contracts, but, in any event, with respect to the Hedging Counterparty, excluding any Excluded Hedging Obligation; and

d. any and all expenses that may be paid or incurred by either Beneficiary in the collection of all or any portion of such Guarantor's obligations hereunder or the exercise or enforcement of any one or more of the other rights, powers, privileges, remedies and interests of the Beneficiaries under the Loan Documents, or the Hedging Contracts, including, without limitation, reasonable attorneys' fees, irrespective of the manner or success of any such collection, exercise or enforcement, and whether or not such expenses constitute part of the Borrower's obligations but, in any event, with respect to the Hedging Counterparty, excluding any Excluded Hedging Obligation.

3. <u>Unconditional Guaranty.</u> This Guaranty is an absolute, unconditional, present and continuing guaranty of payment and performance and not of collection and is in no way conditioned or contingent upon any attempt to enforce any of either Beneficiary's rights against Borrower or to collect from the Borrower or upon any other condition or contingency. Beneficiaries shall have the right to proceed against any Guarantor immediately upon (a) any "Event of Default" under any Loan Document, and (b) any "Event of Default," termination event or similar event under the Hedging Contracts, in each case, without taking any prior action or proceeding to enforce any of the Loan Documents, the Hedging Contracts or any of them, or for the liquidation or foreclosure of any security Beneficiaries at any time hold pursuant thereto. Each Guarantor hereby waives and releases any claim (within the meaning of 11 U.S.C. §101) which such Guarantor may have against Borrower arising from a payment made by such Guarantor under this Guaranty and, except as set forth in Section 8 hereof, agrees not to assert or take advantage of any subrogation rights of such Guarantor or any right of such Guarantor to proceed against Borrower, another Guarantor or any Other Guarantor for reimbursement. It is expressly understood that the waivers and agreements of each Guarantor constitute additional and cumulative benefits given to Beneficiaries for their security and as an inducement for their respective extension of credit to Borrower. Each Beneficiary may at any time and from time to time take any and/or all actions and enforce all rights and remedies available to it hereunder or under applicable law to collect from any Guarantor any amounts then due and payable hereunder by any Guarantor and/or to cause any Guarantor to fulfill his, her or its obligations hereunder. Notwithstanding anything to the contrary in this Guaranty, the Note, any of the Loan Documents or the Hedging Contracts, neither of the Beneficiaries shall be deemed to have waived any right which either of them may have under Section 506(a), 506(b), 1111(b) or any other provisions of the Bankruptcy Code to file a claim for the full amount of the Indebtedness or to

require that all collateral shall. continue to secure all of the Indebtedness owing to either Beneficiary in accordance with the Loan Documents and the Hedging Contracts, as the case may be.

4. Liability Unimpaired. No Guarantor's liability hereunder shall in any way be limited or impaired by, and each Guarantor hereby consents to and agrees to be bound by, any amendment or modification of the provisions of any of the Loan Documents, the Hedging Contracts or any other instrument or agreement made to or with any Beneficiary by Borrower or any Guarantor, or any Person who succeeds Borrower as owner of all or part of the Property prior to foreclosure of the Mortgage or exercise of any power of sale contained therein. In addition, no Guarantor's liability hereunder shall in any way be limited or impaired by (i) any extensions of time for performance required by any of said documents, (ii) any sale, assignment or foreclosure of the Note or Mortgage or any sale or transfer of all or part of the property covered by the Mortgage, (iii) any exculpatory provision in any of said documents limiting either Beneficiary's recourse to the Property or to any other security, or limiting either Beneficiary's rights to a deficiency judgment against Borrower, (iv) the release of Borrower, any Guarantor, any Other Guarantor or any other Person from performance or observance of any of the agreements, covenants, terms or conditions contained in any of said documents for any reason, including by the applicable Beneficiary's election, by operation of law (including, but not limited to the Commodity Exchange Act) or otherwise, (v) the release or substitution in whole or in part of any security for the Loan or Hedging Obligations, (vi) either Beneficiary's failure to record the Mortgage or file any UCC financing statements (or the improper recording or filing of any thereof) or to otherwise perfect, protect, secure or insure any security interest or lien given as security for the Loan or Hedging Obligations, (vii) the invalidity, irregularity or unenforceability, in whole or in part, of any of the Loan Documents, the Hedging Contracts, this Guaranty or any other instrument or agreement executed or delivered to either Beneficiary in connection with the Loan or the Hedging Contracts, except to the extent that there is a final adjudication by a court of competent jurisdiction of a valid defense to Borrower's obligations under the Loan Documents or the Hedging Contracts to payment of the Indebtedness, (viii) the inaccuracy of any of the representations and warranties made by Borrower in the Mortgage, the other Loan Documents or Hedging Contracts, or (ix) any other action or circumstance whatsoever that constitutes, or might be construed to constitute, a legal or equitable discharge or defense (except full payment and satisfaction) of Borrower for its obligations under any of the Loan Documents or the Hedging Contracts or of any Guarantor under this Guaranty; and, in any such case, whether with or without notice to any Guarantor and with or without consideration.

5. Defined Terms. As used herein, the following terms shall have the meanings ascribed thereto below:

(a) **"ADA"** shall mean the Americans with Disabilities Act of 1990, as amended and supplemented from time to time.

(b) **"Affiliate"** shall mean with respect to any Person, (a) any Person which, directly or indirectly through one or more intermediaries controls, or is controlled by, or is under common control with such Person, or (b) any Person who is a director or officer (i) of such Person, (ii) of any Subsidiary of such Person, or (iii) any person described in clause (a) above. For purposes of this definition, control of a Person means the power, direct or indirect, (x) to vote 5% or more of the ownership interests having ordinary voting power for the election of directors (or comparable equivalent) of such Person, or (y) to direct or cause the direction of the management and policies of such Person whether by contract or otherwise; control may be by ownership, contract, or otherwise.

(c) **"Commodity Exchange Act"** shall mean the Commodity Exchange Act (7 U.S.C. §1 et seq.), as amended or supplemented from time to time, and any successor statute or any other rule, regulation or order of the Commodity Futures Trading Commission (or the application or official interpretation of any thereof).

(d) **"Enforcement Costs"** shall mean any and all expenses that may be paid or incurred by either Beneficiary in the collection of all or any portion of any Guarantor's obligations hereunder or the exercise or enforcement of any one or more of the other rights, powers, privileges, remedies and interests of the Beneficiaries under the Loan Documents, the Hedging Contracts or under this Guaranty, including, without limitation, reasonable attorneys' fees, irrespective of the manner or success of any such collection, exercise or enforcement, and whether or not such expenses constitute part of the Borrower's obligations.

(e) **"Environmental Law"** shall mean any present and future federal, state and local laws, statutes, ordinances, rules, regulations and the like, as well as common law, relating to the safety, welfare and protection of human health or the environment or any natural resource, relating to any Hazardous Materials (as defined in the Mortgage), relating to liability for or costs of other actual or threatened danger to the safety, welfare or human health or the environment or any natural resource and includes, but is not limited to, the following statutes, as amended, any successor thereto, and any regulations promulgated pursuant thereto, and any state or local statutes, ordinances, rules, regulations and the like addressing similar issues: the Comprehensive Environmental Response, Compensation and Liability Act of 1980, as amended (as amended, including, without limitation, the Superfund Amendments and Reauthorization Act of 1986, **"CERCLA"**), 42 U.S.C. §9601 et seq.; the Emergency Planning and Community Right-to-Know Act of 1986; the Hazardous Substances Transportation Act; the Resource Conservation and Recovery Act (including but not limited to Subtitle I relating to underground storage tanks); the Solid Waste Disposal Act; the Clean Water Act; the Clean Air Act; the Toxic Substances Control Act; the Safe Drinking Water Act; the Occupational Safety and Health Act; the Federal Water Pollution Control Act; the Federal Insecticide, Fungicide and

Rodenticide Act; the Endangered Species Act; the National Environmental Policy Act; and the River and Harbors Appropriation Act. The term **"Environmental Law"** also includes, but is not limited to, any present and future federal, state and local laws, statutes ordinances, rules, regulations and the like, as well as common law conditioning transfer of property upon a negative declaration or other approval of a governmental authority of the environmental condition of the Property; requiring notification or disclosure of releases of Hazardous Materials or other environmental condition of the Property to any governmental authority or other Person, whether or not in connection with transfer of title to or interest in property; imposing conditions or requirements in connection with permits or other authorization for lawful activity; relating to nuisance, trespass or other causes of action related to the Property; and relating to wrongful death, personal injury, or property or other damage in connection with any physical condition or use of the Property.

(f) **"Other Guarantor"** shall mean any Person executing a guaranty (other than this Guaranty) in favor of either Beneficiary.

(g) **"Person"** shall mean any individual, corporation, partnership, limited liability company, joint venture, estate, trust, unincorporated association, any other entity, any federal, state, county or municipal government or any bureau, department or agency thereof, and any fiduciary acting in such capacity on behalf of any of the foregoing.

(h) **"State"** shall mean the State of New York.

6. Preservation of Loan Documents and Hedging Contracts. Each Guarantor will cause Borrower to maintain and preserve the enforceability of the Loan Documents and Hedging Contracts as the same may be modified and will not permit Borrower to take or to fail to take actions of any kind which might be the basis for a claim that such Guarantor has a defense to such Guarantor's obligations hereunder.



7. Security; Guarantor's Events of Default.

(a) As security for any and all of the obligations of each Guarantor under this Guaranty, now existing or hereafter arising hereunder or otherwise, each Guarantor hereby grants to the Lender for itself and as agent for the Hedging Counterparty a lien upon and a security interest in any and all moneys or other property (i.e., goods and merchandise, as well as any and all documents relative thereto; funds, securities, choses in action and any and all other forms of property whether real, personal or mixed, and any right, title or interest of the Guarantor therein or thereto), and the proceeds thereof, which have been, or may hereafter be, deposited or delivered to the Lender (or with any third party acting on either Beneficiary's behalf) by or for the account or credit of such Guarantor whether for safekeeping, custody, pledge, deposit, transmission, collection or otherwise. All remittances and property shall be deemed delivered to the Lender as soon as put in transit to the Lender by mail or carrier.

(b) Upon the occurrence of any of the following events with respect to any Guarantor (each a **"Guarantor's Event of Default"**): (i) such Guarantor defaults under this Guaranty or any other agreement with either Beneficiary to which such Guarantor is a party; (ii) any representation or warranty made by such Guarantor herein or in any other agreement with either Beneficiary to which such Guarantor is a party is false or untrue as of the date such representation or warranty is made; (iii) such Guarantor commences any case, proceeding, or other action under any law of any jurisdiction relating to bankruptcy, insolvency, reorganization, or relief of debtors or seeks to have an order for relief entered with respect to such Guarantor or seeks to be adjudicated a bankrupt or insolvent, or seeks reorganization, arrangement, adjustment, liquidation, dissolution, composition or other relief with respect to such Guarantor or such Guarantor's debts, or seeks the appointment of a receiver, trustee, custodian, or other similar official for such Guarantor or for all or any substantial part of such Guarantor's property; (iv) such Guarantor makes a general assignment for the benefit of creditors; (v) there is commenced against such Guarantor, any case, proceeding or other action of the type referred to in clause (iii) above or seeking the issuance of a warrant of attachment, execution, distraint, or similar process against all or any substantial part of such Guarantor's property, which case, proceeding or other action results in an entry of an order for relief or is not dismissed, discharged or bonded within fifteen (15) days of the commencement thereof; (vi) such Guarantor takes any action indicating such Guarantor's consent to, approval of, or acquiescence in or in furtherance of, any of the acts set forth in clauses (iii) and (v) above; (vii) the death or incapacity of such Guarantor, if an individual; (viii) such Guarantor admits in writing such Guarantor's inability to pay such Guarantor's debts as they mature; (ix) such Guarantor terminates or dissolves or suspends such Guarantor's usual business activities or conveys, sells, leases, transfers or otherwise disposes of all or a substantial part of such Guarantor's property, business or assets other than in the ordinary course of business; or (x) the existence or occurrence at any time of one or more conditions or events that, in the sole opinion of either Beneficiary, has resulted or is reasonably likely to result in a material adverse change in the business, properties or financial condition of such Guarantor; then, in any such case, and irrespective of whether there is any "Event of Default" under any Loan Document or the Hedging Contracts, any or all of the obligations of such Guarantor shall, at the applicable Beneficiary's option become (for the purpose of this Guaranty) immediately due and payable by such Guarantor, without demand or notice. In addition, upon the occurrence of any Guarantor's Event of Default, the Beneficiaries shall have all of the rights and remedies provided to a secured party by the Uniform Commercial Code as in effect in the State at that time. Each Guarantor agrees that, in the event that notice is necessary, written notice mailed to such Guarantor at the address given below five (5) days prior to the date of public sale of the property subject to the lien and security interest created herein or prior to the date after which private sale or any other disposition of said property will be made shall constitute reasonable notice, but notice given in any other reasonable manner or at any other reasonable time shall be sufficient.

8. Indemnification; Payments; Certain Waivers. Each Guarantor (i) waives any right or claim of right to cause a marshalling of Borrower's assets or to cause either Beneficiary to proceed against any of the security for the Indebtedness, including, without limitation, the Loan, the Hedging Obligations or the other obligations guaranteed hereby before proceeding against such Guarantor, (ii) agrees that any payments required to be made by such Guarantor hereunder shall become due on demand in accordance with the terms of Section 2 (and if applicable Section 3) hereof and without presentment to Borrower or such Guarantor, demand for payment or protest, or notice of non-payment or protest, and (iii) except as hereinafter provided, expressly waives and relinquishes all rights and remedies accorded by applicable law to guarantors. Without limiting the generality of the foregoing, each Guarantor hereby waives all rights (x) to participate in any claim or remedy either Beneficiary may now or hereafter have against Borrower or in any collateral which any Beneficiary, now has or hereafter may acquire for the obligations guaranteed hereby and (y) except as provided below, to contribution, indemnification, set-off, exoneration or reimbursement, whether from Borrower, another Guarantor, any Other Guarantor, or any other Person now or hereafter primarily or secondarily liable for any of Borrower's obligations to either Beneficiary, and whether arising by contract or operation of law or otherwise by reason of such Guarantor's execution, delivery or performance of this Guaranty. No Guarantor waives and each Guarantor hereby retains all rights of subrogation, contribution, indemnification, set-off or reimbursement against Borrower or another Guarantor or any Other Guarantor that such Guarantor may have (the **"Undersigned's Rights"**); provided however that (i) this Guaranty shall neither be contingent upon the existence of the Undersigned's Rights nor subject to any claims or defenses whatsoever which may be asserted in connection with the enforcement or attempted enforcement of the Undersigned's Rights including, without limitation, any claim that the Undersigned's Rights were abrogated by any acts of either Beneficiary, and (ii) until the Indebtedness and all other amounts guaranteed hereunder (including, without limitation, the Loan and Hedging Obligations) shall have been paid in full, each Guarantor hereby postpones and subordinates (A) the exercise of any and all of the Undersigned's Rights to each Beneficiary's rights against such Guarantor under this Guaranty, against Borrower under any of the Loan Documents and the Hedging Contracts, as the case may be, or any Other Guarantor and (B) any of the Undersigned's Rights to any collateral securing the Indebtedness, including, without limitation, the Loan and the Hedging Obligations.

9. Reinstatement. This Guaranty shall continue to be effective, or be reinstated automatically, as the case may be, if at any time payment, in whole or in part, of any of the obligations guaranteed hereby is rescinded or otherwise must be restored or returned by either Beneficiary (whether as a preference, fraudulent conveyance or otherwise) upon or in connection with the insolvency,

bankruptcy, dissolution, liquidation or reorganization of Borrower, another Guarantor, any Other Guarantor or any other Person, or upon or as a result of the appointment of a receiver, intervenor or conservator of, or trustee or similar officer for, Borrower, another Guarantor, any Other Guarantor or any other Person or for a substantial part of Borrower's, another Guarantor's, any Other Guarantor's or any of such other Person's property, as the case may be, or otherwise, all as though such payment had not been made. Each Guarantor further agrees that in the event any such payment is rescinded or must be restored or returned, all costs and reasonable expenses (including, without limitation, reasonable legal fees and expenses) incurred by or on behalf of either Beneficiary in defending or enforcing such continuance or reinstatement, as the case may be, shall constitute Enforcement Costs, the payment of which is guaranteed by such Guarantor pursuant to Section 2 above and covered by such Guarantor's indemnity pursuant to Section 8 above.

10. Litigation Compliance with Judgments. Each Guarantor represents and warrants with respect to itself that there are no actions, suits or proceedings pending or threatened against or affecting such Guarantor, at law, in equity or before or by any governmental authorities that would have a material effect on such Guarantor's ability to perform its obligations hereunder; to the best of such Guarantor's knowledge, such Guarantor is not in default with respect to any order, writ, injunction, decree or demand of any court or governmental authorities.

11. Authorization and Enforceability; No Conflicts. Each Guarantor represents and warrants that it has the full power and authority to enter into and perform its obligations under this Guaranty and this Guaranty is a legal, valid and binding instrument, enforceable against such Guarantor in accordance with its terms. Each Guarantor that is not an individual hereby represents and warrants that the execution, delivery and performance of this Guaranty has been authorized by all proper and necessary actions of such Guarantor. Each Guarantor represents and warrants with respect to itself that the consummation of the transactions contemplated hereby and the performance of this Guaranty has not resulted and will not result in any breach of, or constitute a default under, any mortgage, deed of trust, lease, bank loan or credit agreement, corporate charter, by-laws, partnership agreement or other instrument to which such Guarantor is a party or by which such Guarantor may be bound or affected.

12. Compliance with Laws. Each Guarantor represents and warrants with respect to itself that such Guarantor is in compliance with, and the transactions contemplated by the Loan Documents or the Hedging Contracts and this Guaranty do not and will not violate any provision of, or require any filing, registration, consent or approval under, any federal, state or local law, rule, regulation, ordinance, order, writ, judgment, injunction, decree, determination or award, including the Commodity Exchange Act, the ADA and any Environmental Law presently in effect having applicability to such Guarantor (collectively, the **"Laws")**, and agrees that such Guarantor will comply promptly with all Laws now or hereafter in effect having applicability to such Guarantor.

13. Accuracy of Information; Full Disclosure. Each Guarantor represents and warrants with respect to itself that neither this Guaranty nor any documents, financial statements, reports, notices, schedules, certificates, statements or other writings furnished by or on behalf of such Guarantor to either Beneficiary in connection with the negotiation of this Guaranty, the Loan Documents or the Hedging Contracts or the consummation of the transactions contemplated thereby, or required herein or by the other Loan Documents or the Hedging Contracts to be furnished by or on behalf of such Guarantor, contains any untrue or misleading statement of a material fact; there is no fact which such Guarantor has not disclosed to the Beneficiaries in writing which materially affects adversely any of the property covered by the Mortgage or the business affairs or financial condition of such Guarantor, or the ability of such Guarantor to perform this Guaranty.

14. Financial Statements. Each Guarantor represents, warrants and covenants with respect to itself as follows:

(a) The most recent financial statements heretofore delivered by such Guarantor, if any, to either Beneficiary are true and correct in all respects, have been prepared in accordance with sound accounting principles consistently applied and fairly present such Guarantor's financial condition as of the date thereof, and no material adverse change has occurred in the financial condition reflected therein since the date thereof.

(b) If such Guarantor is other than an individual, such Guarantor shall deliver to the Beneficiaries:

(i) annually, as soon as available, but in any event within two hundred seventy (270) days after the last day of each calendar year, copies of its Federal and state tax returns from the prior calendar year; and

(ii) promptly after written request by Lender therefor, company-prepared interim financial statements and gallon reports, in each case as may be acceptable to Lender from time to time.

(c) If such Guarantor is an individual,

(i) such Guarantor shall deliver to the Beneficiaries annually, as soon as available, but in any event within two hundred seventy (270) days after the last day of each calendar year, (x) the signed, personal financial statement of such Guarantor, on Lender's standard form or such other form as may be acceptable to the Lender from time to time, together with supporting documentation acceptable to Lender verifying such Guarantor's liquidity as set forth therein and (y) the Federal and state tax returns from the prior calendar year; and

(ii) promptly after written request by Lender therefor, a Schedule K-1 with respect to each entity owned by such Guarantor.

(d) Promptly after a written request therefor, such Guarantor shall deliver to the Beneficiaries such other financial data or information as either Beneficiary may reasonably request from time to time.

(e) Each Guarantor authorizes the Lender to make or have made any credit, employment or investigation inquiry that the Lender determines appropriate for the extension of credit, periodic evaluation of the Indebtedness or the collection of amounts owed to the Lender (and if applicable any Affiliate Counterparty) on the Indebtedness, or for any other legitimate purposes associated with the Indebtedness, including without limitation, obtaining one or more business or consumer credit reports. This authorization will also apply to the Lender's agents, affiliates, successors, and assigns.

15. Eligible Contract Participant Status. Each Guarantor, in its own capacity and in its capacity as guarantor for and on behalf of Borrower, represents and warrants to the Beneficiaries that, on and as of the date hereof and on each date on which a "Swap Transaction Event" (as defined in the ISDA August 2012 OF Supplement, as published on August 13, 2012) occurs between Hedging Counterparty and Borrower, it is an "eligible contract participant" within the meaning of Section 1a(18) of the Commodity Exchange Act as amended from time to time, and applicable regulations thereunder.

16. Non-Waiver Remedies Cumulative. No failure or delay on either Beneficiary's part in exercising any right, power or privilege under any of the Loan Documents, the Hedging Contracts, this Guaranty or any other document made to or with either Beneficiary in connection with the Loan or the Hedging Obligations, shall operate as a waiver of any such privilege, power or right or shall be deemed to constitute either Beneficiary's acquiescence in any default by Borrower or Guarantor under any of said documents. A waiver by either Beneficiary of any right or remedy under any of the Loan Documents, this Guaranty or the Hedging Contracts, on any one occasion shall not be construed as a bar to any right or remedy which either Beneficiary otherwise would have on any future occasion, and any such waiver by one Beneficiary shall not be deemed to be a waiver by the other Beneficiary. The rights and remedies provided in said documents are cumulative, may be exercised singly or concurrently and are not exclusive of any rights or remedies provided by law.

17. Transfers of Interests in Loan. Each Guarantor acknowledges that Lender, at Lender's sole discretion, may sell, assign or transfer interests in the Loan, this Guaranty and the other Loan Documents to one or more participants, purchasers and/or assignees (collectively, **"Participants")** and agrees in connection therewith, all Loan Documents and other documentation, financial statements, appraisals and other data, or copies thereof, relevant to Borrower, each Guarantor, the Premises, the Improvements or the Mortgage, may be provided to and retained by any such participant, purchaser or assignee or prospective participant, purchaser or assignee. Each Guarantor agrees that Lender shall have no obligation to give any Guarantor written notice of any sale, assignment or transfer of any interest or participation in the Loan or any part thereof.

18. Separate Indemnity. Each Guarantor acknowledges and agrees that the Beneficiaries' respective rights (and such Guarantor's obligations) under this Guaranty shall be in addition to all of such Beneficiary's rights (and all of such Guarantor's obligations) under any indemnity agreement executed and delivered to such Beneficiary by Borrower and/or such Guarantor in connection with the Loan or the Hedging Obligations, and payments by such Guarantor

under this Guaranty shall not reduce any of such Guarantor's obligations and liabilities under any such indemnity agreement.

19. Severability. Any provision of this Guaranty, or the application thereof to any Person or circumstance (including any invalidation of any Guarantor's or Other Guarantor's obligations under or in connection with the Commodity Exchange Act), that, for any reason, in whole or in part, is prohibited or unenforceable in any jurisdiction shall, as to such jurisdiction, be ineffective to the extent of such prohibition or unenforceability without invalidating the remaining provisions of this Guaranty (or the remaining portions of such provision) or the application thereof to any other person or circumstance, and any such prohibition or unenforceability in any jurisdiction shall not invalidate or render unenforceable such provision (or portion thereof) or the application thereof to any person or circumstance in any other jurisdiction.

20. Entire Agreement; Amendments. This Guaranty contains the entire agreement of the parties with respect to the subject matter hereof and supersedes all prior oral or written agreements or statements relating to such subject matter, and none of the terms and provisions hereof may be waived, amended or terminated except by a written instrument signed by the Person against whom enforcement of the waiver, amendment or termination is sought.

21. Successors and Assigns. This Guaranty shall be binding upon and shall inure to the benefit of the Beneficiaries and each Guarantor and their respective heirs, personal representatives, successors and assigns. This Guaranty may be assigned by either Beneficiary with respect to all or any portion of the obligations guaranteed hereby, and when so assigned each Guarantor shall be liable under this Guaranty to the assignee(s) of the portion(s) of the obligations guaranteed hereby so assigned without in any manner affecting the liability of any Guarantor hereunder to the Beneficiaries with respect to any portion of the obligations guaranteed hereby retained by the Beneficiaries.

22. WAIVER OF TRIAL BY JURY. EACH GUARANTOR, AND BY ITS ACCEPTANCE HEREOF, LENDER AND HEDGING COUNTERPARTY, EACH HEREBY KNOWINGLY, VOLUNTARI LY AND INTENTIONALLY WAIVES THE RIGHT TO A TRIAL BY JURY TO THE EXTENT THAT ANY SUCH RIGHT SHALL NOW OR HEREAFTER EXIST IN RESPECT OF ANY LITIGATION BASED ON THIS GUARANTY, ARISING OUT OF, UNDER OR IN CONNECTION WITH THIS GUARANTY OR ANY OTHER LOAN DOCUMENTS CONTEMPLATED TO BE EXECUTED IN CONNECTION HEREWITH, OR ANY HEDGING CONTRACTS, OR ANY COURSE OF CONDUCT, COURSE OF DEALINGS, STATEMENTS (WHETHER VERBAL OR WRITTEN) OR ACTIONS OF ANY PARTY. THIS WAIVER IS INTENDED TO ENCOMPASS INDIVIDUALLY EACH INSTANCE AND EACH ISSUE AS TO WHICH THE RIGHT TO A TRIAL BY JURY WOULD OTHERWISE ACCRUE AND CONSTITUTES A MATERIAL INDUCEMENT FOR BORROWER AND LENDER AND HEDGING COUNTERPARTY TO

ENTER INTO THE TRANSACTIONS CONTEMPLATED HEREBY. LENDER AND HEDGING COUNTERPARTY ARE EACH HEREBY AUTHORIZED TO FILE A COPY OF THIS PARAGRAPH IN ANY PROCEEDING AS CONCLUSIVE EVIDENCE OF THIS WAIVER.

23. ADDITIONAL WAIVERS IN THE EVENT OF ENFORCEMENT/ CONSENT TO JURISDICTION AND VENUE. EACH GUARANTOR HEREBY EXPRESSLY AND UNCONDITIONALLY WAIVES, IN CONNECTION WITH ANY SUIT, ACTION OR PROCEEDING BROUGHT BY OR ON BEHALF OF LENDER OR HEDGING COUNTERPARTY ON THIS GUARANTY, ANY AND EVERY RIGHT SUCH GUARANTOR MAY HAVE: (I) TO OBJECT TO THE JURISDICTION OR VENUE OF ANY STATE COURT SITTING IN KINGS OR NEW YORK COUNTY OR ANY FEDERAL COURT LOCATED IN THE STATE, (II) TO INJUNCTIVE RELIEF, (III) TO INTERPOSE ANY COUNTERCLAIM THEREIN (OTHER THAN COMPULSORY COUNTERCLAIMS), AND (IV) TO HAVE THE SAME CONSOLIDATED WITH ANY OTHER OR SEPARATE SUIT, ACTION OR PROCEEDING. EACH GUARANTOR HEREBY AGREES AND CONSENTS TO, IN ADDITION TO ANY METHODS OF SERVICE OF PROCESS PROVIDED FOR UNDER APPLICABLE LAW, SERVICE OF PROCESS IN ANY SUCH SUIT BEING MADE UPON SUCH GUARANTOR BY MAIL AT THE ADDRESS SET FORTH HEREIN AND SERVICE SO MADE SHALL BE COMPLETE FIVE (5) DAYS AFTER THE SAME SHALL HAVE BEEN SO MAILED. THE FOREGOING WAIVERS ARE GIVEN KNOWINGLY AND VOLUNTARILY BY EACH GUARANTOR. LENDER AND HEDGING COUNTERPARTY ARE EACH HEREBY AUTHORIZED TO FILE A COPY OF THIS PARAGRAPH IN ANY PROCEEDING AS CONCLUSIVE EVIDENCE OF ANY OR ALL OF THE FOREGOING WAIVERS.

24. Governing Law. This Guaranty and the rights and obligations of the parties hereunder shall in all respects be governed by, and construed and enforced in accordance with, the laws of the State without regard to the State's principles of conflicts of law.

25. Section Headings. Any section headings and captions in this Guaranty are for convenience only and shall not affect the interpretation or construction hereof.

26. Liability Unaffected by Release. Any Guarantor or other Person liable upon or in respect of any obligation hereby guaranteed may be released without affecting the liability of any other Guarantor hereunder.

27. Joint and Several Obligations. If more than one Person comprises Guarantor, then each such Person's obligations and liability under this Guaranty shall be joint and several.

28. Notices. Notices shall be given in the manner provided in the Mortgage and with respect to each Guarantor at the address set forth below.

29. Principles of Construction. All references to sections, paragraphs, schedules and exhibits are to sections, schedules and exhibits in or to this Guaranty unless otherwise specified. Unless otherwise specified, the words "hereof," "herein" and "hereunder" and words of similar import when used in this Guaranty shall refer to this Guaranty as a whole and not to any particular provision of this Guaranty. The recitals to this Guaranty shall be deemed a part hereof and all exhibits and schedules attached hereto, if any, are incorporated herein by reference for all purposes. Unless otherwise specified, all meanings attributed to defined terms herein shall be equally applicable to both the singular and plural forms of the terms so defined and "including" means including without limitation. Whenever the context requires, each gender shall include all other genders.

30. Patriot Act Notice. Lender is subject to the requirements of the USA Patriot Act (Title Ill of Pub. L. 107-56) (signed into law October 26, 2001)) (the "Act") and hereby notifies the Guarantor that pursuant to the requirements of the Act, it is required to obtain, verify and record information that identifies the Guarantor, which information includes the name and address of the Guarantor and other information that will allow Lender to identify the Guarantor in accordance with the Act.

31. Counterparts. This Guaranty may be executed in any number of counterparts, each of which shall be an original and all of which shall constitute together but one and the same agreement. Any signature delivered by a party by facsimile or email transmission shall be deemed to be an original signature hereto.

**IN WITNESS WHEREOF,** each Guarantor has executed or caused this Guaranty to be duly executed and delivered by its duly authorized official as of the date first above stated.

*Debby Day*
Debby Day, Individually

Address of Guarantor:
13 Adams Street, Apt. 7C
Brooklyn, New York 11201

FOLDER VII

# RECENT LEGAL DEVELOPMENTS

## Castigliola v. Commissioner

United States Tax Court
T.C. Memo. 2017-62 (Apr. 12, 2017)

Respondent determined deficiencies in petitioners' Federal income tax and section 6662(a) accuracy-related penalties, as follows:[1]

| Petitioners | 2008 | 2009 | 2010 |
|---|---|---|---|
| Vincent J. and Marie Castigliola | | | |
| Deficiency | $8,278.00 | $5,566.00 | $4,013.00 |
| Sec. 6662(a) penalty | 1,655.60 | 1,113.20 | 802.60 |
| John and Deborah Banahan | | | |
| Deficiency | 9,196.00 | 8,477.00 | 6,418.00 |
| Sec. 6662(a) penalty | 1,839.20 | 1,695.40 | 1,283.60 |
| Harry B. and Marie A. Mullen | | | |
| Deficiency | 4,168.00 | 3,692.00 | 3,126.00 |
| Sec. 6662(a) penalty | 833.60 | 738.40 | 625.20 |

The issues for decision are whether: (1) Mr. Castigliola, Mr. Banahan, and Mr. Mullen, as member-managers of a limited liability company, are each entitled to benefit from the self-employment income exclusion for limited partners under section 1402(a)(13) for a portion of their partnership distributions; (2) Mr. Castigliola, Mr. Banahan, and Mr. Mullen had additional income in 2010 in the form of undistributed funds held in a trust account; and (3) petitioners are liable for accuracy-related penalties under section 6662(a) for 2008, 2009, and 2010.

### FINDINGS OF FACT

Petitioners timely filed joint Forms 1040, U.S. Individual Income Tax Return, for 2008, 2009, and 2010, and they resided in Mississippi when the petitions were timely filed.

Mr. Castigliola, Mr. Banahan, and Mr. Mullen are, and were at all relevant times, attorneys licensed to practice law in the State of Mississippi. Originally, they practiced law through a general partnership, but on July 12, 2001, they reorganized their law firm as a professional limited liability company—Bryan, Nelson, Schroeder, Castigliola & Banahan, PLLC (PLLC).[2] In 2005 the PLLC's office

1. All section references are to the Internal Revenue Code in effect for the years at issue, and all Rule references are to the Tax Court Rules of Practice and Procedure, unless otherwise indicated.

2. Under Mississippi law, a professional limited liability company is a type of limited liability company that may be formed only for the purpose of rendering certain professional services, including legal services. Miss. Code Ann. sec. 79-29-902(f) and (g) (2009). All the members must be authorized by law to render the services that the professional limited liability company offers. Id. sec. 79-29-909(1). Formation of a professional limited liability company requires an additional provision in the certificate of formation electing professional limited liability company status. Id. sec. 79-29-903.

and many of its records were destroyed in Hurricane Katrina, but the members recovered and continued their practice.

Throughout the years at issue Mr. Castigliola, Mr. Banahan, and Mr. Mullen were engaged in the practice of law solely through the PLLC. They were members of the PLLC during the years at issue, and the PLLC is, and has always been, member-managed. The PLLC has never had a written operating agreement. The PLLC timely filed Forms 1065, U.S. Return of Partnership Income, for 2008, 2009, and 2010.[3]

For the years at issue, the members' compensation agreement required guaranteed payments to each member; the guaranteed payments were commensurate with local legal salaries as determined by a survey of legal salaries in the area.[4]

Any net profits of the PLLC in excess of amounts paid out as guaranteed payments were distributed among the members in accordance with the members' agreement.

Petitioners and the PLLC shared the same certified public accountant (CPA).[5] The CPA was an accountant for many years and served in several positions in the National Association of State Boards of Accountancy, including a three-year term on the board of directors. He also served eight years with the Alabama State Bar of Accountancy. Around the time the PLLC was formed in 2001, the members met with the CPA to discuss the new PLLC entity. The CPA had prepared Federal income tax returns for petitioners (and for the general partnership that preceded the PLLC) for many years and was familiar with the history of their law firm as a result. The members explained their situation to the CPA and asked for advice on how to report payments from the PLLC to the members. On the basis of the CPA's advice, they reported all guaranteed payments from the PLLC to the members as self-employment income subject to self-employment tax, but they did not remit self-employment tax on the excess of their distributive shares over the guaranteed payments they received.

At all relevant times the PLLC maintained a Mississippi Bar Foundation Interest on Lawyer's Trust Account at a local bank (trust account). For the years

3. A Form 4605-A, Examination Changes - Partnerships, Fiduciaries, S Corporations, and Interest Charge Domestic International Sales Corporations (Unagreed and Excepted Agreed), was issued on March 13, 2012, to the PLLC for the years at issue. Petitioners' notices of deficiency resulted from the partnership adjustments.

4. The members received the following guaranteed payments for each of the years at issue:

| Member | 2008 | 2009 | 2010 |
|---|---|---|---|
| J. Banahan | $150,000 | $150,000 | $150,000 |
| V. Castigliola | 150,000 | 150,000 | 150,000 |
| H. Mullen | 125,000 | 125,000 | 125,000 |

5. Petitioners' CPA passed away before trial.

at issue, as part of the legal practice, the PLLC handled subrogation payments for State Farm Mutual Automobile Insurance Co. (State Farm). The PLLC negotiated payment plans with uninsured individuals involved in automobile accidents with State Farm policyholders. When these uninsured individuals made payments to the PLLC, it deposited the payments into the trust account. Approximately twice per year the PLLC disbursed subrogation payments from its trust account to State Farm. When it disbursed a subrogation payment to State Farm, the PLLC also transferred the compensation due to the PLLC from its trust account to its operating account. At the end of 2010 the trust account held $15,167 of undistributed funds; the members do not know to whom this amount belongs.

## OPINION

The Commissioner's determinations in a notice of deficiency are generally presumed correct, and the taxpayer bears the burden of proving those determinations erroneous by a preponderance of the evidence. Rule 142(a); *Welch v. Helvering*, 290 U.S. 111, 115 (1933). Yet where the standard of proof is preponderance of the evidence (as it is for all issues in this case), the Court may decide the case on the weight of the evidence and not on an allocation of the burden of proof. *Knudsen v. Commissioner*, 131 T.C. 185, 189 (2008); *Estate of Bongard v. Commissioner*, 124 T.C. 95, 111 (2005).

### I. Self-Employment Tax

Section 1401(a) imposes a tax on the self-employment income of every individual for a taxable year (self-employment tax). Self-employment income is defined as "the net earnings from self-employment derived by an individual * * * during any taxable year" excluding (1) the portion in excess of the Social Security wage base limitation for the year[6] as well as (2) all earnings from self-employment if the total amount of the individual's net earnings from self-employment for the taxable year is less than $400. Sec. 1402(b).

Section 1402(a) defines net earnings from self-employment as

> the gross income derived by an individual from any trade or business carried on by such individual, less the deductions allowed by this subtitle which are attributable to such trade or business, plus his distributive share (whether or not distributed) of income or loss described in section 702(a)(8) from any trade or business carried on by a partnership of which he is a member * * *.

6. The Social Security wage base limitation was $102,000 for 2008, and $106,800 for 2009 and 2010.

Section 1402(a)(13) provides the following exclusion from self-employment income:

> [T]here shall be excluded the distributive share of any item of income or loss of a limited partner, as such, other than guaranteed payments described in section 707(c) to that partner for services actually rendered to or on behalf of the partnership to the extent that those payments are established to be in the nature of remuneration for those services * * *.

Petitioners contend that this exclusion applies to the amounts of the members' distributive shares in excess of their guaranteed payments. Respondent argues that the members were not limited partners for the purposes of section 1402(a)(13), and that, therefore, the exclusion does not apply.

Section 1402(a)(13) was originally enacted in 1977 (as section 1402(a)(12)), before limited liability companies were widely used or generally treated as partnerships for Federal tax purposes.[7] Social Security Amendments of 1977, Pub. L. No. 95-216, sec. 313(b), 91 Stat. at 1536; *Renkemeyer, Campbell, & Weaver, LLP v. Commissioner* (*Renkemeyer*), 136 T.C. 137, 148 (2011). As the Court noted in *Renkemeyer*, no statutory or regulatory authority defines "limited partner" for the purposes of section 1402(a)(13). *See id.* at 148-149. Because the term is not defined, the Court applies accepted principles of statutory construction to ascertain congressional intent. It is a well-established rule of construction that if a statute does not define a term, the term is to be given its ordinary meaning at the time of enactment. *Gates v. Commissioner*, 135 T.C. 1, 6 (2010); *see Perrin v. United States*, 444 U.S. 37, 42 (1979).

*Renkemeyer* indicated that the meaning of "limited partner" is not necessarily confined solely to the limited partnership context. *See* 136 T.C. at 146-150; *cf. Garnett v. Commissioner*, 132 T.C. 368, 377-378 (2009) (finding that under section 469(h)(2) "limited partner" is not necessarily confined to the limited partnership context). Therefore, following the approach taken in *Renkemeyer*, our first inquiry is whether the person claiming the section 1402(a)(13) exemption held a position in an entity treated as a partnership for Federal tax purposes that is functionally equivalent to that of a limited partner in a limited partnership. Mr. Castigliola, Mr. Banahan, and Mr. Mullen were all members of a member-managed PLLC. Consequently, the issue is whether a member of such a PLLC is functionally equivalent to a limited partner in a limited partnership.

A limited partnership has two classes of partners, general and limited. *E.g., Garnett v. Commissioner*, 132 T.C. at 375. General partners typically have management power and unlimited personal liability. 1 Bromberg & Ribstein, Partnership, sec. 1.01(B)(3) (2015-3 Supp.). On the other hand, limited partners typically lack

---

7. The first statute authorizing limited liability companies (LLCs) was adopted in Wyoming in 1977, but the Federal tax treatment of LLCs remained relatively unclear until 1988, when Rev. Rul. 88-76, 1988-2 C.B. 360, clarified that properly organized LLCs would be treated as partnerships. 1 Ribstein & Keatinge, Limited Liability Companies, sec. 1:2 (December 2016 update). Today all States have LLC statutes and the LLC form is widely used. Id.

management power but enjoy immunity from liability for debts of the partnership. *Id.* More specifically, the exact meaning of "limited partner" may vary slightly from State to State. The Uniform Law Commission drafted the Uniform Limited Partnership Act in 1916 (ULPA (1916)), and the Revised Uniform Limited Partnership Act in 1976 (RULPA (1976)). Amendments were added to RULPA (1976) in 1985 (RULPA (1985)). Versions of these uniform acts have been adopted in most States, sometimes with modifications.

Section 7 of ULPA (1916) states: "A limited partner shall not become liable as a general partner unless, in addition to the exercise of his rights and powers as a limited partner, he takes part in the control of the business." ULPA (1916) allowed limited partners a narrow set of rights but did not specifically define which activities a limited partner could perform without losing limited partner status. See id. sec. 10 (allowing limited partners the rights to inspect books, demand an accounting of partnership affairs, and receive a share of the profits and return of capital, and also allowing limited partners the same right as general partners to request dissolution and winding up of the partnership).

Section 303(a) of RULPA (1976) provides—in terms almost identical to those of ULPA (1916)—that a "limited partner" would lose limited liability protection if "in addition to the exercise of his rights and powers as a limited partner, he takes part in the control of the business." With regard to the meaning of "limited partner", the essential difference between ULPA (1916) and RULPA (1976) is that RULPA (1976) enumerates certain activities that a limited partner may perform without taking part in control of the business; for example, section 303(b)(5)(i) and (ii) of RULPA (1976) explicitly permits limited partners to vote on the dissolution of the partnership or the sale of substantially all of the partnership's assets.

In 1987 Mississippi adopted RULPA (1985) with some modifications. *See* 1987 Miss. Laws, ch. 488, sec. 303 (effective from Jan. 1, 1988); Miss. Code Ann. sec. 79-14-303 (2009). In terms almost identical to those of ULPA (1916) and RULPA (1976), the version of the limited partnership act that Mississippi adopted in 1987—and which was effective throughout the years at issue—provided that a "limited partner" would lose limited liability protection if "in addition to the exercise of his rights and powers as a limited partner, he participates in the control of the business." Miss. Code Ann. sec. 79-14-303. Like RULPA (1976), Mississippi's version provides safe harbors for various activities a limited partner may perform without losing limited liability protection. *Id.* Common to each of the definitions of "limited partner" discussed above are the primary characteristics of limited liability and lack of control of the business. In this case, the respective interests in the PLLC held by Mr. Castigliola, Mr. Banahan, and Mr. Mullen made each a member of the PLLC, which was member-managed.[8] Therefore management power over the business of the PLLC was vested in each of them through the interest each held. See id. sec. 79-29-302 (effective after July 1, 1994). The PLLC had no



8. There is no evidence to suggest that any member held a different type of interest in the PLLC or held more than one type of interest in the PLLC.

written operating agreement, nor is there any evidence to show that any member's management power was limited in any way. Furthermore, all members participated in control of the PLLC: For example, they all participated in collectively making decisions regarding their distributive shares, borrowing money, hiring, firing, and rate of pay for employees. They each supervised associate attorneys and signed checks for the PLLC. On the basis of the foregoing facts, the respective interests held by Mr. Castigliola, Mr. Banahan, and Mr. Mullen could not have been limited partnership interests under any of the limited partnership acts. Therefore, they were not limited partners under section 1402(a)(13).

Moreover, a limited partnership must have at least one general partner. *See, e.g.*, Miss. Code Ann. sec. 79-14-801 (2009) ("A limited partnership is dissolved and its affairs must be wound up upon the first of the following to occur: * * * (4) An event of withdrawal of a general partner unless at the time there is at least one other general partner[.]"). This is logical, because limited partners, as discussed above, cannot participate in control of the business and maintain their limited liability. Because there must be at least one partner who is in control of the business, there must be at least one general partner. The members testified that all members participated equally in all decisions and had substantially identical relationships with the PLLC. There was no PLLC operating agreement or other evidence to suggest otherwise. But since by necessity at least one of the members must have occupied a role analogous to that of a general partner in a limited partnership, and because all of the members had the same rights and responsibilities, they must all have had positions analogous to those of general partners in a limited partnership. This conclusion is affirmed by the history of the PLLC: Before the members organized the PLLC, they operated as a general partnership; and there is no evidence that organizing as a PLLC was accompanied by any change in the way they managed the business.

Accordingly, Mr. Castigliola, Mr. Banahan, and Mr. Mullen may not exclude any part of their distributive shares from self-employment income under section 1402(a)(13).

## II. Unreported Income

Respondent argues that $15,167 of undistributed funds remaining in the PLLC's trust account at the end of 2010 is income to the members for 2010 and should have been reported on petitioners' joint income tax returns.

Mr. Banahan testified credibly that the funds in the trust account were not PLLC funds and could not be withdrawn as fees by the members. He was not sure to which clients the funds belonged but was certain that it would be a violation of professional ethics to withdraw the money as fees (the consequences of which might have included disbarment). He was not sure how the discrepancy arose but stated that it may have been attributable to losing the PLLC's office in Hurricane Katrina. He also stated that at some point the money might be deposited into Mississippi's fund for unclaimed moneys. Mr. Banahan's testimony was corroborated by the credible testimony of Mr. Castigliola.

The members testified credibly that the funds respondent identified do not belong to the members. Rule 1.15 of the Mississippi Rules of Professional Conduct requires that a lawyer keep client funds—and funds the ownership of which is disputed—separate from the lawyer's own property. Petitioners argue that, because the members know they do not own these funds, the funds must be kept separate in the trust account. Respondent has offered no evidence or arguments to support his contention that the members are entitled to withdraw these funds as fees. The Court therefore finds that the funds in the trust account do not belong to them. Consequently, the funds remaining in the PLLC's trust account are not income to petitioners for 2010.

### III. Section 6662(a) Penalties

Section 6662(a) and (b)(1) and (2) imposes a penalty of 20% of the portion of an underpayment attributable to any one of various factors, including "negligence or disregard of rules or regulations" and "any substantial understatement of income tax". Respondent contends that petitioners are liable for accuracy-related penalties for the years at issue because they had underpayments due to substantial understatements of income tax or negligence. Under section 7491(c) the Commissioner bears the burden of production with regard to penalties. *UI*, 116 T.C. 438, 446 (2001). To meet that burden the Commissioner must come forward with sufficient evidence indicating that it is appropriate to impose the penalty. *Id.*

There is a substantial understatement of income tax for any taxable year if the amount of the understatement for the taxable year exceeds the greater of 10% of the tax required to be shown on the return for the taxable year or $5,000. Sec. 6662(d)(1)(A). Petitioners did not substantially understate their income tax for any year at issue.

The deficiencies determined by respondent were as follows:

| Petitioners | 2008 | 2009 | 2010 |
|---|---|---|---|
| Banahan | $9,196 | $8,477 | $6,418 |
| Castigliola | 8,278 | 5,566 | 4,013 |
| Mullen | 4,168 | 3,692 | 3,126 |

Respondent determined that the income tax required to be shown on the Banahans' and the Castigliolas' returns was as follows:

| Petitioners | 2008 | 2009 | 2010 |
|---|---|---|---|
| Banahan | $157,463 | $150,368 | $85,340 |
| Castigliola | 154,168 | 144,074 | N/Ax |

The Mullens had deficiencies that were less than $5,000 for every year, and the Castigliolas' deficiency was less than $5,000 for 2010. The deficiencies respondent calculated for the Banahans and the Castigliolas are less than 10% of the respective amounts respondent determined were required to be shown on the Banahans' and the Castigliolas' tax returns for 2008, 2009, and 2010. Therefore, petitioners did not substantially understate their income tax for any year at issue, and respondent has not met his burden of production on this issue.

Negligence includes any failure to make a reasonable attempt to comply with the provisions of the Internal Revenue Code, and "disregard of rules or regulations" includes any careless, reckless, or intentional disregard. Sec. 6662(c). Negligence is determined by testing a taxpayer's conduct against that of a reasonable, prudent person. *Zmuda v. Commissioner*, 731 F.2d 1417, 1422 (9th Cir. 1984), *aff'g* 79 T.C. 714 (1982).

A penalty will not be imposed under section 6662(a) if the taxpayer establishes that he acted with reasonable cause and in good faith. Sec. 6664(c)(1). Circumstances that indicate reasonable cause and good faith include reliance on the advice of a tax professional. Sec. 1.6664-4(b), Income Tax Regs.; *see Higbee v. Commissioner*, 116 T.C. at 449. For a taxpayer to rely reasonably upon advice so as to negate a section 6662(a) accuracy-related penalty determined by the Commissioner, the taxpayer must prove by a preponderance of the evidence that the taxpayer meets each requirement of the following three-prong test: (1) the adviser was a competent professional who had sufficient expertise to justify reliance, (2) the taxpayer provided necessary and accurate information to the adviser, and (3) the taxpayer actually relied in good faith on the adviser's judgment. *Neonatology Assocs., P.A. v. Commissioner*, 115 T.C. 43, 99 (2000), *aff'd*, 299 F.3d 221 (3d Cir. 2002).

All of these requirements are met. Petitioners' CPA, who had over 40 years of experience and had served in positions on State and National boards of accountancy, was a competent professional who had sufficient expertise to justify reliance. On the basis of the entire record, the Court is satisfied that petitioners' CPA was given all the necessary information to prepare their collective tax returns and that the information provided was accurate. Furthermore, the CPA had prepared the law firm's tax returns for many years and so was intimately familiar with the business. Finally, the testimony presented—which was all credible—clearly showed that petitioners relied in good faith on the advice that the CPA had provided. Therefore, petitioners reasonably relied on the advice of their CPA. Additionally, there were no regulations or administrative or judicial guidance to assist the members at the time: "Limited partner" has never been defined by statute or regulation; Renkemeyer was a case of first impression on the issue, and it was decided in 2011—after the years at issue in this case. Also, the members adopted a fairly conservative (though incorrect) reporting position: They remitted self-employment taxes on the guaranteed payments they received, the amounts of the guaranteed payments were calculated on the basis of a survey of legal salaries in the area, and these guaranteed payment amounts were reasonable on the basis of the survey information. For these reasons the Court concludes that petitioners acted with reasonable cause and in good faith.[9]

Therefore, petitioners are not liable for any penalties under section 6662(a) for the years at issue. The Court has considered all of the arguments made by the parties, and to the extent they are not addressed herein, they are considered unnecessary, moot, irrelevant, or without merit.



9. Because of the Court's conclusion regarding the reasonable cause exception under sec. 6664(c), the Court does not reach the issue of whether petitioners were negligent under sec. 6662(b)(1).

## Hardy v. Commissioner

United States Tax Court
T.C. Memo. 2017-16 (Jan. 17, 2017)

Dr. Stephen P. Hardy is a plastic surgeon who performs surgeries in various facilities, including Missoula Bone & Joint Surgery Center, LLC (MBJ). Dr. Hardy owns a minority interest in MBJ, but he has no day-to-day management responsibilities. Beginning with 2008 the Hardys reported the income from MBJ as passive after having reported the income as nonpassive for previous years. [That treatment was the primary issue in the case.] At trial the Hardys moved to amend the pleadings to conform to the evidence, arguing that they overpaid self-employment tax for 2008 and 2009. We will grant this motion.

* * *

## FINDINGS OF FACT

### I. The Hardys

The Hardys were married during 2008 through 2010, the years in issue.

Dr. Hardy is a plastic surgeon. Since the early nineties he has practiced as a plastic surgeon specializing in pediatric reconstructive surgery. Dr. Hardy conducts his medical practice through Northwest Plastic Surgery Associates, a single-member PLLC, which Mrs. Hardy runs as the chief operating officer.

Before joining a surgery center, Dr. Hardy operated on his patients at his office or at two local hospitals. Dr. Hardy can operate at his office only if the procedure requires local anesthesia. If a procedure requires general anesthesia, Dr. Hardy operates at a hospital. And if a procedure requires an overnight stay, then the procedure must be performed at a hospital. Dr. Hardy will explain to his patients the options for where a surgery can take place, and the practice manager will give them a cost estimate for different locations. His patients determine where a surgery will be performed. Because of the limited availability of operating rooms, however, Dr. Hardy struggles to obtain space at a hospital for the procedures.

Dr. Hardy is paid for the surgeries that he performs. Surgical procedures generally have three fee components: (1) a fee for surgical services provided by the surgeon; (2) a fee for anesthesia services provided by the anesthesiologist; and (3) a fee for the use of a surgical facility and its accompanying services. Patients pay the facility fee separately from Dr. Hardy's fee as a surgeon. Facility fees typically include the use of medical equipment, supplies, and staff, who include the front office clerk and the nurses who provide pre- and post-operative care.

In 2001 the Hardys first considered opening their own surgery center. The Hardys believed that a surgery center would benefit patients because it would provide a cost-efficient alternative to having surgeries performed at a hospital, and it would provide Dr. Hardy with greater latitude in scheduling those surgeries.

The following year, the Hardys purchased land and drew up plans to build a surgery center. Before the Hardys began construction, representatives of MBJ and two other surgery centers approached Dr. Hardy about his becoming a member. The Hardys determined that it would be a wiser business decision to join an already operational surgery center because of the expenses of constructing, staffing, certifying, and operating the center.

## II. MBJ

MBJ was a limited liability company formed by a group of practicing physicians in 2004 for the purpose of operating a surgery center. It is treated as a partnership for Federal income tax purposes. In 2005 MBJ began operating a surgery center.[10] MBJ provides patients with a cost-efficient alternative to having procedures performed at a hospital. MBJ is equipped for doctors to perform procedures that require local or general anesthesia; however, complex procedures and procedures that require an overnight stay must be performed at a hospital.

MBJ is professionally managed. MBJ hires its own employees and does not share any employees with Northwest Plastic Surgery. Like hospitals, MBJ directly bills patients for facility fees. MBJ then distributes to each of its members his or her share of the earnings based on the facility fees less expenses. MBJ uses a third-party accounting firm to prepare the Schedules K–1, Partner's Share of Income, Deductions, Credits, etc., for the members. MBJ does not pay physicians for their procedures.

In 2006 Dr. Hardy purchased a 12.5% interest to join seven other practicing physicians in MBJ. He paid $163,974 for his interest. Dr. Hardy cannot sell his interest in MBJ to a third party. The following year, the Hardys built an office next to MBJ for Northwest Plastic Surgery.

Dr. Hardy has never managed MBJ, and he has no day-to-day responsibilities there. Although he meets with the other members quarterly, he does not have any input into management decisions. He generally is not involved in hiring or firing decisions. His role and participation in MBJ have not changed since he became a member.

Dr. Hardy performs surgeries on patients at MBJ on Mondays. Rarely, Dr. Hardy will operate at MBJ on other days of the week. Dr. Hardy does not pay rent to perform surgeries at MBJ; the patients pay the facility fees directly. In 2008 and 2009 Dr. Hardy performed 11% of the surgeries at MBJ. In 2010 Dr. Hardy performed 9% of the surgeries at MBJ. He also had designated alternating Tuesdays as his surgical days at two area hospitals. On the other days of the week, Dr. Hardy continued to perform surgeries at his medical practice. He performed approximately 50% of his surgeries at his office, 20% at MBJ, and the remainder at other facilities.



10. MBJ Orthopedic Center is a separate entity that was formed by some of the same doctors as MBJ. It is in the same building as MBJ. Dr. Hardy has no interest in the orthopedic center.

Dr. Hardy receives a distribution from MBJ regardless of whether he performs any surgeries at the surgery center, and his distribution is not dependent on how many surgeries he performs at MBJ. MBJ does not have a minimum surgery requirement to receive a distribution.

After 2010 Dr. Hardy hired another surgeon at Northwest Plastic Surgery.

If that surgeon's patient chooses, the surgeon performs the surgery at MBJ. That surgeon does not hold an interest in MBJ.

### III. Reporting

Since 2004 the Hardys have been hiring Walter Kero, a partner and tax director at Junkermier, Clark, Campanella, Stevens, PC, to prepare and file their Forms 1040, U.S. Individual Income Tax Return. Mr. Kero is a certified public accountant with over 40 years of experience.

For 2006 and 2007 the Hardys reported their MBJ income as nonpassive. Using his training and experience, Mr. Kero tries to identify income as either payroll, passive, or portfolio. Mr. Kero determined that the income from MBJ was nonpassive by relying on the Schedule K–1. The Schedule K–1 stated that the income was from a trade or business and included self-employment tax. He did not group Dr. Hardy's ownership interest in MBJ with Dr. Hardy's medical practice activity, and he did not consider the grouping regulations.

The Hardys filed their 2006 return and attached a Schedule E, Supplemental Income and Loss, reporting $279,988 of nonpassive income from MBJ. They attached a Form 8582, Passive Activity Loss Limitations, reporting a total unallowed loss of $58,786. They did not attach any statement reporting that [*9] they had grouped Dr. Hardy's ownership interest in MBJ with his medical practice activity.

The Hardys filed their 2007 return and attached a Schedule E, reporting nonpassive income from MBJ of $199,121. They attached a Form 8582, reporting a total unallowed loss of $119,615, which included carryover losses from the previous year of $58,786. They did not attach any statement reporting that they had grouped Dr. Hardy's ownership interest in MBJ with his medical practice activity.

In 2008 Mr. Kero determined that the income from MBJ was passive, and he began reporting it as such. Mr. Kero learned that Dr. Hardy was not involved in the management of MBJ and was not liable for the debts of MBJ. In determining that the income was passive, he went through a checklist of passive activity criteria and obtained corroborating information from the Hardys. He determined that the relationship of Dr. Hardy to MBJ was passive.

Mr. Kero did not amend the Hardys' return for 2006 or 2007. Mr. Kero understood that the difference between passive and active characterization can have a profound effect on a taxpayer's income. However, because he did not believe the change would be material, he did not amend the Hardys' return for 2006 or 2007.

The Hardys filed their 2008 return and attached a Schedule E, reporting passive income from MBJ of $250,494. They attached a Form 8582, reporting a total passive activity loss of $256,411, which included carryover losses from previous years of $119,615. After netting their passive income against their passive losses, they also reported an allowable loss of $250,494, leaving $5,917 as a suspended loss. Additionally, the Hardys reported self-employment tax of $26,745 from the income Dr. Hardy received from Northwest Plastic Surgery and MBJ.

The Hardys filed their 2009 return and attached a Schedule E, reporting passive income from MBJ of $245,012. They attached a Form 8582, reporting an allowed passive activity loss of $104,224, which included a $5,917 carryover loss from the previous year. Additionally, the Hardys reported self-employment tax of $26,530 from the income Dr. Hardy received from Northwest Plastic Surgery and MBJ.

The Hardys filed their 2010 return and attached a Schedule E, reporting passive income from MBJ of $270,521. They attached a Form 8582, reporting an allowed passive activity loss of $157,187.

### IV. Notice of Deficiency

The Commissioner issued a notice of deficiency for tax years 2008 through 2010 on June 24, 2014. For each year, the Commissioner disallowed the Hardys' passive activity loss deduction and itemized deduction for charitable contributions and determined a section 6662(a) accuracy-related penalty.

* * *

Trial was held in Cleveland, Ohio, on December 4, 2015. During trial the Hardys moved to conform the pleadings to the evidence, arguing that they overpaid self-employment tax for 2008 and 2009. After trial the parties submitted a stipulation of settled issues, resolving the remaining charitable contribution deduction dispute for 2008 and 2010. Subsequently, the Internal Revenue Service (IRS) released a technical advice memorandum which presented the same issues as this case.[11] We ordered supplemental briefs, which the parties filed.

## OPINION

We must decide whether the Hardys properly reported Dr. Hardy's income from MBJ as passive. If so, we must decide whether the Hardys may deduct a passive activity loss carryover from previous years and whether they overpaid their self-employment tax. Finally, we must decide whether the Hardys are liable for section 6662(a) accuracy-related penalties.

* * *



11. Tech. Adv. Mem. 201634022 (Aug. 19, 2016).

## II. Whether the Hardys May Deduct Portions of Their Passive Activity Losses

In most passive activity loss cases, taxpayers claim a deduction for certain business and investment expenses under sections 162 and 212. The Commissioner determines that the activity is passive under section 469 and disallows a deduction. The Hardys reported income as passive for 2008 through 2010 and absorbed a passive activity loss carryover from previous years, and the Commissioner has determined that the activity is nonpassive. Accordingly, each party is advancing a position that is more commonly argued by the other side.

* * *

[Regarding the treatment of income as passive, the court c]oncluded that Dr. Hardy may treat his ownership interest in MBJ as passive. That leads us to the inescapable conclusion that the Hardys erroneously treated Dr. Hardy's income from MBJ as nonpassive for 2006 and 2007.

* * *

[The court also recognized that h]ad the Hardys properly reported the MBJ income as passive for 2006 and 2007, it would have fully absorbed their passive losses [from other sources] and there would have been no passive loss to carry forward to 2008. Accordingly, they are not entitled to the full passive activity loss deduction claimed.

* * *

## III. Whether the Hardys Are Liable for Self-Employment Tax on Dr. Hardy's Distributive Shares of Income From MBJ

* * *

### B. Limited Partners Acting as Investors

Section 1401(a) and (b) imposes a tax on self-employment income. "Self-employment income" generally means net earnings from self-employment,[12] which in turn means gross income less allowable deductions from a taxpayer's trade or business plus the "distributive share (whether or not distributed) of income or loss described in section 702(a)(8) from any trade or business carried on by a partnership of which he is a member".[13] Section 702(a)(8) provides that in determining income tax, each partner must take into account separately his distributive share of the partnership's taxable income or loss. Therefore, a partner must generally include his distributive share of partnership income in calculating his net earnings from self-employment.

Section 1402(a) provides several exclusions from the general rule. In particular, section 1402(a)(13) excludes "the distributive share of any item of income or loss

12. Sec. 1402(b).

13. Sec. 1402(a).

of a limited partner, as such, other than guaranteed payments described in section 707(c) to that partner for services actually rendered to or on behalf of the partnership to the extent that those payments are established to be in the nature of remuneration for those services". The Commissioner argues that the section 1402(a)(13) exclusion does not apply in this case. He argues that because Dr. Hardy performs surgeries at MBJ, he is not acting as a limited partner. We disagree.

The Code does not define "limited partner" for purposes of section 1402(a)(13). However, we discussed the definition of limited partner in *Renkemeyer, Campbell & Weaver, LLP v. Commissioner*, 136 T.C. 137 (2011). In that case, the partners were lawyers operating out of a law firm, which was formed as a limited liability partnership.[14] The law firm received revenue from the partners' legal fees, but the firm did not report those revenues on the firm's tax return as net earnings from self-employment.[15] The Commissioner determined that the partners' distributive shares of the law firm's net business income were subject to self-employment tax.[16] We agreed.[17] Because section 1402(a)(13) was enacted before limited liability entities were contemplated and the term "limited partner" remained undefined, we interpreted the statute by looking at legislative history and explained that

> [t]he intent of section 1402(a)(13) was to ensure that individuals who merely invested in a partnership and who were not actively participating in the partnership's business operations (which was the archetype of limited partners at the time) would not receive credits toward Social Security coverage. The legislative history of section 1402(a)(13) does not support a holding that Congress contemplated excluding partners who performed services for a partnership in their capacity as partners (i.e., acting in the manner of self-employed persons), from liability for self-employment taxes.[18]

We held that because the revenue was derived from legal services performed by the partners in their capacity as partners, they were not acting as investors in the law firm. Thus, we held that they were liable for self-employment tax.

Dr. Hardy is an investor in MBJ, which is distinguishable from the limited liability partnership formed by the partners in the law firm in *Renkemeyer, Campbell & Weaver, LLP v. Commissioner*. MBJ owns and operates a surgical center. MBJ is equipped for doctors to perform surgeries that require local and general anesthesia. MBJ bills patients for the use of the facility. Although Dr. Hardy performs surgeries at MBJ, he is not involved in the operations of MBJ as a business. In contrast to the partners in *Renkemeyer, Campbell & Weaver, LLP*, who are lawyers practicing law and receiving distributive shares based on those fees from practicing



---

14. *Renkemeyer, Campbell & Weaver, LLP v. Commissioner*, 136 T.C. 137, 138–139 (2011).
15. *Renkemeyer, Campbell & Weaver, LLP v. Commissioner*, 136 T.C. at 140.
16. *Renkemeyer, Campbell & Weaver, LLP v. Commissioner*, 136 T.C. at 141.
17. *Renkemeyer, Campbell & Weaver, LLP v. Commissioner*, 136 T.C. at 146.
18. *Renkemeyer, Campbell & Weaver, LLP v. Commissioner*, 136 T.C. at 148–150.

law,[19] Dr. Hardy is receiving a distribution based on the fees that patients pay to use the facility. The patients separately pay Dr. Hardy his fees as a surgeon, and they separately pay the surgical center for use of the facility in the same manner as with a hospital. Accordingly, Dr. Hardy's distributive shares are not subject to self-employment tax because he received the income in his capacity as an investor.

## IV. Section 6662

Section 6662(a) and (b) imposes a 20% accuracy-related penalty on any portion of an underpayment of tax that is due to, among other things, any negligence or disregard of rules or regulations or a substantial understatement of income tax. The term "negligence" includes any failure to make a reasonable attempt to comply with the provisions of the Code, and the term "disregard" includes any careless, reckless, or intentional disregard.[20] Negligence has been further defined as a "lack of due care or failure to do what a reasonable and ordinarily prudent person would do under the circumstances."[21] Additionally, a taxpayer is negligent if he fails to maintain sufficient records to substantiate the items in question.[22] An understatement of income tax is "substantial" when that understatement exceeds the greater of 10% of the tax required to be shown on the return or $5,000.[23]

The Commissioner bears the burden of production for this penalty before the burden shifts to taxpayers to prove that the penalty should not apply.[24] The Commissioner has not proven that the Hardys acted negligently. The Commissioner did not provide any evidence that any portion of the underpayment of tax was due to the Hardys' failure to make a reasonable attempt to comply with the Code, lack of due care or failure to do what a reasonable and ordinarily prudent person would do, or failure to maintain sufficient records. Accordingly, the Commissioner has not met his burden regarding negligence.

However, in accordance with this opinion, the Hardys' exact underpayment for each year depends on the Rule 155 computations. If these computations establish a substantial understatement of income tax for any year, the Commissioner will have met his burden of production with respect to that year.[25]

If the Rule 155 computations establish a substantial understatement of income tax for any year, the accuracy-related penalty will not apply to any portion of the underpayment where the taxpayers establish that they had reasonable cause

---

19. *Renkemeyer, Campbell & Weaver, LLP v. Commissioner*, 136 T.C. at 138–139.

20. Sec. 6662(c).

21. *Neely v. Commissioner*, 85 T.C. 934, 947 (1985) (quoting *Marcello v. Commissioner*, 380 F.2d 499, 506 (5th Cir. 1967), *aff'g in part, remanding in part* 43 T.C. 168 (1964) *and* T.C. Memo. 1964–299).

22. *See Higbee v. Commissioner*, 116 T.C. 438, 449 (2001); sec. 1.6662–3(b)(1), Income Tax Regs.

23. Sec. 6662(d)(1)(A).

24. *See* sec. 7491(c); *Higbee v. Commissioner*, 116 T.C. at 446–447.

25. *See Olagunju v. Commissioner*, T.C. Memo. 2012–119; *Jarman v. Commissioner*, T.C. Memo. 2010–285.

and acted in good faith.[26] Taxpayers may establish that they had reasonable cause and acted in good faith through reliance on the advice of a tax professional.[27] The reliance must have been reasonable and in good faith under all the circumstances.[28] To demonstrate that the reliance was reasonable and in good faith, the taxpayer must prove by a preponderance of the evidence that "(1) [t]he adviser was a competent professional who had sufficient expertise to justify reliance, (2) the taxpayer provided necessary and accurate information to the adviser, and (3) the taxpayer actually relied in good faith on the adviser's judgment."[29]

Taking into consideration all the facts and circumstances, we find that the Hardys reasonably relied on Mr. Kero in good faith regarding the portion of the underpayment for 2008 that is attributable to the passive activity loss carryover. Mr. Kero has 40 years of experience. He prepared the returns for 2006 through 2010. He reported the income from MBJ as nonpassive for 2006 and 2007 and passive for 2008 through 2010, and the Hardys provided him with corroborating information. Although he understood that characterizing income as passive or nonpassive can have a profound effect on a taxpayer's income, he did not take into account the proper characterization of Dr. Hardy's income from MBJ when considering the amount of the passive activity loss carryover. The Hardys relied on his advice and experience in preparing their returns. Accordingly, the Hardys had reasonable cause and acted in good faith through reliance on the advice of a tax professional.

The Hardys did not provide any evidence regarding the portion of the underpayment for each year that is attributable to the disallowed charitable contribution deduction. Accordingly, they have not established that they had reasonable cause and acted in good faith with respect to the portion of the underpayment for each year arising from that item.

## V. Conclusion

The Hardys may treat their income from MBJ as passive. However, they have not established that they may deduct the passive activity loss carryover from years in which they treated the income as nonpassive. For 2008 and 2009 the Hardys overpaid their self-employment tax because Dr. Hardy's distributive share from MBJ is excluded from net earnings from self-employment. The Commissioner did not meet his burden of production regarding the section 6662(a) accuracy-related penalties for negligence; however, he may have met his burden of production for underpayments attributable to substantial understatements of income tax



---

26. Sec. 6664(c)(1).

27. *Neonatology Assocs., P.A. v. Commissioner*, 115 T.C. 43, 98 (2000), aff'd, 299 F.3d 221 (3d Cir. 2002); sec. 1.6664-4(c), Income Tax Regs.

28. *Neonatology Assocs., P.A. v. Commissioner*, 115 T.C. at 98–99; sec. 1.6664-4(b)(1), (c), Income Tax Regs.

29. *Neonatology Assocs., P.A. v. Commissioner*, 115 T.C. at 99.

if the Rule 155 computations establish substantial understatements of income tax. If that threshold is met for any year, no penalty applies to the portion of the underpayment for that year attributable to the passive activity loss carryover because the Hardys established that they had reasonable cause and acted in good faith through reliance on the advice of a tax professional. Because the Hardys did not provide any defense for any of the years in issue for the portion of the underpayment that is attributable to the charitable contribution deduction, they have not established any defense to a penalty attributable to that portion of the resulting underpayment.

# Choice-of-Entity Analyses: Effective Tax Rates

Bradley T. Borden

Professor of Law, Brooklyn Law School[1]

The Tax Cuts and Jobs Act of 2017 changes the choice-of-entity calculus by changing the corporate tax rate, creating the deduction for qualified business income (QBI), and reducing the rates that apply to individual income. Corporate income is now subject to a 21% rate, and QBI can qualify for a deduction equal to 20% of the QBI. These changes create different effective tax rates for income from different types of businesses and different types of entities. Analyses of the various rates often compare effective rates using the highest marginal rates. Such analyses are not helpful for the vast majority of the population (those with less than $1,000,000 of taxable income) who have income that falls far short to be taxed at the highest marginal rates. To the extent that the lower incomes are subject to different effective rates, business owners with lower income are not served well by considering the maximum rates.

Computing effective federal tax rates requires considering all types of taxes that apply to income. Those taxes include income tax, employment tax, and net investment income tax. Income tax applies to taxable income of a business.[2] Employment taxes apply to self-employment income and wages.[3] Net investment income applies to passive-type income, such as dividends.[4] Because this analysis is illustrative and each situation will require a separate analysis, this analysis focuses only on the effective income tax rate, considering only income tax.

## BACKGROUND

At the maximum rates, the effective tax on distributed corporate income is 36.8%. This is derived by deeming a corporation to recognize $100,000 of income. With a 21% tax rate, the tax on that income would be $21,000 at the corporate level, leaving $79,000 to distribute. Assuming the distribution is qualified dividend income,[5] the highest income tax rate that would apply to it would be 20%. The tax on the distribution at that rate would be $15,800 ($79,000 x 20%). The total tax on the distributed corporate income would be $36,800 ($21,000 + $15,800) or 36.8% ($36,800 ÷ $100,000). This effective tax rate is close to the top individual marginal rate of 37%. For business owners who qualify for the QBI deduction, the maximum individual tax rate is 29.6%, computed by assuming the individuals have $100,000 of tax, take the 20% QBI deduction, and compute their tax liability on



1. The original version of this article was published by LexisNexis Inc. in its product, Lexis Practice Advisor–Tax, and is reproduced here with permission of the publisher. Copyright 2018 by LexisNexis, Inc.

2. *See* I.R.C. §§ 1, 11, 61(a)(2).

3. *See* I.R.C. §§ 1401, 3101, 3111.

4. *See* I.R.C. § 1411(a), (c)(1)(A)(i).

5. *See* I.R.C. § 1(h)(1), (11).

the remaining $800,000 of taxable income at 37%. The tax under those assumptions would be $296,000 ($800,000 × 37%), so the effective tax rate would 29.6% ($296,000 ÷ $100,000). This simplified analysis of effective tax rates does not apply to most taxpayers for several reasons.

First, owners of closely-held corporations generally participate in management and must cause the corporation to pay them reasonable compensation. That compensation will be taxed at ordinary rates. Thus, the effective tax rate on corporate income cannot simply take into account the corporate-level tax and the tax on corporate distributions.

Second, corporations often do not distribute all of their taxable income. One study found that corporations distribute only about 25% of their taxable income. Consequently, the double tax on corporate income generally only applies to a fraction of corporate income. If the double tax only applies to a fraction of corporate income, the effective tax rate on corporate income will be less than the 36.8% possible maximum.

Third, graduated rates can apply to corporate dividends. If a shareholder has no income other than the dividend from a corporation, the first $77,200 (for joint filers) of dividend is not taxed.[6] The amount of the dividend between $77,200 and $479,000 is taxed at 15%, and any additional dividends are taxed at 20%.[7] Thus, if the dividends are less than $479,000, and the shareholder has no other income, no portion of the dividends would be taxed at 20%. The amount of the dividend would have to be significant under these assumptions for the effective tax rate on the dividend to approach 20%.

Fourth, the effective tax rate on individual income almost never approaches 37%. Because of the graduated individual rate structure, only income over $600,000 (for joint filers) is subject to the 37% rate.[8] All income below $600,000 is subject to lower rates, so even if taxpayers have more than $600,000 of income, the effective tax rate on that income will be less than 37%. A couple's taxable income must approach $10,000,000 for the effective tax rate to approach 37% (at that level of income, the effective tax rate is 36.42%).

Fifth, more than 99% of the population has less than $1,000,000 of taxable income.[9] The effective tax rate on a couple's $1,000,000 of taxable income is about 31%, the effective tax rate for most individuals is less than 37%. The following table illustrates the computation of the effective tax rate on a couple's $1,000,000 of ordinary taxable income.

---

6. *See* I.R.C. § 1(h)(1)(B); I.R.C. § 1(j)(5)(B)(i)(I).

7. *See* I.R.C. § 1(h)(1)(C), (D); I.R.C. § 1(j)(5)(B)(ii)(I).

8. *See* I.R.C. § 1(j)(2).

9. *See* Internal Revenue Service, *SOI Tax Stats—Individual Statistical Tables by Size of Adjusted Gross Income. All Returns: Adjusted Gross Income, Exemptions, Deductions, and Tax Items* (2015).

| | Brackets | Income | Tax Rate | Tax | Effective Rate |
|---|---|---|---|---|---|
| | | $19,050 | 10% | $1,905 | |
| | 19,050 | $58,350 | 12% | $7,002 | |
| | $77,400 | $87,600 | 22% | $19,272 | |
| | $165,000 | $150,000 | 24% | $36,000 | |
| | $315,000 | $85,000 | 32% | $27,200 | |
| | $400,000 | $200,000 | 35% | $70,000 | |
| | $600,000 | $400,000 | 37% | $148,000 | |
| Total | | $1,000,000 | | $309,379 | 30.94% |

Because the maximum tax rates do not represent the effective tax rates for most taxpayers, most taxpayers must do a more sophisticated analysis to determine the effective tax rates that apply to their respective businesses under different scenarios. The following graph presents the effective income tax rates on a married couple's $1,000,000 of taxable income of a QTB, corporate income (with 100% distribution of after-tax income and 25% distribution of such income), and taxable income of an SSTB. These are the effective income tax rates that apply to more than 99% of the population at the respective income levels.

This graph shows that for income up to about $350,000, passthrough structures provide the most favorable effective tax rate. Passthrough structures for QTBs provide the most favorable effective tax rates for income up to about $700,000. This graph only accounts for income taxes, so it does not provide a complete picture of the entity's tax situation. At least some portion of the income of a QTB will be

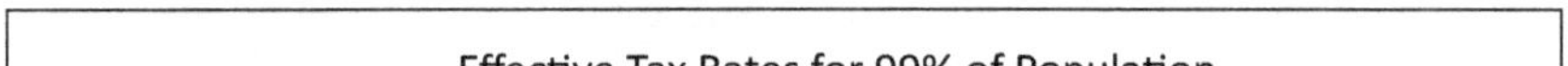

subject to employment tax, and corporations must pay reasonable compensation to their shareholders, which is subject to employment tax.

The employment tax is 15.3%,[10] so it will shift the SSTB and QBI lines up by about that many percentage points, but because a portion of the payment also qualifies for a deduction,[11] the adjustment is not exactly equal to the percentage-point change. Employment tax will also affect the effective tax rate of corporate income. If business owners operate their business in a corporation, they must cause the corporation to pay them a reasonable compensation. That reasonable compensation will be subject to the ordinary income tax rates and employment taxes. Thus, the computation of effective tax rates must account for such taxes. Dividends are also subject to the tax on net investment income, so the analysis must adjust to account for those taxes.

## TAKEAWAY

The Tax Cuts and Jobs Act undermines the general choice-of-entity concepts that applied generally under the old regime. Now the choice is situational and depends upon numerous factors. For instance, income level, amount of wages paid, the amount of earnings the owners withdraw, the type of business, and other factors affect the choice- of-entity. The situational nature of choice-by-entity will often require modeling the effective tax rates of different alternative business forms. To obtain the lowest effective tax rate possible, business owners may have to mix entities in new and creative ways. For instance, business owners who do not wish to withdraw profits from a business may choose to run the business in a corporation that hires the business owners' management company to operate the business. The management company would most likely be a passthrough entity, so the owners would have to determine whether it should be an S corporation or a partnership.

In the past, business owners often used S corporations for service-oriented businesses because such structures allowed the owners to cause the S corporation to pay the owners a reasonable compensation and distribute the remaining S corporation income as dividends. With such a structure, only the compensation was subject to employment tax. After the Tax Cuts and Jobs Act, compensation income does not qualify for the QBI deduction, so business owners may prefer to avoid the S corporation structure and use a partnership as the management company. Perhaps all of the management company's income will be subject to employment tax, but it will also qualify for the QBI deduction. If the owners use a limited partnership for the management company, only the income allocated to them as general partners

---

10. *See* I.R.C. §§ 1401, 3101, 3111.

11. *See* I.R.C. §§ 162(a), 164(f).

would be subject to employment tax, but it should still qualify for the QBI deduction. To qualify for the QBI deduction, however, the management company must pay compensation to third parties. Otherwise, the owners must choose between qualifying for the QBI deduction and paying employment taxes on the amount of reasonable compensation.

## Choice-of-Entity Considerations: Reasonable Compensation versus Passthrough

Bradley T. Borden

Professor of Law, Brooklyn Law School[12]

*IRC Section 199A* provides a deduction equal to 20% of an individual's qualified business income (QBI). The QBI deduction is subject to a wage limit equal to 50% of the wages paid with respect to the qualified trade or business (QTB).[13] QBI does not, however, include (1) reasonable compensation paid to a business owner, (2) guaranteed payments from partnerships to partners, or (3) payments to partners for services provided in a non-partner capacity.[14] This analysis refers to these three types of income as compensatory business income. The exclusion of compensatory business income from QBI means that such income does not qualify for the QBI deduction. That disqualification and the wage limit may affect business owners' choice of entity. As with other choice-of-entity decisions related to Section 199A, the choice regarding compensatory business income will most likely be situational. After a quick review of the relevant aspects of the QBI deduction, consider how different situations may lead to different choices

### BACKGROUND

The QBI deduction applies to all business income below the threshold amount ($315,000 for married individuals filing jointly).[15] Self-employment income is subject to the Social Security and Medicare employment taxes,[16] as is wage income.[17] Corporations must pay reasonable compensation to their shareholders who participate in management of the corporation.[18] Income allocated to general partners comes within the definition of self-employment income, but income allocated to limited partners, if not a guaranteed payment for services, does not come within the definition of self-employment income.[19] Allocations to members of LLCs may or may not come within the definition of self-employment income, depending on

---

12. The original version of this article was published by LexisNexis Inc. in its product, Lexis Practice Advisor–Tax, and is reproduced here with permission of the publisher. Copyright 2018 by LexisNexis, Inc.

13. *See* I.R.C. § 199A(b)(2)(B).

14. *See* I.R.C. § 199A(c)(4), I.R.C. § 199A(e)(2).

15. *See* I.R.C. § 199A(c)(3)(A) (eliminating the wage limit if a taxpayer's taxable income is below the threshold); I.R.C. § 199A(d)(3) (including specified service trades or businesses (SSTBs) in the definition of qualified trade or business (QTB) and allowing the full QBI deduction, if the taxpayer's income is below the threshold amount).

16. *See* I.R.C. § 1402.

17. *See* I.R.C. § 3101, I.R.C. § 3111.

18. *See*, e.g., *David E. Watson, P.C. v. United States*, 757 F. Supp. 2d 877 (2010).

19. *See* I.R.C. § 1402(a), I.R.C. § 1402(a)(13).

members' management authority.[20] Three situations illustrate how business owners might prefer compensatory business income in some situations, but not others.

### Situation 1: Income Is Less Than the Threshold Amount

If taxpayers' taxable income is less than the threshold amount, business income will qualify for the QBI deduction. Compensatory business income does not qualify for the QBI deduction, regardless of income level. Thus, business owners who have taxable income below the threshold amount will want to ensure that the income is not compensatory business income. Because corporations must pay their shareholders reasonable compensation, the owners would have compensatory business income if they operate the business in a corporation. They would lose the QBI deduction on the portion of the business income paid to them from the corporation as compensation. To avoid receiving compensation and losing the QBI deduction on that portion of their income, the owners may consider operating the business as a sole proprietorship, or through a partnership.

Moving away from S corporations may be difficult for some business owners. For years, without additional planning, such income would be subject to employment taxes, but would qualify for the QBI deduction. Business owners have used S corporations to reduce employment taxes. They reduce employment taxes by causing the S corporation to pay reasonable compensation to the members that is less than the S corporation's taxable income. The amount paid as compensation is subject to employment tax, but the corporation's residual taxable income flows through to the members free of employment taxes. The residual income would come within the definition QBI and qualify for the QBI deduction in this situation, but the reasonable compensation would not. For business owners who have taxable income below the threshold amount, they would lose the QBI deduction with respect to the reasonable compensation paid by the corporation. They could, however, retain the employment-tax benefits of an S corporation without losing the QBI deduction, if they operate the business in a limited partnership.

The owners of a limited partnership who structure to minimize employment tax and maximize the QBI deduction would hold both limited partner and general partner interests in the limited partnership. State law allows a single person to hold both limited partner and general partner interests in a limited partnership.[21] Income allocated to the owners in their general partner capacities will come within the definition of self-employment income and be subject to the employment tax.[22] The income allocated to them in their limited partner capacities will not come within the definition of self- employment income, so it will not be subject to the



20. *See, e.g.*, *Castigliola v. Commissioner*, T.C. Memo 2017-62 (Apr. 12, 2017); *Hardy v. Commissioner*, T.C. Memo 2017-16 (Jan. 17, 2017).

21. *See* UNIF. LTD. P'SHIP ACT § 109 (2001, as amended in 2013).

22. *See* I.R.C. § 1402(a).

employment tax.[23] To ensure that the allocated income qualifies for the QBI deduction, the owners must ensure that the allocations are not compensatory business income, i.e., not guaranteed payments or payments for services the owner provides in a non-partner capacity. If the allocations are a percentage of the partnership's income, they would not be guaranteed payments.[24] The legal distinction between partner and non-partner capacity is not clear, so the business owners must study the existing law to ensure that the allocations of income and any payments received from the partnership are not for non-partner services.[25] If the IRS respects the allocations, the limited partnership's income should be QBI and qualify for the 20% deduction, and only a portion of it would be subject to employment taxes. The owners can avoid liability related to the general partner interests by forming an LLC to be the general partner.

### Situation 2: Income Is Greater Than the Threshold Amount, No Employees

Now consider a choice-of-entity analysis for business owners whose taxable income exceeds the threshold amount plus $100,000 for joint filers (threshold-plus amount) and who have no employees. In this situation, the nature of the business will affect the application of the QBI deduction. If the business is a specified services trade or business, it will not qualify for the QBI deduction.[26] SSTBs include service businesses in areas such as health, law, accounting, performing arts, and finance.[27] The income of the specified services trade or business will be taxed to the owners like compensation (i.e., be subject to employment tax and not qualify for the QBI deduction). If the business is a QTB, it will qualify for the QBI only if the business owners can clear the wage limit. When business owners' taxable income exceeds the threshold-plus amount, the QBI deduction cannot exceed 50% of the wages the QTB pays or the sum of the 25% of the QBI's wages and 2.5% of the unadjusted basis of its assets.[28] Assume the QTB has assets with nominal unadjusted basis.

In this situation, the QTB has no employees, so the business owners can only qualify for the QBI deduction through entity restructuring that creates wages for the QTB. Partners are not considered employees, so amounts allocated or paid to them are not wages.[29] Notice that although guaranteed payments and payments for non-partner services are excluded from the definition of QBI, they do not come within the definition of wages for purposes of determining the QBI wage limit.[30]

---

23. *See* I.R.C. § 1402(a)(13).

24. *See* I.R.C. § 707(c) (defining guaranteed payment as one that is determined without regard to the partnership's income).

25. *See, e.g., Pratt v. Commissioner*, 550 F.2d 1023 (5th Cir. 1977); Rev Rul 81-301, 1981-2 CB 144; Prop. Treas. Reg. § 1.707-2.

26. *See* I.R.C. § 199A(d)(2), I.R.C. § 199A(d)(3).

27. *See* I.R.C. § 199A(d)(2)(A), I.R.C. § 1202(e)(3)(A).

28. *See* I.R.C. § 199A(b)(2).

29. *See* I.R.C. § 199A(b)(4) (defining wages); Rev Rul 69-184, 1969-1 CB 256.

30. *See* I.R.C. § 199A(b)(4) (defining wages).

Consequently, business owners cannot create wages by operating a QTB through a partnership and paying themselves guaranteed payments. Furthermore, if they run the business through a partnership, at least a portion of the income will be subject to employment taxes, and all of the income could be subject to employment tax, if they choose an LLC.

In this situation, the business owners should be able to qualify for at least a portion of the QBI deduction running the QBT through an S corporation and causing the S corporation to pay them reasonable compensation. The compensation will be subject to employment tax, but it can free up the deduction for the portion of the business income that is not compensation. The compensation paid must be reasonable. If the amount of compensation that is reasonable comes within a range, then the business owners should do an analysis to determine the amount of compensation that will result in the lowest effective tax rate. Assuming reasonable compensation covers a range of values, the business owners should seek a value within that range that minimizes their tax liability.

Finding the optimal amount of wages to pay the owners will be a challenge. Every dollar of compensation that the S corporation pays to the owners frees up fifty cents of QBI deduction, until 50% of the deduction equals 20% of the income minus the compensation. That equation reveals that the inflection point for compensation is two-sevenths of QBI prior to compensation. To recognize that two-sevenths is the inflection point, imagine that the QBI is $700,000. If wages were $100,000 (i.e., one-seventh of pre-wage income), QBI would be $600,000 ($700,000 – $100,000). The QBI deduction could be $120,000 ($600,000 × 20%), but $50,000 wage limit ($100,000 × 50%) caps the deduction at $50,000. If wages were $300,000 (i.e., three-sevenths of pre-wage income), QBI would be $400,000 ($700,000 – $300,000). Thus, when wages are less than two-sevenths, the wage limit prevents business owners from taking the maximum QBI deduction, even though they pay employment tax on a relatively small amount of wages. An example illustrates the trade-off of paying compensation to business owners in the current situation. Assume the business owners have $700,000 of QBI and pay no wages in a member-managed LLC that the owners manage. The wage limit will prevent the business from claiming the QBI deduction, the entire $700,000 of QBI will be taxable income under these facts. Because the income passes through a member-managed LLC, it will also be subject to employment tax. To obtain the optimal QBI deduction, the owners should run the business through an S corporation and pay $200,000 of wages ($700,000 × 2/7 = $200,000). Only the $200,000 of wages will be subject to employment tax, providing a tax savings over the LLC form under which all $700,000 of income was subject to employment tax. Even though the $200,000 of wages will not be QBI, they will free up $100,000 ($200,000 × 50%) of QBI deduction. Setting compensation at two-sevenths of the pre-wage income appears to provide the optimal tax situation. The wages paid to shareholders must, however, be reasonable. If wages equal to two-sevenths of the pre-wage income is not reasonable, the business owners will lose some of the tax benefits for which they would otherwise qualify.

### Situation 3: Income Greater Than Threshold Amount, Compensation Paid to Third Parties

If a QTB has third-party employees, the optimal business structure might be a limited partnership. As with wages paid to owners, a QTB maximizes the benefit of its QBI deduction if wages paid to third parties equal two-sevenths of the QTB's pre-wage income. Assuming third-party wages are at that target, owners would not want to create wages for themselves, but would want to minimize employment taxes they pay on their income from the business.

If the owners operate the business as a general partnership, the entire amount of QBI would be subject to employment tax. If they operate the business through an S corporation and cause the S corporation to pay them reasonable compensation, the reasonable compensation will be excluded from the definition of QBI and not qualify for the QBI deduction. Thus, the owners should consider operating the business in a limited partnership with the owners holding both limited partner and general partner interests. Income allocated to the members in their general partner capacities should be subject to employment tax, but income allocated to them in their limited partner capacities should not be subject to employment tax. All income allocated to them by the limited partnership should be QBI and qualify for the QBI deduction.

## TAKEAWAY

Compensatory business income and employment taxes will dictate the preferred entity choice in many situations. The preferred choice is situational. This analysis shows the preferences vary in three different situations as follows:

*Situation 1 Takeaway: If taxable income is below the income threshold, do not run business income through an S corporation.*

*Situation 2 Takeaway: If a QTB pays no wages to third parties and its income exceeds the income threshold, the owners should be able to minimize their effective tax rates by forming an S corporation to pay the owners reasonable compensation. If reasonable compensation equals two-thirds of the business's pre-wage income, the owners should cause the S corporation to pay that amount of wages.*

*Situation 3 Takeaway: If a QTB's income exceeds the threshold amount and the QTB pays wages to third parties, the business owners may prefer operating the business in a limited partnership to avoid wage income and reduce their employment taxes.*

## Carried Interests Tax

Bradley T. Borden

Professor of Law, Brooklyn Law School[31]

The Tax Cuts and Jobs Act of 2017 created a new *I.R.C. Section 1061* that alters the character of some income recognized with respect to certain types of partnership interests. The operative provision of Section 1061 modifies the definition of long-term gain with respect to certain types of partnership interests by extending the required holding period of capital assets from one to three years.[32] The mechanics of the new provision raise some questions. This article considers some of those questions. Before examining the provision, consider the situations to which the new law might apply.

### BACKGROUND

Managers of real estate ventures and promoters of financial partnerships (together managers), such as private equity funds, find investments assets, raise capital, form ventures, manage assets, and oversee the disposition of the assets. In return for the services they provide, managers typically also take a carry (private equity) or promote (real estate), which grants the managers an interest in the back-end profit of the venture following payment of the investors' preferred return and return of capital (i.e., carried interest). Even though carried interests relate to services provided by managers, they grant the services provider an interest in profits so the managers typically would not be taxed upon receipt of the carried interests.[33] The character of income related to the carried interest passes from the venture to the manager when the venture recognizes sufficient income to fund the interest. Typically, a venture has such funds when it sells fund assets so the character of income associated with a carried interest is capital gain. If the fund has held an asset for at least one year, the character should be long-term capital gain and qualify for favorable tax treatment.[34] Commentators have debated the proper characterization of income allocated to holders of carried interests, but such income had retained the character established at the partner level.[35] Section 1061 was enacted to recharacterize some of the gain allocated to real estate and fund managers.

31. The original version of this article was published by LexisNexis Inc. in its product, Lexis Practice Advisor–Tax, and is reproduced here with permission of the publisher. Copyright 2018 by LexisNexis, Inc.

32. *See* I.R.C. § 1061(a)(2).

33. *See* Rev Proc 93-27, 1993-2 CB 343.

34. *See* I.R.C. § 1(h)(1).

35. *See* Profits-Only Partnership Interests, 74 Brook. L. Rev. 1283 (2009) (discussing the difficulty of changing the character of income that flows from a partnership to a partner); Victor Fleischer, Two and Twenty: Taxing Partnership Profits in Private Equity Funds, 83 N.Y.U. L. Rev. 1, 57–58 (2008) (recommending that at least a portion of the partnership profits allocated to holders of profits-only partnership interests be taxed as ordinary income); Gregg D. Polsky, Private Equity Management Fee Conversion, *122 Tax Notes 743* (Feb. 9, 2009) (arguing that the conversion of management fees from compensation income to capital gain income lacks support in the law and violates fundamental principles of equity); see also Fair and Equitable

Section 1061 recharacterization only applies to a taxpayer's long-term capital gain with respect to an applicable partnership interest.[36] The rule requires computing the taxpayer's total long-term capital gain with respect to an applicable partnership interest and the amount of that long-term capital gain that is attributable to property held less than three years. The excess of the total long-term capital gain over the long-term capital gain attributable to property held less than three years is treated as short-term capital gain.[37] Thus, application of the provision requires knowing what is an applicable partnership interest and what gain occurs with respect to such interest.

An applicable partnership interest is any interest that is transferred to (or held by) the taxpayer in connection with the performance of substantial services by the taxpayer, or a related person, in any applicable trade or business.[38] This definition does not apply to an interest held by a person who is employed by another entity that is conducting a non-applicable trade or business and only provides services to such other entity.[39] An applicable trade or business consists, in whole or in part, of raising or returning and performing at least one of four other functions.[40] The other function can be either investing in specified assets, disposing of specified assets, identifying specified assets for investing or disposition, or developing specified assets.[41] A specified asset means securities, commodities, real estate held for rental or investment, cash or cash equivalents, options or derivative contracts with respect to any of the forgoing, and an interest in a partnership to the extent of the partnership's proportionate interest in any of the forgoing.[42] Partnership interests held by corporations and certain capital interests do come within the definition of applicable partnership interest. [43]

---

Tax Policy for America's Working Families: Hearing Before the H. Comm. on Ways & Means, 110th Cong. 58 (statement of Darryll K. Jones, Professor, Stetson U. College of Law) (recognizing the injustice of a person who makes $70,000 of compensation a year paying tax at ordinary income rates while fund managers make millions and pay tax at long-term capital gains rates); Carried Interest, Part II: Hearing Before the S. Comm. on Finance, 110th Cong. (2007) (statement of Joseph Bankman, Professor, Stanford Law School) (supporting taxing carried interests as compensation to "increase economic welfare and make the tax law more equitable"); Carried Interest: Hearing Before the S. Comm. on Finance, 110th Cong. (2007) (statement of Mark P. Gergen, Founder Chair, U. of Texas School of Law) (commenting that the unfairness of the current law is evident and recommending that income allocated to a partner who provides services to a partnership should be ordinary income when the amount allocated is compensation); but see David A. Weisbach, The Taxation of Carried Interests in Private Equity, 94 Va. L. Rev. 715 (2008) (arguing generally that the nature of partnerships supports partnership- level characterization); see also Leo L. Schmolka, Taxing Partnership Interests Exchanged for Services: Let Diamond/Campbell Quietly Die, 47 Tax L. Rev. 287, 288 (1991) (preferring the law to not tax profits-only partnership interests, but if it does, to use a constructive loan method to tax only a portion that is treated as interest on a constructive loan to the service provider).

36. *See* I.R.C. § 1061(a).

37. *See* I.R.C. § 1061(a) (flush language).

38. *See* I.R.C. § 1061(c)(1).

39. *See* I.R.C. § 1061(c)(1).

40. *See* I.R.C. § 1061(c)(2)(A), I.R.C. § 1061(c)(2)(B).

41. *See* I.R.C. § 1061(c)(2)(B).

42. *See* I.R.C. § 1061(c)(3).

43. *See* I.R.C. § 1061(c)(4).

This definition of applicable trade or business would include private equity funds, venture capital funds, and most real estate ventures. The recharacterization rule would apply to managers who receive a carried interest in exchange for substantial services.

Participants in such arrangements will undoubtedly seek clarity on the definition of a term such as "substantial services," and they will also be interested to know what constitutes long-term capital gain with respect to an applicable partnership interest. This article focuses on the latter issue.

Section 1061 does not define how gain occurs with respect to a partnership interest. Feasibly, the section may refer to gain a partner recognizes on the disposition of a partnership interest or upon receipt of a cash distribution that exceeds the basis the partner has in a partnership interest. It may also refer to gain allocated to the partner with respect to a partnership interest. Timing related to acquisitions and dispositions of partnership property and interests in the partnership may affect the application of Section 1061.

## TAKEAWAY

The new Section 1061 applies to long-term capital gain with respect to applicable partnership interests held by the taxpayer at any time during the taxable year.[44] Conceivably, gains can occur with respect to a partnership interest when the partner sells a partnership interest or when the partnership sells assets and allocates gains to the holder of a partnership interest. Four transactions could affect the character of gain that occurs with respect to a partnership interest: (1) a manager's acquisition of a partnership interest through contribution or purchase, (2) the partnership's acquisition of an asset, (3) the disposition of an interest in a partnership through sale of the interest or distribution from the partnership, and (4) the partnership's disposition of an asset. The timing of these four transactions can affect the character of gain that a partner recognizes and would appear to affect the application of Section 1061. Consider how Section 1061 might apply to various combinations of those four transactions, assuming in every instance that any gain or loss recognized will be capital gain and the arrangement otherwise satisfies the Section 1061 conditions.

### Situation 1: Partner and Partnership Transactions Are Concomitant

The application of Section 1061 is most obvious when the partner and partnership transactions occur concomitantly. In such situations, the investors contribute to acquire interests and the partnership immediately invests contributed proceeds in an asset. When the partnership sells the asset, it immediately distributes the proceeds to the partners in complete liquidation of their interests. The partnership allocates gain it recognizes on the disposition of the assets to the partners. If



44. *See* I.R.C. § 1061(a).

any gain is to be recognized on the distribution of sale proceeds, the distributee partners recognize such gain immediately after the sale of the asset. Both the gain from the sale of the asset and the distribution would appear to be with respect to the partnership interest. Any gain that results from allocations of the partnership's sale of the assets or from distributions received from the partnership will be of the same character, either short-term or long-term gain. If the partnership held the assets for less than three years, the gain would be short-term.

### Situation 2: Partner Disposes of a Partnership Interest Before the Partnership Disposes of the Asset

A partner may dispose of an interest in a partnership before the partnership disposes of its assets. For instance, an original investor in a fund might dispose of an interest in the fund before the fund disposes of its investment asset. If that happens, the gain that the member recognizes on the disposition of the partnership interest would appear to occur with respect to the partnership interest. If the partner had not held the interest for at least three years, the gain recognized by the partner could be short-term capital gain under Section 1061(a).

### Situation 3: Partnership Disposes of an Asset and Reinvests Proceeds

A partnership may dispose of an asset and reinvest the proceeds. If so, the partnership will allocate any gain it recognizes on the disposition of its assets to the partners. That gain would appear to occur with respect to the partners' interests in the partnership so presumably Section 1061 would apply to the gain. If the partnership had held the asset for less than three years, the gain would be short-term capital gain under Section 1061.

### Situation 4: Partner Acquires Interest After Partnership Acquires Assets

A partner may acquire an interest in a partnership through contribution or purchase from another partner at some time after the partnership acquires assets. In such situations, the partnership's holding period in the assets would exceed the partner's holding period in the partnership interest. Within three years after the partner acquires the interest in the partnership, the partnership might sell an asset that it has held for more than three years. Because the gain and the character of the gain are determined at the partnership level, the application of Section 1061(a) in this situation would appear to apply at the partnership level. Because the partnership held the asset for more than three years, the gain would appear to retain its long-term character.

Section 1061 changes some long-term capital gain to short-term capital gain. Take care when advising clients regarding the character of gain that will be allocated to them. Members who have been with an applicable partnership (one that conducts an applicable trade or business) since its inception will be motivated, for tax reasons, to defer the disposition of the partnership assets until after the three-year threshold in Section 1061. That preference may differ from the investors' preference. Because gain allocated to them will qualify for the favorable treatment one year after an asset's acquisition, they will have no tax incentive to hold property beyond that point. The parties should be aware of and sensitive to their respective interests when making decisions related to the disposition of property.

www.ingramcontent.com/pod-product-compliance
Lightning Source LLC
LaVergne TN
LVHW080032210926
848481LV00011B/3162
*9781543809329*